The Irish Experience Since 1800

A Concise History

Third Edition

Thomas E. Hachey *and* Lawrence J. McCaffrey

Routledge
Taylor & Francis Group
LONDON AND NEW YORK

First published 2010 by M.E. Sharpe

Published 2015 by Routledge
2 Park Square, Milton Park, Abingdon, Oxon OX14 4RN
711 Third Avenue, New York, NY 10017, USA

Routledge is an imprint of the Taylor & Francis Group, an informa business

Library of Congress Cataloging-in-Publication Data

Hachey, Thomas E.
  The Irish experience since 1800 : a concise history / by Thomas E. Hachey and
Lawrence J. McCaffrey. 3rd ed.
    p. cm.
  Rev. ed. of: The Irish experience. Rev. ed. 1996.
  Includes bibliographical references and index.
  ISBN 978-0-7656-2510-6 (cloth : alk. paper)
  1. Ireland—History. I. McCaffrey, Lawrence John, 1925– II. Hachey, Thomas E. Irish
experience. III. Title.

DA910.H33 2010
941.508—dc22   2009037869

ISBN 13: 9780765625113 (pbk)
ISBN 13: 9780765625106 (hbk)

To our spouses,

Jane
and
Joan

With Gratitude

Contents

Preface to the Third Edition
    Thomas E. Hachey and Lawrence J. McCaffrey   ix

Acknowledgments   xiii

Part I. From Colony to Nation-State
    Lawrence J. McCaffrey   1

1. Ireland Before the Union: England's Conquest of Ireland   3
The Tudor/Stuart Plantation of Ireland   7
Penal Laws   13
Landlordism   16
The Rise and Fall of the Protestant Nation   18

2. Catholic Emancipation, 1801–1829   28
The Life of Rural Catholic Ireland   28
The Emergence of Daniel O'Connell   32
The Catholic Association and the Beginnings of Modern
    Irish Nationalism   36
The Catholic Victory   37
The Consequences of Catholic Emancipation   39

3. Repeal and British Politics, 1830–1845   41
O'Connell in the House of Commons   41
The Whig Alliance   43
Lobbying for Repeal   46
Young Ireland and Cultural Nationalism   47
The Surge of Repeal   51
Combating the Rising Tide   54
The Defeat of Repeal   55
Peel's Effort to Integrate Ireland into the United Kingdom   57

4. Famine and Fenianism, 1845–1870   61
The Irish Confederation   62
Repeal to Revolution   64

Famine	65
The Consolidation of Irish Catholicism	67
Land and Politics	70
The American Dimension	73
Fenianism	76
Gladstone's Initial Response to the Irish Question	79

5. Home Rule and the Land War, 1870–1882 — 82

Isaac Butt and Home Rule	82
The Emergence of Charles Stewart Parnell	87
The New Departure	89
The Decline of Butt's Version of Home Rule	91
The Land War	93

6. Home Rule and British Politics, 1882–1906 — 97

The Irish Party: Strong and Solid at Last	97
Gladstone's Pursuit of Home Rule	99
Aspects of the Irish-Liberal Alliance	100
The Fall of Parnell	102
The Ebb and Flow of Home Rule Enthusiasm	106
Trying to Kill Home Rule with Kindness	108

7. Currents and Crises in Irish Nationalism, 1880–1914 — 111

A Reunified but Aging Irish Party	111
English and Irish "Racism"	112
Irish-Ireland	113
An Alternative to Home Rule	116
Labor Restiveness	117
Reform Under the Liberals	118
The House of Lords Crisis and Home Rule	121
The Brink of Civil War	122
The Union Temporarily Preserved by a Foreign War	126

8. Wars of Liberation, 1914–1921 — 128

Blood Sacrifice	128
The Anglo-Irish War	134
End of a War, Start of a Nation	136

Part II. From Free State to Republic
Thomas E. Hachey — 141

9. The Irish Free State, 1922–1932: A Reluctant Dominion — 143

Establishing the New State	143
Irish Economic, Cultural, and Religious Life in the 1920s and Early 1930s	153

The Irish Constitution: Blueprint for Democracy at Home and
    Equality Abroad   159

10. The de Valera Era, 1932–1959: Continuity and Change in Irish Life   165
Dismantling the Treaty and Supplanting the Free State   165
The Anglo-Irish Agreements of 1938   174
Social and Political Unrest in the 1930s   177
Irish Neutrality and World War II   181
Irish Life and Politics During the Emergency   185
The Irish Republic, 1948–1959   188

11. Modern Ireland, 1959–1998: Adjusting to a European Future   194
Abandoning Economic Self-Sufficiency   194
New Challenges and Opportunities   196
Social and Political Responses to the New Realities   200
Ireland Confronts Modernity   203
The Old Boy Network of Irish Politics   206
Church-State Relations in the 1990s   207
Irish Catholicism and Irish-Ireland: Cultural Identities in Transition   209

**12. The Northern Specter, 1920–1998: A Continuing Crisis in
the Conflict of Cultures**   214
Early Background to the Modern "Troubles"   214
The Northern Ireland Civil Rights Movement   218
Attempts at Power-Sharing and Devolution   220
The New Ireland Forum and the Anglo-Irish Accord   225
Irish-American Familiarity with the Ulster Issue   228
IRA Propaganda in America and the Problem of Perception for Britain   230
NORAID and the American Connection with Ulster   231
Concern and Constraint in Confronting the Ulster Crisis   232

13. Ireland into the Twenty-First Century   235
The Genesis of the Peace Process   236
Decade of the Celtic Tiger   244
Old-Age Politics in a New-Age Nation   247
Popular Culture in the New Ireland   250
Education: Liberating or Limiting?   251
The Celtic Tiger and Cultural Change   252
Irish Neutrality in the Twenty-First Century   254
Economic Collapse and the Prospect of an Uncertain Future   255

Recommended Reading   263
Index   273
About the Authors   288

Preface to the Third Edition

George Santayana famously warned that "Those who cannot remember the past are condemned to repeat it." In the case of the Irish, both in Ireland and among the Diaspora, the tendency was rather to be obsessed with the past, with its injustices and miseries, frustrating realistic, hopeful concentration on the present and future. These memories motivated James Joyce to write: "History is a nightmare I am trying to escape." A distinguished historian of Victorian Britain, G.M. Young, observed that what "England could never remember, Ireland could never forget." Of course, losers have longer memories than winners do. But many recent Irish historians, frequently labeled revisionists, have complained that much of Irish historical memory is afflicted with mythology rather than enlightened objectivity, agreeing with José Ortega y Gasset that "We have need of history in its entirety, not to fall back into it, but to see if we can escape from it."

Of course, there were justifications for an Irish persecution complex. Ireland did experience centuries of colonialism, which denied the Catholic majority basic civil liberties. In addition, British occupiers stole their property as well as their political influence. Most of them lived in virtual slavery as well as poverty. The Great Famine of the 1840s killed over 800,000 and forced at least a million to leave the country, mostly to North America. During the Great Hunger, British religious and racial prejudices and heartless economic theory influenced the Westminster government to inadequately relieve distress in part of the United Kingdom. In the United States, Irish immigrants suffered from extensive bigotry. Admittedly, these ignorant often-undisciplined pioneers of urban ghettos were a social blight, but their Catholicism, more than their conduct, fostered hate. Even after religious morality, better jobs and higher family incomes, and education lifted them from the lowest levels of American society, anti-Catholic nativism still restricted or blocked Irish social and professional advancement. Seldom were Irish Americans visible in the worlds of banking, big business, and prestigious positions in the professions. That is why some of their best and brightest sought power and prestige in the church, politics, and the labor movement. As late as the 1960s, many colleges and universities refused them academic appointments, even in state institutions of higher learning they paid taxes to support.

Things have improved for Irish and other Catholic Americans since post–World War II prosperity; an increasing number of college and university graduates, a result of the G.I. Bill; and John F. Kennedy's election as president of the United States. His popularity in office diminished anti-Catholicism. Irish Americans became more comfortable and confident, abandoning much of their negative defensiveness. With Kennedy occupying the White House, they shared movie director John Ford's sentiment that he now felt like a first-class citizen. Now the American Irish can be found at the highest levels of academia, business, and the professions. The British–American alliances in World War II, the cold war, and, more recently, in the Middle East have lessened anti-British sentiments among the Irish as well as others in the United States.

While the peace process in Northern Ireland is occasionally disrupted by ongoing sectarian violence, incremental progress toward political and economic normalization is being made. By contrast, the south has enjoyed a period of notable economic prosperity that provided, at least during the recent era of the "Celtic Tiger," well-paid employment and higher standards of living; and the country's international visibility has turned much public attention, particularly among the young, away from old wrongs and toward an optimistic future.

Unfortunately, loss of memory can be as dangerous as remembrance. Historical realities have great value not only for understanding current events and instilling pride in Ireland's successful efforts to evolve from colony to nation-state and its significant cultural achievements, especially in literature. And the Irish should understand that they have had almost as much impact in shaping British history as the British have had in molding theirs. In the United States, the Diaspora Irish have used the Irish experience to influence politics, religion, and economics. Throughout the English-speaking regions and other places on the globe, Irish history has served as an inspiration and guide to other countries seeking to banish colonialism.

British influences in Ireland have been positive as well as negative. Although many Irish-Ireland nationalists have viewed the English language as representing English conquest and Irish submission and as an alien force, subverting a unique Irish culture, it has enabled a large number of writers in Ireland to produce some of the world's great prose, poetry, and theater, establishing Dublin as a leading literary capital. Speaking English was an important asset to emigrants, giving them a head start over other nationalities in new homelands.

Anglo-Irish colonists provided Ireland with the concept and reality of a political nation. Through the agency of nationalism, in time it evolved from exclusive, only Protestant, to inclusive, although Catholics enjoyed more political and religious status. In general, British politics provided Irish leaders with traditions and techniques to liberate themselves. British legal and political institutions have persisted during Free State and Republic. Following the British mode, the United States and Ireland are rare examples of revolution producing liberal democracy rather than tyranny. Irish immigrants experienced in the tactics and techniques of the British political system, like their use of English, made them significant forces in new environments. In the United States it brought them power as leaders of the Catholic Church, ethnic political coalitions, and organized labor. Emigration was a horrible family experience, represented by the American wake, where people drank, ate, sang, and danced the night before daughters and sons left home under the assumption that they would never return. But what was the alternative in an overpopulated country without enough economic versatility or social dynamic to keep them at home? It took time, but the Irish adapted to the United States with patriotic zeal as they did to Canada, Australia, and New Zealand. Their control of Catholicism throughout the English-speaking world and more primitive colonies led to an Irish spiritual empire.

While negative British influence in Ireland had some positive aspects, Irish influences on Britain were also beneficial. Reacting to Irish pressure and hoping to quell Irish discontent and preserve the union, by the beginning of the twentieth century British Liberal and Conservative governments had eliminated economic and social grievances that had fueled the fires of Irish nationalism. And remedies for Ireland established precedents aiding constructive change in Britain. Emancipation for Catholics in Ireland also applied to coreligionists in Britain. Political chaos in 1870s Ireland brought about the secret ballot. Various Irish land acts on the road to peasant proprietorship also enhanced the existences of rural populations and throughout the United Kingdom while establishing that property, while private, had responsibilities. Many British government efforts to provide employment and raise standards of living in Ireland were previews of the welfare state.

Charles Stewart Parnell's Irish Parliamentary party was so unified, disciplined, and well-organized in constituencies and the House of Commons that British Conservative and Liberal politicians tried to accomplish similar unity in their organizations. Home Rule politicians were probably the most talented in Irish history and enhanced parliamentary debates with eloquent, tough, and witty oratory. Their alliance with British Liberals aided economic, social, and political reform. It reduced the veto power of the House of Lords, a significant step in expanding political power for an increasing larger share of the British population. The Irish-Liberal Alliance also ideologically clarified British politics, driving right-leaning Whigs into the Conservative, renamed Unionist fold, freeing Liberals to pursue a more leftist agenda. With the House of Lords' veto reduced to three sessions of Parliament and the alliance in control of the House of Commons, Home Rule seemed to be guaranteed in 1914. However, Ulster Protestant resistance, with threats of violence, posed a serious threat to British constitutional government, delaying Irish self-government and making some form of partition inevitable.

Despite demands for repeal and then Home Rule, Irish constitutional nationalists were friends of the British empire, and defended and expanded it. A large portion of the British armed forces were Irish soldiers and sailors. Although Ireland remained neutral in World War II, many Irish men fought in the trenches, in the air, and on sea against Germany, Italy, and Japan. More Northern Irish Catholics than Protestants were in Britain's military efforts. Irish civilians, men and women, worked in British defense plants. The Royal Irish Constabulary served as a model for law enforcement agencies throughout the empire. Irish Catholicism also played a significant role in preserving and expanding British rule in various places. Its missionaries educated, Christianized, and "civilized" native populations and helped accept British rule and institutions. Irish sovereignty also altered the shape of the empire. At Commonwealth Conferences, Free State representatives led forces that redefined and increased dominion independence. Irish nationalist ideas and strategies also affected colonies not yet dominions. For example, the Anglo-Irish war was the twentieth century's first guerrilla war of liberation. It was evidence that armed citizens, not necessarily numerous, working with the support of local populations could frustrate and sometimes defeat traditional armies.

Since the 1960s, thanks largely to the Clancy Brothers and Tommy Makem and other folk performers, a large number of Irish Americans, in a proud search for their identity, have taken a considerable interest in things Irish—history, literature, music, dancing, theater. Libraries, here and in Ireland, serve many in their attempts to trace their ancestors. Unfortunately, too many stop short of combining all these interests into a comprehensive understanding of Ireland past and present. History can provide a contextual integrating instrument for all aspects of the Irish experience. We hope that this book will achieve that goal while providing an interesting and instructive guide to general readers as well as academic specialists and their students.

Now that this Preface has previewed the intentions of the authors and explained why we believe that Ireland's history has many dimensions and is significant to an understanding of all aspects of Irish life and culture and to the heritage they bequeathed to the Diaspora, let us begin the story.

Thomas E. Hachey
Lawrence J. McCaffrey

Acknowledgments

The authors express their deep appreciation for the considerable help afforded them in the production of this edition by two professionally skilled graduate assistants: Alissa Condon provided the critical double-checking of the dates and names added to this new edition and offered substantial editorial oversight; Lauren Hoehlein was unfailingly resourceful in procuring essential data for the new and updated chapters. They are equally grateful to Michael Burns for his guidance on diacritical and punctuation usage; to Jane Hachey, who proofread the manuscript for spelling and syntax, and to M.E. Sharpe's Makiko Parsons, who capably oversaw every stage of manuscript preparation for this new edition, as well as Angela Piliouras, who oversaw the production process. We, of course, assume full responsibility for any and all errors that might have survived that collective scrutiny.

Thomas E. Hachey
Lawrence J. McCaffrey

ATLANTIC
OCEAN

North Channel

Lough Foyle

(London-
Derry derry)
LONDONDERRY
ANTRIM
Lifford
Strabane
• Belfast
Lough
Neagh
Donegal Bay
DONEGAL
TYRONE
DOWN
FERMANAGH
ARMAGH
MONAGHAN
Sligo
LEITRIM
CAVAN
Dundalk
SLIGO
• Carrick
LOUTH
Irish
Sea
MAYO
ROSCOMMON
LONGFORD
• Drogheda
Westport
CONNAUGHT
WESTMEATH
MEATH
GALWAY
OFFALY
KILDARE
DUBLIN
Galway
★ Dublin
ARAN IS.
R. Shannon
LEINSTER
Wicklow
CLARE
LAOIGHIS
WICKLOW
Shannon
TIPPERARY
Kilkenny
CARLOW
Limerick
KILKENNY
WEXFORD
LIMERICK
Tipperary
Tralee
Wexford
KERRY
WATERFORD
Killarney
MUNSTER
Waterford
St. George's Channel
Dingle Bay
CORK
• Cork
Youghal
Cobh
Bantry Bay

IRELAND

0   25   50   75   100
MILES

— NORTHERN IRELAND (U.K.)
····· — REPUBLIC OF IRELAND

SCOTLAND

IRELAND
ENGLAND
WALES

FRANCE

Part I

From Colony to Nation-State

Lawrence J. McCaffrey

1

Ireland Before the Union

England's Conquest of Ireland

Although Ireland became England's first colony, English imperialism did not commence as a planned adventure. It began when Dermot MacMurrough went to Wales to recruit help to regain his Leinster throne, which he had lost in an Irish war. He persuaded Richard fitz Gilbert de Clare, Earl of Pembroke, known as Strongbow, a vassal of Henry II patrolling the Welsh border, to assist him. In exchange, Mac Murrough promised his daughter in marriage and succession to the recovered Leinster monarchy.

In 1169, when Strongbow's Normans arrived in Ireland, they confronted a culturally united enemy but a country in political chaos. Whereas the rest of western Europe was developing nation-states, Ireland was divided into provincial and petty kingdoms, which in turn featured clan territories. Clannishness or tribalism assured defeat. Another factor aiding Norman victory was superior military skills, tactics, and weapons: They used armor, horses for mobility, and employed castle fortresses to secure conquered territory.

Because Irish resistance was ineffective, Strongbow's forces moved beyond Leinster, upsetting Henry II, who feared that his vassals might establish a rival Norman-Irish kingdom on the other side of the Irish Sea. Therefore, in 1171 he came to Ireland and received homage from his vassals and some native chieftains and bishops as Lord of Ireland. In 1156, Pope Adrian IV (Nicholas Breakespear), an Englishman, had originally conferred that title on the English monarch.

Papal interference in Anglo-Irish affairs indicates that Ireland suffered from a variety of imperialisms: political, economic, cultural, and religious. Inspired by continental European models, pre-Norman Ireland was in transition. Elements of feudalism were apparent when petty kings became vassals of provincial monarchs but the latter's powers were so evenly balanced that none of them could unify the whole country. A reformation affected Irish Christianity with the creation of diocesan structures and an importation of religious orders from abroad. Although earlier Viking invasions resulted in a sharp quality decline in Irish learning, a cultural renaissance of no small significance occurred in the eleventh and twelfth centuries. But despite Ireland's changing character, from English and continental perspectives, it appeared a primitive, even savage place, with an archaic clan system and a decadent, disorganized, and immoral Christianity remote from Roman authority. The Norman English hoped to seal their conquest through Anglicization and Romanization. Their colony began with an attitude of superiority over the conquered, one that persisted.

For a number of reasons, during the fourteenth century, the Norman English found themselves on the defensive. Irish chieftains adopted their military tactics and weapons. In remote areas many colonists married Irish women, adopting a Gaelic life-style, while others, tiring of Ireland's cold and damp, returned to England. In doing so, many turned estate management over to agents, beginning a pattern of absentee landlordism. Because they remained divided, without a concept of political nationhood, the Irish failed to exploit English weaknesses and drive them out of the country.

From the mid-fourteenth until the early sixteenth century, English colonists in Ireland concentrated on survival rather than expansion. In 1366, the Statutes of Kilkenny expressed defensiveness. An early example of cultural apartheid, these laws forbade associating with the Irish, marrying their women, wearing their style of dress, speaking their language, adopting their children, or seeking the services and consolations of their priests. In 1509, when Henry VIII became king of England, he was lord of three Irelands: the Pale, or Anglo-Irish-held territory, a miniature England in language, culture, and institutions; Gaelic Ireland, where native culture existed in its purest form; and an ambiguous in-between where Irish and English coexisted and sometimes blended. The Pale essentially was Leinster, Ulster was Gaelic Ireland, Munster and Connacht represented cultural assimilation.

Tudor England emerged as a significant power with a budding overseas empire, providing a rationale for increasing control in Ireland. Its monarchs decided that Ireland's chaos and the defensive position of its colony posed a security threat to England. They feared that Irish turbulence invited an invasion threat by a continental enemy, and worried that Ireland under foreign control would endanger England by diminishing the importance of its position as an island defended by a strong navy.

Instead of spending large sums of money to stabilize Ireland militarily, Henry VIII (1491–1547) chose a more subtle strategy for extending English hegemony beyond the Pale. He persuaded clan chiefs to surrender lands to him and receive them back with territorial titles to administer as his vassals: for example, O'Neills became earls of Tyrone and O'Donnells earls of Tyrconnell. Certainly, this arrangement weakened foundations of the Gaelic order and spread common law at the expense of Brehon law. In 1541, Anglicization made progress when Ireland's Parliament elevated Henry to king rather than lord of Ireland and when feudalism penetrated Gaelic territory. However, these innovations were more superficial than real. Outside the Pale, particularly in Ulster, Ireland remained Gaelic and politically decentralized.

Henry's religious policy affected Ireland more than did efforts to feudalize it. In 1534, when he failed to obtain a papal annulment of his marriage to Catherine of

Aragon, Henry broke with Rome. Both the English and Irish Parliaments endorsed this move and declared him head of the Church. Because Because Henry's rift with Rome had little relevance in Ireland, which had less loyalty to the papacy than England, Anglo-Irish feudal lords and Gaelic clan chiefs accepted the new state religion. Like the governing class throughout western Europe, Irish leaders believed that *cuius regio, eius religio*: People should embrace the prince's religion in the interest of public order and tranquility. In addition, changing spiritual leadership from pope to king did not really touch people's lives. Although Henry confiscated wealth and property from monasteries, retaining much of the spoils for the royal treasury and distributing the remainder among loyal Anglo-Irish feudal lords and Irish chiefs, his rejection of papal supremacy did not interrupt traditional Catholic devotionalism.

Long-range effects of Henry VIII's Reformation did not become apparent until the reigns of his son, Edward VI (1547–1553), and daughter, Elizabeth I (1558–1603), when the state religion evolved liturgically and theologically into Protestantism. Most Irish (Anglo and Gaelic) were offended by this cultural attack, a more pernicious imperialism than previous English political and military adventures in their country. Irish leaders negotiated with continental powers, first Spain, then France, to support their resistance to English domination. Religious dimensions of the contest between English imperialism and Irish objection altered Irish Catholicism's character and significance, gradually transforming it into a main feature of Irish identity, the nucleus of an incipient nationalism. Jesuits and Franciscans poured into Ireland as agents of the Counter-Reformation.

By creating an impassible barrier between English and Irish, Protestantism disrupted cultural assimilation, protecting Ireland from complete conquest by its stronger neighbor. Catholicism symbolized a besieged Irish civilization, Protestantism Anglo-Saxon aggression. While equally Irish, Anglo and Gaelic Catholic slowly melded into one identity, to uphold cultural and political autonomy, England justified conquest and control in Ireland as a protection against popery's alien, tyrannical, and subversive presence.

During the sixteenth and seventeenth centuries, England waged war against Spain and France to achieve and maintain its status as a first-rate power. Because their enemies were Catholic, English leaders cultivated Protestant nativism as an ideology and weapon against their enemies. They also insisted that they had to conquer and subdue Ireland so that it could not host a back-door to invasion. Military strategy harnessed Protestant nativism to England's national security, the main outlines of an Irish policy that would remain in place for centuries.

Throughout her long reign, Elizabeth coped with Irish insurrection. O'Neills, O'Donnells, and Maguires in Ulster, and Anglo-Irish Fitzgeralds, earls of Desmond in Munster, and sometimes combined forces from north and south were in revolt. In 1590, armies led by Hugh O'Neill and Hugh O'Donnell, assisted by Spanish intrigue and intervention, came close to victory. O'Neill's guerrilla tactics and his troops, trained in up-to-date weaponry, baffled Elizabeth's generals, Sir Henry Bagenal and

The Borders of the English Pale, 1500 and 1600

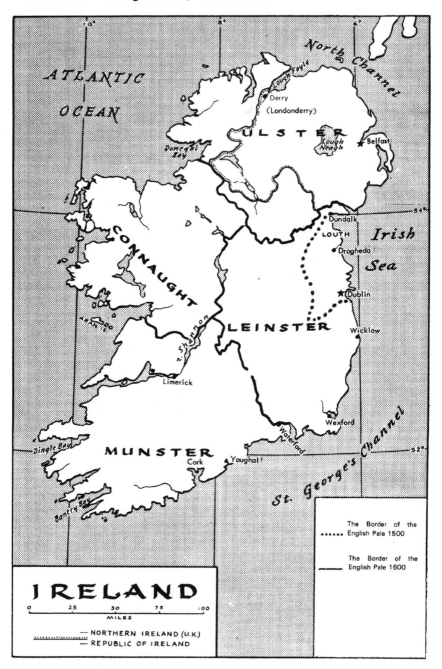

the earl of Essex. In August 1598, his startling victory at Yellow Ford frightened England's government and inspired support for independence in Ireland.

In 1601, Spain sent four thousand troops to assist the Irish rebels. In September, when they landed in Kinsale, an English army quickly attacked them. Irish efforts to relieve their allies failed, and the Spanish returned home. O'Donnell surrendered shortly afterward, while O'Neill returned to Ulster, fighting all the way, but defeat was inevitable. On March 30, 1603, he formally submitted to Mountjoy, the queen's deputy, six days after her death. O'Neill's submission was a fatal blow to Gaelic Ireland and jeopardized Catholic Ireland.

The Tudor/Stuart Plantation of Ireland

During the reign of Henry VIII, Lord Leonard Grey, representing him in Ireland, advised the king that the best way to secure English authority there would be to confiscate rebel property and transfer it to supporters of the crown. Catholic Mary Tudor (1553–1558) was the first monarch to employ plantation as a strategy. She seized O'Moore's land in Leix and O'Connor's in Offaly, shired and renamed them King's and Queen's Counties, and gave them to Anglo-Irish lords friendly to English interests, setting a precedent for territory in and out of the Pale.

In subduing Munster, Elizabeth awarded large estates to English adventurers in the royal army. She also shired Connacht and Ulster (Munster and Leinster were previously reorganized), creating present-day county borders. Under the new arrangement, authorities, particularly from 1606 to 1608, abolished Irish customs and institutions, replacing Brehon with common law.

In the wake of O'Neill's surrender, James I (1603–1625), the first Stuart king, permitted him and O'Donnell to retain their properties and titles as earls of Tyrone and Tyrconnell. But in 1607, fearing an English conspiracy to murder them, both chiefs fled to the continent, and in the end both died in Rome. The flight of the earls provided James with an opportunity to further pacify and control Gaelic Ulster. Previous plantation in the south and west were superficial, only transferring ownership of large estate from rebels to loyalists while Catholics remained on the land. In Ulster, James employed a policy used by the Stuarts to humble Gaelic chiefs in the Scottish Highlands. In 1610, he seized O'Neill and O'Donnell territory, extending over most of present-day Armagh, Cavan, Derry, Donegal, Fermanagh, and Tyrone, planting them with complete Protestant colonies: landlords, tenants, tradesmen, artisans, and merchants. James invited Anglicans from England and Presbyterians from Scotland to settle in Ulster. The thoroughness and density of the Protestant Ulster plantations made that province unique.

Not all post-Reformation Catholics in Ireland were native to the soil. Most of the Old English colony retained the faith. Duel loyalties to pope and king placed them in a difficult and dangerous position, losing ground to a growing influence of New English who had acquired Irish estates through conquest and plantation. But they continued to think of themselves as culturally and politically English. After

Plantations

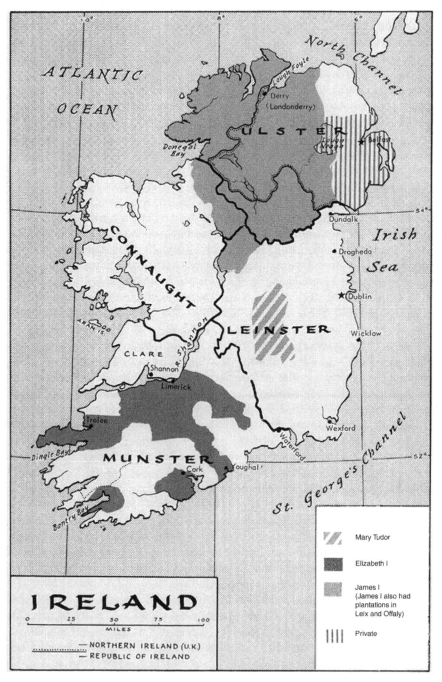

1613 they became a minority faction in Ireland's Parliament and were liable to heavy fines for fidelity to Rome. During the reigns of James and his son, Charles I (1625–1649), English governments, by insisting on religious conformity as a loyalty test, gradually weakened differences between Old English and Irish Catholic. From an English perspective they were both offensive "papists."

In 1641, taking advantage of an English civil war between king and Parliament, Old English and Irish joined forces in rebellion. By spring 1642, they controlled most of Ireland, except for Dublin, Cork City and large portions of the county, Drogheda, Carrickfergus, Belfast, Enniskillen, Coleraine, Derry, North Down, South Antrim, and parts of north Donegal. In October 1642, Catholic bishops, Old English leaders, and clan chiefs met in Kilkenny to establish a provisional government. The Confederation of Kilkenny announced a commitment to freedom of private conscience, a right to practice openly in the church of one's choice, Ireland's independence, and loyalty to the King. The saying *Pro Deo, pro rege, pro patria Hibernia unanimis* (For God, for king, for country—Ireland united) summed up these principles.

Unfortunately, unity between the Old English and Irish Catholics was too fragile to survive. The Old English still considered themselves more English than Irish. They were intensely loyal to the Stuart monarchy and fought to maintain their property and place in Ireland's Parliament. Irish Catholics wanted a comprehensive revolution, one that would restore the Gaelic order. They never had a significant parliamentary role and already had lost most of their property. Giovanni Battista Rinuccini, papal legate, and James Butler, earl of Ormond, the king's deputy, manipulated and increased Confederation conflicts. Rinnuccini encouraged the native Irish to serve as a sword of the Counter-Reformation; Butler attempted to lure the Old English into the Stuart camp in its war against Parliament.

Confederation disputes and Ormond and Rinuccini intrigues divided military strategy; inadequate weapons, short supplies, and inadequately trained soldiers prevented military success. Meanwhile, antagonism among Ormond, a pro-English Parliament, and Ulster Presbyterians divided English interests in Ireland and prevented victory. In 1649, before Ormond and Confederation leaders agreed on coalition, Oliver Cromwell had already triumphed over Charles I. He then proceeded to Ireland, and when he left in 1650 he had mostly broken Catholic resistance. Within two years his lieutenant, Henry Ireton, completed the task.

Massive confiscations and plantations followed Cromwell's victory. Previously, despite Elizabethan and Stuart plantations, Catholics, mostly Old English, had managed to retain two-thirds of Irish property. Cromwell reduced that proportion to one-fourth. In addition to new plantations, war diminished the Catholic population by one-third. Some Catholics were transported to the West Indies in chains and put on the slave market. Others, including a large portion of the Catholic aristocracy and gentry, sought new homes in Connacht's rugged and infertile terrain.

After the Stuart restoration (1660), Irish Catholics supported the monarchy in quarrels with England's Parliament. They believed that Charles II (1660–1685)

Catholic Land Ownership, 1641

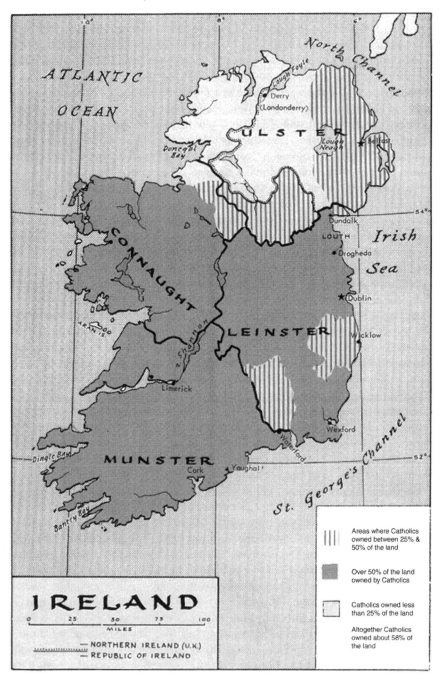

sympathized with their religious convictions and hoped that he would restore land that Cromwell had "stolen." Charles did have a tolerance for things Catholic and returned a small amount of confiscated land. However, he had no intention of provoking British and Anglo-Irish hostile to the crown by repealing the Cromwellian settlement. His Catholic brother, James II (1685–1688), was openly friendly to Irish members of his faith. His Catholic deputy in Ireland, Richard Talbot, earl of Tyrconnell, found places for them in the Irish army and government.

James's pro-Irish Catholic attitude and conduct were factors, though not as important as the birth of a Catholic son and heir, in Parliament's decision to depose him and invite his Protestant daughter Mary and her Dutch husband, William of Orange, to become England's joint rulers (1650–1702). James abandoned England without a fight, deciding to make a stand in Ireland, where he had majority backing. War in Ireland between William and James fit into a wider European context as part of a conflict between Louis XIV of France and the Grand Alliance, a coalition of the Dutch, Hapsburgs, and some Italian and German forces that William led. The alliance attempted to frustrate Louis's maneuvers to place a Bourbon on the Spanish throne and his territorial ambitions in the Rhenish Palatinate. With soldiers and money, Louis encouraged James to fight in Ireland as a strategy to occupy William's attention and exhaust his resources. A dispute between Pope Alexander VIII and the French king concerning an opening for Cologne's Archbishopric, and the Pope's friendship with Holy Roman Emperor Leopold, meant that Rome endorsed the Grand Alliance and Protestant William against Catholic James.

On July 12, 1690, William's army of 36,000 Englishmen, Irish Protestants, French Huguenots, Dutchmen, and Danes defeated James's force of 25,000 Irish Catholics, supplemented with French officers on the banks of the Boyne, deciding the outcome of the war. James fled to France, leaving Irish Catholics to fight on against impossible odds. After William failed to take Limerick, defended by Patrick Sarsfield, he returned to England, leaving the campaign in the hands of trusted lieutenants. Before the end of 1690, the earl of Marlborough had conquered Cork and Kinsale.

Feuds and jealousies among its commanders weakened Stuart supporting Jacobite solidarity. When the war recommenced in 1691, little harmony existed between Tyrconnell, James's leading lieutenant; the marquis de St. Ruth, Louis XIV's representative; and Sarsfield, the Limerick hero. On June 30, 1691, Godbert de Ginkel, one of William's generals, prevailed over St. Ruth and took Athlone, opening the west for conquest. St. Ruth decided to defend access to Galway at Aughrim, near Ballinasloe in east Galway. He died there on July 12, demoralizing his soldiers, reversing the tide of battle in the midst of victory, and opening Galway to defeat and occupation on July 21. The remainder of the Irish army then retreated to Limerick. In August Tyrconnell died, of poisoning by enemies, according to rumors, but Sarsfield again managed to defend the city and preserve morale at a reasonably high level. However, the situation was hopeless. An English fleet prevented help or escape by sea.

Catholic Land Ownership, 1688

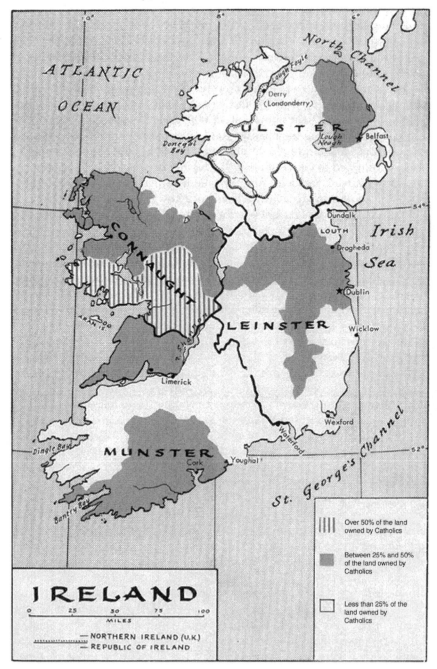

Because he was dealing with more pressing matters—consolidating his rule in England and the continental campaign against Louis XIV—William considered Irish events of minor significance. In order to free his soldiers for action against Louis, he offered Catholics in Limerick honorable surrender terms, which they accepted. According to the Treaty of Limerick, signed by both parties on October 1, 1691, Irish and Anglo-Irish Catholic leaders could leave their country for service with continental Catholic monarchs with a guarantee that their coreligionists who remained behind would be free to practice their religion as in the days of Charles II and remain secure in their property. In late 1691, important Catholic leaders and their retainers sailed to France, leaving dependents protected by a vaguely worded document, resting on William's integrity, England's Parliament, and Protestant planter tolerance.

The Penal Laws

William of Orange was a man of politics, not a bigot. He intended to honor the Treaty of Limerick. His own country, the Dutch Republic, adopted religious tolerance as a pragmatic alternative to civil war. William was prepared to apply a similar approach in Britain and Ireland as a path to reconciliation, peace, and stability—goals that he considered more important than Protestant ascendancy. Unfortunately, Irish and British Protestants did not share his point of view; they chose punishment. Carefully weighing British and Irish Protestant "no-popery" fanaticism, William decided it would be impolitic to resist popular demand and consented to anti-Catholic laws in both kingdoms.

During reigns of William and Mary, Anne (1702–1714), and the first two Georges (1714–1760), Parliament enacted Irish Penal Laws, harsher than those in England, touching every aspect of civil and religious life. They banished Catholic bishops and religious orders and forbade secular priests from abroad entry into Ireland. They required resident secular clergy to register, pay a fee, remain in their parishes, and take an oath abjuring Stuart pretenders. The Penal Laws disarmed Catholics, excluded them from Parliament and the legal profession, and denied them a vote. They prohibited Catholics from establishing schools or sending children abroad for education. They allowed them to lease property for thirty-one years, but not to purchase it. On an owner's death, a Catholic's property had to be divided among all his sons. If the eldest turned Protestant, he acquired the land, reducing his father to life tenancy.

British and Irish Protestants considered themselves highly enlightened possessors of a Whig representative government and constitutional tradition. They branded Spain's Inquisition, the Edict of Nantes, and French persecution of Huguenots as typical examples of Catholic oppression. Penal Laws in Britain, Ireland, and the American colonies contradicted their enlightenment claim. How did British and Irish Protestants defend anti-Catholic policies that exceeded religious persecutions in Catholic areas of western Europe? They maintained that anti-Catholic laws were necessary for security, insisting that popery's malignant and subversive nature excluded it from tolerance. To them, Catholicism epitomized anti-intellectualism and

Catholic Land Ownership, 1703

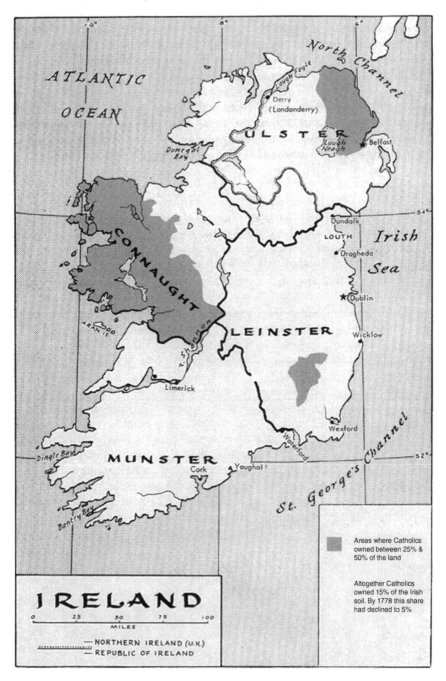

superstition, an expression of authoritarianism and treason. Catholics accepted the temporal authority of a foreign ruler, the pope, and had extended aid and comfort to England's enemies.

Penal Laws neither destroyed nor weakened Irish Catholicism. Government authorities lacked the will, resources, or personnel to enforce all their religious clauses. In 1709, Rome commenced appointing new bishops. By mid-century, many diocesan priests and members of religious orders—Franciscans, Dominicans, Carmelites, Capuchins, and Jesuits—served Irish communities. Candidates to the priesthood studied at Louvain, Antwerp, Douay, Paris, Nantes, Lille, Barcelona, Santiago, Seville, Salamanca, Rome, and other seminaries in continental Europe. Prominent and prosperous aristocrats and middle-class families also sent sons abroad for education. Although the Irish Catholic masses were theologically ignorant and often negligent in practicing their faith, by 1760 Irish Catholicism was healthier institutionally than it had been before the days of Penal Law.

Although penal legislation did not significantly drive ordinary people to convert from Catholicism to Protestantism, legal pressures, property considerations, concern for heirs, status, and political ambitions encouraged most of the Catholic aristocracy to shift religious allegiance. However, adversity did not alter the faith of the rural masses, and quite a few native and Old English aristocrats also remained Catholic.

If the purpose of the Penal Laws was the destruction of Irish Catholicism and the mass conversion of its believers, they obviously failed. But that was not their main intent. Intimidation was their purpose, not proselytism—an expression of Protestant fear, insecurity, and hatred, a tactic to humiliate, demoralize, and humble the enemy. Military victories in sixteenth- and seventeenth-century wars left Protestants a privileged minority with a monopoly of power that they were unsure they could maintain. They lived in the midst of dangerous natives, constantly fearing insurrection. Mass defections of Irish Catholics were not likely or desirable—someone had to serve and do menial labor. The Penal Laws were an updated version of the Statutes of Kilkenny, a method of neutering a conquered people so that they would accept their servility as hewers of wood and drawers of water. On this level, the Penal Laws were a remarkable success. Catholic aristocrats, members of the gentry, middle class, and peasantry all bowed to Protestant ascendancy. Catholic agitation was directed toward tolerance rather than equality. Catholic committees representing the aristocracy, gentry, and middle class pleaded for civil and property rights, but humbly renounced intentions of subverting Protestant dominance.

The Penal Laws completed Ireland's division into separate societies: Protestants and Catholics, conquerors and conquered, powerful and powerless. Not all Protestants were aristocrats or gentry members, however. Some were merchants, tradesmen, even tenant farmers and agricultural laborers. And some Protestants did not belong to the Established Church of Ireland. About 15 percent of Ireland's population was Nonconformist, mostly Ulster Presbyterians. A Sacramental Test Clause attached to a 1704 Popery Act excluded Nonconformists from civil and military office. While a series of Toleration and Indemnity Acts eased their legal burdens, they still resented being less than first-class citizens. During the eighteenth century, a large number left for North America.

Not all Irish Catholics were impoverished. Often assisted by friendly Protestant neighbors, a few in the upper classes held on to their property. Actually, Penal Laws encouraged the growth of a relatively significant Catholic middle class. Denied opportunities to purchase property or pursue legal or political careers, many bright and ambitious young men pursued banking and commerce, particularly the lucrative provisions trade, and many Protestant landlords employed Catholic agents to manage their estates and collect rents. Often these agents acquired wealth and standing in rural Ireland. There were also a number of Catholic "strong farmers," perhaps a hundred thousand or so, who rented 30 acres or more, frequently subleasing parts of their holdings, and had their own tenants and agricultural laborers. Nevertheless, by the mid-eighteenth century, a Catholic majority of 75 percent possessed less than 10 percent of Irish landed property and was excluded from the affairs of their own country. Despite political and economic grievances against the Protestant Ascendancy, middle-class urban and rural peasant Nonconformists shared its hatred and fears of Catholicism. In fact, rigid Calvinist theology tended to make Presbyterians more intense than Established Church members in their "no-popery."

Landlordism

Landlordism shaped the Ascendancy personality. An irresponsible system bred irresponsible people. Irish aristocracy and gentry acquired reputations for charm, gaiety, wit, hospitality, and courage. But their charm was restricted to peers, gaiety often featured inebriation, hospitality was frequently profligacy, wit could be cruel, and courage often was a euphemism for recklessness. Many landlords showed indifference to their income sources, ignored the welfare of their estates, and wasted the country's resources on an exorbitant standard of living and decadent life-style. Maria Edgeworth's *Castle Rackrent* (1800) is a classic literary description of landlord irresponsibility.

Many members of the Ascendancy preferred not to live in Ireland. Highly talented graduates of Trinity College, such as Edmund Burke and Oliver Goldsmith, fled provincial Dublin to seek fame and fortune in London. Despite good hunting and fishing, and some attractive big houses, many landlords abandoned rural Ireland for a more exciting life-style in England, leaving agents to manage their estates. There is no convincing evidence that absentee landlords as a group were more hard-hearted than those who remained in the country or that their estates were less efficient. However, absenteeism did deprive Ireland of potential talented leadership, widen the gap between sectarian communities and landlord and tenant, and drain money from the economy. Collected rents in Ireland spent in England retarded the growth of local crafts and industries.

In contrast to comfortable resident and absentee landlords, most Catholic peasants, usually illiterate, residing in the south and west, and Irish- rather than English-speaking, experienced abject poverty and the threat of raised rents and eviction. They were the most miserable examples of their class in western Europe. The reasons for, and the extent and consequences of rural poverty, are discussed in Chapter 2.

English and foreign observers tended to blame rural wretchedness on "alien" landlords. Since the early nineteenth-century, Irish nationalists have echoed this charge. But many historians failed to examine its authenticity. Actually, Protestant planters were no more improvident or indifferent to the peasantry than the native or Old English Catholics whom they replaced, who also had been notorious for drinking, gambling, hunting, and agricultural ignorance. It could be argued that eighteenth- and nineteenth-century Protestant proprietors were examples of the English in Ireland becoming more Irish than the Irish. There were incidents of mutual loyalties, even affection, if sometimes patronizing, between Protestant landlords and Catholic tenants. Despite peasant Ireland's miserable standards, hunger among the lower class, insecurity, and exploitation existed in other parts of Europe, if not as widespread. Institutionally, the legal position of tenant farmers and agricultural laborers in Britain was similar to that in Ireland, and many also existed on the edge of survival. In Ireland, however, shared religious beliefs might have resulted in more interclass understanding and kindness. Ireland's land question was cultural as well as economic or social. Issues were also British and Irish, Protestant and Catholic, colonial and native. Eighteenth-century Irish peasants were not sophisticated about politics or economics, and they had not acquired a national self-consciousness, but they knew emotionally and instinctively that the landlord system represented English conquest and their servitude.

In the late eighteenth century, Britain, Ireland, and much of continental Europe experienced rapid rises in population. In Britain, health benefits associated with industrial, agricultural, and transportation revolutions helped stimulate population growth: improved sanitation, fresh water, inexpensive clothing, better and less costly food, and smallpox vaccinations prolonged life and reduced infant mortality. But Ireland did not experience industrial or agricultural change, and medical care was primitive and rarely available. Famine and disease were endemic.

Often landlords were more victims than promoters of a vicious agrarian system. Until after the French Revolution, they were reluctant to halt subdivisions, slow to comprehend that the multiplication of smallholdings was largely responsible for inefficient farming, reducing the potential for profit. And they had to confront pressures of tenant needs and, to a lesser extent, British mercantilist restrictions on Irish trade, preventing the development of dynamic urban economies to siphon off surplus rural residents. Intelligent, efficient landlords, determined to improve the quality of their estates by rational, hardheaded measures would have inflicted burdens on their tenants. By forbidding subleasing, they would have destroyed social patterns of rural life and antagonized those not averse to sharing poverty with others. Collecting rents without interfering with peasant mores, even if such timidity encouraged eventual disaster, was an easy way out for proprietors.

In the north, conflict was more likely to occur between Catholics and Protestants than between landlords and tenants or agricultural laborers and tenants. Sectarian tensions, especially west of the River Bann, inspired the creation of rival secret societies. During the 1780s, the Protestant Peep O' Day boys terrorized Catholics, who responded with the Defenders, their secret society. In the 1795 Battle of the Diamond in County Armagh between Peep O' Day Boys and Defenders, Protestants prevailed and thereafter instituted the Orange Order. It quickly gained adherents and terrorized Ulster Catholics, driving many of them out of the province, frequently to the west. Realizing the potential of "no-popery," Protestant Ascendancy upper classes took command of the Order, armed its members, and persuaded government officials that religious bigotry and intimidation were effective instruments of law and order. Orangeism remained a permanent Protestant Ascendancy weapon, a prototype of future Anglo-Protestant nativism in Ireland, Britain, and North America.

Although the Defenders' main concern was Catholic protection, they also were involved in protests against excessive rents and tithes to the established Church. Early in the nineteenth century, the Ribbon Society absorbed them. Despite its origins in Ulster, Ribbonmen were more concerned with economic rather than sectarian issues and thus spread into Leinster and Munster. Ribbonism appealed to agricultural laborers, sharpening class divisions among peasants. Until the Great Famine of the late 1840s rapidly and radically reduced rural numbers, agricultural laborers outnumbered tenant farmers. The latter often exploited the former as landlords had abused them. Agricultural laborers worked more for tenant farmers than aristocracy or gentry. To feed families they rented small potato patches—conacre—sometimes in lieu of wages. A late eighteenth-century tendency to switch from tillage to raising cattle in order to satisfy the meat needs and desires of urban Britain was particularly hard on agricultural labor. Finding difficulty in obtaining work or conacre, they often relied on Ribbonmen to defend their interests against tenant farmer employers.

Secret societies did not represent the budding of revolutionary Irish nationalism. They did not attempt to destroy either Protestant Ascendancy or landlordism. Instead, their intention was to reform both. Hope and rising expectation breed revolutionaries. Irish Catholics were too demoralized to wave flags of insurrection. They had not melded their religion, language, customs, and values into a coherent ethnic identity to challenge Protestant Ascendancy. They were Catholic rather than Irish, finding salvation and significance within religious confines. Still, men angry enough to use a cudgel or spike, burn a building, shoot a landlord or his agent or tithe collector had revolutionary potential. All the Irish Catholic masses needed for social, economic, and political liberation was hope, discipline-specific goals, an ethnic identity, and charismatic leadership. They had to wait until the nineteenth century to find them.

The Rise and Fall of the Protestant Nation

During the eighteenth century, Britain's Irish colony evolved into a Protestant nation. With the Penal Laws' success in degrading and demoralizing Catholic

Ireland, Protestants felt more secure and less dependent on Britain for survival. They began to resent British political and commercial restrictions. During Mary Tudor's reign, Poynings Law (1494), limited the Irish Parliament's role to the submission of bills to the king and his Privy Council in Britain for approval, veto, or amendment. Irish legislators could only accept or reject British amendments. If they attempted to improve or alter a bill, it became new legislation and had to be resubmitted to London. In 1720, the British Parliament's Declaratory Act, the sixth of George I, further restricted Irish sovereignty, insisting on Britain's right to legislate for the country. In legal cases, appellate jurisdiction by Britain's House of Lords also pointed up Ireland's subordination.

Irish commercial interests did well through association with the world's richest empire. During most of the eighteenth century, landlords, merchants, and manufacturers profited and raised standards of living through the connection. But they complained that British mercantilism regulated the Irish economy to serve British interests. Short on natural resources, Ireland could not seriously compete with Britain, but it had a few small industries (i.e., woolen textiles and glass making) that might, if encouraged, have served as useful employment and investment alternatives to a primitive agrarian economy suffering from overpopulation. Concentrated in the Belfast area, linen manufacturing prospered with the consent of both the Irish and British Parliaments.

Like those in North America, Anglo-Protestants in Ireland developed into a self-conscious community that complained that absentee landlords drained Irish talent, leadership, and potential investment. They argued that if more men of property remained in the country that furnished them with incomes, they might develop a concern for its rights and progress. They also protested the expenses of a large military establishment and Hanoverian exploitation of a large Irish pension list to reward favorites, depriving Ireland of funds better used in economic development.

Like North American agitators, those in Ireland expressed grievances in Lockian rhetoric. William Molyneux, a friend of John Locke and the first Irish Protestant patriotic theoretician, insisted that only an Irish Parliament could represent his people because laws and institutions had to reflect their wishes, not a British consensus. Jonathan Swift, dean of St. Patrick's Cathedral and the most articulate of the patriot propagandists, argued in his 1724 *Drapier Letters* that "all Government without the consent of the Governed is the very *definition* of *slavery*." He told the Anglo-Irish "that by Laws of God, of nature, of nations, and of your country, You Are and ought to be a Free a people as your Brethren in England."

Although Protestant patriots' discontent continued to mount, forces independent of Irish public opinion sustained British interests in Ireland. They included English-born primates (Archbishops of Armagh) of the Church of Ireland and about half its hierarchy. They defined their Church's mission as promoting and advancing British interests. British loyalties also attracted a good number of Irish aristocrats and gentry. British lord lieutenants played minor roles and spent little time in Ireland. In their absence three lord justices, usually including primates and speakers of Ireland's House of Commons, represented the crown. They spoke for landed magnates and through patronage controlled a majority of parliamentary seats. As long as Westminster politicians avoided conflict with their Irish agents, they could depend on them to pursue and protect British interests.

In 1767, Britain appointed Lord Townshend as lord lieutenant, instructing him to diminish the influence of Ireland's aristocracy and gentry. Evidently, London decided that ruling Ireland through Anglo-Irish middlemen was too expensive. Under the new policy, lord lieutenants had to reside in Ireland and directly control patronage. The promotion of lord lieutenants and demotion of Anglo-Protestant leaders clarified Ireland's colonial status and persuaded many aristocrats and gentry that there were deep conflicts between Irish and British interests. But lord Lieutenants could still employ patronage to maintain a pro-British parliamentary majority in Dublin's College Green.

Beginning in 1775, the strategies and objectives of Anglo-Irish Protestantism merged with those of Anglo-America to reduce British influence in their countries. In October of that year, the Irish government asked Parliament to brand American patriots as rebels in a war to preserve the empire. Because so many Irish MPs benefited from crown patronage, a parliamentary majority agreed. But the American cause had Irish friends, particularly in Ulster, who sympathized with Benjamin Franklin's appeal for Irish support against a common "tyranny." Fifty-four Ulster MPs voted against Britain's request.

America's 1777 victory at Saratoga, which brought Bourbon France and Spain into the war as allies, intensified British anxiety concerning Irish discontent. Now it had to fear Irish Protestant as well as Catholic sentiment. Grumbling in Ireland grew louder when Britain placed an embargo on its exports, except to specified countries, to prevent supplies from reaching American rebels. Anglo-Irish patriots blamed the embargo for an expanding Irish debt, which had reached 3 million pounds. They argued that the embargo made it difficult to find new sources of revenue, eliminated some already existing sources, and impoverished quite a few taxpayers. The British prime minister, Lord North, would have liked to soothe Anglo-Irish discontent with a few concessions to their grievances, but leaders of British commerce pressured him to change his plans. The Anglo-Irish interpreted North's surrender as evidence that Britain never would tolerate a vigorous, varied, or competitive Irish economy.

Because Anglo-Irish patriots could not overcome a patronage-loaded parliamentary majority, they were forced to employ strategies outside the regular political processes. War in America provided such an opportunity. Most Irish soldiers were overseas in Britain's army while the combined French and Spanish fleets commanded the surrounding seas, leaving Ireland vulnerable to attack and invasion. The lord lieutenant, Lord Buckinghamshire, responded to a Belfast citizen's petition requesting troop protection with a frank admission that war in America made it impossible to honor his request. Petitioners then organized a volunteer force for their defense. This initiative set an example for other parts of the country. Soon a national Volunteer movement integrated companies throughout Ireland. Many Anglo-Irish who could afford to purchase arms became Volunteers. Although Protestants did not want to arm Catholics, in 1780 they relented and permitted respectable gentry and middle-class papists to become Volunteers. The Earl of Leinster and Lord Charlemont commanded Volunteer forces, and parliamentary patriots served as officers in local units. When Leinster realized that patriots had something in mind beyond Ireland's safety, he reduced his commitment, leaving Charlemont as sole commander. British government representatives in Ireland distrusted Volunteers but indirectly armed them by distributing guns and ammunition to county lord lieutenants as a deterrent to an invasion. Because most of them also led Volunteer companies, these weapons were soon in patriot hands.

The American war not only aided Anglo-Irish patriots, but also slightly improved the lot of Irish Catholics. Even before hostilities began across the Atlantic, the Enlightenment spirit, growth of Irish Protestant self-confidence, respectability of an increasing large Catholic middle class, and papist loyalty to Hanoverian monarchs during the 1715 and 1745 Stuart disturbances in Scotland increased prospects for some concessions to Penal Law opponents. In 1774, when Britain extended toleration to French-Canadian Catholics, coreligionists in Ireland had permission to demonstrate loyalty by taking an oath of allegiance to the king. Although this oath conferred no benefits, it acknowledged the existence of Catholic subjects and hinted of future concessions. When France and Spain became American allies, Ireland's Protestant Ascendancy opposed remedies to Catholic grievance because they because they might encourage more demands and expectations . English Whigs, however, believed "no-popery" fostered, not discouraged, treachery. In 1777, George III (1760–1820) favorably received an Irish Catholic petition to mitigate the Penal Laws, and Whigs in Britain told those in Ireland that it was time to relax sectarian tensions.

Fearing British exploitation of the religious issue, Henry Grattan, leader of the patriot cause in and out of Parliament, decided that it would be a positive strategy to encourage Catholic civil liberties. He advised coreligionists that "the Irish Protestant could never be free until the Irish Catholic ceased to be a slave." At the urgings of Grattan and British Whigs, Ireland's Parliament passed a Relief Bill permitting Catholics to lease land for 999 years and to pass it on through primogeniture. It also eliminated the threat that an apostate son might acquire his father's property. Although Catholics remained excluded from political influence associated with direct property ownership, for all practical purposes a 999-year lease amounted to permanent possession.

In 1779, patriots applied Volunteer pressure on the free-trade issue. When the Irish Parliament met on October 12, Grattan moved for an amendment to the king's address, stating that Ireland's economic problems originated in British mercantilism. On November 4, Volunteers celebrated William III's birthday with a display of military force. They assembled in College Green with two cannons and raised placards warning "Free Trade or This." Having gotten the message, Ireland's Parliament voted the government only six months of supplies. Impressed and intimidated by Volunteer strength and determination, harassed by war in America, worried about a possible French invasion, and urged by opposition Whigs to compromise, Lord North persuaded the British Parliament to permit Irish exportation of glass and woolen products and trade with British colonies without restrictions.

Encouraged by this major concession, Grattan decided to push for his ultimate objective, self-government. Once more he relied on Irish opinion and a Volunteer menace to convince Ireland's Parliament and Britain's government that increasing Irish sovereignty was prudent and necessary. On December 18, 1781 Irish MPs called for an end to Poynings' Law and the Declaratory Act. Two months later Volunteer leaders met at Dungannon to ratify a set of resolutions demanding: (1) an independent Irish Parliament, (2) unrestricted free trade, (3) control of Ireland's judiciary by the Irish Parliament, (4) repeal of the Penal Law.

The last resolution expressed Grattan's conviction that a successful Irish nation demanded full equality of Catholics, Protestants, and Nonconformists. Patrick Flood, his colleague and patriot rival, led the opposition to repeal, insisting that it would result in Catholic power at the expense of the Protestant constitution and destruction of Anglo-Irish culture. Claiming to be an enlightened advocate of tolerance, Flood said the Protestant Ascendancy protected liberty against popery's authoritarianism and bigotry. Subsequent events revealed that Flood's antipathy toward Catholicism was more in tune with Anglo-Irish opinion than Grattan's inclusive patriotism.

Political change in Britain was as important as Volunteer pressure in advancing patriot goals. In March 1782, Whigs came to power with the Marquis of Rockingham as prime minister and Charles J. Fox as the leader in the House of Commons. Because they shared Locke's ideology, British Whigs urged compromise with their Irish brethren, but were reluctant to abandon all control over the neighboring island. However, the Duke of Portland, the viceroy in Ireland, informed Rockingham and Fox that Grattan and friends would accept nothing less than an independent Parliament in Dublin. Britain's international troubles added weight to Portland's information.

In the late stages of the American Revolution, combined French and Spanish fleets controlled and sailed up and down the English Channel and blockaded Chesapeake Bay and the mouth of the York River. This blockade prevented supplies from reaching Marquess Charles Cornwallis, the British major-general quartered at Yorktown. After Cornwallis's surrender in October 1781 ended the American conflict, Bourbon powers remained confident. In 1782, they captured Minorca and laid siege to Gibraltar, but the tide of war changed in April 1782, when Admiral George Rodney Bridges defeated and captured his opponent, Admiral François Joseph Paul de Grasse, Marquis de Grassetilly, in the West Indies. Nevertheless, war against France and Spain, joined by the Dutch, had Irish implications, causing anxieties in Westminster. On May 15, 1782, Fox introduced a series of proposals to Parliament, which received assent from both Houses. They amended Poyning's Law and repealed the Declaratory Act. These alterations meant that lord lieutenants and their advisors could no longer initiate Irish legislation, monarchs could veto bills but not alter them, British Parliaments could not legislate for Ireland, and Irish judges had secure tenures and Irish courts final jurisdiction. In 1783, under pressure from Anglo-Irish patriots, the British Parliament passed a Renunciation Act abandoning any present or future claim to legislate for Ireland.

British concessions to Anglo-Irish patriotism were less than those granted to Anglo-Americans at the 1783 Treaty of Paris. Irish sovereignty was restricted in two significant ways: lord lieutenants were responsible to British, not Irish, governments, and royal vetoes depended on the advice of British, rather than Irish, ministers. Nevertheless, Britain's somewhat limited surrender to Irish Protestant patriotism was an advance on the road to Ireland's liberation, and by any standard the first ten years of the new relationship between Ireland and Britain comprised a record of achievement for the former. Ireland increased its manufacturing, trade, and consumption of goods. Only members of the Catholic peasantry did not share in this new prosperity. An expanding economy and the importance of Ireland's Parliament had a positive effect on Irish culture. The founding of the Royal Academy and construction of architecturally splendid buildings such as the Four Courts and Customs House along the Liffey indicated energy and confidence. Dublin began to wear the vestments of a capital city. Although Irish talent continued to emigrate, absenteeism declined. Numerous aristocrats decided Irish life was exciting and Irish politics deserved their involvement. They also found Dublin's social and intellectual climates stimulating. Quite a few built attractive townhouses in or on the fringes of the city. A large resident upper- and an affluent middle-class encouraged a taste for luxury goods and skilled artisans to cater to sophisticated demands.

During the 1780s and 1790s Catholic upper and middle classes also improved their status, mostly through British rather than Irish Protestant initiatives. Wars of the French Revolution revived fears of Ireland as a potential danger to Britain, which pressured the Irish Parliament to make some gestures of goodwill toward Catholics. In 1792, it responded by removing Catholic disabilities connected with mixed sectarian marriages, granting Catholics permission to open schools, and permitting them to become solicitors and barristers. A year later, Catholics received municipal and parliamentary franchises. They could also bear arms and became eligible for minor civil and military positions. A Catholic franchise was a shadow, not substance, of political influence. Religious loyalty oaths continued to bar them from Parliament and urban governments. Without a secret ballot, 40-shilling freehold voters expanded political dominance of the Protestant ascendancy, which led to more subdivision, expanding numbers of inefficient units of agriculture, and more votes for Protestant landlord candidates. If a tenant failed to vote his landlord's choices, he risked eviction.

As French revolutionary armies swept the continent, British and Irish governments grew concerned over Irish Catholic clerical education. Many continental seminaries training Irish young men for the priesthood had to close or bend to winds of radical anticlerical Jacobin ideology. Irish bishops and Irish and British politicians feared ordained priests would return home as revolutionary agents. To prevent this, British leaders encouraged the Irish Parliament in 1795 to establish a Roman Catholic seminary at Maynooth, County Kildare, and finance it with an annual grant. "No-popery" bowed to expediency. Successful British efforts to lead the Irish Parliament away from extreme anti-Catholicism revealed the Protestant nation in retreat from its 1782 victory. In the 1790s, economic dimensions of war with France restricted Irish trade, ending the economic boom of the 1780s. Deeply in debt, Ireland became a dependency of Britain. Loans from Britain revived its influence in Irish affairs.

Political instability magnified economic hard times and opened the door to British interference. Feuds, disputes, and rivalries forced both Grattan and Flood from the political arena. Dublin's Parliament was a cockpit of selfish interests. Upper classes dominated both the House of Lords and the House of Commons, and lord lieutenants manipulated competing cliques. Grattan and Flood had believed that a patriot victory would not be a complete reality until Parliament represented a wider spectrum of opinion, and their followers continued to urge parliamentary reform. But the landed aristocracy's stubborn resistance to constitutional change drove patriot reformers farther to the left. In 1791, some of them organized the Society of United Irishmen. Members admired Jean-Jacques Rousseau, and their organization was a Jacobin imitation that advocated a democratic republic as a desirable alternative to Protestant Ascendancy. United Irishmen were prepared to employ physical force to achieve a government representing the General Will.

With a middle-class Ulster Protestant base, United Irishmen represented Anglo-Irish patriotism evolving into Irish nationalism. They wanted a democratic Ireland without sectarian divisions. Theobald Wolfe Tone, a Dublin Protestant, emerged as the society's dominant personality. From 1792 until 1793, he served as secretary of the Catholic Committee as part of a strategy to unite Catholics and Protestants in a common revolutionary cause. Tone had little respect for timid Catholic upper- and middle-classes, but he considered exploited Catholic peasants excellent revolutionary material, potential allies of radical, middle-class Ulster Nonconformists.

Sensing unrest, Irish authorities reacted with coercion rather than reform. In 1796, Parliament approved legislation restricting civil liberties, increasing police powers, and suspending habeas corpus. Since the government distrusted the loyalties of Catholic-loaded militia companies, it armed landlord-recruited yeoman corps filled with Orangemen. But there was no reason to distrust Catholic soldiers; they did their duty. In 1797, they served General Gerard Lake when he moved into Ulster and smashed a United Irishmen Belfast organization and damaged others in the province. Seeing that coercion and terror were effective in Ulster, authorities applied them to the rest of the country. Zealous about crushing "treason," Orange yeomen were guilty of numerous atrocities in the Catholic south. Orange terrorism frightened many Catholics but drove others into Defender ranks as United Irishmen allies.

In March 1798, authorities arrested most Dublin-area United Irishmen leaders. Having gone to France in an attempt to raise an expeditionary force in support of an Irish insurrection, Tone escaped. Although Lord Edward Fitzgerald, the society's most prestigious member, managed to avoid the March dragnet, he was mortally wounded two months later while resisting arrest. Government repression destroyed United Irishmen's efficiency but failed to stop rebellion. On May 26, 1798, in Wexford Father John Murphy launched a peasant revolt. He won some victories but pikes were no match for guns, and on June 21 government troops crushed Murphy and his followers at Vinegar Hill. Although Lake's excursion crippled Ulster's United Irishmen, in June 1798 they rose in revolt in Antrim and Down. They fought courageously, but government forces defeated them and executed their leaders.

The United Irishmen originally called for a coordinated national revolution, but the risings in Wexford, Antrim, and Down were spontaneous and without joint planning. When General Jean Joseph Humbert's small French army of about a thousand landed in Killala Bay, County Mayo, in August 1798, it arrived too late with too little. Still, for a short time, Humbert's troops, joined by a contingent of pike-armed Connacht peasants, outmaneuvered and outfought its enemies. However, in September they ran out of supplies and space to maneuver. Humbert surrendered to General Packenham, who slaughtered a large number of Catholic peasants but let French soldiers return home. In 1815, Humbert had his revenge when he joined Andrew Jackson to defeat Packenham at New Orleans. In October 1798, Wolfe Tone, having attained the rank of adjutant general in the French army, failed in an attempt to invade Ireland. Captured off Donegal's coast, Tone committed suicide in a Dublin cell as an alternative to being hanged as a traitor.

Irish nationalist mythology distorted the meaning of events in 1798 . Events in Northern Ireland since 1969 have perpetuated misinformation. According to the nationalist canon, that year represented an ecumenical happening: Protestants from the north joined Catholics from the south in a heroic effort to free their country and protect civil liberties. But United Irishmen were not typical Irishmen. Most were Enlightenment Deists, scornful of all organized religions and oblivious to the sectarian passions culturally as well as religiously separating Catholics from Protestants. In reality, Orangemen were more representative of Protestant Ulster than United Irishmen. Rebels in Antrim and Down did not share a community spirit with those who fought in Wexford and Mayo. Catholics who murdered Wexford Protestants, and in turn and fell victim to Orange Yeomen, participated in a peasant revolt rather than a crusade for an independent, democratic, nonsectarian Irish Republic. Catholics who joined Humbert in Mayo fought for pope and Blessed Virgin rather than the rights of man. Throughout the turmoil of 1798, militia Catholics remained loyal to the king and the Protestant government. They furnished most of the troops that smashed the uprisings.

The year's developments diminished, not expanded, prospects for Irish independence. Even before the events of that year, British politicians at Westminster were disturbed by Ireland's instability. Insurrections in Wexford, Antrim, Down, and Mayo, plus French involvement, convinced Prime Minister William Pitt (the Younger) that Ireland had to join the United Kingdom. An influential segment of Irish Protestants, led by John Fitzgibbon, earl of Clare, whose father had converted to Protestantism, agreed with Pitt. Once a patriot, Clare decided that Catholic discontent wedded to Jacobin radicalism could destroy Protestant Ascendancy, which he and his friends agreed was more important than an independent Irish Parliament. In a United Kingdom, Protestants could rely on the British military to preserve their power monopoly.

In advocating union with Britain, Clare was candid about Ireland's class and religious realities. He told Whig opponents in the Irish Parliament that reform idealism jeopardized their status. Clare said that there could never be democracy and civil rights in Ireland because Protestants descended from the conquerors who had robbed natives of their property and then enslaved them. Therefore, it would be unreasonable not to expect an emancipated Catholic majority to insist on the restoration of what once was theirs.

Pitt instructed the lord lieutenant, Lord Cornwallis, who had surrendered at Yorktown, and his chief secretary, Lord Castlereigh, to prepare ground for union. Like Pitt, both favored Catholic Emancipation. They assured Irish Catholic bishops that union with Britain would advance the interests of their religion because a British Parliament would be more objective than the Protestant Ascendancy Irish legislature. Cornwallis and Castlereigh promised the prelates that they and Pitt would try to persuade the British Parliament to concede Catholic Emancipation once the union existed. While they were courting the Catholic hierarchy, other English politicians guaranteed Lord Clare and his friends that the union would sustain Protestant Ascendancy.

Late in 1798 both houses of the British Parliament agreed to principles of a United Kingdom, but in January 1799, Ireland's House of Commons rejected a pro-union paragraph in Cornwallis's address. For the remainder of the year, Irish MPs and pamphleteers debated merits and demerits of a union in an atmosphere clouded by rumors of French invasion plots and the presence of martial law. Both operated as pro-Union intimidation factors.

Advocates of a British connection argued that the Irish political system had failed to maintain stability or security from foreign intervention, insisting that Ireland's integration into the United Kingdom was necessary to defend it from internal chaos and external enemies and as a guarantee of continued Protestant Ascendancy. Led by Grattan, patriots responded that such an arrangement would reduce Ireland's status from a nation to a province, warning that Britain would sacrifice Irish to British interests. And they predicted that after Ireland lost its independence, the aristocracy would abandon the country, industries would collapse, and trade would decline.

Anticipating that a British Parliament would make concessions to Catholic agitation, few Orangemen favored the union. Some Catholic merchants and lawyers shared Protestant patriot concerns that a United Kingdom would wreak havoc on the

Irish economy. But most Catholic bishops and lay leaders believed Pitt's promise that it would be a prelude to Catholic Emancipation.

While the upper and middle classes debated the pros and cons of a British linkage—peasants found the issue irrelevant—Cornwallis and Castlereigh were busy employing persuasion and patronage in constructing an Irish parliamentary majority for an intended union. They concentrated on the large number of MPs who had remained neutral in January 1799. After the lord lieutenant distributed peerages, granted pensions, and agreed to compensate holders of seats in Ireland's Parliament, in February 1800 the House of Commons endorsed a union by a 43-vote majority, 158 to 115. Support for a union was more substantial in the House of Lords, 75 to 26. In March, Ireland's Parliament approved specific articles for an Act of Union; the British Parliament followed suit two months later. On December 31, 1800, Ireland's Protestant political nation ceased to exist. Nationalists continued to complain that Cornwallis's and Castlereigh's tactics defied Irish public opinion, but they were common to both Irish and British politics of the time.

In the 1920s, infuriated by Catholic-dominated Dáil legislation discriminating against Protestant consciences and privacy, the senator and poet William Butler Yeats described his coreligionists as one of the stocks of Europe, the people of Jonathan Swift, Oliver Goldsmith, Edmund Burke, George Berkeley, Thomas Davis, and Charles Stewart Parnell. In a pioneering effort in his country's intellectual history, *The Irish* (1969), Sean O'Faolain looked at pre-union Anglo-Irish Protestants from a different perspective: "They resided in Ireland—their country, never their nation—so that their achievements were, for the most part, so remote from the life of the native Irish (now utterly suppressed) that they ultimately became part of the English rather than the Irish cultural record."

While setting an early example in apartheid colonialism, the Anglo-Irish made important and permanent additions to Ireland's cultural and political personality. They decorated Irish cities with attractive and graceful architecture, created the first Irish political nation, and endowed subsequent Irish nationalism with some liberal, democratic values. Ireland's Protestant nation and patriotism have had a prominent place in the history and mythology of Irish nationalism, inspiring the imagination and encouraging nineteenth- and twentieth-century constitutional and violent liberation efforts.

2

Catholic Emancipation, 1801–1829

The Irish Parliament held its last session in College Green on August 2, 1800. On January 28, 1801, one hundred Irishmen took seats in the 658-member British House of Commons, and thirty-two Irish peers, including four Protestant bishops, entered the 360-member House of Lords. Despite the existence of a UK Parliament at Westminster, the merger of the Churches of Ireland and England, and the 1815 amalgamation of the two treasuries, Ireland was not as thoroughly integrated into the United Kingdom as were the other two portions of the Celtic fringe, Scotland and Wales. The continuation of such positions as lord lieutenant, chief secretary, lord chancellor, and chancellor of the exchequer, over twenty government agencies supervising a multitude of civil servants, a military department, and separate courts and prison systems were remnants of nationhood.

The most glaring contrast between Ireland and Britain was the condition of the Irish Catholic majority. The Penal Laws had coerced most of the Catholic aristocracy and gentry into Protestantism, and restrictions on the acquisition of land had expanded the Catholic merchant and shopkeeper middle class. Although the position of the small Catholic upper class and the growing middle class had substantially improved by the time of the union, they were still deprived by remaining Penal Laws that kept them from a role in Irish political life and the professions. Both worked for Catholic emancipation to achieve equality with Anglo-Irish and British Protestants. In their effort to liberate themselves, upper- and middle-class Catholics had little empathy for the plight of the rural masses.

The Life of Rural Catholic Ireland

The overwhelming majority of Irish Catholics were attached to the land as tenants at will or agricultural laborers. Few tenants had farms bigger than 15 acres. Far more numerous than farmers, agricultural laborers were fortunate to have a patch of land on which to erect a crude mud hut and to plant a potato garden. Small tenant farmers' cottages were often no better than those of the laborers. The floors were dirt, and vermin infested the thatch roofs. Windows to let in a bit of fresh air were rare. Because a pig was a valuable possession, in bad weather animals and people shared hearth and home. Such living conditions bred disease, resulting in an extremely high mortality rate, particularly among infants. If a person managed to

DANIEL O'CONNELL, 1775–1847

Daniel O'Connell built modern Irish nationalism on the foundations of the agitation for Catholic emancipation. As a champion of human rights and freedom throughout the world, he implanted the values of liberal democracy in the soil of Irish nationalism. (Photo painted and engraved by R.M. Hodgetts, courtesy of the National Gallery of Ireland)

survive childhood, the scourges of scurvy, cholera, tuberculosis, and malnutrition threatened to prevent the attainment of middle age. Defying poverty and disease and the lack of significant medical care, Ireland from the mid-eighteenth century until the Great Famine of the 1840s experienced a massive population increase. In

1781 the estimated number of people living in the country was 4,048,000. Sixty years later the census recorded the population at 8,175,000, a gain of slightly more than 100 percent.

Ireland's population explosion indicated frequent marriage and high fertility. Throughout time and place, poverty has increased the need for shared misery and stimulated sexual urges. Living within the confines of their religious and agrarian mores, Irish Catholics satisfied desires inside the marriage bond. For people as poor and as miserable as rural Irish Catholics, sex, the companionship of wives and husbands, and the joy of children, like good and even bad whiskey, were comforts and escapes in a normally hopeless existence.

Potatoes also figured in Ireland's population boom. An easy-to-cultivate vegetable that flourished in less than excellent soil, the nutritious potato dominated the rural Irish menu. By the time of the Great Famine, most of the people ate only potatoes with a little milk or buttermilk to wash them down. Sometimes they were consumed half-cooked to prolong the digestive process. Potatoes made it possible to feed many with few resources, encouraging the young to marry and begin large families. But such reliance on a single food source posed the danger of crop failures. Beginning in the 1820s, Ireland experienced a series of famines, culminating in the "holocaust" of the 1840s.

The population explosion put too much strain on an already weak agrarian economy. Because there was no industry outside northeast Ulster to absorb the surplus population, tenant farmers had to emigrate, suffer downward mobility by joining the ranks of agricultural labor, or subdivide already-too-small holdings. As Irish farms decreased in size, agriculture gained in inefficiency. Following the decline in grain prices after the French Revolution and continuing for the rest of the century, Irish farming became more pasture than tillage, adding to the land shortage. Due to land hunger, landlords were able to raise rents beyond the value of farms and still find desperate souls willing to pay. Tenants with exorbitant rents were anxious to sublease parts of their holdings, also at excessive rates, to meet obligations to landlords.

Land pressure and its exploitation fostered avarice, evictions, class war, and violence. Because the landlords commanded the law and the authorities, secret societies such as the Ribbonmen, Whiteboys, Molly Maguires, Terry Alts, and Defenders flourished. In individual instances and in epidemics of violence, they burned hayricks and maimed cattle to punish landlords for high rents and landgrabbers who occupied the farms of evicted tenants; they shot bailiffs of enemy landlords, harassed tithe collectors for an established Church that served only 13 percent of the population, and even punished Catholic priests with reputations for charging too much for baptisms, weddings, and funerals. While tenant farmers and agricultural laborers frequently united in opposition against the landowning class, secret societies were organized by laborers to protest the wages offered and conacre (potato patch) rents demanded by farmers.

In the form of fiction, William Carleton presented an insider's portrait of pre-famine rural Ireland. His *Wildgoose Lodge* describes how agrarian terrorists could be cruel and indiscriminate in their violence at the expense of innocents. But secret societies did enforce a sort of moral economy where and when legal and political structures were indifferent to the plight of the rural masses.

Government responses to Irish violence indicated that Ireland was much more a colony than an integral part of the United Kingdom. Insurrection acts and coercion bills with house searches, curfews, sentences without jury trials, and suspensions of habeas corpus violated traditional British constitutional rights. In 1813 Sir Robert Peel, Irish chief secretary and Tory leader in the House of Commons, introduced a professional police force into Ireland. By 1867 it had evolved into the Royal Irish Constabulary (RIC). The half-police, half-soldier barracks-dwelling RIC became a model security force for the empire. The government also used the military in Ireland for purposes of law and order. Among their police duties, soldiers assisted in tithe collection and escorting electors to the polls in hotly contested elections.

In Irish nationalist mythology and in British reformism, Irish landlords were the arm of British economic and social colonialism and the source of rural discontent and misery. As in Maria Edgeworth's *Castle Rackrent,* some landlords were reckless, improvident, and indifferent to the welfare of their estates. A considerable number were absentees living in Britain off their Irish rents. Absenteeism probably aggravated the social and economic dimension of the Irish question. Although it was not always the case, resident landlords were more likely to be interested in the quality of agriculture on their estates and the good of their tenants. It is difficult to prove that absentees were not as humane as residents, but they did deny to Ireland income derived from their property, thus hampering the development of domestic trades and industries. Absentees were more British than Irish in perspective, and the loss of such a large proportion of the aristocracy retarded the development of a vital, intelligent, and influential Irish political, cultural, and economic opinion.

Irish nationalism and British reformism exaggerated landlord evils. They were scapegoats for complex social and economic problems. Many were kindly disposed toward their tenants. Often well-intentioned landlords caused economic disasters. Reluctant to interfere with the mores of their tenants, they ignored farm subdivisions and inefficient farming. But the main problem with Irish landlordism was its alien rather than economic character. The landed aristocracy and gentry in other sections of the United Kingdom were often cruel to their tenants, but they shared religious and cultural values with them. They received natural acceptance as the leaders of British rural society. In Ireland, landlords and tenants were separated by religious and cultural barriers. Landlordism symbolized the passing of the Gaelic order, the oppression suffered by Catholic Ireland, and the triumph of British colonialism.

Relations between landlord and tenant were more cordial in Ulster than in Leinster, Munster, and Connacht. Ulster custom permitted a tenant to sell his interest in the farm, the result of improvements, when he left it. This was some protection against unfair rent increases and evictions. But in the south and west, if a tenant added to the value of his farm by draining, fencing, or fertilizing his fields or by repairing buildings, the landlord might raise his rent and evict him with no compensation if he could not meet the new demand. Consequently, Leinster, Munster, and Connacht farmers seldom improved their holdings, and the quality of Ulster agriculture was higher than in the remainder of the country. No doubt landlord-tenant contacts in Ulster were also more cordial because many farmers were Protestants (Anglicans) or Nonconformists like their landlords, and religious differences did not add to class and economic conflicts. In that way large areas of Ulster were more like Britain than Ireland.

Although the unhealthy condition of rural Ireland was apparent to all intelligent and impartial observers, politics, religion, and economic dogmas obstructed remedies. Both Whigs and Tories fought limitations on property rights, arguing that the Irish agrarian issue was moral rather than political. Laissez-faire dogmatism, so important in Whig and Radical circles, opposed proposed government emigration and public work programs to ease Irish poverty burdens. However, the British left was willing to give the Irish a greater voice in their own destiny through political reform, and it was sympathetic to equality between Catholic and Protestant peoples and their churches. But Tories were adamant in resisting any changes that might diminish Protestant ascendancy. They considered objections to the privileged position of Irish Protestantism and landlordism assaults on property and traditional institutions. Concessions to Catholic grievances would encourage further Irish discontent and open doors to new demands for change. Radical victories in Ireland would jeopardize the union and inspire agitation against the status quo all over the United Kingdom.

The Emergence of Daniel O'Connell

Before Irish gentry and middle-class Irish Catholics could transform Whig and Radical good intentions into a constructive Irish policy and overcome Tory obstinacy, they had to mobilize the Catholic masses behind the demand for justice and equality. Demoralized farmers and laborers, whose hopes did not extend much beyond survival in this world and salvation in the next, were poor political material. Catholic Ireland needed a leader with the genius to lift its spirits and provide it with the expectations and confidence necessary for effective agitation. Daniel O'Connell was such a person. He created an Irish national opinion that forced British politicians to choose between the unpleasant alternatives of reform and a revolution endangering political, social, and economic structures throughout the United Kingdom.

O'Connell was more than the creator of modern Irish nationalism. No other Irish leader has had as much international importance. His main concern was Ireland, but the principles he defended, the goals of his efforts, and his agitation techniques had favorable consequences for liberal democracy throughout the world. In the reactionary age of Metternich, O'Connell was the most successful tribune of the people. He translated democratic theory into practice by mobilizing the Irish rural masses into a powerful nationalist bloc. Applying this new force, he forced concessions from an arrogant, aristocratic British government. In early nineteenth-century Europe, O'Connell was a much-discussed personality: To the embattled left, he was a symbol of hope and a promise for the future; to the ascendant but nervous right, he was the enemy threatening entrenched privilege.

O'Connell was most hated by the British and Anglo-Irish establishments. Their newspapers and periodicals portrayed him as a mendacious, avaricious vulgarian inciting discontent in the public mind to collect money from ignorant, impoverished peasants. Conservative journalists and Tory politicians told the British public that O'Connell was the instigator of a vast conspiracy to subvert the empire and the constitution by detaching Ireland from Britain and by imposing popery on the British Isles. Because anti-Catholicism was the core of British nativism, O'Connell was a natural target for Tories manipulating Protestant passions to prevent economic and social change and to preserve the union with Ireland.

O'Connell's entry onto the public stage made the Irish question the leading emotional issue dividing British political forces and public opinion. He instructed British politicians in the techniques of political organization and activity. His successors at the helm of Irish nationalism continued the lesson.

O'Connell was born on August 6, 1775, the son of Morgan and Catherine O'Connell, members of the Kerry Catholic gentry. Through the goodwill of Protestant neighbors, the O'Connells managed to hold on to their property through the Penal Law years. They increased the family fortune through smuggling activities along the Kerry coast. Because Catholics were denied opportunities in Ireland, some O'Connells served Hapsburgs and Bourbons on the continent. O'Connell's uncle, Count Daniel, was a French general.

Following an Irish Catholic upper-class custom, Morgan and Catherine placed their infant son as a foster child with peasants for nursing and rearing. Learning and speaking the Irish language, participating in the religious devotions, games, and customs, and sharing the values of the people were good training for the future leader of Irish nationalism.

When O'Connell was still a boy, his childless uncle Maurice, head of the clan, adopted him as his heir. In 1791 Maurice sent his nephew to the continent for his secondary education. After the armies of the French Revolution closed two schools that he attended, St. Omer and Douai, O'Connell transferred to a London academy in 1793. Because by then the Irish Parliament had opened the practice of law to Catholics, the young man decided to become a barrister, and in 1794 he enrolled in Lincoln's Inn. He transferred to the King's Inn, Dublin, two years later. In 1798 O'Connell was admitted to the Irish bar.

In O'Connell's day, legal studies were not rigorous, and he had time and leisure to read history, biography, fiction, poetry, theology, and essays on political and economic thought. William Godwin's belief that democratic moral force could change society impressed the young student. Thomas Paine bolstered his democratic faith and led him away from orthodox Christianity to Deism. Adam Smith made him an advocate of laissez-faire. Although O'Connell eventually recovered his Catholic faith, he never rejected his commitment to human rights, democracy, religious tolerance, freedom of conscience, separation of church and state, and economic individualism. During the 1830s and 1840s he argued those causes in the British Parliament.

In Dublin, O'Connell became grand master of a Masonic lodge, visited the Irish Parliament, projected himself as a Catholic version of Henry Grattan liberating his people, and dabbled with the Society of United Irishmen, while at the same time drilling with a lawyer's yeoman corps organized to defend law and order. In 1798 O'Connell fled Dublin to avoid arrest. When the revolutions commenced, he was sick with fever in Kerry, but in his diary he denounced the events in Wexford: "Good God! What a brute man becomes when ignorant and oppressed! Oh liberty! what horrors are perpetrated in thy name! May every virtuous revolutionary remember the horrors of Wexford." O'Connell concluded that the Irish people were "not yet sufficiently enlightened to bear the sun of freedom." Revolution had released destructive passions in ignorant, frustrated people. Britain and the Irish establishment had responded to their rage with cruel repression and with the Act of Union. The uprising of '98 had contracted rather than expanded Ireland's freedom.

O'Connell was not an ideological pacifist. He praised the leaders of the American Revolution and contributed money and the services of a son to Simón Bolívar, the liberator of Latin America. Believing that the British would always crush a peasant mob and then further restrict Irish liberties, O'Connell rejected physical force as the route to Irish freedom. He continued to argue that the only way Catholics should earn civil rights, and Ireland's independence, was through the pressures of moral force. He condemned secret agrarian societies and had little use for Robert Emmet, who became one of Ireland's most beloved heroes.

A younger brother of Thomas Addis Emmet, one of the founders of the Society of United Irishmen, Robert Emmet in 1803 led a Dublin insurrection crushed by the authorities. He was tried, convicted, and executed for treason. Before being sentenced, Emmet made a speech defending his honor and condemning British oppression. He asked the young men of Ireland to listen to their country's cry for freedom and to vindicate his work and justify his sacrifice: "When my country takes her place among the nations of the earth, then and not until then, let my epitaph be written." Emmet's words and Thomas Moore's poetic tribute, "Oh Breathe Not His Name," made Emmet a martyr for Irish nationalists, but not to O'Connell. He wrote to a friend, "A man who could so coolly prepare so much bloodshed—so many murders—and such horrors of every kind has ceased to be an object of compassion."

In 1802 O'Connell married a distant cousin, Mary O'Connell. They had seven children who survived to adulthood. She provided him with a great deal of love, wise political advice, and the peace and security of a happy home. He loved her with passion and constancy.

When O'Connell began practicing his profession, times were difficult for

Catholic lawyers. They had to be content with unimportant cases and small fees. But O'Connell worked hard and used his knowledge of the Irish people, as well as a quick mind, devastating wit, and oratorical skills, to become the best cross-examiner and persuader of juries in Ireland. His practice became so large that by 1828 he was earning over 6,000 pounds a year.

In the courtroom, O'Connell promoted Irish nationalism. In addressing juries, he blamed British rule and the oppression of Catholics for Irish crimes and disorders. In 1805 O'Connell joined the Catholic Committee, working through petitions to Parliament to open political office for Catholics. He gave it much of his time and income. By 1812 he had replaced John Keogh as the most influential member of the organization.

Henry Grattan, leader of the Protestant nation and foe of the union, championed the cause of Catholic emancipation in the House of Commons. He presented Catholic Committee petitions to his parliamentary colleagues. Emancipation enlisted the support of most Whigs and Radicals, and even a few Tories. On occasion it could command a House of Commons majority. But the Tory government, in its resistance to Irish and British Catholic and parliamentary opinion, could count on the king's Protestant conscience, the House of Lords, and British nativism to frustrate the Catholic civil rights effort. There was one possibility that Catholic emancipation might become law: a compromise that would give the government or a committee of respectable and loyal Catholic laymen a veto over papal appointments of bishops in the United Kingdom. This security was acceptable to most prominent Catholics in Britain and Ireland, a few of the Irish Catholic hierarchy, Grattan and the British Whigs, and even the pope. Many governments in Catholic countries controlled appointments to the episcopacy. Britain, however, was a Protestant country with an established church. But the pope wanted cordial relations with one of the world's major powers.

In 1813 Grattan introduced a Catholic emancipation bill with securities. Most of the leadership of the Catholic Committee approved of the measure. Joining a majority of the Irish Catholic hierarchy, O'Connell opposed Grattan's bill, killed it, and split the Catholic Committee. Why? He argued that government intervention in the affairs of the Catholic Church would be detrimental to religion. His opposition to the veto was consistent with his Benthamite commitment to the separation of church and state, but his decision to oppose Grattan had political implications beyond the religious issue. O'Connell wanted to use the Catholic cause to create Catholic solidarity as a step toward national self-consciousness. The Catholic Church, its hierarchy, and its clergy were instruments of nationality. Because most bishops and priests came from the strong farmer and shopkeeper classes, they had an affinity with the people. As a group they had been prevented by the Penal Laws from political participation, but their position made them natural leadership rivals to Anglo-Irish Protestant landlords. If the government could establish some influence over the appointment of Irish bishops, they could be turned into agents of British rule. It would be difficult, perhaps impossible, to organize an effective nationalist movement without the endorsement of the Catholic hierarchy and clergy. Therefore, O'Connell reasoned, it would be better to postpone emancipation to preserve the potential of something even more important, national freedom.

The Catholic Association and the Beginnings of Modern Irish Nationalism

In 1823 the division in the Catholic emancipation leadership ended when O'Connell and two of the leaders of the pro-security wing, Sir Thomas Wyse and Richard Lalor Sheil, met at the home of O'Connell's son-in-law in the Wicklow Mountains and initiated a new organization, the Catholic Association. It took some time for the association to catch on. For a while it was difficult to gather a quorum. Then, in 1824, O'Connell decided to broaden the base of the Catholic movement and at the same time add to its financial resources. He invited peasants and workers to join the organization as associate members for only a shilling a year. They could pay it off a penny a month or only a farthing a week. Every Catholic parish in Ireland became a recruiting station for the Catholic Association. In sermons, priests told their flocks that they had an obligation to participate in the campaign for civil liberties and urged them to contribute their shillings, pennies, and farthings to the association. Outside chapels, Catholic rent collectors set up tables to harvest the fruits of these sermons. A shilling was a small amount of money, but contributed by many, the result was thousands of pounds in the association treasury. And to an Irish tenant farmer or a city or town worker, a shilling was a considerable expenditure. To make it, many had to give up tobacco or liquor, two escapes from the misery of poverty. Their sacrifice committed passions and emotions.

Most of the Irish masses could not even afford a shilling for Catholic emancipation. However, even agricultural laborers became moral supporters of the association. Their presence at mass meetings added to the formidability of the emancipation agitation. Through it O'Connell took degraded and demoralized people, lifted them from their knees, and gave them hope, dignity, and meaning to their lives. He disciplined their enthusiasm, arranged them into a powerful instrument of public opinion, educated them in the techniques of agitation, and grafted a nationality onto a religious loyalty, thus creating modern Irish nationalism. O'Connell, the Liberator, became the uncrowned king of Ireland.

From the beginning, it was evident that the Catholic Association was an unofficial Irish parliament. In addition to emancipation, it demanded repeal of the union, justice and security for tenant farmers, the end of tithes, and a democratic electorate voting by secret ballot. O'Connell insisted that his followers use constitutional methods to achieve Catholic liberties and national independence, moral rather than physical force. But the emancipation agitation had revolutionary implications. Never before had a British government confronted a united, mobilized, and disciplined Catholic Ireland with high morale, commitment to a cause, and national determination. O'Connell's nonviolence implied the opposite. He warned British politicians that if they were not prepared to deal with men of moderation, the Irish masses might turn to leaders who advised physical force.

When the government outlawed the Catholic Association, O'Connell used his legal dexterity to reorganize it under new names and then expand its activities. The association became a grievance committee, a propaganda agency against tithes, and a support group for mass education, tenant rights, expanded suffrage, the secret ballot, and parliamentary reform. In the process of agitating for Catholic emancipation, Irish nationalism took on its leader's liberalism.

While O'Connell was enlisting mass enthusiasm for Catholic emancipation, Thomas Wyse organized liberal clubs around the movement in cities and towns. They would continue to affect Irish politics long after the civil rights issue was settled. A superb tactician, Wyse decided to apply the power of the Catholic Association to the general election of 1826. In Waterford, the association endorsed a pro-emancipation Protestant, Villiers Stuart, against Lord George Beresford. The Beresford family considered the Waterford seat private property. Priests helped the association steel the courage of 40-shilling freehold voters to defy the wishes of their landlords. The Beresfords were defeated, and the Waterford example encouraged a number of other constituencies (Louth, Monaghan, Westmeath, Armagh, Cork City, Galway) to make emancipation a test for candidates. Again priests successfully competed with landlords for the farmer vote. The victories of 1826 elated the association, added to the confidence of the Irish Catholic people in their leaders, frightened the Irish Protestant aristocracy, and worried the Tory government. Wellington and Peel understood that O'Connell had permanently diminished the influence of landlordism, rivaling it with Catholic clerical power. The former decided that emancipation would have to be the price of a successful United Kingdom. However, he wanted to avoid the appearance of surrender to agitation, and he hoped to work out an arrangement guaranteeing the loyalty of the Catholic clergy to Britain as part of an emancipation package.

Six months after the general election, Lord Liverpool resigned as prime minister for health reasons. George Canning took his place. Because he was sympathetic to Catholic emancipation, O'Connell slowed the pace of agitation to give him time to create and introduce a Catholic relief bill. But within months Canning was dead, and O'Connell's old enemies, Wellington, "the stunted corporal," and "Orange" Peel, were back in office as prime minister and home secretary, respectively. Peel also led government forces in the House of Commons.

The Catholic Victory

Wellington appointed C.E. Vesey Fitzgerald, MP for Clare, to the Board of Trade presidency, forcing him to recontest his seat in a by-election. Fitzgerald was a popular landlord and a friend of Catholic emancipation. However, the Catholic Association decided to confront the issue of Catholic exclusion directly. Wyse and others persuaded O'Connell to challenge Fitzgerald. With the help of the priest-led 40-shilling voters, O'Connell defeated the government- and landlord-supported candidate.

The Clare results left Wellington and Peel with a variety of unpleasant questions and alternatives. After their great victory, would Irish Catholics passively stand aside if the government denied them civil equality and crushed the association? More likely, they would become involved in a massive agitation to destroy the union. And there was a possibility that they might turn away from O'Connell's constitutional tactics toward physical force. In any event, if the government did not grant Catholic emancipation, governing Ireland would become an even more difficult task than it already was. If suppression of the Catholic movement and denial of its demand resulted in insurrection, many pro-emancipation MPs in the House of Commons would blame the government, not Irish Catholics. In addition, there was considerable economic and social discontent in Britain, the consequence of industrialism and urbanization. It took the form of rioting, machine breaking, and demands for parliamentary reform. There was always the chance that rebellion in Ireland would increase British lawlessness.

To preserve peace and stability in Britain and Ireland, Wellington and Peel decided to ignore British no-popery and the right wing of their party and concede Catholic emancipation. The prime minister wanted to accompany it with payment of the Catholic clergy as a loyalty-wooing gesture. Peel talked him out of such a defiance of British nativism. Instead, the Catholic relief bill of 1829 revealed the government as a poor loser. In exchange for the Catholic opportunity to sit in Parliament, hold government office, and achieve professional distinctions, the 40-shilling freeholders lost their vote. Because landlords could no longer control it, tenant farmer suffrage seemed dangerous to the government. O'Connell accepted this defeat, arguing that the 40-shilling franchise without a secret ballot was not a free or reliable vote. He probably had other reasons for not defending the people who routed the Anglo-Irish Protestant ascendancy in 1826 and 1828. Knowing that upper- and middle-class British and Irish Catholics were more interested in their prospects than the rights of the people, he did not want to smash the Catholic Association as he had the Catholic Committee.

In addition to eliminating the 40-shilling franchise, there were other nasty reservations in the Wellington-Peel concession. The government forced O'Connell to recontest Clare (he won again, but at great expense), outlawed the Catholic Association, and forced Catholic MPs to take an insulting oath of allegiance before taking seats at Westminster.

After the relief bill came into force, Catholics could sit in the House of Lords and House of Commons and fill all offices in the United Kingdom except regent, lord chancellor, and lord lieutenant and lord chancellor of Ireland. Without the 40-shilling freeholders, the Irish electorate declined from over 100,000 to about 16,000. Even so, it was possible that Catholic voters could return a substantial number of their own to the House of Commons. Wellington expected emancipation to produce sixty Catholic MPs. However, because members of Parliament did not receive salaries, and, given the high cost of political campaigns and London living, few Irish Catholics had the economic resources or the leisure to seek parliamentary careers. As late as 1874, after considerable franchise extensions and the secret ballot, a general election returned only forty-nine Catholic MPs from Ireland. Fortunately, there were a few Protestant nationalists and liberals to speak at Westminster for Ireland's Catholic majority. Unfortunately, they were too few to make much difference.

The Consequences of Catholic Emancipation

Although Catholic emancipation did make Irish Catholic opinion somewhat more important in Parliament, its immediate impact was greater on British than Irish politics. Right-wing Tory extremists fought Catholic relief to the bitter end, appealing to the anti-Catholic core of British nativism. When they lost, they never forgave Wellington and Peel, especially the latter, for their betrayal of the Protestant constitution. Peel had to give up his Oxford seat and find another one in Westbury. A number of the ultras began to urge parliamentary reform, claiming that the people were more dependably conservative than parliamentary aristocrats. They said that Parliament had surrendered to popery against the wishes of public opinion. And they joined the Whigs in 1830 to topple Wellington's government, clearing the way for a reform Parliament. Ultra-Tories in their pique were only playing with parliamentary reform because their instincts were as hostile to British democracy as they were to Irish nationalism. Whereas their flirtation with radicalism was of the moment, their distrust of Peel was permanent. It opened a fissure among the Tories that never closed completely, deepened under the stresses of Irish and economic policies during the 1840s, and finally divided them into progressive and reactionary factions.

Catholic emancipation changed British liberalism and radicalism as well as British conservatism. The Catholic Association became a model for popular movements and agitations in the United Kingdom. In their successful campaign for parliamentary reform, British radicals imitated O'Connell's ways of mobilizing public opinion, collecting funds, and intimidating the government with reform or revolution alternatives. Later, free traders successfully borrowed O'Connell's tactics in their eventually successful effort to repeal the Corn Laws.

Catholic emancipation nourished democracy beyond parliamentary and other reforms. It triumphed over George IV and the House of Lords, lessening the significance of monarchy and aristocracy. The Irish Catholic campaign for civil rights involved an early engagement in the long-term worldwide struggle for popular sovereignty. Daniel O'Connell in Ireland joined with Andrew Jackson in the United States as cocreators of modern political democracy.

Wellington and Peel conceded Catholic emancipation to preserve the union. But political equality had been delayed too long, granted under pressure and not as an act of justice, and enacted with humiliating strings attached. It therefore failed to merit the gratitude of Irish Catholics or divert them from nationalism.

Emancipation had little effect on the day-to-day lives of ordinary Catholics. It did not alleviate their poverty or economic insecurity or eliminate famine situations. They were not going to sit in Parliament or hold political office. But the events of the

1820s did introduce an element of hope into bleak lives. O'Connell and his success had demonstrated the potential of the pressure of organized mass opinion. Perhaps emancipation would be a prelude to economic improvements, social equality, democracy, even an Irish nation-state. The struggle for emancipation did establish and shape the structure and principles of modern Irish political nationalism. And thanks to the work of Wyse and others, it also contributed grass-roots organizations that would continue to be factors in reform and nationalist activities.

Unfortunately, emancipation's linkage of Irish and Catholic identities intensified sectarian bitterness in Ireland. After 1829, what was left of Protestant patriotism quickly faded. Certain that emancipation-derived nationalism represented a priest-led democracy, Protestants became fanatically attached to the union as security.

Although the campaign for Catholic emancipation and its triumph added to religious hostilities in Ireland, O'Connell had little choice but to emphasize the Irish-Catholic connections to mobilize a mass agitation to win Catholic civil rights and to initiate Irish nationalism. And it was necessary for him to bring in the priest as a local recruiting agent and as a counterforce to landlord influence.

It is true that post-1829 clericalism has often had a baneful impact on Irish affairs, but early nineteenth-century priests in Ireland were quite different from those on the continent. Originating from an oppressed people and serving an oppressed church, they were not defenders of the economic, social, or political privileges of the aristocracy. Two French travelers in Ireland, Gustave de Beaumont and Alexis de Tocqueville, observed how close priests were to their parishioners and how strongly they preached the political doctrine of popular sovereignty. They were disciples of John Locke rather than Bossuet.

Critics of the Irish clergy often exaggerate and misunderstand its role in politics. The respect the clergy received in religion did not carry over to politics. Priests were more lieutenants than leaders of popular movements. In that role, most of them accepted the liberal values of Irish nationalism. They learned that they had more standing with the people when they rode with rather than against the tides of nationalist sentiment. Clericalism surfaced as a problem only in the absence of strong lay leadership, as in the period after O'Connell. When Irish Catholics committed themselves to a leader, the bishops and priests tagged along.

O'Connell's partial if not total integration of the values of Irish Catholicism with those of British liberalism had repercussions for the New World as well as the Old. Because of political lessons and values taught by O'Connell the Liberator, Irish pioneers of the American urban ghetto were able to overcome poverty, lack of technological skills, and the hostility of Anglo-American nativism to acquire power. Politics opened doors to economic opportunity and, eventually, respectability. By the close of the nineteenth century, Irish-American priests, politicians, and labor leaders were in charge of a powerful, city-based Catholic America. Because the Irish center of this force was Anglicized as well as Romanized, it could accommodate Catholicism in the United States to the American situation. The Irish played an important role in shaping a culturally pluralistic America by embracing a liberal political consensus.

3

Repeal and British Politics, 1830–1845

O'Connell in the House of Commons

When O'Connell entered the House of Commons in 1829, most British political experts predicted that, at fifty-four, he was too old to launch a successful parliamentary career. They said that a man had to be a skilled speaker and debater to command attention at Westminster and that O'Connell's earthiness, blarney, and invective might impress Irish peasants but would only antagonize British gentlemen.

Political pundits underestimated their man. O'Connell was immediately a powerful presence in the House of Commons. He played the parliamentary game with skill and dexterity. Occasionally his speeches were scurrilous—a tactic to bait opponents while pleasing the folks back home—but in general he adjusted his style to the House of Commons. Even his enemies had to concede that he was one of its leading debaters. He used his beautiful speaking voice to argue Irish grievances passionately and reasonably to plead the case for Irish reform and repeal of the union.

O'Connell was also an advocate of British radicalism, serving as a spokesman for his friend, Jeremy Bentham, in Parliament. He was active in a variety of causes: a democratic electorate with a secret ballot, abolition of the House of Lords, an expansion of public participation in municipal government, laissez-faire and hostility to labor combinations as restraints on trade, prison and legal reform, Jewish emancipation, and the abolition of slavery throughout the British empire, with full civil rights for blacks. O'Connell's Benthamism was appropriate to the British parliamentary and industrial systems but largely irrelevant to the needs of Irish Catholics suffering the burdens of manorialism. Still, they remained loyal to him. O'Connell had British political ambitions, sometimes fantasizing about the premiership, but British MPs and their constituents could not hide their contempt for the tribune of Irish papists.

O'Connell commanded almost forty Repeal MPs in the House of Commons. They constituted Ireland's first parliamentary party. In the early 1830s, when O'Connell emphasized the Repeal issue, Tory and Whig governments were equally determined to preserve the union. In fact, the Whig administration that took office in 1830 demonstrated more diligence in curtailing Irish nationalism than did the

Duke of Wellington and Sir Robert Peel. Whig leaders courted O'Connell's support with offers of government office, but Lord Anglesey, the lord lieutenant, and Lord Stanley, the chief secretary, outlawed all his political organizations.

Whigs owed O'Connell for the passage of the 1832 reform bill. His influence was both direct and indirect. Radicals who led the reform agitation in Britain modeled their organizations on the Catholic Association. Their newspapers reported and exaggerated discontent in Britain, warning the government that it had two choices: parliamentary reform or revolution. Not everyone in the government was convinced that revolution would follow a failure to reform, but like Wellington and Peel in 1829, they could not afford to take a chance.

O'Connell directly furthered parliamentary reform by supporting it with speeches and the votes that he and his followers cast in the House of Commons. O'Connell fought for the reform bill out of democratic principles and because he hoped that an improved British Parliament might concede justice to Ireland. However, the results of the measure were disappointing.

The Irish reform bill increased the Irish electorate to around 93,000 and Irish representation in the House of Commons to 105. But the numbers of voters were still smaller than before emancipation, and, compared to other members of the United Kingdom, Ireland was shortchanged. A franchise including twenty-year leaseholders of property worth at least 10 pounds as well as owners of property of the same value for tax purposes, did not radically increase the number of voters or begin to diminish aristocratic influence. As a result of the reform bill, 1 person in 115 voted in Irish county elections, compared with 1 in 24 in England, 1 in 23 in Wales, and 1 in 45 in Scotland. In cities, the Irish franchise was one in twenty-two, in England and Wales it was one in seventeen, and in Scotland one in twenty-seven. British politicians replied to O'Connell's complaint that an increase of five MPs did not adequately represent Ireland's rapidly multiplying population with the argument that Parliament represented property more than people. Despite his disappointment with Ireland's share of the reform bill, O'Connell stuck with the Whigs because he was sure that the Tories would be worse for Ireland, and he had hopes that the administrations of Lords Grey and Melbourne might see value in treating his country fairly.

Against his better judgment, at the urging of Fergus O'Connor, the future Chartist leader, O'Connell introduced an 1834 Repeal motion in the House of Commons. The support of only one British MP persuaded him that Parliament would never consider self-government for Ireland until it commanded the support of organized, massive, and disciplined agitation.

The first five years of the O'Connell-Whig collaboration brought few benefits to Ireland. Only Lord Stanley's 1831 Irish education bill establishing a state-supported system of national elementary schools was significant. To minimize religious conflict, they offered nondenominational instruction in secular subjects, but the various sects could supplement this with religious training for their own people. Protestants objected to this system of "Godlessness," which deprived them of an education monopoly. At the time, most bishops and priests welcomed the opportunity to raise the literacy and cultural levels of Catholics. Later, when the boldness and self-confidence of the hierarchy had increased, Archbishops Paul Cullen of Armagh and then Dublin, an ultramontane, and John MacHale of Tuam, a nationalist, led a fight against the schools. Cullen called them agents of Protestant proselytism; MacHale added the charge that they promoted British rule. Throughout the nineteenth century, cultural nationalists blasted the national schools as vehicles of Anglicization and destroyers of the Irish language. When Catholics began to attack the system, Protestants began to defend it to prevent what Cullen and MacHale wanted, government aid for schools, which would be mostly Catholic. In reality there was little to criticize about the system. No doubt in 1831 the British government decided that after Catholic emancipation it was necessary to Anglicize the Irish masses. And to a certain extent the schools did that. In his autobiography *An Only Child*, Frank O'Connor (born Michael Francis O'Connor O'Donovan), the writer and critic, discussed how the schools he attended in early twentieth-century Cork City had given him English life-style models. Speaking of a later time, John Montague, the poet, in "A Grafted Tongue" complained that his school in Tyrone had caused his stutter by substituting English for his native language. However, English values also contained the liberal-democratic principles of O'Connell's nationalism. And the literacy that trained Irish emigrants to survive in more competitive societies also gave a reading audience to Irish political and cultural nationalism. National schools did spread English at the expense of Irish, but economic connections between Ireland and Britain and emigration to the English-speaking world doomed Irish as the vernacular anyway. Even religious complaints against the schools lacked validity. By the mid-nineteenth century they had in fact become denominational. In Catholic districts the priest headed the school board, while in Protestant or Dissenter territory the vicar or minister performed that function.

Ireland's system of national education also had British implications. In Ireland the government imposed state-supported, theoretically secular education at a time when it was afraid to take such a risk in Britain. The Irish experiment was a British Radical victory, increasing pressure for a program for state-financed nondenominational schools in Britain.

The Whig Alliance

For five years the Whigs enjoyed the benefits of Irish nationalist support without the inconvenience of an open alliance. Then in 1835 the balance of political forces in the House of Commons compelled Whig leaders to come to specific terms with O'Connell. The Lichfield House Compact between Whigs and Repealers promised O'Connell Irish reforms in exchange for his efforts to keep the former in office and his promise to aid them in governing Ireland. This meant that O'Connell was abandoning repeal in return for reform. Tories denounced the Lichfield Compact as a corrupt bargain, and some Irish nationalists agreed. Lords Russell and Melbourne replied that the agreement with the Irish did not violate Whig principles, and O'Connell insisted that his arrangement with the Whigs was designed to advance Irish interests.

O'Connell's advocacy of repeal contained no inherent or unbending objections to the union in theory. He wanted an Irish Parliament because he believed that only a local legislature could solve the political, religious, social, and economic problems unique to Ireland. He knew that an Irish House of Commons would be dominated by members of the Protestant ascendancy. They were the only people in the country who could afford the luxury of political careers with heavy election expenses and service without compensation and who had the leisure to sit in Parliament. Protestants in an Irish Parliament, however, would have to respond to Catholic opinion and a Catholic electorate. Therefore, Irish Catholics would have more influence on a Parliament in Dublin than on one at Westminster. O'Connell also expected that time and pressure would bring changes increasing Catholic strength in an Irish legislature.

The Irish leader complained that under the union, Irish needs took second place to British concerns, but he was willing to let British politicians prove otherwise. O'Connell often told Irish audiences that he would accept the union as a permanent arrangement on the following conditions: Britain must treat Ireland as an equal partner, Parliament must discuss and solve Irish problems in an Irish, not a British context, and the United Kingdom must endeavor to promote Ireland's prosperity.

Except when stump-speaking to the Irish masses, O'Connell was not fanatical in his Irishness. He was little touched by the romantic cultural nationalism that began in the early nineteenth century on the continent, spread to Britain, and reached his own country in the form of the group known as Young Ireland. O'Connell was more concerned with the personal liberty, happiness, and economic security of his people than in such abstractions as national sovereignty or the folk soul. Although he doubted that the Protestant-dominated UK Parliament involved with Britain's booming industrial economy would ever have the patience, the sympathy, or the insight to cope with the difficulties of Catholic, underdeveloped, agrarian Ireland, in the Lichfield House Compact O'Connell gave British politicians another opportunity to demonstrate that the union could work for his country.

Melbourne's administration was responsible for the passage of three important pieces of Irish legislation. In 1838 Parliament commuted the tithe to a land tax, theoretically freeing most Catholics from the irritation of financing an alien religion, and enacted a law affecting the Irish poor that did not go into effect until 1842. The Irish municipal reform bill of 1840 opened city government to Catholic participation.

Like emancipation, the tithe act demonstrated the role of the Irish question as a catalyst defining and molding British politics. In its early form, it would have applied surplus revenues of the Protestant Church of Ireland to Irish social needs. Lords Stanley and Graham considered such a proposal a despoliation and left the Whig fold. After a short period of independence, they became stalwarts in Peel's Conservative party.

Of the three Whig measures, the poor law was the best example of the insensitivity of a British Parliament legislating for Ireland. In 1833 the prime minister, Lord Grey, appointed an Irish commission to investigate the extent of poverty in Ireland and to recommend solutions. It included prominent Catholic, Protestant, and Presbyterian clergy (both the Catholic and Protestant archbishops of Dublin were members). After two years of carefully gathering and evaluating evidence, the commission submitted a report rejecting for Ireland the British poor law system of placing paupers in government-supported workhouses. It noted that in Ireland poverty was not a disgrace and that the pauper had a social place in Irish society. Wandering beggars brought news and entertainment to rural cottages and offered the people an opportunity to practice Christian charity. The commissioners said that the Irish people would resent the government's locking the poor up in workhouses as if they were guilty of a crime. And the report emphasized that Ireland could not afford to imitate the British system. About 2.5 million Irish people, almost one-third the population, were impoverished. To institutionalize them would drain the financial resources of an extremely underdeveloped country, increasing rather than diminishing Irish poverty. Instead of a poor law, commissioners asked for more voluntary relief agencies and urged government public works and emigration projects. The former would provide employment and develop the economic potential of the country; the latter would siphon off the surplus population.

Lord John Russell, the Whig leader in the House of Commons, ignored the report. His utilitarian logic insisted that what was good for Britain would serve Ireland. He sent George Nicholls, a British poor law official, to conduct another poverty investigation in Ireland. After only six months there, Nicholls recommended the British poor law system, and Parliament concurred.

O'Connell expressed dissatisfaction with the results of the Whig alliance. The tithe act fell far short of his demand for the disestablishment of the Protestant Church in Ireland, and it did not prevent landlords from raising rents as a source for their tithe contribution. O'Connell was also disappointed when the government dropped the idea of applying surplus church revenue to social needs. His agreement with the Whigs prevented him from attacking the poor law with all the anger that he felt. However, he did say that the bill was inappropriate to Irish conditions and voted against it. O'Connell also complained that the Whigs had done nothing to expand the Irish parliamentary franchise or to increase Irish seats in the House of Commons and not enough to destroy the Protestant monopoly of power in Dublin Castle.

O'Connell realized that Thomas Drummond, the Whig undersecretary, had made efforts to bring a sectarian balance to the Irish situation. He told landlords that they had duties as well as rights and appointed Catholics to government, magisterial, and legal positions. Drummond also drove the anti-Catholic Orange Order underground, but the liberal and tolerant spirit in the Irish administration died with him in 1840.

Lobbying for Repeal

O'Connell decided to warn Melbourne in 1838 that from then on, Whigs would have to earn the support of Irish nationalist MPs. He started the Precursor Society as a prelude to resuming agitation for repeal and again demanded substantial Irish reforms. When by 1840 it was evident that the Whigs would not author any constructive Irish legislation, O'Connell implemented his threat by creating the National Association, rechristened a year later as the Loyal National Repeal Association. Only a hundred people attended the first meeting at the Corn Exchange in Burgh Quay, Dublin, and just fifteen applied for membership. This apathy indicated that many nationalists feared that O'Connell's association with the Whigs revealed an insincerity regarding repeal and that the new organization was only an instrument to intimidate the Whigs.

O'Connell modeled the Repeal Association on its Catholic predecessor. Members paid annual dues of one pound. Contributors of 10 pounds or more became Volunteers and could wear uniforms similar to those of the 1782 Irish Volunteers. To achieve the same mass enthusiasm for repeal that emancipation had enjoyed, O'Connell again offered to farmers and workers an associate membership in his organization with dues of only one shilling. In city, town, village, and rural parishes, repeal wardens, selected by the local clergy and approved by the association, collected dues and sent them along with the names of contributors to Dublin headquarters. Wardens also established reading rooms where Repealers and potential recruits could read nationalist newspapers and pamphlets.

During its first three years, the Repeal Association had little impact on Irish opinion. Most of the energetic and bright Catholic lawyers who assisted O'Connell in the campaign for emancipation were now successes in their profession and were uninterested in repeal. Many, such as Richard Lalor Sheil, were House of Commons Whigs. Some held government office. Irish Catholic bishops remained nationalist in sentiment. But few of them believed that the British government would ever abandon the union. Prelates such as Daniel Murray, archbishop of Dublin, worried that repeal raised false expectations among the people and distracted them from the realities and duties of their lives. Murray, and the majority of bishops who agreed with him, thought that O'Connell should concentrate his energies on the practical, winning Irish Catholic advances in the United Kingdom.

John MacHale, archbishop of Tuam, led the minority wing of the bishops active in the repeal agitation. To keep their support and to win more converts from among the hierarchy, O'Connell became a vigorous opponent of government-sponsored nondenominational education. From that time on, Irish nationalism would be wedded to Catholic educational interests.

Young Ireland and Cultural Nationalism

Fortunately for O'Connell and repeal, a new talent source replaced the lawyers and bishops who defected from nationalism. On October 15, 1842, the first issue of the *Nation* appeared. This nationalist weekly was the product of the combined talents of Thomas Osborne Davis, John Blake Dillon, and Charles Gavan Duffy, three young men in their twenties, trained in the law and experienced in journalism. Davis was Anglo-Irish Protestant; Dillon and Duffy were Catholics; Davis and Dillon had attended Trinity College, Dublin; Davis was from Dublin, Dillon from Mayo, and Duffy from Monaghan; all three were nationalists educated, to a large extent through Thomas Carlyle, in the romantic movement. They gave Irish nationalism the most powerful and influential newspaper voice that it ever had or ever would have, and they provided it with a cultural ideology.

Duffy, Dillon, and Davis launched the *Nation* to create an Irish cultural nationalist opinion and "to make it racy of the soil." They insisted that a nation was a spiritual as well as a geographic and political entity. Even more important than political independence, nationhood demanded cultural sovereignty. Young Irelanders, as those associated with the *Nation* were called, emphasized the spiritual qualities of peasant Ireland and ridiculed the materialism of urban, industrial Britain. They wanted to save their country from the cultural as well as the political and economic dimensions of British colonialism. They championed the Irish language as a defense against Anglicization, advocating its preservation where it still was the vernacular, and its revival where it had faded or disappeared. Since Young Irelanders viewed the national school system as a strategy to replace the Irish with a British heritage, they took on the responsibility of educating the people to know and appreciate their culture and history.

The *Nation* attracted the talents of Thomas MacNevin, Daniel Owen Madden, John Mitchel, John O'Hagan, Thomas D'Arcy McGee, and Thomas Meagher. They extolled the quality of pre-Christian and early Christian Celtic culture and discussed the contributions of Irish missionaries to the spread of civilization. They wrote about Irish patriots who defended their country's independence against Danes, Normans, and Saxons. In addition to extolling the glories of an Irish past, Young Ireland tried to encourage a cultural revival in the present that would shape a promising future. The *Nation* printed the best in contemporary Irish writing, including William Carleton's prose and James Clarence Mangan's poetry. And it invited readers to submit stories, essays, poems, and ballads. Many of the nationalist songs that still stir Irish emotions at home and abroad first appeared in the *Nation* of the 1840s.

THOMAS OSBORNE DAVIS, 1814–1845

Thomas Osborne Davis cofounded the Young Ireland Movement. In his editorial columns and his ballad poetry published in the *Nation*, he helped define the spirit and contents of Irish cultural nationalism. (*Source:* Sir Charles Gavan Duffy, *Thomas Davis: The Memoirs of an Irish Patriot, 1840–46* [London, 1890])

Dillon, Duffy, Davis, and their associates wanted to differentiate between the Catholic and Irish identities. In the *Nation,* the contributions of Protestants and Nonconformists to Ireland received treatment equal to that of those of Catholics. Young Irelanders pleaded for harmony between religious groups and stressed the common interests of Irish people from all creeds. This ecumenical spirit was expressed in Davis's "Anglo-Saxon and Celt":

What matters that at different shrines

We pray unto one God?

What matters that at different times

Our fathers won this sod?

In fortune and in name we're bound

By stronger links than steel;

And neither can be safe nor sound

But in each other's weal.

News coverage played a secondary role to the *Nation*'s cultural nationalism. It usually borrowed news stories from other papers. The *Nation* featured poetry, historical essays, biographical sketches, patriotic ballads, reviews, and exceptionally well-written editorials. Its columns preached cultural and political nationalism, supported the Repeal Association, encouraged cooperation among Irishmen of all religions, classes, and ethnic origins, and advocated tenant rights, cultural and vocational education for the Irish people, and political change consistent with liberal democracy. Young Ireland's cultural nationalism had such an immediate impact on Irish national opinion that the *Nation* became a topic of discussion in Parliament. British MPs recognized the talent of Young Irelanders but condemned their radical nationalist, anti-British ideology.

O'Connell welcomed Young Irelanders to the Repeal Association and the *Nation* to repeal reading rooms, but he was a bit suspicious of his young allies and new lieutenants. Because O'Connell's nationalism concerned the bread-and-butter issues of politics, he never really understood the passionate, uncompromising cultural nationalism of Young Ireland. On political platforms, O'Connell told the Irish people that they were the most virtuous, handsome, and intelligent people in the world, living in its most beautiful and potentially fruitful country. His praise was designed to lift spirits demoralized by centuries of ignorance, poverty, and oppression. While O'Connell genuinely loved his own kind, he did not hate England, its people, or its culture. He admired Britain's technological leadership, constitution, political institutions, and liberal tradition and wanted them for his own country.

O'Connell's love of Ireland and the Irish—Catholic, Protestant, and Nonconformist—did not include preoccupation with the Gaelic tradition. He was so concerned with Ireland's present and future that he had little interest in its past. He refused to emote over former defeats and misery. His modernist and utilitarian views were illustrated by his attitude toward the Irish language. Unlike the Young

Irelanders, he was a native speaker. Occasionally he spoke Irish at political meetings, sometimes to confuse police reporters, but he did not encourage efforts to preserve or revive Irish. To him it was a symbol of inferiority and an obstacle to progress.

Because the cosmopolitan O'Connell could not relate to the xenophobic spirit of cultural nationalism, which had spread throughout Europe and entered his own country, he distrusted the militant tone of the *Nation* and at times ridiculed its literary efforts and style (perhaps a reflection of his admiration of Charles Dickens). Young Irelanders, in turn, were often impatient with O'Connell's pragmatic flirtations with the Whigs, which compromised repeal for reform possibilities, with his vulgarity, and with his despotic control of Irish nationalism. They also thought that he antagonized Protestants through his linkage of Irish and Catholic.

On specific issues, such as Chartism, Corn Law repeal, and federalism, Young Ireland and O'Connell came to disagree. Young Ireland viewed the Chartists as representatives of the British democracy, a natural ally of Irish nationalism against the common enemy, British aristocracy. Chartists wanted to solve the social and economic problems of urban industrialism through political reform. Their "People's Charter" called for universal male suffrage, a secret ballot, equal electoral districts, the end of property qualifications for political office, annual Parliaments, and salaries for MPs. O'Connell approved of these goals, but he accused Chartists, particularly Fergus O'Connor, an old political foe, of advocating violence to achieve them. His attack on the Corn Laws was consistent with his utilitarian, free trade beliefs. The *Nation* argued that free trade benefited British industry but endangered Irish agriculture. A *Nation* editorial once suggested that a federal arrangement between Ireland and Britain might be a worthy substitute for repeal. Young Ireland withdrew from that position but said that it was prepared to work with Irish federalists in a common front against British rule. When in 1844 O'Connell announced that he would be inclined to accept a federal restructuring of the United Kingdom if British politicians made such an offer and Irish opinion was agreeable, the *Nation* denounced federalism as inadequate.

Despite Young Ireland's efforts and intention to blend the interests of Catholic, Protestant, and Nonconformist, Anglo-Irish, Scots-Irish, and Celt, the overwhelming majority of non-Catholics considered the group's cultural nationalism as much a bid for Catholic power as O'Connell's political nationalism. Their Britishness excluded any pride in things Irish before the English colonial presence. And for them, Irish history after that was a constant struggle for survival against the Catholic majority. To the Anglo-Irish and Scots-Irish, Celtic Ireland was Catholic Ireland. Their loyalty and their interests—religious, political, and economic—were invested in Britain.

While Young Ireland cultural nationalism made little impression on the Anglo-Irish or Scots-Irish community, it had massive appeal for members of the Catholic middle class. Their literary expression in the works of Gerald Griffin and John Banim revealed a serious identity crisis. They enjoyed economic prosperity but suffered the disdain of the Protestant aristocracy and middle class. And they had no affinity for Catholic peasants and agricultural laborers. Young Ireland told them that they were important people with a dignified and glorious historical tradition and cultural heritage.

The Surge of Repeal

Despite differences in temperament, policy, and procedure, Young Irelanders realized that O'Connell had the allegiance of the Irish masses and that without him the national movement would lose momentum. Therefore, they were gentle in criticizing him. They submitted to his leadership, and the *Nation* made a major contribution to the revival of national enthusiasm. Its influence extended beyond the 8,000 weekly subscribers. The *Nation* was in repeal reading rooms, and throughout Ireland illiterates crowded into thatch-roofed cottages to listen to the local scholar, often the national schoolteacher, read its poems, essays, and editorials.

During 1842, repeal activities were practically suspended while O'Connell served as first Catholic lord mayor of Dublin. When 1843 began, O'Connell had completed his term, Sir Robert Peel was prime minister of a Conservative government, and the Repeal Association was meeting weekly at the Corn Exchange. But few people in Ireland or Britain considered the repeal movement a serious threat to the continuation of the United Kingdom. British newspapers and periodicals described O'Connell as a deteriorating demagogue promoting repeal to keep his name before the Irish people so that he could line his pockets with their contributions. If that was his motive, he was unsuccessful. The Repeal Association's meager income showed public apathy to its work. Only the *Nation*'s success indicated the potential of Irish nationalism.

No doubt the sorry condition of the Repeal Association irritated O'Connell. He did love the limelight, and he needed the annual tribute he had received from the Irish people since Catholic emancipation. Their donations had permitted him to concentrate on their welfare instead of his law practice. The amount of the tribute had declined with repeal enthusiasm. However, for O'Connell, financial self-interest was of far less importance than the future of Ireland. And he worried that without mass energy and involvement in repeal, he could not effectively pressure the British government for change. So in January 1843 he decided to launch one more giant agitation for the restoration of the Irish Parliament or at least a considerable improvement in the Irish situation. He believed that he had the necessary ingredients at his disposal to rouse the Irish people from their lethargy.

Poverty, Protestant ascendancy, and peasant insecurity remained to perpetuate tensions between Irish Catholics and the British government. When the poor law went into effect in 1842, it raised a storm of opposition from all classes and creeds. There was resentment toward the workhouse test for poor relief and toward paying rates to support the new system. Repealers, Tories, and Whigs joined in denouncing the administration of the poor law, mainly the despotic power of the Central Board of Poor Law Commissioners, and complained about the expenses of operating a project designed for an industrial rather than an agrarian country.

The upper and middle classes expressed disapproval of the poor law in petitions to Parliament, platform orations, and letters to newspapers. Farmers often resorted to more spectacular and sometimes more violent methods. In many sections of the country they refused to pay rent, even when the army came to collect them. O'Connell recognized how anti-poor law feelings stimulated anti-British passions. So he encouraged the protest, including an anti–poor law plank as a major part of the repeal platform. His strategy worked. In the spring of 1843, as anti-poor law activities tapered off, the Repeal Association grew in numbers and income.

Theobold Mathew, a Franciscan friar, was by 1843 the most popular and influential man in Ireland after O'Connell. He had enrolled between 4 million and 5 million people in a temperance crusade. Almost every small village in Ireland had a local branch of the movement, complete with a reading room and a band with musical instruments and colorful uniforms. Even Protestant ascendancy newspapers praised Father Mathew's efforts to curb the tendency of the Irish masses to escape the realities of poverty in drink. O'Connell considered the discipline and the enthusiasm of temperance as repeal potential. Father Mathew had continued the tradition of mass meetings that had started with the emancipation agitation and declined when O'Connell cozied up to the Whigs. The repeal leader tried to entice teetotalers into repeal by endorsing temperance. He said that it was the most powerful weapon in repeal's arsenal of moral force and predicted that it would discipline Irish nationalism in its struggle against British tyranny.

Father Mathew wanted to avoid mixing temperance with Irish nationalism because it might alienate the British and Irish Protestants who had encouraged his efforts. However, he could not control the political loyalties of his followers or compete with O'Connell's charisma. During the repeal campaign of 1843, temperance bands were an important feature at mass meetings, and the *Nation* was prominent in temperance reading rooms.

After O'Connell had maneuvered the anti-poor law protest and temperance into repeal, he persuaded the Dublin corporation, along with other municipal and public bodies, such as poor law boards, to petition Parliament for repeal of the union. Government officials helped him mobilize Irish opinion behind the antiunion demand by a series of blunders. They awarded the Irish mail coach contract to a Scots company in preference to an Irish concern already holding it, thus forcing thousands of Dublin workers out of jobs in an employment-starved city. Then, without explanation, the government fired Dr. Phelan, one of the two Catholic poor law commissioners. And when Parliament finally amended the poor law, it heeded gentry demands while ignoring the complaints of ordinary people.

During the 1843 repeal agitation, the government pushed through Parliament an Irish arms bill that curtailed civil liberties, and the Irish lord chancellor, Sir Edward Sugden, dismissed magistrates attending repeal meetings, although he conceded their legality. The arms bill and the dismissal of magistrates rallied a large number of Catholic barristers and solicitors to the Repeal Association, returning to O'Connell the support of an influential segment of the Catholic middle class that had largely abandoned him after Catholic emancipation.

In the spring of 1843, O'Connell began to hold public meetings to petition for repeal, choosing a different part of the country every week. They took place on Sunday afternoons, and hundreds of thousands attended. In the early morning roads were packed with Repealers who journeyed considerable distances to listen to the "Liberator." Priests said outdoor masses on the hillsides, and then the people sat down to eat their potato breakfasts. Parish priests and curates, local dignitaries, and temperance bands leading lines of marching Repealers met O'Connell's carriage as it approached the town. People detached the horses and pulled it by hand through the streets as women and children threw flowers in his path.

When he addressed the meetings, O'Connell told his audiences that they were the bravest, strongest, most patient, most virtuous people in the world. He promised them that before the year was out, Ireland would have its Parliament in College Green. They would win the independence of their country through the application of moral force. They would never fight except in self-defense. But that would not be necessary. Peel and Wellington would surrender to Irish national opinion as they did in 1829. O'Connell assured his followers that after Ireland had its own Parliament, there would be a reconciliation between classes and creeds. Tenant farmers would be secure on the land, trade and commerce would flourish, and culture would thrive. There would be freedom of conscience with no religious establishment. A free Ireland loyal to the crown would live in peace with its British neighbor as friends. O'Connell always encouraged loyalty to the queen. He said that even if "Orange" Peel and the "stunted corporal" denied justice to the Irish people, Victoria, who loved them, would use her royal prerogatives to establish an Irish legislature (it is difficult to accept that O'Connell actually believed such nonsense). In preparation for independence, O'Connell promised to summon a preliminary Parliament, the Council of Three Hundred, the same number as the old Irish Parliament, to meet in Dublin. He also announced his intention to establish arbitration courts so that the people could seek and find Irish rather than British justice. By the fall of the year, the arbitration courts were in operation, with surprising effectiveness.

The Monster Meetings, as the *Times* of London labeled them (the term caught on even among Repealers), were tremendous successes. Dues poured into the Repeal Association. For a time in the late spring and summer, the weekly repeal rent exceeded 2,000 pounds. Some of this money came from the Irish in Britain and the United States, although quite a few Irish Americans were offended when O'Connell denounced slavery as a vile institution. They said that he should keep his nose out of American affairs. He replied that he did not want to liberate the Irish with money made from exploiting black slaves. O'Connell insisted that Irish nationalism represented a universal cry for human liberty and equality.

The surge of repeal indicated by the Monster Meetings and the flow of shillings, pounds, and dollars to O'Connell's agitation horrified Irish Protestants. To preserve the union and to protect Protestant ascendancy, they demanded that the government suppress repeal. Earl de Grey, the anti-Catholic lord lieutenant, endorsed their plea.

Combating the Rising Tide

Peel and even de Grey were strangely unaware of the gradual but steady increase of repeal enthusiasm in the early spring of 1843. Not until May did the prime minister realize the extent of O'Connell's challenge to British authority. When he did, Peel told the House of Commons that he would preserve the union at all costs. Wellington made the same pledge to the House of Lords. But the government found it difficult to deal directly with the agitation. Legislation designed to suppress the Repeal Association would also embrace the Anti–Corn Law League modeled on O'Connell's tactics for mobilizing public support. Peel did not want to unite radicals, free traders, and Irish nationalists in a common defense of civil and political liberties. Such an alliance would make O'Connell respectable in Britain and both the anti–corn law and repeal agitations more difficult to control.

Since Peel had to reject an anti-repeal strategy that could provide O'Connell with a British constituency, he was forced to respond to revitalized Irish nationalism with a public pose of calculated indifference. His refusal to react to O'Connell's boasts with coercive legislation or military might infuriated the reactionary, anti–Irish Catholic core of the Tory wing of the Conservative party, but his seeming indifference masked a strategy to destroy O'Connell's influence in Ireland and to eradicate the roots of Irish nationalism. By refusing to acknowledge the significance of repeal by either coercion or immediate conciliation, Peel hoped to demonstrate to Irish Catholics that the scarcely veiled threats of their antiunion agitation would not intimidate the government into conceding repeal or reform. He hoped that after they realized that O'Connell could not deliver on any of his promises, they would lose confidence in him and his methods. Repeal would then dwindle into insignificance, and the British army could cope with any hotheads.

While Peel and the home secretary, Sir James Graham, waited for calculated indifference to deflate repeal's balloon, they plotted a long-range Irish policy to satisfy some of the ambitions and needs of various components of the nationalist coalition, thus destroying anti-unionism by eliminating the grievances that had created and nourished it. But Peel and Graham had no intention of initiating reform while repeal was at full strength. Such a move would encourage Irish Catholics to believe that the government was susceptible to intimidation. They would then invest more loyalty in O'Connell, and he would intensify agitation. Peel wanted a coherent, long-term Irish policy, not an ill-considered, fearful response to Irish discontent. He wanted to lay the Irish question to rest permanently and to make the United Kingdom a true community of interests and allegiances.

Of course, there was the danger that O'Connell, faced with the necessity of retaining his influence with Irish Catholics, might commit himself to revolutionary conspiracy. There was also the possibility that he might lose the reins of Irish nationalism to more militant Repealers. To forestall these contingencies, Peel and Graham took out insurance policies against the failure of calculated indifference. They dispatched troops, weapons, ammunition, and other military supplies to Ireland, and arms were stored for possible use by Protestant yeomen. The prime minister and home secretary also decided to punish O'Connell and his chief lieutenants for their audacious challenge. Graham instructed Irish legal authorities to collect evidence indicating the seditious character of repeal.

When Peel told Parliament in May that he was prepared to use military force to preserve the union, and when Sugden acted on this pledge by dismissing repeal magistrates, O'Connell decided that the government was going to crush his movement. In an effort to persuade Westminster to reconsider the use of soldiers and to maintain the enthusiasm and confidence of his followers, he added a militant tone to his speeches. While addressing an audience in Mallow, County Cork, in June, O'Connell went so far as to suggest that he would lead a defensive war against British oppression.

By late summer, however, it dawned on O'Connell that Peel was out to demolish repeal by undermining Irish Catholic confidence in his ability to deliver on promises of freedom and reform. He feared that if the prime minister's strategy succeeded, Repealers might reject constitutional agitation for physical force. To save them from the bullets and bayonets of the military, O'Connell softened the tone of his public statements, no longer guaranteeing repeal in the near future. He said that it would be impossible to summon the Council of Three Hundred before the end of 1843. Instead of promising quick victories, O'Connell now asked Irish nationalists to support him in a long struggle for freedom. He warned them against counsels of violence, insisting that moral force could and would triumph over anti-Irish opinion in Britain.

The Defeat of Repeal

By early autumn it was apparent that Peel's strategy of calculated indifference was wearing down repeal. O'Connell was preparing his followers for short-term defeat, the repeal rent had declined, and Irish farmers were neglecting agitation to concentrate on bringing in an abundant harvest. Now that the enemy was in retreat, the prime minister made ready to assume the offensive. He decided to institute prosecution for sedition against the repeal leadership and sent Lord de Grey and Sugden to Dublin to supervise the arrest and trial of O'Connell and his lieutenants. They also received instructions to prevent the Clontarf repeal rally on Sunday, October 8. It was to be the last Monster Meeting of 1843. A tremendous crowd was expected in the Dublin suburb. A large number of British Repealers were coming.

Late on Saturday, October 7, de Grey proclaimed the Clontarf meeting on the grounds that the original announcement—written and distributed when O'Connell was not in Dublin—indicated that it was designed as a military demonstration to intimidate the government. Rather than risk a confrontation between soldiers and Repealers, O'Connell canceled the meeting. A week later, he and six others, including Charles Gavan Duffy, were arrested and charged with sedition and attempting to subvert the loyalty of her majesty's soldiers stationed in Ireland. (Because many soldiers in the British army were Irish, the government was always concerned that they could be infected with Irish nationalism.) In speeches O'Connell said that noncommissioned officers and privates would not heed orders to shoot their own people. In February 1844 a jury brought in a verdict of guilty, and the court sentenced the repeal defendants to a year in prison and payment of a stiff fine. In September the law lords, in a 3-to-2 decision (three Whigs and two Tories), reversed the decision because the prosecution's indictment was improperly drawn, and the defendants were tried before a packed jury that excluded Catholics. O'Connell and his friends were released from Richmond Gaol. He received a hero's welcome. People pulled his carriage from the prison to his Merrion Square residence. Bonfires of celebration were lit on the hills of Ireland. But after his prison experience, though brief and comfortable, O'Connell lost his zeal for agitation. His decision to abandon the Clontarf meeting and his failure to exploit his legal vindication by intensifying nationalist activity did much to crush the repeal spirit and to undermine confidence in constitutional methods. However, the 1843 repeal defeat was not the consequence of faulty tactics so much as the Irish leader's misreading of the temper of the times.

Like many political leaders, O'Connell became a captive of past successes. In 1843 he expected Peel and Parliament to react to repeal as they had to Catholic emancipation. In 1829 he had convinced Wellington and Peel that if they did not concede Catholic civil rights, extremists might push him aside, take control of popular agitation, and substitute physical for moral force. During the repeal year he seemed to assume that if Peel again had to face the choices of concessions to Irish discontent or the chaos of rebellion, he would once more select the former. And if the prime minister refused to bow to expediency, perhaps, O'Connell hoped, the Whigs would exploit the Irish crisis to embarrass and perhaps topple the Conservative government. Once in power, he thought, Lords Russell and Palmerston would try to calm troubled Irish waters with a conciliation policy and a resumption of the Irish nationalist–Whig alliance.

Apparently, O'Connell failed to understand that although the Irish situation in 1843 was similar to that in 1829, things in Britain were different. During the 1820s and earlier, there was a considerable body of enlightened parliamentary opinion favorably disposed toward emancipation. In 1829 Peel and Wellington knew that attempts to suppress the Catholic Association without conceding its objective would receive a rough reception in the House of Commons. Therefore, Irish physical resistance to government coercion would enjoy the sympathy of a respectable body of British opinion, and the seeds of rebellion might spread and take root in socially, economically, and politically disturbed Britain. Catholic emancipation was an Irish issue with implications for the United Kingdom.

In 1843 no respectable Tory, Whig, or Radical MP accepted repeal as a solution to the Irish question. Both Tories and Whigs argued that an independent Ireland would weaken Britain's defenses and initiate a collapse of the empire. Tories also insisted that repeal would place the Catholic democracy in a position to take revenge on the Protestant ascendancy. Radicals maintained that a properly managed union would bring peace and prosperity to Ireland. During the 1843 repeal crisis, British anti-Catholic and unionist parliamentary opinion opposed Irish nationalism. Although Whigs and Radicals did not hesitate to exploit Irish discontent to embarrass the government with attacks on and inquiries into its administration of Irish affairs, Peel could depend on their support in his determination not to compromise the union.

When Peel challenged O'Connell on the Clontarf meeting, the Irish leader had no realistic choice but to back down. His nonviolent convictions, commitment to constitutionalism, and common sense would not permit him to lead his followers to slaughter in an engagement with British soldiers. But by surrendering to the government's ultimatum, O'Connell lost one of constitutional nationalism's most effective persuaders—the implied threat of rebellion if the government refused concessions to moderate opinion.

Peel's Effort to Integrate Ireland into the United Kingdom

Early in 1844 Peel and Graham were confident that repeal had faded as a significant factor in Anglo-Irish affairs, and they could proceed with a comprehensive policy to destroy Irish nationalism by integrating Ireland into the United Kingdom. Although it included concessions to each of the clerical, agrarian, and middle-class components of the repeal coalition, the main focus was the detachment of priests from popular agitations. Peel accepted a thesis, popular in British intellectual and political circles, that the Catholic hierarchy and clergy in Ireland had to promote the activities of demagogues because they were dependent on the ignorant anti-British masses for financial support. Before they could be persuaded to withdraw from politics, the government would have to provide them and their church with guaranteed incomes. But separating priests from nationalism presented risks. If not handled with tact and diplomacy, it would alienate British no-popery, Tories in the Conservative party, the Irish Catholic hierarchy and clergy, and even Rome.

The government began implementing its Irish policy by asking the pope, Gregory XVI, to forbid further excursions of bishops and priests into politics. Realizing the implications for all of Europe, and particularly for the multiethnic Hapsburg empire, of a radical and nationalist Catholic hierarchy and clergy in Ireland, Prince Metternich, the Austrian chancellor, endorsed the British request to Rome. Peel's emissary there told the pope that if the British government could obtain the cooperation of Irish bishops and priests in efforts to maintain the union and to preserve the social order, the prime minister's Irish initiatives might culminate in the endowment of the Church in Ireland. Papal officials welcomed this prospect and the opportunity to establish friendly relations with the world's greatest power. So Cardinal Fransoni, prefect of propaganda, the agency supervising Catholicism in the United Kingdom, wrote to the Irish hierarchy advising against clerical political involvement and urging the concentration of priestly energies on spiritual matters. But only a handful of prelates paid heed to the Roman directive.

In the fall of 1844 the government launched the legislative phase of its Irish policy with a bill that permitted the Catholic Church to inherit and bequeath property. The charitable bequests act was intended as a signal of the government's intention to extend justice to Irish Catholics. Peel also hoped to use bishops on the charitable bequests board as agents in his effort to convince Catholic clerical and middle-class opinion that cooperation with the British government promised more benefits than opposition did.

O'Connell attacked the charitable bequests act because its provisions were inadequate in terms of inheritance and because it opened up the Catholic Church in Ireland to British influences. Archbishop MacHale and a number of his allies in the hierarchy also criticized the act. Archbishop Murray of Dublin and his friends among the bishops accepted the British offer and agreed to sit on the charitable bequests board. This division intensified a split that had begun over the national schools in the 1830s. The feud in the hierarchy was bitter and personal, with MacHale accusing Murray of being a Dublin Castle bishop, a tool of British interests. Both sides frequently appealed to Rome.

In the spring of 1845 the government made another friendly gesture to the Irish Catholic clergy when it introduced a bill to increase the annual grant to the seminary at Maynooth and convert it to a permanent endowment. Every year when the grant was up for renewal, it touched off a binge of anti-Catholicism, embittering relations between Britain and Ireland. Peel hoped that the Maynooth bill would remove the seminary as an annual issue and at the same time assure Catholic bishops of the government's friendly intentions, thus smoothing the way for a more extensive endowment of Irish Catholicism. However, the bill generated so much no-popery, in and out of Parliament, that some of the effect of the government's generosity was lost, and Peel realized that he was restricted on what he could do to pacify Irish Catholicism. Nevertheless, he courageously resisted Protestant prejudice expressed by the Tories in his party, and with the support of Whigs, Radicals, and Repealers, he ushered the bill through Parliament.

After Maynooth, Peel directed attention to the educational needs of the Irish Catholic middle class, introducing an Irish colleges bill establishing three provincial colleges, in Cork, Galway, and Belfast, on the principle of nondenominational or mixed education. Peel expected that in a university environment, Protestants and Catholics would meet, socialize, and develop middle-class solidarity. He also thought that an exposure to sophisticated, secular culture might free the sons of Catholic shopkeepers, professionals, and strong farmers from nationalism and clericalism, making them aware that they had interests independent of their religion and more relevant than repeal.

In Parliament, the Colleges Bill met with minimal opposition. In Ireland, however, O'Connell attacked mixed education as offensive to Catholics and forced the hierarchy to condemn the provisions of the bill. Since O'Connell's position on the colleges proposal was inconsistent with his principles concerning freedom of conscience and Catholic-Protestant harmony, he probably opposed Peel's higher education measure to repay MacHale for his support in 1843, cementing the nationalist-Catholic compact.

Young Irelanders approved of mixed education because they believed that the results would contradict Peel's anticipation. They predicted that Catholic-Protestant college contacts would lead Protestants toward nationality rather than lead Catholics away. The conflict over the Colleges Bill in the Repeal Association started an open feud between O'Connell and Young Ireland, eventually leading to the latter's secession.

At the urging of MacHale, the pope in 1847 and 1848 disapproved of the Queen's colleges, the name given to the three provincial institutions. In 1850, at the Synod of Thurles, with Archbishop Cullen presiding, the Irish hierarchy forbade Catholics to attend the colleges or to accept administrative or teaching posts in them. The next year Rome concurred in the Thurles decision. In the 1850s Cullen established a Catholic University in Dublin with John Henry Newman as its first rector. Newman found it impossible to get along with the anti-intellectual Irish bishops. After contributing his brilliant views on higher education in *Idea of a University,* Newman returned to England. The Catholic university continued to exist without a government subsidy. It evolved into University College, Dublin, and in 1907 joined the Queen's colleges in Cork and Galway as a constituent branch of the new National University of Ireland. Queen's College, Belfast, developed into an excellent twentieth-century university.

The Colleges Bill was the last portion of Peel's Irish policy to receive parliamentary approval. He attempted to conciliate Irish farmers by appointing a commission headed by an Irish landlord, Lord Devon, to investigate landlord-tenant relations and to recommend legislation improving the situation. Lord Stanley introduced a bill in the House of Lords, based on the findings of the Devon Commission, designed to establish a moderate tenant right. When many Whig and Conservative MPs made it clear that they would not tolerate even a minor interference with property rights, the government dropped the measure.

In many ways Peel's Irish policy received affirmative results. Rome had condemned the nationalist involvement of bishops and priests, and several prelates were cooperating with government efforts to lighten the financial burdens of their church. The charitable bequests board gave Peel the opportunity to continue negotiations with some members of the hierarchy in his effort to demonstrate the potential benefits of the union. And despite the anti-Catholic bigotry provoked by the Maynooth bill, the Catholic hierarchy and clergy, and even O'Connell, appreciated Peel's intentions and his fortitude in standing up to irrational fanaticism. Finally, although O'Connell and the bishops condemned the Colleges Bill, it did open a split in Irish nationalism, an ideological clash between Young and Old Ireland that eventually destroyed repeal unity.

O'Connell limited Peel's achievements by reducing the success of his Irish policy. During the charitable bequests act controversy, he informed the Irish people that the British government was negotiating an arrangement with Rome at the expense of Irish national interests. This forced the bishops to publish the Fransoni letter, strengthening distrust of the British and creating suspicion of Roman motives. It also forced Archbishop Murray and British spokesmen to deny plans for a London-Rome concordat. By fostering Irish fear of an alliance between the Rome and the British government, O'Connell to a certain extent repaired the breach in Catholic nationalist unity opened by Peel's Irish policy and made the hierarchy cautious about overtures from the British government. British anti-Catholic reactions to the Maynooth bill also aided O'Connell's effort to maintain nationalist solidarity. This exhibition of religious bigotry demonstrated that Peel's Irish policy did not represent British attitudes toward the Irish. Even the split in repeal ranks over the Colleges Bill did not appear all that serious in 1845. Old and Young Ireland were still united on the methods and aims of repeal.

Of course, it is impossible to evaluate Peel's success by the only valid historical measure, its long-range impact on Anglo-Irish affairs. The 1845 potato blight devastated Ireland, inciting agrarian crime and discontent, persuading Peel to abandon, at least for a time, his project of integrating Ireland into the United Kingdom. He sent grain into the country to feed the people and used the famine as evidence that the Corn Laws had to be repealed. However, the prime minister, confronted with a rise in agrarian outrages, decided to substitute law and order for conciliation. In June 1846 he introduced a coercion bill. On the evening of June 29, the same day Corn Law repeal passed the House of Lords, protectionist Tories, in a vengeful mood, joined Whigs, Radicals, and Repealers to topple the Peel government on Irish coercion. But their break with Peel on agricultural protection was the conclusion of a division in the Conservative party that had started with Catholic emancipation and peaked on the Maynooth bill.

Because Peel's abortive effort to sabotage Irish nationalism contributed to the destruction of his administration, no British leader dared to confront all the complexities of the Irish question until William E.H. Gladstone took office in 1868. By that time Irish nationalism had assumed an identity independent from the myriad of grievances that manufactured it. Short of self-government, solving the Irish question was no longer feasible.

4

Famine and Fenianism, 1845–1870

O'Connell's liberal democratic political nationalism and Young Ireland's cultural nationalism complemented each other. Both moved Irish Catholics away from passivity and fatalism inherent in their Gaelic folk and religious traditions. O'Connell demonstrated that mass, disciplined agitation could change things. Young Ireland inspired a new folklore that provided the people with a sense of dignity and self-confidence. But after the collapse of the 1843 repeal effort, differences in perspective and temperament inserted an ever-widening wedge between O'Connell and the young men at the *Nation*. Open conflict started when Davis and O'Connell battled verbally over the Colleges Bill in the Repeal Association. Although that quarrel was patched up, Young Irelanders, rigid in their ideological cultural nationalism, grew increasingly uncomfortable in alliance with the utilitarian O'Connell. When he came out of prison and indicated an indifference toward resuming repeal agitation, began flirting with federalism, and finally resumed his Whig associations, Young Irelanders criticized what they considered a cynical betrayal of nationalist principles.

The conjunction of nationalism with Catholicism was another issue in the O'Connell–Young Ireland controversy. Almost all the Young Irelanders were Catholics, but they believed that it was time to cut the close ties that bound repeal to the Catholic hierarchy and clergy. They argued that this association discouraged Protestants from participating in a coalition against British rule. They insisted that nationalism be Irish, not sectarian. O'Connell believed in freedom of conscience and the separation of church and state, but he also understood political reality. He had invited Protestants to join the national movement, even offering them its leadership. But he comprehended much better than young idealists that Protestants regarded the union as guarantor of their ascendancy position in Ireland. Therefore, it was not in their interest to support repeal. O'Connell, more than anyone, knew that nationalism began in the struggle for Catholic civil rights and that the bishops and priests were the force that did so much to undermine the influence of Protestant landlords. He doubted that nationalism was yet strong enough to exist separately from Catholicism. Because Young Irelanders wanted to reduce the Catholic factor in Irish nationalism, some O'Connellites did not hesitate to portray them as secularists and anticlericals. This tactic turned most of the clergy in the Repeal Association against the young men.

The Irish Confederation

The feud between O'Connell and Young Ireland came to a head in July 1846. Worried that *Nation* articles extolling the patriotism of such revolutionaries as the United Irishmen of 1798 might provoke violence in a country made desperate by famine, O'Connell introduced a resolution in the Repeal Association demanding that every member renounce physical force, no matter what the situation, as a method of achieving Irish freedom. Rather than adhere to the resolution, Young Ireland, led by Charles Gavan Duffy, Thomas Meagher, and William Smith O'Brien (Davis had died of scarlet fever in 1845) walked out of the Repeal Association and in January 1847 established the Irish Confederation as its rival.

William Smith O'Brien, a Protestant landlord from Clare, worked for Irish reform and justice as a Whig in the House of Commons. During the repeal agitation of 1843, he decided that Irish interests would always take second place in the British Parliament. When the government arrested O'Connell and his chief lieutenants in October 1843, O'Brien joined the Repeal Association. His wife and mother pleaded with him not to mingle with nationalist riffraff. Although his mother disinherited him, O'Brien stuck to his principles. He was entrusted with the leadership of the Repeal Association while O'Connell was in prison. Young Irelanders formed a deep attachment to this man of strong conviction. He joined with them in withdrawing from the association and was recognized as the chief of the confederation.

The Irish Confederation had more talent than the Repeal Association and appealed to middle-class people, who formed branches in cities and towns. However, O'Connell retained numbers for the association. Most Irish nationalists followed their priests in remaining loyal to Old Ireland. Apathy marked the activities of the association. O'Connell still placed confidence in the Whigs as Ireland's hope. During the famine crisis, he turned to them for help. In February 1847, as a fading old man with a voice not much louder than a whisper, he rose in the House of Commons and begged the British people to rescue his starving country. British MPs listened and then ignored O'Connell's plea. Brokenhearted and sick, he set out for Rome in late March. In Paris he received homage from French liberals, who expressed their gratitude for his contribution to the advance of democracy. O'Connell never completed his journey. He died in Genoa on May 15, 1847, and was laid to rest in Dublin's Glasnevin cemetery beneath a gigantic round tower, though his heart was buried in Rome. O'Connell's favorite but not most talented son, John, took command of the Repeal Association.

Shortly after its beginning, the confederation suffered a split over tactics. John Mitchel, an Ulster Unitarian and barrister, was at the center of the controversy. Mitchel began contributing to the *Nation* when it started in 1842. After Davis died, Duffy invited him to become assistant editor. He seceded with the other Young Irelanders from the Repeal Association and helped establish the confederation. But by 1847 he had become disillusioned with constitutional nationalism and had lost confidence in the possibility of recruiting Protestants in any numbers for the self-government cause. Mitchel believed that they placed their property interests above all other considerations and that landowners were the economic dimension of British colonialism. Mitchel decided that landlordism had to be destroyed and the property of Ireland distributed among its people. He insisted that a vital Irish nationalism must revolve around the land question.

Mitchel's convictions were inspired by James Fintan Lalor, an occasional contributor to the *Nation*. Lalor came from a prominent nationalist family. His father, Patrick, was an active antitithe agitator in the 1830s. His younger brother, Peter, a Repealer, emigrated to Australia, became an important leader there in the labor movement, and held office as a minister in the Victoria government. A hunchback recluse, Lalor not only lacked the extroverted personality of his father and sibling, but he also did not share their enthusiasm for repeal. He believed that land was the most important aspect of the Irish question and deserved priority over demands for independence. In 1843 Lalor wrote Peel to say that he could derail repeal with concessions to the farmer's need for economic justice and security.

Impressed with Lalor's mind but unaware of his antirepeal advice to the British government, Duffy invited him to express his ideas in the *Nation*. In a series of letters to the paper, Lalor said that the agrarian issue was of more immediate importance than repeal and that the only way that Irish nationalism could hang on to the support of tenant farmers was by endorsing their cause. He ridiculed O'Connell's agitation tactics and his distinction between legal and illegal methods. With considerable insight, Lalor pointed out that because British authorities defined what was legal and what was illegal, constitutional nationalism would always be limited by enemy restrictions. He insisted that the Irish people base their liberation strategy on only one consideration, the best interests of their country. Lalor suggested refusal to pay rents as a stratagem to destroy landlordism, the foundation of British rule in Ireland. Fascinated with this logic, Mitchel in early 1848 recommended a variation of Lalor's plan, a campaign against payment of poor rates.

With his landlord background, William Smith O'Brien was shocked by the ideas of Lalor and Mitchel. He believed in the potential of Protestant nationalism and feared that wild, antiproperty talk would destroy its prospects. When Duffy agreed with O'Brien, Mitchel resigned from *Nation*. In a confederation debate, Duffy opposed nonpayment of rates and suggested an alternate strategy: the formation of an independent Irish party in the British Parliament. It would publicize Irish grievances and attempt to convert British opinion to the necessity of repeal. If the Irish party failed to make an impression at Westminster and if Britain remained hostile to improving the situation in Ireland, then, said Duffy, Irish MPs should retaliate by obstructing the passage of British legislation in Parliament. He recommended that while the Irish party was presenting Ireland's case before the parliamentary forum, nationalists at home should organize and use their voting power to win control over local government agencies. If the Irish MPs were ejected from the House of Commons for obstruction, Duffy indicated that they could return home to an Ireland under nationalist domination. In that case, Britain would have to surrender to a united and disciplined national opinion in charge of parliamentary representation, city corporations, poor law boards, and grand juries and capable of mobilizing effective passive resistance to alien rule in Ireland.

Repeal to Revolution

When the confederation adopted Duffy's proposal, Mitchel resigned and began, with the assistance of Devin Reilly, to publish a nationalist weekly, *The United Irishmen*. It advised readers to prepare for revolution by collecting weapons and practicing their use. Mitchel's editorials insisted that the British be driven out of Ireland and their puppets, the landlords, with them. They preached that in an Irish Republic, "the land of Ireland would belong to the people of Ireland," a slogan coined by Lalor. The February 1848 revolution in France and its spread throughout Europe altered the attitude of Young Irelanders toward physical force. When the news from Paris reached Dublin, they decided that a new day of liberty had dawned for all of Europe, including Ireland. Mitchel rejoined the confederation, *Nation* editorials took on the same militant tone as those in *The United Irishmen,* Smith O'Brien and others attempted to enlist John O'Connell and Irish conservatives in a national front, and contacts were made with friends of Irish freedom in the United States and Britain (the Chartists). O'Brien led a delegation to Paris to congratulate the leaders of the Second Republic on their victory and to secure their aid for an Irish uprising, and confederation clubs throughout the country were advised to gather arms and prepare for combat. Although O'Brien was ready to lead a rebellion against Britain, he had no intention of making war on Irish property. This conservatism decided Mitchel again to leave the confederation.

Attempting to prevent an insurrection, in May the government arrested O'Brien, Mitchel, and Meagher. When juries failed to agree that O'Brien and Meagher were guilty of sedition, the government released them. But a packed jury, applying a new coercion bill, decided that Mitchel had committed treason and sentenced him to fourteen years' transportation in Tasmania. Meanwhile, revolutionary planning made little headway. The confederation did not persuade John O'Connell or Protestant leaders to cooperate in an effort to end British rule; Catholic bishops and priests remained hostile to Young Ireland and loyal to O'Connell's nonviolence; French Republicans, eager to win British recognition of their new government, refused military assistance for Irish nationalism; and Irish peasants, demoralized by hunger, fever, and emigration, were not good revolutionary material.

In July, however, the government's arrest of Duffy, seizure of the *Nation's* office, and suspension of habeas corpus pushed Young Ireland into insurrection, but it had neither the leadership nor the materials for victory. A sincere patriot and a brave man, O'Brien lacked the essential ruthlessness and indifference to property rights to lead a peasant uprising against the landlord establishment. The small number who answered the call to arms came with pikes to battle police and soldiers with rifles. O'Brien told members of his motley army not to cut down trees on landlord property for road barricades and to bring their own food rather than forage in the country. Toward the end of May, the Young Ireland revolution came to a pitiful end. The constabulary routed O'Brien's small force in Widow McCormick's Ballingarry, County Tipperary, cabbage patch and arrested him. After juries decided that he and many of his companions had committed treason and sentenced them to death, the government transported them to Tasmania instead. Other Young Irelanders were on the run, looking for a means of escape to France or the United States. Young Irelanders did not just fade away. They might have failed at revolution, but their accomplishments in many things and in many places proved that they were an extraordinarily talented group. Thomas D'Arcy McGee helped create the federated Dominion of Canada and served it as a cabinet minister. Duffy became important in Australia and was prime minister of Victoria. Thomas Francis Meagher was a brigadier general in the Union army during the American Civil War and was appointed governor of the Montana Territory. John Blake Dillon returned from American exile to play a prominent part in Irish politics during the 1860s. Thomas O'Hagan became lord chancellor of Ireland. John Martin, Mitchel's brother-in-law, was an early leader of the Home Rule movement. Other Young Irelanders, including James Stephens, John O'Mahoney, Michael Doheny, and Charles Kickham, created Irish revolutionary republicanism in the United Kingdom and in the United States. As a journalist in the latter, John Mitchel opposed abolitionism and was a Confederate propagandist in the Civil War. During the 1870s Tipperary voters twice elected him their MP, but as a convicted felon, he was denied a seat in Parliament. Mitchel was an Irish example of the ideological divide between liberalism and cultural nationalism, a distinction made clear on the continent during the revolutions of 1848. Unlike most Irish nationalists, Mitchel could not harmonize nationalism with liberalism. His defense of American slavery indicated that he did not equate individual freedom and dignity with national sovereignty. Mitchel was the complete opposite of O'Connell, who associated the Irish freedom effort with the universal struggle for individual liberty and equality.

In a time of crisis, Young Ireland had been rejected by the priests and people, then defeated by soldiers and the constabulary. But in the history of Irish nationalism, martyrology has been as important as victories. Young Irelanders joined Robert Emmet in the pantheon of defeated but noble and articulate defenders of their country. In the long run, Young Ireland captured the mind of Irish nationalism. While the *Nation's* message would inspire Fenians, Home Rulers, Gaelic Leaguers, writers of the Literary Revival, and Sinn Feiners, in the late 1840s it seemed of little significance to a country devastated by the tortures of famine.

Famine

In 1845 a potato fungus from North America arrived in Ireland via Europe, causing a massive famine that persisted with great intensity until 1849. Its effects lingered into 1851. During the "Great Hunger" at least a million and a half people died of starvation or the side effects of malnutrition—cholera, fever, and scurvy; many millions more came close to death; and at least another million crossed the Atlantic in fever-filled coffin ships or swarmed across the Irish Sea to Liverpool, Glasgow, and Cardiff. Most who arrived in Liverpool went on to America.

Nineteenth-century Irish nationalists argued, and there are still people in Ireland and Irish America who hold this view, that Ireland suffered so much and lost so many people during the famine because the British government used it to solve the Irish question through population extermination. This is too simplistic an explanation for a complex situation. Most of the misery of the famine was the product of an inefficient and unproductive agricultural system that preceded the union. There is no reason to believe, considering the economic ideologies of the time, that the aristocracy and gentry in an Irish Parliament would have responded much differently to the famine than did people from the same classes in the British Parliament. Death, disease, and emigration were also the consequences of a population explosion produced by the agricultural system and dependence on the potato. When the famine began to strike down the Irish people, British officials in Ireland worked energetically to mitigate the disaster. Often they contributed their own money to feed the poor. A number of British physicians fell victim to fever while treating the sick. Britons, including the queen and members of the royal family, donated funds to famine relief. British religious groups, particularly the Quakers, raised relief funds, ministered to the sick, and distributed food to the hungry. The government spent a fortune attempting to soften the blow of the famine. In the first year, Peel's administration spent 8 million pounds on famine relief.

In contrast to Peel's effort, the Whig government's famine response gave Irish nationalists reason to raise the genocide charge. At a time when the Irish were dying of hunger or disease or fleeing the country, Britain was the most prosperous country in the world. Its politicians did not use the full resources of the United Kingdom to save Ireland. Committed to laissez-faire dogmatism, they did not provide enough food to meet the Irish need or design the sort of public works projects that would provide food-buying income while at the same time stimulating the economy. Government officials argued that famine relief should not interfere with normal commercial activity, compete with private business, discourage personal initiative, make the Irish people psychologically dependent on government charity, or interfere with private property or private responsibility. They appeared to believe that the Irish famine was a beneficial Malthusian disaster. In its darkest hours, Nassau Senior, a famous economist high in the counsels of the Whig administration, lamented that in 1848 only a million would die from famine causes, and that was not sufficient to solve the Irish surplus population problem. Charles Edward Trevelyan, undersecretary of the treasury and the person most responsible for the government's relief program, decided that the famine was divine retribution on a wicked, perverse people.

There are similarities between the famine of the 1840s and the Holocaust of the 1930s and 1940s. The Jews and the Irish were both victims of what Albert Camus in *The Plague* described as ideological murder. Certainly the Nazis were more ruthless, heartless, and consistent in the application of racist principles than Trevelyan and his colleagues were in their anti–Irish Catholicism or in their enforcement of the dogmas of political economy. But Irish people dying of hunger or fever or crowded into the bowels of an emigrant ship, abused by heartless captains and crews, exploited by runners and hostel keepers in Liverpool, New York, Boston, and New Orleans, would have had scant consolation in knowing that their predicament was not the result of racism but a price they must pay to retain a free enterprise economy and to restore a "proper" population balance.

The famine was the most significant episode in modern Irish history, destroying whatever chance Peel's policy might have had to conciliate Catholic opinion. It left the Irish with bitter memories and focused and intensified their hatred of British rule as the source of their miseries. These recollections and emotions were passed on to children and grandchildren. The famine also influenced the development and personality of Catholicism in Ireland; pushed the agrarian dimension of the Irish question to the forefront, with important economic and political consequences; and, through emigration, transported Irish nationalism throughout the English-speaking world, especially to the United States.

The Consolidation of Irish Catholicism

When British government pressure in the late eighteenth century persuaded the Irish Parliament to begin rolling back the Penal Laws, Irish Catholicism began to lose its timidity and tentativeness, shedding the trappings of a ghetto religion. (It became less Anglo-Protestant and more continental Catholic in observance.) Devotions such as the rosary and the stations of the cross became popular in the eighteenth century. In the early nineteenth, old chapels were repaired and new ones constructed. Parish missions became increasingly common. Post-Tridentine discipline, dogma, and liturgy spread through Irish Catholicism. The successful campaign for Catholic emancipation instilled confidence and courage in the hier-archy and clergy, completing the change in the Church's stance from defensive to aggressive. Because of indifference, ignorance, and poverty (lack of decent clothes to wear), many people did not attend Mass or receive the sacraments in a church setting (large numbers did at stations held in private homes). Still, the pre-famine Irish were more frequent churchgoers than continental Catholics.

While Irish Catholicism on the eve of the famine was increasingly assertive and devotional, most of the post-Penal religious enthusiasm and reform took place in Anglicized cities, towns, and the prosperous agricultural sections of Leinster and Munster. West of the Shannon, in the poorer, more Gaelic parts of the country, superstition continued to compete with Catholic orthodoxy, religious observance was spotty and casual, and there was a shortage of priests and chapels. Everywhere in Ireland the Church was afflicted by a split in the hierarchy between the Murray and MacHale factions; a clergy that was contentious, insubordinate, and less than well educated; and a laity largely ignorant of Catholic beliefs.

The famine was a catalyst in the movement of Irish Catholicism toward Roman discipline, devotionalism, and centralization. Most of the famine casualties came from the poorest, most unenlightened element in the population, people who knew the least about their religion and practiced it spasmodically. With their passing, through death or emigration, the Church found it easier to instruct and control those who remained, and the clergy and chapel facilities increased in proportion to the decline of the laity. Catholicism also had a role in famine-induced changes in marriage and reproduction patterns. When the famine survivors became aware that overpopulation and subdivision of land contributed to the Great Hunger, they determined to control numbers through a more thoughtful approach to marriage. The result was prolonged periods of and sometimes permanent celibacy. Catholic morality gave spiritual and psychological support for this difficult decision. If social and economic necessities attached the Irish more closely to their Church, it also made puritanism a prominent feature of their religion. Perhaps it contributed to the Irish alcohol addiction as sublimation. Of course, the pub is a great refuge from the depressing damp and cold of the Irish climate as well as a substitute for the company of women. People on the next island, the English, Scots, and Welsh, also drank heavily.

The impact of the famine on Irish Catholicism set the stage for the entry of Paul Cullen. He became the most powerful personality in Ireland in the period between O'Connell and Charles Stewart Parnell. The son of a substantial Kildare yeoman farmer, with priests on both sides of the family, Cullen attended the Propaganda College in Rome for seminary training and doctoral studies. He became a papal court favorite and its adviser on Irish affairs. Appointed rector of the Irish College in 1832, Cullen was the intermediary between the Irish hierarchy and the Curia. More nationalistic in his youth, prior to Mazzini's ouster of the pope from Rome, than in middle or old age, Cullen tipped off O'Connell on the Fransoni Directive. In 1849 Pius IX sent his good friend Cullen back to Ireland as archbishop of Armagh, primate, and apostolic delegate. Three years later he replaced Murray as Dublin's archbishop. In 1866 Cullen became the first Irish cardinal. His importance was apparent in 1870 when he designed Vatican I's papal infallibility formula.

Cullen returned to Ireland determined to engineer an ultramontane triumph over competing forms of Gallicanism: Murray's cooperation with the government, MacHale's alliance with nationalism. With the exception of much of Ulster and MacHale's Tuam, Cullen managed to select bishops and to impose his will on the hierarchy. As part of the Romanization process, he built large numbers of churches and schools; achieved public displays of unity in the hierarchy; improved the discipline and training of priests; promoted a rapid increase in religious vocations, both for Irish and missionary purposes; expanded Catholic education, including the founda-tions of a university; defeated an English-financed Protestant evangelical crusade to proselytize Irish Catholics; and completed a "devotional revolution" that made the Irish the most pious, generous, and dedicated Catholics in western Europe.

Cullen disliked and distrusted the English, even those who were Catholic, and all

PAUL CARDINAL CULLEN, 1852–1878

Paul Cullen's primary commitment to the interests of the Catholic Church made him unpopular with Irish nationalists, but as archbishop of Armagh (1849–1852) and archbishop
of Dublin (1852–1878) he led the "Devotional Revolution" that shaped the spirit, content,
and structure of modern Irish Catholicism. (Courtesy of the National Library of Ireland)

Protestants, but he was also hostile to lay and clerical nationalism. When he came to
Ireland, he associated Young Ireland with Mazzini's anticlericalism. Later he would link
the Fenians with Garibaldi and the Carbonari. In Cullen's opinion, Irish nationalism's
liberal inclusiveness and tolerance constituted a more dangerous threat to ultramontan-
ism than the hereditary Anglo-Saxon and Anglo-Irish Protestant enemies. To him, there

was no distinction between Irish and Catholic identities—faith and fatherland were inseparable. What was good for the Church was good for the country.

What Cullen never understood was that the success of his effort to unify, discipline, and dogmatically and liturgically Romanize the Irish Church owed as much to the advance of Irish nationalism, with its religious and cultural identity connections, as it did to his leadership. The Irish wore their religion as an identity badge. As they increased their commitment to nationality, they intensified their Catholicism. However, stronger Catholics did not mean weaker nationalists. Cullen and other bishops found out that in politics, they could only lead where people wanted to go. The Irish loved their religion, treasuring it as culture as well as faith, and respected their priests, listening to and obeying them on matters of dogma, but retained their allegiance to the principles and objectives of Irish nationalism. At the Dedalus family's Christmas dinner in James Joyce's *Portrait of the Artist as a Young Man*, Mrs. Riordan, bitterly denounces John Casey, the ex-Fenian and Parnellite anticlerical, as a renegade Catholic. In anger, he replies: "And I may tell you ma'am, that I, if you mean me, am no renegade Catholic, I am a Catholic as my father was and his father before him again when we gave up our lives rather than sell our faith."

While Romanization brought discipline and solidarity to the Catholic Church in Ireland and throughout its religious empire, and strengthened and tightened identity bonds between faith and nationality, there were long-term negative aspects. It lessened the spontaneous spirituality of pre-Devotional Revolution Catholicism, substituting an emphasis on rules and regulations, which along with increasing clericalism and Puritanism repressed Irish Catholic creativity, intellectual energy, and healthy social and sexual relations between men and women. A wide gap between clergy and laity would lead to a post-1922 Catholic confessional state and friction between writers and other creative artists concerning the social and political influence of bishops and rigid and often stupid censorship. And clerical haughtiness and superiority complexes no doubt played a role in the sexual and physical abuse scandals that contributed to the falling significance of post-1970s Catholicism.

Land and Politics

Catholicism remained the nucleus of Irish identity, but emancipation and Peel's Irish policy did much to reduce the religious dimension of the Irish question. Because of the famine, land emerged as the most pressing and emotional issue in nationalist politics.

After the fiasco at Ballingarry, Charles Gavan Duffy was the only Young Ireland leader left in the country. The government tried him five times on treason charges, but brilliant courtroom tactics by his attorney, Isaac Butt, and the inability of juries to reach a unanimous decision freed him from prison and saved him from transportation to Van Diemen's Land (Tasmania). After his release, Duffy revived the *Nation* and with new colleagues—Dr. John Gray, Protestant part-owner of the leading daily nationalist newspaper, *The Freeman's Journal*, and Frederick Lucas, owner and editor of the *Tablet*, a Catholic weekly—he set out to combine the ideas of Lalor and Mitchel with the strategy he proposed to the Irish Confederation as a new program for Irish nationalism.

Duffy and his friends proposed an Independent Irish Party in the House of Commons dedicated to a tenant right solution to agrarian discontent. They believed that a concentration on the plight of farmers all over the country would unite Protestants in Ulster in common cause with rural Catholics from all over Ireland. A precedent of Catholic-Protestant cooperation would break down barriers of suspicion and animosity, clearing the way for an ecumenical Irish nationalism incorporating all the people.

Duffy, Gray, and Lucas were appealing to famine-intensified farmer security concerns both north and south, Catholic, Anglican, and Presbyterian. The demand for economic and social justice did not express desperate poverty. In fact, as British political economists predicted, the famine benefited its survivors, especially in the fertile sectors of Leinster, Munster, and Ulster. Famine death and emigration population decreases most affected the agricultural laboring and marginal tenant-farming classes. Continuing emigration kept reducing Irish numbers. After the famine, farmers came to outnumber laborers, and farms grew larger. Throughout the 1850s, 1860s, and well into the 1870s, harvests tended to be good, agricultural prices rose, rents were relatively stable, and evictions were rare. These factors and dollar gifts from sons and daughters in the United States lifted the rural Irish standard of living. Cottages became roomier and sturdier; people wore better clothing and supplemented potatoes with cereals, bread, butter, vegetables, eggs, and occasionally meat and fish. National school education, a demanding Catholicism, and better food and housing produced a much more sophisticated, disciplined, and healthier peasantry than the pre-famine variety.

Tenant right was most consistently advocated in areas where people were experiencing economic and social improvements, rather than along the Atlantic coast or in mountainous Catholic Ulster, where the soil was poor and rocky and fields were small, and the potato still sustained life. Therefore, tenant right organizations articulated rising expectations, a determination not to fall back into a pre-famine survival situation and mentality.

Encouraged by Duffy, Lucas, and Gray, representatives of tenant right clubs from all over Ireland began to discuss shared problems and goals. These conversations resulted in the Irish Tenant League, with the stated objectives of fair rents established by impartial evaluation, secure tenures, and the right of tenants to sell their interest in the farm they occupied when leaving (Ulster custom). The political activation of Irish farmers persuaded a number of MPs to combine in an Irish party committed to independent opposition in the House of Commons and to tenant right. In July 1852 a general election returned forty-eight Irish party MPs, but within a few months of this spectacular victory, it began to disintegrate.

The Achilles' heel of the party was the Tenant League–Irish Brigade coalition. Ridiculed as the "Pope's Brass Band," the brigade was the organized response of a group of Liberal Irish MPs to Lord John Russell's 1851 bill threatening to prosecute and penalize Catholic clergymen who took UK geographic ecclesiastical titles. In exploiting the anti-Catholic hysteria following Pius IX's decision to create a diocesan structure for an Irish-immigrant-enriched British Church, Russell's bill indicated that the Whigs were prepared to outdo the Tories at their no-popery game.

Insulted by the Whig courtship of prejudice, George Henry Moore, MP, son of the George Moore in Thomas Flanagan's novel *The Year of the French* and the father of a future distinguished writer, George Moore, gathered a small group of Irish MPs to punish Russell by voting with the opposition to destroy the government. The passage of the Ecclesiastical Titles Bill (it was never really enforced, and the Catholic Church used different geographic titles from the Church of England's) so aroused Irish Catholic opinion that Moore decided to retain the brigade as an independent influence. To give it constituency backing, in August 1851 brigade MPs established the Catholic Defense Association of Great Britain and Ireland.

Gray's *Freeman's Journal* endorsed the brigade and its constituency organization. Duffy respected Moore's integrity and talent but did not find the same qualities in some of his brigade colleagues. However, in August 1851 he helped William Sharman Crawford, MP, an Ulster Protestant champion of federalism and the outstanding parliamentary promoter of tenant right legislation, complete an alliance between the brigade and the Tenant League. It gave the league additional strength in Parliament without associating the nondenominational tenant right movement with the brigade's Catholic concerns.

Shortly after the general election, two brigade members of the independent Irish party, William Keogh and John Sadlier, broke their independent opposition pledge and accepted office in Lord Aberdeen's Peelite-Whig coalition government. This apostasy did not offend Archbishop Cullen or some other bishops. They wanted cooperation with Aberdeen, hoping to win concessions for the Catholic Church, particularly in education, and were pleased to have Catholics such as Sadlier and Keogh in office.

Duffy blamed the defection of Sadlier and Keogh and the anti-independent opposition stance of prominent members of the Catholic hierarchy for the collapse of the Irish party. By 1855 he had lost confidence in the movement and in his ability to shape the future of Irish nationalism. Duffy sold the *Nation* to A.M. Sullivan, a young nationalist from West Cork, and sailed to Australia, where he played an important part in that nation's political development. When an old man, he returned to Ireland as Sir Charles Gavan Duffy, blessed the Home Rule movement, and molded Irish popular history in books on Thomas Davis, Young Ireland, and the Independent Irish party.

Duffy's historical interpretations made Cullen a villain in the mythology of Irish nationalism. While it is true that the approval of Cullen and other prelates of the Sadlier-Keogh "treachery," their enmity to independent opposition, and Cullen's instructions to Irish priests to stay out of politics did damage Irish party prospects, other factors, perhaps more important, contributed to its demise. Aberdeen's government attracted considerable support from Ulster Protestant tenant farmers. Common famine suffering created common cause, but when times improved, ancient sectarian animosities reemerged and defeated peasant-class solidarity. And it must be remembered that relations between landlords and tenants were more harmonious in Ulster than in the other provinces.

Landlordism also had a political resurgence in the 1850s. With the Catholic hierarchy split on such matters as independent opposition and the priority of tenant right, landlords were able to muster the votes to return fifty-seven Conservative Irish MPs in the general election of 1859. Tenant insecurity, their deference to the upper classes, and the absence of a secret ballot meant that the owners of large estates could still control Catholic as well as Protestant votes.

Landlord success in the 1859 general election also owed something to the pro-Cavour, antipapal position of Lords Palmerston and Russell. Reacting to this Whig support for Italian nationalism's menace to the papal states, Nicholas Patrick Cardinal Wiseman, archbishop of Westminster, and some Irish prelates urged Irish voters in Britain and Ireland to support Lord Derby and the Conservatives.

In addition to the conduct of bishops and priests, the Independent Irish party's difficulty in finding quality candidates assisted the resurgence of landlord political power. As previously observed, prohibitive election costs and London living expenses without a salary made politics an upper-class avocation. Most Irishmen in a position to pursue parliamentary careers were landlords hostile to the economic, political, and religious interests of Irish Catholics. Candidates willing to gamble small fortunes to represent nationalist, tenant right, or Catholic causes could not be expected to keep pre-election pledges once separated from constituents by the Irish Sea. Irishmen eager for status, prestige, and wealth often sold their services to any government in exchange for office.

By 1858 the Independent Irish party numbered an ineffectual twelve. A year later it was officially dissolved. Led by John Blake Dillon, most of its MPs moved to the Liberal benches in 1866. In the 1860s a number of Irish Liberal MPs, including George Henry Moore and Dillon, cooperated with Cullen and other bishops in the National Association. Its goals were government aid to Catholic education, disestablishment of the Protestant church, and tenant right. Because of Cullen and the bad experience of the Independent Irish party, the association lacked a mass constituency, but through its alliances with John Bright's Reform League and the Society for the Liberation of the Church from State Patronage and Control, two British radical organizations, it did influence William E.H. Gladstone's perspective on the Irish question. However, in the 1860s Irish nationalism was moving in an anticonstitutional direction, and emigration was instrumental in this shift.

The American Dimension

Irish emigrants were scattered throughout the English-speaking world, but most ended up in the United States. Before 1820 the majority of those who left Ireland for North America were Ulster Presbyterians irritated by British restrictions on Irish economic development and the ascendancy of the Church of Ireland. After that date, periodic famines, rural violence, and population pressures on a primitive and static economy transformed emigration into a primarily Catholic affair. The famine institutionalized it as a safety valve, with parents raising most of their children for export. From 1845 to 1891 more than 3 million Irish, mostly young and single, entered the United States. By the end of the nineteenth century, more women than men were leaving for America.

Irish emigrants were not prepared psychologically or vocationally for life in industrial societies. As the most underprivileged people in urban Britain and the United States, they did the hard, unpleasant work that Anglo-Americans and Britons were too proud or perhaps too weak to do. The Irish dug canals; built railroads; mined coal, silver, gold, and copper; lifted cargo on the docks; soldiered all over the British empire and on the American frontier; and scrubbed the floors, washed the dishes, and took care of children in the homes of the well-to-do. Anglo-Protestants in Britain and in Boston, New York, and Philadelphia despised dirty, ignorant Irish Catholics, and the British and American working class did not welcome their labor competition. Rejected by host communities, the Irish huddled in slum ghettos, spawning a large proportion of juvenile delinquents, petty thieves, alcoholics, depressives, and schizophrenics. Many immigrants blamed their American misfortunes on the British oppression that forced them into exile. And they responded to alienation with a nationalism more fanatic than the Irish-in-Ireland variety; as Thomas N. Brown has observed: "in the alembic of America the parochial peasant was transformed into a passionate Irish nationalist."

This emigration-scattered Irish nationalism multiplied its challenge to Britain. Although economic realities necessitated emigration as an Irish safety valve, nationalist leaders blamed the diaspora on British misgovernment. When the Irish began to achieve economic and social mobility in the United States, their success also fed Irish nationalist propaganda. It argued that Irish genius flourished when emancipated from British tyranny.

Irish Catholicism's acceptance of liberal democracy and the political skills Irish immigrants brought from Ireland led to Irish-American progress. O'Connell's instructions on Anglo-Protestant political values and on operating within its constitutional traditions and structures made it possible for the Irish to adjust to the American political system and consensus and then lead other Catholic ethnics into a similar accommodation. Political power and the leadership of Catholic America resulted in economic and social advances and eventual respectability, but the process was long and uneven.

In early Irish America the dominant impulse of nationalism was an alienation response to poverty, social disorder, and Anglo-American Protestant nativism. Because Anglo-Americans emphasized Catholicism as the main feature of the "ugly" Irish cultural and social profile, and because in the United States nativism destroyed fraternal links between Irish Catholics and Irish Protestants and Dissenters, the twin identities, Irish and Catholic, became stronger than in the United Kingdom. Consequently, Irish nationalism evolved to become more exclusively Catholic in America than in Ireland. Anglo-Irish and Scots-Irish Americans melded into Anglo-America. When it came, economic progress in the United States did not necessarily eliminate the Irish inferiority complex. Irish Americans with substantial incomes and good educations were classical examples of what the Chicago school of sociology in the 1920s described as marginal men. They longed to participate in the social activities of Anglo-Protestant America. When rejected, they returned to the subordinate Irish cultural community as leaders, determined to demonstrate its significance and achieve its acceptance. Young Ireland's cultural nationalism was as good for the ego of Irish Americans as it was for the Irish in Ireland. It told them that they were an honorable people with a cultural heritage as rich and a history as glorious and values more spiritual than Anglos. So in economically and socially mobile Irish America, nationalism developed a respectability as well as an anti-British purpose. Associating their status problem with Ireland's bondage, many middle-class Irish Americans believed that the liberation of their homeland would culminate in American acceptability.

Irish-American nationalism employed two strategies. One pressured U.S. foreign policy to move in an anti-British direction; the other used the United States as a supply station for freedom efforts in Ireland. Although Irish Americans have been the most talented politicians in the United States, they have not been particularly effective in influencing foreign policy. Occasionally non-Irish candidates for office have played to an Irish grandstand to gather votes, but Anglo-American Protestants have defeated Irish-American maneuvers to provoke antagonism between the United States and their cultural mother country, Britain.

Irish strategic successes compensated in part for Washington failures. Without the American connection, nationalism in Ireland might have perished. In addition to organization, passion, dollars, and pressures on Britain, Irish America affected the personality of Irish nationalism. Nationalist commitments in Ireland to demo-cratic principles and values were strengthened through associations with American republicanism and democracy. In 1887 Lord Spencer, an influential Liberal peer, discussed the importance of the Ireland-America connection:

> The Irish peasantry still live in poor hovels, often in the same room with animals; they have few modern comforts; and yet they are in close communication with those who live at ease in the cities and farms of the United States. They are also imbued with the advanced political notions of the American republic and are sufficiently educated to read the latest political doctrines in the press which circulates them. Their social condition at home is a hundred years behind their state of mental and political culture.

Anglo-Irish landlords and Catholic priests were also apprehensive about the impact of American examples. After 1860 they observed that people had become more assertive and less deferential to their social or religious betters, attributing this arrogance to the American contents of Fenianism.

Fenianism

Fenianism emerged in 1858 from the New York–based Emmet Monument Association, dedicated to writing Robert Emmet's epitaph in the form of an Irish nation. John O'Mahony and Michael Doheny, veterans of 1848, led the association. They and James Stephens managed to escape British clutches after Ballingarry. Doheny made it to New York; Stephens and O'Mahony found work, respectively, as a translator and an English teacher in Paris, where they absorbed the teachings of 1848 refugees from other European revolutions.

In Paris, O'Mahony and Stephens decided on a revolutionary movement to establish a democratic Irish republic. Ideologically socialists, they agreed to submerge economic issues, still entertaining the Young Ireland notion that Protestant property owners could become Irish nationalists. This fantasy deprived republicanism of a significant economic content.

Invited by Doheny, O'Mahony left Paris in 1854 for New York to recruit Irish Americans for revolutionary conspiracy. Stephens concentrated his mobilizing efforts in Ireland and Britain. In 1858 he initiated the Irish Republican Brotherhood (IRB) and incorporated Jeremiah O'Donovan Rossa's Cork-centered Phoenix Society. It represented the dashing Gaelic speaker's determination to raise Ireland from the ashes of British conquest. This was in the same year that O'Mahony transformed the Emmet Monument Association into the American branch of republicanism. Because he was a Gaelic scholar and an admirer of the legendary sagas featuring warriors called Fianna, O'Mahony decided to name it the Fenian Brotherhood. *Fenianism* became the popular term for Irish republicanism on both sides of the Atlantic.

To ensure secrecy, Stephens and O'Mahony organized Fenianism into circles commanded by a center. Circles were subdivided into cells under the command of captains with authority over sergeants in charge of privates. Lower-rank Republicans knew only cell comrades. IRB members took secrecy oaths. To avoid offending American Catholic bishops, Fenians took a pledge. Despite security measures, informers and spies infested and infiltrated republicanism.

Stephens was head center of the IRB and chief organizer of the Irish Republic. O'Mahony was Fenian head center. Stephens considered himself in charge of the total Republican movement. Irish Americans did not always honor that claim.

The IRB in Ireland and the Fenians in the United States both had about 50,000 members, but many more Irish Americans were contributing sympathizers. In 1865 the American Irish donated about $228,000 to the cause. The next year they increased their contribution to over $500,000. During the Civil War, many Irish Americans enlisted in the Union and Confederate armies, hoping to use their combat training and experience against the British at some later date.

Fenianism was more than politics and nationalism. As previously mentioned, in the United States it involved working-class alienation and a quest for middle-class respectability. Like Young Irelanders, many IRB leaders were journalists.

Striving for fame and glory, these lower-middle-class young men were blocked by the O'Connellite and Young Ireland establishments. By moving beyond repeal and independent opposition to revolutionary republicanism, they found a position in Irish nationalism.

Despite the reluctance of Stephens and O'Mahoney to emphasize the economic aspects of the Irish question, republicanism did exhibit class frustrations and interests. In the United States it included unskilled working-class rage and the expectations of the economically mobile. In Ireland city and town artisans and shop assistants, suspended between the working and middle classes, joined the IRB. In the late 1860s it took root in rural Ireland, particularly Connacht and Catholic Ulster, whence it became a significant force in the Land War of the 1870s and 1880s.

In Ireland and the United States, Fenianism also offered recreational opportunities for fun-starved people. Life in class-structured, agrarian, Catholic, puritan Ireland was dull and monotonous. This, as well as economic hardship, stimulated emigration. Fenians sponsored athletic activities, reading rooms with discussion groups, outings, and walking tours in the mountains. They gathered at horse races and fairs and formed musical organizations. In the United States, the Fenian Brotherhood, and later the Clan na Gael, sponsored picnics and clambakes with barrels of beer to wash down the food. After the meal, there were colorful patriotic speeches and, even better, music and dancing. Finley Peter Dunne, the Chicago journalist initiator of American urban ethnic literature, observed in the 1890s that if Ireland could have been liberated by picnics, it would have become an empire.

In Ireland the IRB did not get the approval of John Martin or William Smith O'Brien, two returnees from Australian exile. In the United States, other Young Irelanders, such as Thomas Meagher, condemned Fenianism. John Mitchel first opposed, then later approved. Because of his hostility, Fenians assassinated Thomas D'Arcy McGee in 1867 on the steps of the Canadian Parliament in Ottawa. In the *Nation,* A.M. Sullivan identified the IRB with agrarian secret societies in a blanket denunciation of physical force. Catholic bishops, led by Cullen, were the most powerful enemies of republicanism. They attacked its secret character and commitment to the violent destruction of British rule. To Cullen, Fenians were dangerous secularists, enemies of throne and altar, radicals inspired by the excessively democratic and turbulent environment of the United States, and Irish disciples of Mazzini, Cavour, and Garibaldi. The Catholic hierarchy also had high hopes that Gladstone's Liberal party would disestablish the Protestant Church and endow Catholic education. They feared that violent nationalism in Ireland would so alienate British opinion that Gladstone would shy away from Irish reform. No doubt the bishops also were concerned with the recreational side of Fenianism. They did not approve of social functions outside the control of the parish priest, particularly if they involved contact between young men and women. David Moriarity, bishop of Kerry, said that "hell wasn't hot enough or eternity long enough" to properly punish Fenians.

Clerical hostility introduced a strong anticlerical note into republicanism. In its newspaper, *The Irish People,* Charles J. Kickham replied to the hierarchy. Kickham, a devout Catholic, was author of such popular novels as *Knocknagow* and *Sally Cavanaugh.* His descriptions of peasant Ireland were much more romantic than those of Carleton, but insightful all the same, and they contributed to the mainstream of Irish cultural nationalism. Kickham ranked with Thomas Moore and Thomas Davis in the hearts of Irish exiles in America. Speaking then from a position of powerful influence, Kickham said that the Irish people should respect and listen to bishops and priests when they discussed religion but that clerical authority stopped on the frontiers of politics. He reminded readers that bishops had supported the treachery of Sadlier and Keogh and warned that some of them would sell the liberty of their country for government educational grants. He advised Irish Catholics to love God and His Church but also to love their country. He assured them that there was no conflict in these affections.

From the original condemnation of the Fenians in 1858 until 1865, Cullen managed to keep his fellow bishops and priests away from republicanism. However, there were a few exceptions. Because most of the clergy came from the farmer and shopkeeper classes, they shared the grievances of their kin. Some were bold enough to defy superiors by offering prayers for and sympathy to the IRB. In 1861, for example, Patrick Lavelle, a Mayo priest, spoke at the Glasnevin burial of Terence Belew McManus after Cullen displayed coolness to a Fenian-staged Catholic funeral for the 1848 veteran who had died in San Francisco. Lavelle was shielded by Archbishop MacHale, who, though he never went so far as to endorse Fenianism, remained on good terms with Republicans and accepted their charity.

After the surrender at Appomattox that ended the Civil War, Fenians began to prepare for war on Britain. Irish Americans who had recently commanded troops in the War between the States infiltrated Ireland and began to train members of the IRB. John Devoy initiated an effort to recruit Irish soldiers in the British army stationed in Ireland for the IRB. Several thousand may have joined. American pressure forced Stephens to plan an uprising for 1866, but a factional dispute in American republicanism cut off supplies to Ireland. In 1865 a national Fenian convention in Philadelphia adopted a new constitution abolishing the head center, replacing him with a president responsible to a general congress divided into a senate and a house of delegates. Colonel William R. Roberts, head of the Senate, dictated a new strategy for Fenianism. Instead of participating in an Irish revolution, American Fenians would attack British Canada, holding it hostage for Ireland's freedom, leaving the Irish in Ireland to conduct and supply their own war against the British. Efforts to attack Canada failed and lacking proper equipment, Stephens refused to repeat the fiasco of 1848. Meanwhile, a spy in the offices of *The Irish People* turned over incriminating evidence to the government. The authorities shut down the paper and arrested its staff, along with Stephens. Devoy engineered the head center's prison escape. Stephens then went to the United States to end the feud between O'Mahony and the Senate wing and to obtain weapons for an Irish revolution. However, his arrogant and abrasive personality exacerbated rather than ended conflict within American Fenianism. Blaming Stephens for indecisiveness in regard to an Irish revolution, in December 1866 American Fenians deposed him as Republican head center. An Irish American, Colonel Thomas J. Kelly, took his place.

While Stephens's American mission was collapsing, the government took the IRB by surprise. It transferred Irish soldiers stationed in their own country elsewhere, suspended habeas corpus, and arrested a number of Republican leaders. In a futile gesture of defiance, Kerry Fenians took the field in February 1867, and others in Dublin, Cork, Tipperary, Limerick, and Clare followed the next month. Without adequate weapons, these little Fenian bands were easily routed by the British army and the Royal Irish Constabulary.

After 1865 a growing number of priests, influenced by traditional grievances, particularly those concerned with land, a decreasing American influence on the IRB, and the fact that republicanism had been defeated and was more a legend than a reality, began to view Fenianism with some sympathy. Cullen feared that the clergy was becoming unmanageable on the issue. When news got out that British prison authorities were brutal to Fenian convicts, and when in 1867 the British legal system executed three young Irishmen (W.P. Allen, Michael Larkin, and Michael O'Brien), after a trial in an atmosphere of tremendous anti-Irish feeling, for allegedly killing a police constable in a Manchester rescue of Colonel Kelly from a police van, there was a massive wave of pro-Fenian sentiment in Ireland. Prayers rose from Catholic altars for the Manchester martyrs. Some bishops joined the Amnesty Association working to commute prison sentences for Republicans. But the British government was active in Rome. Assisted by Bishop Moriarity, and with promises of benefits to the church in Ireland, Lord Odo Russell, the British representative, persuaded Pius IX to issue an official condemnation of the IRB.

Actually, Rome's pro-British interference in Irish affairs antagonized Irish nationalism, making the Fenians more popular. Trying to exploit a friendlier climate of opinion and to increase efficiency, Republicans reorganized their movement on both sides of the Atlantic. Violent nationalism best represented Irish America's approach to liberating Ireland from British colonialism. In Ireland people came to respect Fenians for their sacrifice and their bravery—they were added to the list of martyred patriots, but revolutionary republicanism was and remained a minority voice. Fenianism added democratic and egalitarian impulses to Irish nationalism, but its mainstream continued to seek self-government with some British connection by constitutional means. After 1870 it found expression in Home Rule.

Gladstone's Initial Response to the Irish Question

Fenianism not only colored the personality of Irish nationalism, but along with the alliance between the National Association and the British Liberation Society, it decided William Ewart Gladstone, who organized the Liberal party from a coalition of Whigs, Radicals, and Peelites, to address the Irish question. Taking office after the 1868 general election, he decided to follow the lead of his mentor, Peel, by initiating a policy of attempting to destroy Irish nationalism by eliminating the social, economic, and religious grievances of its constituency. In 1869 the prime minister disestablished the Protestant Church of Ireland. The next year he pushed a Land Act through Parliament. It was a conservative effort to achieve tenant farmer security by forcing landlords to compensate evictees for improvements they had made and inconvenience they had suffered. The Land Act applied in all instances of eviction except for nonpayment of rent. Gladstone believed that the expense of ousting tenants from their holdings would force landlords to think twice before clearing estates. Both the disestablishment and Land Acts contained land purchase possibilities. The government offered tenants on church property loans to buy their holdings. John Bright added an important clause to the Land Act, providing government loans up to two-thirds of the purchase price for tenants who wanted their own farms.

As an instrument of security, the Land Act failed. Because landlords could evict tenants without compensation if rents were not paid, it encouraged them to raise rents to get rid of poor tenants. Loans provided by the Disestablishment Act created about 6,000 peasant proprietors, but the terms of the Bright Clause did not attract much tenant farmer enthusiasm. In fact, with the severe agricultural depression that began in the late 1870s, peasant conditions worsened, and many tenant farmers were evicted for nonpayment of rent.

Though inadequate for its purpose, the Land Act was a precedent that weakened resistance to government control of property rights, paving the way for more meaningful legislation in the 1880s. And the Disestablishment Act and Bright Clause pointed to a final solution of the land problem, peasant proprietorship. The Disestablishment Act was a British liberal rejection of Protestant ascendancy in Ireland. And the refusal of dual establishment by Cullen and other Catholic bishops, despite the wishes of Rome, meant that Irish Catholicism had accepted the separation of church and state, a principle of Irish nationalism. The Land Act was the first major government reversal of the traditional rights of landed property, so it had major implications for Britain as well as Ireland. By expanding government areas of responsibility, the Land Act was a significant step in the progress of British liberalism from its early nineteenth-century laissez-faire start to its late nineteenth- and early twentieth-century collectivist climax.

Although Gladstone agreed with Irish Catholic complaints that they were denied higher education opportunities and facilities, as leader of a party dependent on the votes of British Nonconformists, he could hardly endow the Catholic University in Dublin. And it would be imprudent and inconsistent to follow the disestablishment of Irish Protestantism with an endowment of Catholic education. In 1873 the prime minister presented to Parliament a solution to the Irish higher education dilemma. His Irish University Bill proposed converting Dublin University from a Protestant institution to a national one by expanding it to include a Catholic college as well as Trinity. The university would offer no lectures or examinations in such controversially sectarian subjects as theology, history, or moral philosophy. The affiliated colleges, however, would be free to offer courses and diplomas in them.

Because the Irish Catholic hierarchy had been fighting nondenominational higher education beginning with the Queen's colleges in the late 1840s, they rejected Gladstone's offer as inadequate. They argued that because the government supported Protestant Oxford and Cambridge and the Disestablishment Act left Trinity a well-financed center of Protestant studies, a non-endowed Catholic college within Dublin University would be a disadvantaged institution without funds to attract good students or faculty. Influenced by the bishop's criticism of the University Bill, a large number of Irish Liberal MPs voted against and defeated it, forcing Gladstone to call a general election in January 1874. Expanded by the 1867 Reform Bill and emancipated by the 1872 Ballot Act, the British electorate returned a Conservative majority. Benjamin Disraeli succeeded Gladstone as prime minister. In Ireland, the contest between Liberals and Conservatives was of minor importance compared to the success of Home Rule, which sent fifty-nine MPs to the House of Commons.

5

Home Rule and the
Land War, 1870–1882

Isaac Butt and Home Rule

Isaac Butt created the Home Rule movement. He was born in 1813, the son of a Protestant rector in Donegal. At Trinity College, Dublin, Butt was a brilliant student, and he cofounded and edited *Dublin University Magazine,* the best of nineteenth-century Irish conservative periodicals. After graduation in 1836, Butt stayed on at Trinity to teach political economy while he studied law at the King's Inn. As a young barrister, his was the most intelligent voice of Irish unionism and Protestant ascendancy. In 1843 Alderman Butt debated repeal with O'Connell in the Dublin Corporation, arguing that by including Ireland in the United Kingdom, the union promoted it from province to world power. At the same time that Butt exalted the union, he complained that British laissez-faire endangered the Irish economy. From an economic protectionist he evolved into a political nationalist. This process was evident in Butt's 1847 pamphlet *Famine in the Land.* In it, he attacked the Whig laissez-faire approach to hunger and death in Ireland. As a substitute, he recommended strong government action, including public works to provide employment while advancing Ireland's economic potential, improved transportation facilities to encourage Irish industry and agriculture, and a government-sponsored and -financed emigration program to relieve population pressure.

In 1848 Butt defended Young Ireland rebels, telling juries that British insensitivity to the famine disaster had exasperated the patience of idealists. He insisted that the Irish people had a constitutional right to agitate for repeal. He also suggested that an Irish legislature supervising local affairs might be the best solution to the Irish question.

As a liberal Conservative MP in the 1850s and a pamphleteer in the 1860s, Butt abandoned Protestant ascendancy and proposed constructive unionism. He suggested tenant right, denominational education, and a dual Catholic and Protestant religious establishment as conservative responses to Irish religious pluralism and economic discontent. During those two decades, Butt worked closely with Catholic bishops and the leaders of tenant right organizations.

In 1867, without charge, Butt defended Fenians in court. Then he became president of the Amnesty Association, petitioning for their parole from prison. By this time convinced that the Westminster Parliament could not reconcile the priorities of industrial Britain with those of agrarian Ireland, Butt came out for a local legislature to manage Irish business. As a conservative in the school of Edmund Burke, he also believed that a domestic parliament might isolate Ireland from the secularism and radicalism sweeping Britain. But he did not want self-government to come through the democratic, egalitarian, and violent auspices of Fenianism. It was time, he believed, for a conservative constitutional attempt at legislative independence.

Butt discussed his ideas with George Henry Moore. Together they decided that constitutional nationalism should replace repeal with federalism as its objective. Since the Union victory in the American Civil War, federalism had developed a clientele among British intellectuals and politicians. They were responsible for the 1867 North American Act establishing the Dominion of Canada with a federal constitution to harmonize relations between the Anglos and the French. Moore and Butt thought that Britain might be prepared to apply the same logic to the Irish situation.

Moore died in early 1870, leaving Butt with the task of founding a federalist organization. He met with forty-nine prominent Dubliners, mostly Protestants, on May 19, 1870, and their discussion led to the Home Government Association (HGA), which had its first meeting at the Rotunda on September 1. The HGA was a private organization dedicated to uniting Irish Catholics and Protestants behind Home Rule and persuading British and Irish opinion that a federal arrangement between the two islands would be a permanent and satisfactory conclusion to centuries of animosity. To secure the allegiance and allay the fears of Irish Protestants, the HGA confined itself to one issue, Home Rule. All other subjects were barred from its meetings.

In *Irish Federalism* (1870), Butt assured Irish and British readers that Home Rule was a conservative proposal. He pointed out that their religion made Irish Catholics orderly and deferential. Frustrations with British misrule had led them into paths of rebellion. But once governed by their own Parliament, they would be the most loyal members of the British empire, following the lead of a Protestant aristocracy and gentry. He told the British that Home Rule meant Irish-British friendship and Irish Protestants that it would lead to religious and class reconciliation in Ireland. Butt informed his coreligionists that they would have significant influence in an Irish House of Commons and control over an Irish House of Lords. This would prevent the domination of the Catholic majority. But he warned them that if they rejected this opportunity to join Catholics in a common national cause, they could expect little consideration in a future Irish state.

Irish republicanism responded to federalism in a variety of ways. Charles J. Kickham, president of the IRB's Supreme Council, did not oppose alternatives to Irish freedom. He told Butt that he would neither publicly endorse nor oppose Home Rule. Therefore, many IRB members worked in the HGA. Some, such as

Joseph Biggar and John O'Connor Power, were Home Rule MPs while serving on the Supreme Council. Irish Republicans in Britain admired Butt for his legal defense of the Fenians and his work with the Amnesty Association. They established a number of HGA branches in British cities. Things were different in America. Founded by Joseph Carroll in 1867, the Clan na Gael superseded the Fenian Brotherhood. Under the direction of John Devoy, who arrived in the United States in 1871 after his release from a British prison, the clan refused to cooperate with the "corruptions" of parliamentary nationalism. Because Irish-American money funded Republicanism in Ireland, the clan forced Kickham in 1876 to expel IRB members trafficking in federalism.

From the beginning, federalism enjoyed successes. The Dublin Corporation, poor law boards, town councils, tenant right organizations, and many newspapers, including the influential Protestant Tory *Evening Mail,* came out for Home Rule. In England and Scotland branches of the HGA multiplied so rapidly that in 1873 it was necessary to create an umbrella organization, the Home Rule Confederation of Great Britain, with Butt as president. From January 1871 to August 1873 federalism acquired a parliamentary representation of fourteen. Eight came from by-election victories; six were converts from Liberal ranks. Turmoil in the by-elections between Home Rulers and pro-Gladstone priests convinced Parliament in 1872 that it was time to legislate the secret ballot.

Home Rule advances were limited by its failure to enlist significant numbers from the Protestant community or from the Catholic hierarchy and clergy. Fondly recalling their eighteenth-century nation, hating Gladstone's liberalism, thinking that their position might be more stable in an Irish than a British Parliament, in its early days some Protestants, mostly from the commercial class but a few from the aristocracy and gentry, signed on with the HGA. Later, when they decided that an expanded Irish suffrage combined with a secret ballot and an aggressive and assertive Catholicism projected a Catholic peasant democracy beyond the control of the Protestant upper and middle class, they returned to staunch unionism.

Butt's main recruiting focus was Protestant Ireland, but he also bid for the participation of the Catholic hierarchy and clergy, knowing their importance to the advance of any nationalist movement. Convinced, however, that he would endow the Catholic University in Dublin, the bishops were in Gladstone's camp. They worried that Irish nationalism diverted attention from the education issue, and some of them rejected Home Rule as a Protestant effort to diminish Catholic influence and to frustrate Gladstone's effort to bring religious and social justice to Ireland. Hierarchical antipathy discouraged many priests from association with the HGA. Some politicians also avoided a movement displeasing to the bishops. As previously mentioned, at by-elections Home Rule candidates often encountered clerical opposition. They usually won but their victories and the accompanying bitterness and violence (some priests were stoned) did nothing to improve the bishops' opinion of federalism.

Gladstone's University Bill disappointed the expectations of the hierarchy, warming some to Home Rule. Several prelates said that legislative independence was the best route to government-sponsored denominational education. A few went so far as to praise Butt and his program, encouraging priests to enroll in the HGA.

A number of federalists interpreted by-election victories, and clerical approval of Home Rule principles, as indications that it was time to replace the HGA with an organization more open to the public. In October and early November 1873 some 25,000 people signed a requisition summoning a national conference to discuss and organize Home Rule's future. From November 18 to 21, the national conference was in session in Dublin's Rotunda. Nine hundred delegates approved a resolution calling for a federal arrangement between Ireland and Britain, insisting on the responsibility of nationalist MPs to their constituents and future national conferences and replacing the Home Government Association with the Home Rule League, with Butt as president. League dues were a pound a year, but borrowing from O'Connell, it established an associate membership for only a shilling.

The inadequacies of Gladstone's Irish legislation promoted public support for federalism. In addition to the disappointment of bishops and priests with the University Bill, tenant farmers soon realized that the Land Act did little to increase their security. Although the mild platform of the league did not address economic, religious, or social issues, priests and farmers sought an outlet for their frustrations in federalism. They appeared to accept its idealistic assumptions that an Irish Parliament would be able to create an Ireland united in spirit and purpose.

In January 1874 Gladstone called a general election. In Britain the Liberals lost, and Benjamin Disraeli became prime minister of a Conservative government. In Ireland voters returned fifty-nine Home Rulers. Shortly after the election, they met in Dublin and organized the Irish Home Rule parliamentary party. It mirrored the conservatism of Butt, who as chairman rejected Charles Gavan Duffy's idea of a completely independent, strongly disciplined Irish party voting as a bloc on all Irish matters. He said that Home Rule MPs were not of one mind on British, imperial, or even Irish issues and that independent opposition would signal that they were allied to the Liberals. According to Butt, tight discipline would force inflexibility on land and religion, convincing Protestants that Irish nationalism was inextricably tied to Catholic ambitions and agrarian radicalism. He asked party members to function as a unit only on federalism. In other things they could vote according to private interests and consciences.

Butt realized that his efforts to avoid offending Protestant concerns might anger Catholics. To compensate, he urged Home Rule MP s as individuals, not party members, to support his efforts to amend the Land Act, enlarge the Irish suffrage, and gain government funds for Catholic education. Butt's strategy was too subtle. Not many nationalists or unionists made the effort to sort out the differences between individual parliamentary conduct of Home Rule MPs and their party's public image.

To impress British parliamentary and public opinion with Home Rule's conservative character, Butt's House of Commons strategy was conciliatory. He instructed Irish party MP s to be gentlemen in debate and discussion, always to respect parliamentary procedures and traditions, and to demonstrate loyalty to the crown, empire, and constitution.

Two years after its spectacular start, the Irish party was in shambles. It suffered from weak leadership, unsatisfactory personnel, and a restricted platform. Butt was an intelligent and generous man lacking leadership qualities. He was too kind and jovial to be a disciplinarian, and he admired the British and their system too much to oppose them effectively. An extravagant and dissolute lifestyle left him financially embarrassed. During the 1860s he spent time in debtor's prison. Because of shaky finances, Butt had to spend much time practicing law, to the neglect of Home Rule. The Irish people did not contribute with the same generosity to a Butt tribute as they had to O'Connell's. Because of his drinking and womanizing, Butt's Home Rule colleagues were afraid to send him on an American fund-raising tour. To remain solvent, he had to rely on the generosity of Mitchel Henry, Galway landowner, and William Shaw, Cork banker, two Protestant conservative Home Rule MPs.

In recruiting parliamentary candidates, the Home Rule party was in the same fix as the Tenant Right party of the 1850s. They both had to accept whoever came along. Election expenses, London residences while Parliament was in session, and the lack of salary excluded many sincere, talented nationalists from politics. Often those who declared themselves as such in election campaigns were opportunists. Once elected, their love of Ireland lessened and their self-interest increased. Absenteeism became a notorious party problem. A number of Irish reform bills were defeated for lack of Home Rule votes. And Butt did not chastise party members who failed in their duties.

When tested, Butt's conciliation policy failed. British politicians were not impressed with Home Rule's logic, considering it just another attempt to destroy the union and disrupt the empire. The freedom of action of Irish party MP s offended all shades of Irish opinion. Most Protestants remained convinced that Catholicism, agrarian radicalism, and nationalism were one package. The vast majority of Irish Catholics insisted that tenant right and religious education were part of the national demand. They found it increasingly difficult to give their enthusiasm to a movement that isolated political from other grievances.

Criticisms of the Irish party performance that began in 1874 were widespread by the close of the 1876 parliamentary session. Tenant righters and their newspaper, *The Kilkenny Journal*, and denominational education advocates, through *The Galway Vindicator*, accused Home Rule MPs of indifference to their causes. Some suggested shelving federalism for a national movement more involved in agrarian and Catholic issues. T.D. Sullivan, of the *Nation*, still the most important voice of nationalist journalism, branded Butt's parliamentary policy of conciliation a failure and suggested obstruction as an alternative. He said that it would be an appropriate response to the indifference of British politicians to the Irish question. Most other nationalist newspapers seconded the *Nation*. And when the Home Rule Confederation of Great Britain held its annual convention in Dublin in July 1876, delegates passed a resolution expressing loyalty to Butt but demanding more discipline and energy from the Irish party. Butt assented to the resolution, committing Home Rule MP s to a more resolute course of action in the next session of Parliament.

The Emergence of Charles Stewart Parnell

Butt did not keep his promise. In 1877 his leadership of the Irish party remained passive, and the conduct of most of its members apathetic. But the obstructive tactics of Joseph Biggar and Charles Stewart Parnell diverted attention from the sorry record of so many of their colleagues. Biggar, head of a Belfast Protestant provision firm, was a member of the IRB's Supreme Council when he joined the HGA. Cavan voters elected him their MP in 1874. In 1877 the IRB expelled him for his association with constitutional nationalism. That same year he became a Catholic. During the parliamentary session of 1875, Biggar experimented with obstruction by reading at length from blue books to delay passage of an Irish coercion bill. Butt was outraged that the MP from Cavan disregarded his instruction that Home Rulers should be gentlemen and play the British parliamentary game.

Charles Stewart Parnell was born in 1846 at Avondale, County Wicklow, into an Anglo-Irish Protestant gentry family. Parnell's great-grandfather Sir John was active in the eighteenth-century Protestant patriot Parliament. In 1793 he objected to concessions to Catholics. Seven years later he opposed the Act of Union. Parnell's grandfather William and his father, John Henry, played the role of country gentlemen rather than politicians. They were nationalist in sympathy, friendly to Catholicism, and good to their tenants. Parnell's mother, Delia Tudor Stewart, was an American from New Jersey. Her father was a retired commodore in the U.S. Navy. Parnell attended Magdalene College, Cambridge, concentrating on mathematics. Because of a tussle with a railway porter, he was dismissed before earning a degree. Despite his Cambridge experience, English speech patterns, love of cricket, and an aloof manner associated with the British establishment, Parnell inherited his family's antipathy to things English and devotion to Irish interests.

When Parnell contested County Dublin in 1874, Butt welcomed the young Protestant landlord as the ideal Home Ruler. He lost, but in 1875 Meath electors chose him to take the place of the deceased Joseph Martin, secretary of the Home Rule League. During the first two years of his parliamentary experience, Parnell seldom spoke, but he was always present for debates and divisions, and he kept close contact with his constituents. In this period he was studying the parliamentary process and learned his lesson well. He was particularly impressed with Biggar's obstruction tactics in 1875.

During the 1877 Parliament, Parnell and Biggar, joined by a handful of other Home Rule MPs, impeded Disraeli's legislative schedule with motions to adjourn or to report progress and with amendments to almost every bill on the docket. Although some of the amendments were constructive, they forced long discussions that seriously delayed the government's timetable.

CHARLES STEWART PARNELL, 1846–1891

As president of the National Land League and chair of the Irish Parliamentary Party, Charles Stewart Parnell made Home Rule and the Irish question the dominant issue in British politics. His decline and fall led to a messiah myth and cult that inspired Irish literature and a new generation of intense nationalists. (*Source:* R. Barry O'Brien, *The Life of Charles Stewart Parnell* [London, 1910])

Responding to their tactics, British newspapers and periodicals characterized Parnell and Biggar as uncouth Irish ruffians. Butt accused them of insubordination and party disunity. He said that obstruction was a negative approach that would increase anti-Irish British nativism by encouraging the opinion that the Irish were too savage and incompetent for self-government.

In a debate conducted mainly in the columns of *The Freeman's Journal,* Parnell and Biggar denied that their consistent attention to parliamentary duties, frequent motions, and numerous amendments were attempts to paralyze the British government. They insisted that they were working to achieve proper and detailed consideration of important issues at times when people were attentive and in their seats in the House of Commons. Parnell argued that if thoughtful analysis and discussion of legislation delayed the government's schedule, this was evidence that the docket was too crowded. He suggested a solution: Home Rule for Ireland and other portions of the United Kingdom. He, like Butt, thought that the Scots, the Welsh, and the English should also manage their affairs in local legislatures with common interests supervised by the imperial Parliament.

In defending what he and Biggar were doing in the House of Commons, Parnell ridiculed Butt's notion that reason and politeness would persuade British politicians to concede reform and legislative independence to Ireland. He said that Liberals and Conservatives seldom took the time to listen to Irish points of view, no matter how well presented. What really counted in the House of Commons was party strength and discipline, and the Irish party was small, demoralized, and disorganized. Parnell pointed out that the only way Home Rule could triumph in Parliament was through the support of one of the British parties. He said that could be achieved through intimidation, not reason. Parnell argued that Home Rule MPs had to make their presence felt by dedicated attention to duty and by influencing legislation that directly touched Britain and the empire. They had to present Parliament with clear choices: Home Rule for Ireland or persistent Irish interference in British and imperial affairs. Parnell told the Irish people that if his active parliamentary policy failed, they might as well abandon hope in constitutional methods.

Obstruction or conciliation was the issue discussed in newspapers, nationalist organizations, Irish party meetings, and tenant right societies and on political platforms. Butt fought with unusual energy, though with decreasing effect, as Parnell's attraction grew within nationalist opinion. Most Home Rule newspapers praised the man who stood up to the British and recommended his defiance to the Irish party. In 1877 the Home Rule Confederation of Great Britain ousted Butt as its president and elected Parnell in his place. Sensing the mood of nationalist Ireland, a growing number of Butt's friends urged him to compromise with Parnell by adopting a more vigorous parliamentary strategy. It was the despised absentee and Whig elements in the party that remained loyal to the chairman. Parnell partisans forced the Home Rule League to summon another national conference to decide the question of parliamentary strategy. Held in January 1878, it retained Butt as president but instructed him to unify the party and to pursue an energetic parliamentary effort.

The New Departure

The popularity of Parnell and Biggar with the Irish people compelled the Clan na Gael to reevaluate parliamentary nationalism. Clan leaders decided that an Irish party led by a man with Parnell's qualities could advance Irish freedom. They were interested in reaching an understanding with him as part of a "New Departure" strategy. Clansmen such as John Devoy and John Boyle O'Reilly, editor of *The Boston Pilot*, a Catholic nationalist publication, were sure that Britain would actively take the Turkish side in the war against Russia. This would give Irish nationalism the opportunity to exploit Britain's preoccupation with a foreign enemy. They hoped to repeat 1782, when Britain, fighting for survival against Bourbon France and Spain in the American Revolution, submitted to armed Ireland's demand for parliamentary sovereignty. American republicans were in a poor position, however, to mobilize the Irish people. Too many years of subterranean conspiracy had cut them off from the mainstream.

Patrick Ford, Galway native and editor of *The Irish World,* a paper published in New York but widely circulated in both Ireland and Irish America, advised a way for the republican movement to capture the hearts and minds of the people. He rejected the notion of William Smith O'Brien, James Stephens, and Isaac Butt that Irish nationalism should avoid offending Protestants by espousing causes associated with the Irish Catholic majority. He agreed with O'Connell, James Fintan Lalor, John Mitchel, and the Charles Gavan Duffy of the 1850s that Irish nationalism could recruit mass enthusiasm only by concentrating on the economic and social concerns of its constituency. Ford, a Henry George single-tax socialist, appealed to Irish Americans by attacking industrial capitalism and courted the Irish in Ireland by denouncing landlordism. According to Ford, Irish-American and Irish national- isms on both sides of the Atlantic had a common enemy, exploitative property. He finally persuaded Devoy and other Clan leaders that the only way republicanism could enlist and mobilize mass support for revolution in Ireland was through a war on landlordism.

Ford's view was particularly appropriate to the Irish situation of the late 1870s. Inexpensive American and Canadian grain swamped a free trade UK market, reduc- ing the prices of agricultural goods and thereby ending prosperity for British and Irish farmers. Conditions were particularly bad in Ireland, where horrible weather resulted in a series of meager harvests. People on the small farms and rocky soil of the overcrowded, potato-dependent west suffered most from the economic downturn. But times were difficult all over. Many tenants could not pay rents and suffered evictions. Emigration nearly approached famine-era proportions. This new economic calamity increased the irrelevancy of the one-issue Irish party.

The New Departure emerged as a two-dimensional effort to bring the Republican movement into association with majority nationalist opinion. A campaign against landlordism was designed as a device to arouse passion among a politically apathetic peasantry in the throes of agricultural depression. Republican involvement in the troubles of the rural masses was also an approach to an alliance with the Parnell segment of the Irish party. According to the New Departure design, Ireland would be free when the peasant masses became ardent nationalists and a significant number of Irish MPs committed to separation from Britain. At the right time, perhaps 1882, the centenary of the Protestant patriot victory, Parnell would demand immediate Home Rule in the House of Commons. When the British refused, as they surely would, he and his colleagues would withdraw from Westminster and establish an Irish republic supported by a militant peasantry armed by Irish America.

In October 1878 the Clan na Gael offered Parnell alliance terms, including the substitution of a general commitment to self-government for federalism; energetic efforts to replace landlordism with peasant proprietorship, while accepting legislation to abolish arbitrary evictions as an interim concession; an Irish party united on all Irish and imperial issues pursuing an aggressive policy in the House of Commons; and "advocacy of all struggling nationalities in the British empire and elsewhere."

Parnell was not as interested in, sympathetic to, or informed about tenant farmer problems as Butt was. However, he did realize the merit of combining the agrarian and Home Rule movements and recognized the importance of Irish-American funds for Irish nationalism. But he was reluctant to conclude an alliance with the clan on its terms. Parnell did not want to become a pawn of Irish Americans or to offend Catholic bishops by a close association with revolutionary republicanism. While waiting for a more favorable time to reach an accord with Irish America, Parnell and his colleagues in the active wing of the Irish party became involved in the agrarian phase of the New Departure. At one tenant right meeting, John O'Connor Power, ex-IRB Supreme Council MP for Mayo, echoed James Fintan Lalor's slogan, "The Land of Ireland for the People of Ireland." Copying Patrick Ford's American theme, some Parnellites, speaking in the cities of England and Scotland, said that it was time for an alliance between the British working class and Irish tenant farmers in a democratic thrust against the enemies and exploiters of the poor: Irish landlords and British industrialists.

The Decline of Butt's Version of Home Rule

Although Parnell never concluded a working relationship with the clan until 1879, Butt in 1878 already believed that such a compact existed and that it was designed to destroy constitutional nationalism. In the autumn he addressed a manifesto to the Irish people, warning that obstruction would lead to the expulsion of Irish MPs from the House of Commons, the disenfranchisement of nationalist voters, and the resurgence of physical-force nationalism followed by bloody defeat on the battlefield.

Butt's message had a small audience. His parliamentary activities in 1878 did much to discredit him with nationalists. In exchange for an Irish intermediate education bill, providing scholarships for Catholic secondary school students, he pledged support for the government's foreign and imperial policies. True to his bargain and to his pro-imperial convictions, Butt defended Disraeli's actions at the Congress of Berlin against verbal jabs from the Liberal benches. In December, when Parliament discussed a crisis in Afghanistan involving tensions between Britain and Russia, he rejected a suggestion by some Home Rule MPs that the party add an amendment to the queen's speech asking for a redress of Irish grievances. Butt said that it would jeopardize national security and cast doubt that Irish nationalists were patriotic supporters of crown and empire.

Nationalist newspapers expressed shock that the champion of Home Rule would defend Tory imperialism. Even newspapers that had previously sided with Butt in his conflict with Parnell disowned him for encouraging a British administration "avowedly hostile to the claims of Ireland."

When the annual meeting of the Home Rule League convened on February 4, 1879, T. D. Sullivan gave notice of two resolutions. The first censured Butt for violating the Irish party pledge by personally negotiating with the government on the education question; the second insisted on increased activity and vigilant parliamentary attendance from Home Rule MPs. Butt persuaded Sullivan to drop the censure move, but the second resolution passed by eight votes. Butt left the meeting an ill man, leaning on the arm of his son. He died of a stroke on May 5, 1879.

Parnell made no move to replace Butt as president of the impoverished, tottering Home Rule League or as chair of an apathetic, lackluster Irish party. He concentrated on the land agitation and on the energetic Irish in Britain and Irish-American wings of Irish nationalism. Command of Home Rule in Ireland could wait for a more auspicious occasion.

Home Rule MPs elected William Shaw, MP from Cork, Nonconformist clergyman and successful banker, to succeed Butt as party head. He failed to improve its undistinguished performance. Meanwhile Parnell, pointing to the next general election, helped Michael Davitt launch the National Land League in October 1879. Davitt, a native of County Mayo, moved as a child to Britain with his family. An industrial accident deprived him of an arm but did not keep him from Fenianism. In 1870 he was sentenced to fifteen years of penal servitude but was released in 1878. During an American lecture tour he became a convert to the New Departure, returning to Ireland to initiate its agrarian phase with the Land League of Mayo. It evolved into the National Land League. Realizing that Parnell had more charisma than he and that an Anglo-Protestant landlord would make a good front man for the league, Davitt turned over its presidency to the Home Ruler.

From January to March 1880, Parnell was in the United States completing an alliance with the Clan na Gael on his own terms and soliciting funds for the Land League. During his stay he spoke to a joint session of Congress on the Irish situation and established an American branch of the league. Parnell arrived back in Ireland in time to contest and win three seats in the general election. Altogether, Irish voters returned sixty-one Home Rulers, most of them Parnellites. In the April 26 election for party chair, Parnell defeated Shaw twenty-three votes to eighteen, ending the era of Butt's conciliation policy, commencing the ten-year Parnell domination over the forces of Irish nationalism at home and abroad.

Shaw and about twenty of his followers could not accept the new regime. They sat in the House of Commons as independent nationalists tied to the Liberals. Most lost to Parnellites in the 1885 general election. In the 1880s, John O'Connor Power and F. Hugh O'Donnell, two of his former obstructionist colleagues, decided that they were more qualified for leadership than Parnell and seceded from the party.

The Land War

When Parnell took charge of the Irish party, he was focused more on the land agitation than on Home Rule. Irish Americans were so generously endowing the Land League that by March 1880 it had a balance in excess of 20,000 pounds. Davitt's solution to the agrarian aspect of the Irish question was land nationalization, but the league asked for peasant proprietorship. However, as the prosperous farmers from Leinster and Munster joined the agitation and outnumbered the league's first recruits, the more radical peasants from the rocky fields of Connacht, the old and more conservative tenant right demand became more prominent. Because the league inherited the traditions of secret societies and Fenianism, the agrarian agitation sometimes crossed the frontier of violence. Although Parnell and his lieutenants did a remarkable job of limiting bloodshed and destruction, they urged tenants to hang on to their farms, not to occupy those of evicted members of their own class and not to pay unjust rents. In July 1880 John Dillon, twenty-nine-year-old son of John Blake Dillon, recently elected MP for Tipperary, brilliant Parnell lieutenant, and militant Land Leaguer, advised its members to refuse rent payments, to purchase arms, to march to meetings in military formation, and to hold back their friendship from those involved with landlordism. Two months later, in an Ennis, County Clare, speech, Parnell expanded on Dillon's ideas. He told his farmer audience that they should not use violence against the agents of landlordism or land-grabbers.

> I wish to point out to you a very much better way—a more Christian and charitable way, which will give the lost man an opportunity of repenting. When a man takes a farm from which another has been evicted, you must shun him on the roadside when you meet him—you must shun him in the streets of the town—you must shun him in the shop—you must shun him on the fair green and in the market place, and even in the place of worship, by leaving him alone, by putting him in moral Coventry, by isolating him from the rest of the country, as if he were the leper of old—you must show him your detestation of the crime he committed.

The rent strike and shunning suggestions were melded into a policy and first applied to Lord Erne's estate in Mayo where Captain Charles Boycott was agent. Ostracism was so effective in driving off house servants and field hands that Orangemen from the north, protected by soldiers, had to bring in the harvest at a net loss. The English language had a new word: Shunning became *boycotting*.

Although Parnell had mustered the most powerful agitation in Ireland since the repeal movement of the 1840s, and not even O'Connell had so stirred the west, two important elements in Irish nationalism held back from the land war. Although the Clan na Gael initiated the New Departure and was the senior partner in the Revolutionary Directory (1877) with the IRB, Kickham and the Supreme Council rejected the Land League because they thought it divided Ireland by class and religion. The IRB insisted that nothing must distract Ireland from its priority cause, independence. A sovereign Irish nation would reconcile economic, social, and religious differences. Compared to Catholic bishops and priests in other places, those in Ireland had been liberal on property rights and duties, supporting tenant right. But many thought that abolition of landlordism was too radical, and they were uneasy about the Fenian elements and flashes of violence in the land war. Even John MacHale, the prelate most associated with nationalism, condemned the Land League.

The reluctance of the bishops and priests to become involved with the Land League created a local leadership vacuum filled by shopkeepers in the towns. They had kinship, customer, and money-lending ties with farmers. Most shopkeepers had peasant origins; many continued to till the soil. Their town residences and their economic associations with and visits to cities gave them an aura of sophistication and knowledge that rivaled that of the clergy. When priests discovered that the peasantry was marching on ahead of them with a new class of leaders, they quickly caught up, but they had to share power and influence with the shopkeepers.

Despite the rage of British politicians, journalists, and Irish Protestants and despite government coercion, the land campaign continued, bordering on the fringes of insurrection. Land League militancy and the turbulence in Ireland persuaded Gladstone, who replaced Disraeli as prime minister after the 1880 Liberal election victory, that he must again try Irish reform. He decided to mix kindness with firmness. Despite the obstruction tactics of Irish party MPs, the government passed a strong Peace Preservation Act. After the House of Lords vetoed a measure to compensate evicted tenants, in August 1881 Gladstone, with the queen's influence, maneuvered a Land Act through Parliament. It established the Three Fs so long sought by tenant righters: "fixity of tenure, fair rents, and free sale." Although it did not destroy landlordism, the Land Act, by creating a sort of dual ownership of land, made it untenable. Gladstone's measure also weakened laissez-faire economics throughout the United Kingdom by establishing precedents for government limitations on property rights.

Parnell rejected the Land Act as inadequate because it did not include over 100,000 tenants in arrears on rent (one-third of the farmers in Ireland, two-thirds in Mayo) or leaseholders. Parnell also knew that it was unwise for a leader of Irish nationalism to be enthusiastic about or grateful for British concessions that were considered compensations for part injustices by the Irish people. And he was aware that to radicals in the Land League, the act stopped short of their objective, the destruction of landlordism.

Parnell continued the agrarian agitation even after the Land Act became law, hoping to force further reforms and to influence tribunals to decide on the lowest possible rent obligations. Finally, in October 1881, Gladstone and the Irish chief secretary, W.E. Forster, lost patience and employed the Peace Preservation Act to incarcerate Parnell and his chief lieutenants in Dublin's Kilmainham Gaol. The Irish leader retaliated with orders to Irish farmers not to pay rent. The no-rent manifesto was opposed by influential bishops and priests, and few tenants responded to its appeal.

Imprisonment was a favor to Parnell, increasing his popularity as a victim of British oppression, removing him from the land war when he needed time to ponder the future direction of Irish nationalism. Now that agrarian agitation had mobilized and impassioned the Irish people, and most of them accepted the Tenant Right Land Act, it was time to refocus their attention on Home Rule. To do this, he had to subdue radicals determined to continue the war on landlordism. Gladstone relieved Parnell's problems by outlawing the Land League while Parnell was in Kilmainham.

By the spring of 1882 both Parnell and Gladstone wanted the Irish leader out of prison. Although the no-rent manifesto fell on deaf ears, crimes and outrages increased while Parnell was out of circulation. During that time, there were fourteen murders and sixty-one murder attempts in Ireland. Gladstone realized that Parnell had restrained agrarian violence and that it would be better to have him back in charge of the Irish situation. Although his captivity was relatively comfortable, Parnell's physical and emotional states, never the most stable, were deteriorating under confinement. His superstitious conviction that green was unlucky was constantly provoked by sweaters and scarves in that color knitted by the patriotic women of Ireland and sent to his cell. What troubled Parnell most was the fading health of his infant daughter, Claude Sophie (she eventually died), and the anxiety of her mother, his lover, Katherine O'Shea.

In April, Joseph Chamberlain, a cabinet minister, using his friend Captain William O'Shea, Katherine's husband, as intermediary, began release negotiations with Parnell. What he considered a betrayal of law and order angered Forster, who resigned as chief secretary, but an arrangement, known as the Kilmainham Treaty, was reached. Parnell accepted the 1881 act as "a practical settlement of the land question" and agreed to cooperate with the Liberals in reform efforts in Ireland and other regions of the United Kingdom. In exchange, Gladstone introduced and passed an Arrears Act that guaranteed 800,000 pounds in rent money to restore evicted tenants and to include them and leaseholders in the benefits of the Land Act. There was also a tacit agreement that the Liberals would end coercion. On May 2, 1882, Parnell and his friends left Kilmainham.

The Kilmainham Treaty promised an era of good feeling and cooperation between British Liberals and Irish nationalists. Unfortunately, a shocking incident in Dublin postponed that hope. Although Parnell had captured majority Irish-American opinion and loyalty, elements in the Clan na Gael closely associated with anarchism were sponsoring and subsidizing violence in Ireland. Irish-American money and manpower participation went into schemes to blow up such scenic and historic sites in Britain as London Bridge (the dynamiters demolished themselves instead of the bridge). An IRB breakaway group, the Invincibles, got Irish-American funding for plots to assassinate British officials. Three days after Parnell left Kilmainham, they stabbed to death Lord Frederick Cavendish, Forster's replacement as chief secretary and Gladstone's nephew by marriage, who had just arrived in Dublin that day, and his undersecretary, T.H. Burke, near the viceregal lodge in Phoenix Park. Parnell was so disgusted by this atrocity that he offered to resign as Home Rule leader and to retire to private life. Gladstone persuaded him to stay on as chair of the Irish party, but the prime minister heeded the anger of British opinion by renewing coercion.

6

Home Rule and British Politics, 1882–1906

The Irish Party: Strong and Solid at Last

With the land issue temporarily settled and British reactions to the Phoenix Park murders subsiding, Parnell was ready to redirect Irish attention to Home Rule. Although Gladstone had done him the favor of outlawing the Fenian-tainted Land League in 1881, the Ladies Land League still existed to express agrarian radicalism. Much to the consternation of its president, his sister Fanny, Parnell terminated the organization in 1882. He then appropriated the funds of the defunct Land League and added them to new American money to restructure the Irish party. He recruited bright, energetic young men as parliamentary candidates. In the Young Ireland and Fenian traditions, many of them were journalists. The Irish party paid their election expenses and gave them a living allowance so that they could survive in London when Parliament was in session. An efficient election machinery, Irish-American money, good candidates, the secret ballot, and the 1884 reform bill, which created a household rural male suffrage, guaranteed Irish constitutional nationalism eighty-five Westminster seats. No longer was it hostage to political opportunism. Parnell's party was disciplined. Its MPs pledged solidarity on all Irish issues before the House of Commons. A parliamentary committee of sixteen MPs, dominated by Parnell and his chief lieutenants, determined party policy. During the 1880s, Home Rulers were the most efficient, best-organized party in the House of Commons. Their front benches displayed as much talent as either of the two British parties. They inspired the reorganization of both the Liberals and the Conservatives.

During Butt's leadership, Home Rule nationalism never tapped into the nationalist loyalties of the Roman Catholic hierarchy and clergy. Cullen was still able to concentrate their attention on Catholic interests. Parnell and circumstances changed the situation. At his death in 1878, Cullen left a church structurally, economically, and spiritually sound. Shortly after, Irish Catholicism got caught between Irish nationalism, energized by the land war and Parnell's leadership, and Pope Leo XIII's ambition to achieve a diplomatic relationship with Britain.

In courting the British government, the pope tried to remove Irish bishops and priests from agrarian and nationalist populism. His pro-British policy infuriated many Irish Catholics, threatening the survival of the Irish-Catholic identity blend. To prevent Irish Catholic estrangement from Rome and true to their own patriotism, Archbishops William J. Walsh (Dublin) and Thomas William Croke (Cashel) warned Leo of the danger of sacrificing Irish Catholicism to papal foreign policy and kept the bishops and priests loyal to Irish nationalism.

Croke and Walsh renewed the Catholic-nationalist alliance first negotiated between O'Connell and MacHale in the 1840s. As a result, a large majority of the bishops recognized the Irish Parliamentary party as the voice of the Irish nation and endorsed its effort to liberate Ireland through constitutional means. In exchange, Parnell, like O'Connell, accepted the hierarchy's right to control the spiritual life of the laity through a system of state-financed denominational education.

Parnell knew that the continued health and progress of the Irish party necessitated a strong constituency as well as Catholic support in Ireland and the continued mobilization of Irish nationalism throughout the English-speaking world. He replaced the apathetic, nearly bankrupt Home Rule League with the Irish National League. Irish Americans and the Irish in Britain created branches. In Ireland the league functioned as a powerful election machine. In Britain and the United States it collected funds for Home Rule nationalism. British Home Rulers also worked for the election of English and Scots MPs friendly to Irish self-government. From 1885 until 1921, Thomas Power O'Connor, an Irish journalist working in England, was Home Rule MP for the Scotland division of Liverpool and a power in the Irish party. Irish-American Leaguers tried to influence Washington to take a friendly view toward Home Rule for Ireland.

Obstruction had been a short-range parliamentary tactic to concentrate the attention of the Irish people on the active wing of the Irish party and to discredit Butt's conciliation policy. After New House of Commons procedure rules limited the potential of obstruction, the Irish party, increased in size and improved in efficiency, had a much better strategy, balance of power. In 1885 Home Rule votes forced the Liberals out of office and supported a Conservative minority administration. Its prime minister, Lord Salisbury, promised not to renew the Irish Coercion Bill. The Conservatives also agreed to initiate a new program of land purchase and to investigate some measure of local self-government for Ireland. They appointed Lord Carnarvon, who supported a mild form of Irish Home Rule, as lord lieutenant and passed the Ashbourne Act, providing a tenant loan fund of 5 million pounds at 4 percent interest so that they could purchase their farms.

Liberals won the general election of 1885 in Britain, but eighty-six Home Rule MPs kept the Conservatives in office. Parnell had more confidence in what Randolph Churchill, the champion of Tory democracy and a young man on the move in the Conservative party, might do for Ireland than he did in the intentions of Joseph Chamberlain, the Birmingham radical who appeared to be an heir apparent to Gladstone. Chamberlain's devolved government ideas for Ireland were far short of Parnell's notion of Irish sovereignty. But in December 1885 Herbert Gladstone announced his father's conversion to Home Rule. Since Salisbury had no intention of topping Gladstone's gesture, the Conservatives abandoned their effort to conciliate Irish nationalism. They made preservation of the union the main plank in their platform and introduced an Irish Coercion Bill. The Irish party immediately dismissed them from office, and Gladstone returned as prime minister committed to Irish Home Rule.

Gladstone's Pursuit of Home Rule

Gladstone's adoption of Home Rule gave British Liberalism Irish nationalist support at a time when Tory imperialism had an appeal to the newly enfranchised British masses. However, there was more than opportunism involved in the Gladstone conversion. He had endorsed the efforts of emerging nationalities throughout the world and was on record as saying that British rule should encourage self-government in colonial situations. A post-1885 election report by James Bryce that Ireland was on the brink of social disintegration was the final push in Gladstone's journey to Irish self-government.

Gladstone's historical and philosophical arguments for Home Rule were similar to Isaac Butt's. He focused on the long preunion Irish parliamentary tradition, particularly in the era of Grattan's Parliament, emphasizing its Protestant patriotism. Gladstone argued that the union had magnified class and sectarian divisions in Ireland. He promised that Irish self-government would be a conservative solution to the Irish question because Irish Catholics would follow the guidance of a mostly Protestant aristocracy and gentry. Gladstone agreed with the Irish party that Irish Protestant unionism was narrow Orange factionalism.

Gladstone's 1886 Home Rule Bill proposed a two-order Irish assembly (he did not want to use the word *parliament* because of its separatist connotations). The first order of 103 members would include 28 appointed peers and 75 elected by a narrow, high-property franchise. Democracy was the intended base of the second order, with 204 members representing popular opinion. Although both orders would deliberate collectively, they would vote separately, giving the upper classes a veto over the will of the Irish majority. The proposed assembly was denied the power to legislate on matters dealing with religious endowments, customs, excise, defense, foreign policy, and empire. In time the police would come under the control of the Irish government. It also would select and pay the salaries of judges, but court verdicts would be subject to review by the British Privy Council, which could also decide on the constitutionality of Irish assembly legislation. Although Ireland was to contribute one-fifteenth of the costs of empire, it would lose its parliamentary representation at Westminster unless it became necessary to revise the provisions of the Home Rule Bill. Gladstone wanted to complement Home Rule with a land purchase solution to the agrarian issue, but such a suggestion was far too radical for many members of his own party.

British opponents of the bill and Irish unionists argued that the high Irish contribution to imperial expenses could wreck the Home Rule experiment and make the

Irish more anti-British than ever. They also pointed out that since 40 percent of Irish taxes would be collected by the British government for the imperial contribution, denying that Irish representation at Westminster was taxation without representation. British and Irish unionist enemies of Home Rule had more serious objections to Gladstone's proposal. They said that it was a surrender to Irish extremism and endangered Britain's security and the permanence of empire. Irish party MPs also opposed certain segments of the bill: the denial of tariff protection, the high imperial contribution, temporary British control of the Royal Irish Constabulary, voting by orders in the assembly, and taxation without representation. But Home Rule MPs had little choice but to defend and support Gladstone's proposal. The weakness of Irish constitutional nationalism was that the senior partner in the union, Britain, would ultimately define the quantity and quality of Irish self-government. And the Irish party knew that it was either Gladstone's bill or nothing at all.

Gladstone would have entertained an amendment restoring Irish representation at Westminster, but the first Home Rule Bill never reached the committee stage, suffering defeat on its second reading. The fatal blows came from within the Liberal party. The Whig faction, led by Lord Hartington, refused to stomach Home Rule. And Chamberlain, convinced that Home Rule threatened the continuation of empire, angry that Parnell had rejected devolution as an alternative to Home Rule, and bitter because he thought he deserved more cabinet influence, persuaded some of his radical colleagues to reject Gladstone's proposal. On June 8, 1886, ninety-three Liberals, mostly Whigs, joined British and Irish conservatives in opposing the Home Rule Bill, defeating it, 343 to 313.

After his defeat, Gladstone dissolved Parliament and took the Home Rule issue to the British electorate. Conservatives marshaled anti–Irish Catholic opinion against Liberals. When the votes were tabulated, they won 316 seats, Liberal Unionist defectors from Gladstone 78, Home Rule Liberals 191, and the Irish party 85. With Liberal Unionist support, Lord Salisbury was able to form a Conservative government.

Aspects of the Irish-Liberal Alliance

The events of 1886 indicated that the Irish-Liberal alliance was the most important development in late nineteenth-century British politics. While it made the Irish question the dominant issue, it also compromised the independence of the Irish party. From 1885 on, Home Rule rested on the fortunes of British Liberalism, and Parnell and his colleagues had no other choice but to uphold their allies in the House of Commons. The Irish nationalist–British Liberal compact also redefined British politics.

Many Liberal politicians and some historians have suggested that during and after 1886 Gladstone made a tactical blunder when he tied his party to Irish nationalism. They argue that with the British economy failing after 1870, Liberals would have been better off concentrating on the social question to keep the working-class vote.

However, when Gladstone committed British Liberalism to Irish self-government, he clarified its ideological content. Before 1886 the Liberal party still had too many representatives of the Whig aristocracy to permit an uncompromising commitment to political, social, and economic reform. Policy tensions within the party tarnished its image as a progress vehicle and blocked efforts to enlist the loyalty of the recently enfranchised working class. Whigs who could not tolerate the Home Rule alliance left the Liberal party, called themselves Liberal Unionists, and finally found a home in the Conservative fold. They felt comfortable with people who shared their views concerning class distinctions, property rights, and the glory of empire.

Before the Irish-Liberal alliance, the British party system reflected hereditary allegiances more than principles. By pruning the Liberal party of its Whig–landed aristocracy tradition, Home Rule made social, economic, and imperial issues more significant in the contest between Liberals and Conservatives. Association with Irish nationalism made it easier for Liberals to make commitments to democracy and social change. Home Rule MPs were more interested in the welfare of Irish peasants than British industrial workers and were more committed to denominational education, friendlier to the brewing and distilling industries, and less supportive of free trade than Liberals. However, they were also stronger on democracy and government involvement in social change than their British allies. Thus the Irish-Liberal connection was natural and served mutual interests.

While Home Rule moved Liberals left, it sent Conservatives in the opposite direction. The Whig addition strengthened Conservatives in the House of Commons and reinforced their commitment to property, tradition, aristocracy, and empire. The Liberal commitment to Home Rule gave the Conservatives an opportunity to exploit the prejudices and loyalties of British nativism in the quest for votes. Much of the attack on Home Rule appealed to anti-Catholicism with the slogan "Home Rule Is Rome Rule." And Conservatives insisted that Irish self-government was the beginning of a domino process that would begin with the disruption of the United Kingdom and end in the destruction of the empire. To emphasize that the Home Rule debate involved social structure, the Protestant Constitution, British security, and the empire, Conservatives changed the name of their party to Unionist.

Home Rule polarized politics more clearly in Ulster than in Britain. There the population density of non-Catholics was higher than in other portions of Ireland, slightly over 50 percent, most of it concentrated in the region around Belfast. Because of the even sectarian divide, bitter memories of ancient and modern struggles for land and power, Ulster's politics were the most paranoid in the United Kingdom.

Beginning with eighteenth-century linen factories and shipyards, Belfast and northeast Ulster became an extension of the British industrial complex, adding an economic motive to the contents of Ulster unionism. Wealthy landlords and factory barons led Ulster Toryism. Protestant and Presbyterian tenant farmers, industrial workers, and middle-class professionals despised Catholics but found common social and economic cause with them in the Liberal party.

Starting with Home Rule, some Ulster Catholics, particularly in the border counties where they were most numerous, began to drift to the Irish party, but Ulster Liberalism continued to be significant and ecumenical in numbers if not entirely in spirit. During the Land War, a small number of Protestants and Presbyterians joined the Land League, and, of course, all Ulster tenants profited by its achievement. But when Parnell pulled Irish popular agitation back into the path of Home Rule and concluded an alliance with Gladstone, there were for all practical purposes only two parties in Ireland: nationalist and unionist. After 1886 Ulster politics lost its economic and social content. The fate of the union dominated all other issues.

From the first Home Rule Bill through the third, British Conservatives played the "Orange card" as a key part of their strategy to frustrate the Irish-Liberal alliance, preserve the union, retain the status quo, protect property interests, and maintain the empire. In the general election of 1886, Lord Randolph Churchill, privately contemptuous of Ulster Anglicans and Nonconformists, cynically appealed to their prejudices. He went to Belfast and told them to resist Home Rule to the point of defying Parliament. He said, "Ulster will fight and Ulster will be right." Well into the twentieth century, Churchill clones would make the same appeal to Ulster fanaticism.

Gladstone would continue to publicly interpret Ulster unionist opposition to Home Rule as a contradiction of the Grattan Protestant patriot tradition and as selfish Orange factionalism. Nationalists started out thinking that way but came to realize the almost unanimous Ulster Protestant and Presbyterian antipathy to Irish self-government. But they rejected it as an inadequate expression of Ulster's geography and people. Home Rulers pointed out that five of Ulster's nine counties had Catholic majorities and that the other four had large minorities. Often nationalist MPs had a 17-to-16 majority in the province's parliamentary representation.

Gladstone and the Irish party were anticipating an Ulster Unionist bid for separate treatment in any Home Rule settlement. However, since Ulster Protestants were more interested in preventing Home Rule for any part of Ireland and did not want to desert their coreligionists in other parts of the country, they never presented a partition plan for themselves. Despite their frequent threats of violence, they planned to resist a Dublin government passively before resorting to force.

The Fall of Parnell

After 1886 the Irish party continued to perform effectively for its constituents, but the exigencies of the Liberal alliance restricted its independence and flamboyance. Distracted by his relationship with Katherine O'Shea, Parnell left much of the party leadership tasks to such talented lieutenants as John Dillon, William O'Brien, Timothy Harrington, Thomas Sexton, and Timothy Healy. Because of the Liberal connection, Parnell found it necessary to soften the public tone of Irish nationalism. This caution was evident in his reluctance to support the Plan of Campaign authored by Harrington, Dillon, and O'Brien.

Agricultural hard times did not end with the 1882 Land Act. For many farmers, paying rent was difficult. Harrington, Dillon, and O'Brien advised them to request further rent reductions. If landlords refused to comply, the three MPs suggested that tenants place the rents they were prepared to pay in a fund to assist victims of evictions. This strategy, which became the Plan of Campaign, swept the country. Unionist government coercion and the arrest of the radical Home Rule MPs provoked violence. To avoid antagonizing British public opinion and diverting Irish agitation away from Home Rule, Parnell did not participate in the new war on landlordism. Only grudgingly did he contribute Irish party funds to the relief of evictees.

Parnell's decision not to become involved in the Plan of Campaign did not damage his Irish popularity, and by 1890 he had acquired considerable respectability in British circles. In 1887 the *Times* of London published a series of articles called "Parnell and Crime," claiming that the Home Rule leader and his lieutenants had instigated agrarian outrages in Ireland. One of these articles reproduced a letter supposedly signed by Parnell condoning the 1882 Phoenix Park murders of Cavendish and Burke. The *Times'* attack on Parnell's integrity raised a groundswell of animosity toward him throughout Britain. Indifferent to what the British thought of him, he ignored the Unionist *Times'* effort to discredit him. However, one of Parnell's former Irish party colleagues who became his opponent, F. Hugh O'Donnell, took offense at his inclusion in the *Times'* charges and sued for libel. During the trial, the *Times'* attorney offered more incriminating letters allegedly signed by Parnell.

Parnell decided to take action against the paper. Because he had no confidence in the justice of British courts and juries in cases involving Irish nationalists, he asked the government for a parliamentary committee of inquiry to investigate the authenticity of the letters. The Unionist government said no but did appoint three judges to investigate the total context of the *Times'* accusations against the Irish leader and his movement. The hearing discovered that the *Times* had, in good faith, purchased the Parnell letters from Richard Pigott, a Dublin journalist with shady credentials in nationalist circles. In a February 1889 cross-examination of Pigott, Charles Russell, Parnell's counsel, proved that Pigott had forged the letters. The forger left the courtroom and Britain and committed suicide in a Madrid hotel room. The respectable *Times* was in disgrace. Irish nationalist opinion was jubilant that its leader had evaded and exposed a vile Unionist plot to damage his and Home Rule's reputation. Many Britons with notions of justice and fair play believed that Parnell had almost become a victim of a foul conspiracy involving the *Times,* the Conservatives, and the Liberal Unionists.

When Parnell entered the House of Commons following the exposure of the Pigott forgeries, he received a standing ovation from the Liberal and Home Rule benches. But only ten months after this triumph, Parnell was on the road to ruin. On December 24, 1889, Captain William O'Shea, his one-time friend and former Irish party MP, sued his wife, Katherine, for divorce on grounds of adultery, naming the Home Rule leader as correspondent. Although not a public item, Parnell's relationship with Mrs. O'Shea was not exactly a secret. They had been lovers since 1880 and during that time had three children, two of whom survived. Liberal leaders knew of the relationship, and Mrs. O'Shea played a role in the Kilmainham Treaty negotiations. A number of Home Rule MPs were also aware of the Parnell-O'Shea connection. During the 1886 general election, Joseph Biggar and Timothy Healy went to Galway and told voters to reject Captain O'Shea as a Home Rule candidate because Parnell was prepared to let him avoid taking the party pledge. However, in the Victorian period, there was considerable difference between a quiet affair and a public scandal. A messy divorce case could ruin a political career. It had destroyed the prospects of Sir Charles Dilke, a likely successor to Gladstone as leader of the Liberal party.

After the announcement of the pending divorce case, Parnell told Irish party colleagues that evidence would prove his relationship with Katherine O'Shea honorable. Many nationalists believed that O'Shea's charges, like the *Times'* accusation, was a Unionist scheme to ruin Home Rule and its chief. Some public bodies in Ireland passed resolutions endorsing Parnell's nationalist leadership, and the divorce case dropped from public discussion for over ten months.

In the courtroom O'Shea presented himself as the victim of betrayal by wife and friend. Historical evidence rejects this claim. The Galway seat appears to be a payoff for O'Shea's passive acceptance of his wife's relationship with Parnell. O'Shea's own conduct with other women was far from correct. Katherine intended to divorce her husband and marry Parnell but was reluctant to do so while her wealthy aunt, Mrs. Benjamin Wood, was alive. Mrs. Wood made a substantial financial contribution to the O'Shea household and might have cut Katherine out of her will if she divorced the captain. When Mrs. Wood died in 1889, Katherine agreed to buy a divorce from William for 20,000 pounds. The estate, however, was tied up in legal tangles. Hungry for money and bitter at not getting it, O'Shea decided that Katherine was swindling him out of his silence fee. In vengeance, he initiated the divorce. Chamberlain, bitter against Parnell, encouraged him.

Planning to marry as soon as possible, Parnell and Mrs. O'Shea decided not to contest the divorce when it came to trial. Consequently, O'Shea's testimony, the only evidence presented, portrayed Parnell as an unscrupulous fiend who had invaded a friend's home and seduced his wife. The judge gave the verdict and custody of the O'Shea children, including Parnell's two, to the captain.

Nationalist Ireland's first reaction to the divorce was pro-Parnell. The Irish National League met and pledged continuing loyalty to his leadership. But there were negative reactions. In *The Labour World,* Michael Davitt asked him to resign as party chair. Henry Cardinal Manning, archbishop of Westminster, intermediary in negotiations between Gladstone and the Irish Catholic hierarchy, and resenter of a Protestant leader of Irish nationalism, advised the Liberal leader and the bishops to repudiate Parnell. The most powerful anti-Parnell force was British righteous, Nonconformist opinion, a large part of the Liberal electorate. Its leaders gave Gladstone an ultimatum: disassociate British Liberalism from the adulterous champion of Irish nationalism or lose the next election. Gladstone had to accept political realities.

On November 24, Gladstone informed John Morley, the most pro-Irish Liberal, and Justin McCarthy, prominent essayist and vice-chair of the Irish party, that for the sake of the Irish-Liberal alliance and Home Rule, Parnell had to remove himself as party leader. The next day the Irish party met to elect its chair for the coming parliamentary session. Morley failed to contact Parnell before the gathering, but McCarthy delivered Gladstone's message. Parnell ignored it, and McCarthy did not mention it at the party meeting. Home Rule MPs, unconscious of the issue at stake, unanimously reelected Parnell as leader. When Gladstone made his position public the next day, a large number of Irish MPs persuaded Parnell to call another party meeting on the leadership question. From December 1 to 6, Home Rule MPs gathered in committee room 15 of the House of Commons and vigorously, and at times nastily, debated whether they should retain or reject the man who relit the flame of Irish constitutional nationalism and forced the Liberals into a Home Rule commitment.

If Parnell had been a selfless, dedicated patriot, logic and integrity would have forced his resignation to save Home Rule. He would have continued as a power in the Irish party. Perhaps, as Gladstone suggested, time would have permitted him to regain the leadership. But powerful politicians are seldom selfless. Parnell was a man of intense pride and lust for power. His ego and ruthlessness had carved his political fortune and the success of Home Rule. He considered himself leader of the Irish nation not through election but through conquest. He had triumphed over Butt, the Fenian tradition, and apathy in the ranks of nationalism. He was the "uncrowned king" of Ireland, and he was not going to abandon his throne at the dictate of the British puritan conscience or its public spokesman, William Ewart Gladstone.

John Redmond, Parnell's most articulate party defender, argued that if Home Rule MPs deposed their leader on the orders of Gladstone, they would publicly surrender their independence and acknowledge themselves as Liberal satellites. Parnell told his colleagues that if they were going to sell him out, they had better make sure that Gladstone promised a better Home Rule Bill than the 1886 version as a price. Anti-Parnellites countered that when Parnell consummated the Liberal alliance, the identities and welfare of the Liberal and Irish parties became one; the fate of Home Rule was in the hands of the British Liberal electorate, and it had spoken. Gladstone had no choice but to obey, and the Irish party had no option but to replace Parnell with a new chair.

Some prominent Irish party MPs were fund-raising in the United States during the leadership crisis. The two most prominent, O'Brien and Dillon, could not return home because the government would arrest them under the Crimes Act for their role in the Plan of Campaign. They and most of the other members of the American delegation supported the demand that Parnell resign. On December 6, Justin

McCarthy left committee room 15 with forty-four other Home Rule MPs, leaving Parnell with twenty-seven followers. Anti-Parnellites reassembled in another place and elected McCarthy party chair.

Parnell refused to surrender to the wishes of the party majority, deciding to appeal to the Irish people. His choice interjected the influence of the Catholic bishops and priests into the leadership controversy. On December 4, during the committee room 15 discussion, the bishops had issued a manifesto asking the laity to reject Parnell as their spokesman. It did not affect the Irish party, which made a political, not a moral decision. The hierarchy and clergy, by contrast, emphasized the moral issue rather than the future of the Liberal alliance. They could not be less pious and sanctimonious than British Nonconformists and Protestants, who denounced Parnell as a public sinner and as an enemy of the sanctity of marriage.

In 1891 Parnell put his prestige on the line in three by-elections. Sometimes he appealed to the Fenian element, suggesting that if he failed to achieve self-government through constitutional methods, he would join in a violent attack on British tyranny. Parnell never worked harder or more courageously than he did in campaigning for his candidates. But he could not compete with the combination of bishops and priests, the anti-Parnellite majority in the Irish party, and Gladstone and the Liberal alliance. Parnellite candidates lost all the by-elections, and their chief ruined his health speaking on political platforms in the Irish cold and damp. On October 6, 1891, he died of rheumatic fever in the Brighton, England, residence that he shared with his wife, Katherine. After a large and emotional Dublin funeral, largely managed by his Fenian following, Parnell was laid to rest near O'Connell in Glasnevin. He left behind a shattered Irish party, a disillusioned and divided Irish national opinion, and the powerful myth of martyred messiah to inspire future generations, particularly the literati. Parnell as myth was almost as powerful as the Parnell of reality.

To serious students of Irish history, it seems strange that the cold, neurotic Parnell retains more popularity in contemporary Ireland than the warm, articulate, and charismatic O'Connell. To the champions of physical-force nationalism that finally severed the chains of the union, Parnell appears to be a sterner, more uncompromising foe of British colonialism than O'Connell. And his leadership of the Land League and his last campaign appeal to the Fenian tradition gave Parnell a revolutionary image. To Parnellite writers such as William Butler Yeats, James Joyce, and Sean O'Faolain, their hero was not only a martyr sacrificed on the altar of British anti-Irish nationalism but also a victim of Catholic authoritarianism and puritanism. To them Parnell was a symbol of artistic resistance to the forces of narrow-minded oppression.

The Ebb and Flow of Home Rule Enthusiasm

In 1893, during his fourth and final administration, Gladstone introduced a second Home Rule Bill. Again he proposed a bicameral chamber, one of 48 elected by a restricted franchise, the other of 103 more democratically constructed. Deadlocks between them that lasted two years would be resolved by an absolute majority of the two chambers. Most of the provisions and restrictions of the 1893 bill were similar to those of 1886 except that Gladstone lowered Ireland's imperial contribution from one-fifteenth to one-twentieth and retained Irish MPs at Westminster for discussion of Irish and imperial matters. An amendment to the bill kept Irish MPs in Parliament for all debates and votes. Because of the combined Liberal-Irish majority, Home Rule passed in the House of Commons, but the House of Lords crushed it. Gladstone wanted to dissolve Parliament and take the House of Lords veto power issue to the electorate. When other Liberal leaders disagreed with Gladstone on the House of Lords strategy and on naval expenditures, he resigned as prime minister.

Lord Rosebery, the new prime minister, was an advocate of a strong national defense and of empire, but he was indifferent to Irish nationalism. Shortly after assuming command, he made it clear that Ireland was not a Liberal priority. Rosebery said that his party would not introduce another Home Rule bill until British public opinion clearly favored Irish self-government. But the Liberals were not long for office. Because of divisions within the cabinet, House of Lords vetoes of House of Common bills, and a slim Liberal majority, Rosebery in late 1895 turned over the government to Unionists. A general election confirmed them in office with a large majority.

Opposition strengthened Rosebery's conviction that Home Rule alienated British public opinion. He wanted his party to be associated with concern for social problems resulting from a retreating British industrial economy and nationalism, imperialism, and militarism sweeping through the world following the emergence of Germany, Italy, and Japan as major powers. The conduct of Irish nationalist MPs offended Liberal jingoism. As the first victims of British colonialism, the Irish ridiculed the humanitarian cant and hypocrisy of its apologia. And during the 1899–1902 war in South Africa, Irish nationalist MP sympathy for the Boers angered British majority opinion, propelling some Liberals farther away from the Irish alliance. While most agreed with John Morley that Home Rule was a moral commitment for their party, they believed that it should be postponed until a more favorable time. Now, they decided, the party should address issues dearer to the hearts of the British middle and working classes.

Irish nationalism was in poor condition to respond to the Liberal retreat from Home Rule. The Irish party was in shambles, divided into Parnellite and anti-Parnellite wings. John Redmond led the small Parnellite group of seven MPs in 1892, eleven in 1895. Despite meager parliamentary representation, it had considerable constituency support, much of its coming from the IRB. Justin McCarthy led the anti-Parnellite majority until 1895, when John Dillon succeeded him. The anti-Parnellite faction had serious problems. Nationalists in Ireland, Britain, the United States, Australia, and Canada were disillusioned by the division in the Irish party and were no longer generous in money contributions. Without Parnell's firm hand

and the deference he received from party members, his brilliant lieutenants—Dillon, Tim Healy, and William O'Brien—disagreed on policies. Dillon, once a strong agrarian radical, came to fear that continued emphasis on land distracted attention from Home Rule. But William O'Brien insisted that the party continue to focus on the needs of tenant farmers, particularly in the west. Dillon believed in a strongly centralized Irish party in the O'Connell and Parnell mode. Tim Healy insisted that constituency organizations have more say in the selection of parliamentary candidates and in Home Rule policy. He won much clerical support for his decentralization program by promising priests major roles on the local Home Rule level. While Dillon managed to maintain his control of the party, he did so by forcing Healy and O'Brien to its fringes and sometimes into independent opposition.

Trying to Kill Home Rule with Kindness

With the Liberals lukewarm on Home Rule and Irish nationalism confused, divided, and demoralized, the Unionists decided on a comprehensive Irish program. From 1886 to 1892 and then from 1895 until 1902, Lord Salisbury was prime minister. His nephew, Arthur J. Balfour, was Irish chief secretary from 1887 to 1891. He developed the Unionist Irish strategy and continued to guide it when his brother, Gerald, was chief secretary (1895–1900), and from 1902 to 1905 when he was prime minister. Both Salisbury and the Balfours refused to accept Home Rule as an answer to the Irish question. They believed that the "racial" instability of the Celtic personality made Irish Catholics unfit for self-determination, and they were convinced that Home Rule would begin to unravel the United Kingdom and the empire.

British Unionism pledged a strong commitment to Irish Anglicans and Nonconformists, promising that they would never be placed under the domination of a Catholic majority. Unionists also emphasized law and order. Balfour believed that Ireland needed strong government. His efficient use of the Crimes Act to suppress agrarian outrage and agitation earned him the sobriquet "Bloody Balfour." The insult was a bit unfair. Balfour did not believe that commitments to resolute government and Irish Unionists contradicted the need for Irish reform. Most historians of the period have accepted Gerald Balfour's description of Unionist Irish policy as an attempt "to kill Home Rule with kindness." There was some of that, but it had other, perhaps more tactically important purposes. Salisbury and Balfour were also determined to calm Ireland so that they could more easily govern the United Kingdom and the empire. They also wanted to satisfy the Liberal Unionists who deserted Gladstone on Home Rule but retained a concern for constructive change in Ireland. British Conservative leaders also needed to keep Ulster Protestants divided by religion (Anglican and Presbyterian) and class (landlord and tenant, factory owner and industrial worker) under one Unionist umbrella. Salisbury and Balfour also intended to demonstrate that a British government could deal with Irish problems, proving Home Rule unnecessary. This would diminish its British constituency and hurt the Liberals still associated, if reluctantly, with Irish nationalism.

No matter what its motivation, Unionist legislation transformed the Irish political, economic, and social scene. Despite the 1881 Land Act and another land purchase scheme, the 1885 Ashbourne Act, Irish agriculture remained depressed, with the familiar scenario of agitation, violence, and evictions. In 1887 Balfour introduced a Land Act lowering rents to harmonize with agricultural prices and increased protection against eviction. He followed the next year with another Land Purchase Bill, the first in a series leading to the Wyndham Act of 1903, named after its author, Charles Wyndham, the Irish chief secretary. It encouraged tenants to buy their farms with interest rates so low (3.25 percent) and the repayment period so long (68.5 years) that their financial obligations were no higher than their rents. The government gave the landlords an incentive to sell with a 12 percent cash bonus. In 1909 the Liberal government amended Wyndham's measure with even more generous terms and compulsory sales in certain instances. Land purchase was the final solution to the agrarian dimension of the Irish question. The 1903 and 1909 bills created 200,000 peasant proprietors. Their farms comprised about half of Ireland's arable land.

Balfour realized that poverty in Ireland was a problem that went beyond land-ownership. In 1891 he established the Congested Districts Board to provide poor relief and to stimulate economic growth in the most depressed areas of the country. Most of the board's activities were in Connacht, but Kerry, Cork, and Donegal also benefited. With government subsidies, the board developed cottage industries such as spinning and weaving, fishing, and agriculture. Much of the progress was achieved through technical and agricultural education programs. The board consolidated many small holdings into more efficient ones, placed poor farmers on them, and then taught the new occupants modern agricultural methods. In 1899 Gerald Balfour established the Department of Agricultural and Technical Instruction (DATI) for Ireland with Horace Plunkett, Unionist creator of the Irish Agricultural Cooperative Movement, as vice-president and guiding hand. The department was in charge of agricultural and technical instruction, fisheries, prevention of animal and plant diseases, the National Library, and the National Museum. Perhaps peasant proprietorship, the Congested Districts Board, and the DATI projects retarded modernization by keeping Ireland in an agrarian mold, but they did raise the rural standard of living and introduced some economic vigor. Still, its rocky soil, uneconomic farm units, relatively primitive agricultural methods, conservative resistance to change, and Gaelic-Catholic fatalism kept the west of Ireland one of the most impoverished, unproductive parts of Europe. Although the results did not match its intentions, the Congested Districts Board was probably the most humane example of British rule in nineteenth-century Ireland.

In addition to the various programs associated with the Congested Districts Board and the DATI, Unionists initiated public works projects to provide employment while stimulating and improving the Irish economy. They involved railroad construction, road and bridge building, and drainage. Although their ultimate objective in reform legislation was to encourage rural prosperity through self-help rather than dependence on government intervention, Unionists, who had warned against the socialist implications of Home Rule and the Liberal party's approach to Ireland and the British social problem, established welfare state precedents in Ireland far in advance of anything yet attempted in Britain.

While refusing to relent in their objections to Home Rule, Unionists did make a major concession in Irish demands for self-determination. Their 1898 local government act stripped the Protestant landlord–dominated grand juries of all fiscal and administrative powers and responsibilities, transferring them to urban, rural, and county councils elected by a democratic franchise including women voters. This legislation turned over local government to the Catholic nationalist majority in every section of Ireland except northeastern Ulster, which became the last enclave of Irish Protestant political power. But instead of substituting for an Irish parliament, urban, rural, and county councils gave nationalists political experience and whetted their appetite for more influence over their destiny.

When the Unionists left office in December 1906, their and previous Liberal legislation had eliminated almost all of the economic, political, and religious grievances that combined to manufacture the Irish question and fuel Irish nationalism. Nevertheless, the demand for Home Rule, more muted than in Parnell's time, remained. Irish nationalism by the close of the nineteenth century had assumed an identity independent of the complaints that conceived and sustained it. From O'Connell's time, the Irish nation existed as a Catholic community. Parnell increased its intention to become an Irish state. No British concession, whether Liberal or Conservative, could deter that resolve.

7

Currents and Crises in Irish Nationalism, 1880–1914

A Reunified but Aging Irish Party

After a decade of division, in 1900 the Irish party reunited with John Redmond in the chair. John Dillon graciously agreed to serve as his chief lieutenant. Under the new arrangement, the United Irish League replaced the Parnellite Irish National League and the anti-Parnellite Irish National Federation as the Home Rule constituency organization. William O'Brien created the United Irish League in 1898 to pressure the British government into dividing and distributing large grazing ranches in the west among Irish peasants to slow the rush of emigration.

Not all Home Rule MPs were happily assimilated into the Irish party. Healy still insisted on Home Rule decentralization, with more power to local constituencies. O'Brien continued to focus on the land question, believing that landlord-peasant cooperation on land purchase could lead to collaboration on other issues, including self-government. Redmond wanted to make the party as inclusive as possible but finally bowed to Dillon's determination to maintain a tightly controlled Home Rule organization concentrating on self-government. As a result, the party expelled Healy, and O'Brien left. They, their followers, and a few other dissidents numbered eleven independent nationalists after the last 1910 general election.

Despite the O'Brien-Healy disaffections, the end of the Parnellite-anti-Parnellite feud improved Home Rule prospects in the House of Commons and opened Irish purses at home and abroad to the party. To all appearances, Home Rule nationalism was in a healthy condition. However, a gap was slowly growing between the politicians at Westminster and the people back home, particularly the younger generation.

For all their talent and integrity, Redmond, Dillon, and their colleagues lacked Parnell's charisma. The trauma of Irish nationalism in the 1890s, with its feuds and splits, and the conviction of many that the Irish party had betrayed its leader to appease the Liberals renewed cynicism concerning, constitutional nationalism that did not completely vanish with party unification. And in addition to the O'Brien and Healy independent opposition, after 1890 many problems nagged the Irish party. Some critics said that it was a Catholic lobby; others ridiculed it as a Liberal pawn. Because Home Rule MPs had to insist that the union was a disaster and that only a native parliament could rescue Ireland from injustice and misgovernment, they could not take proper credit for their substantial efforts and successes in the House of Commons. They could not dwell on the reality that they had forced British politicians to pass constructive legislation to improve the condition of the Irish people.

By 1900 the Irish party had lost the bloom of youth and had become a familiar part of the nationalist landscape. Parliamentary experience and the restrictions of the Liberal alliance had transformed the energetic young firebrands, almost revolutionaries, who followed Parnell in the turbulent 1880s into cautious, prudent, sophisticated, practical, and pragmatic politicians. They never sold their convictions for place or profit or shirked their constituent obligations, but over the years Home Rule MPs slowly, almost imperceptibly and unconsciously, were integrated into the British political system. They enjoyed the give-and-take of parliamentary debate, appreciated the corridors of power, admired and respected British institutions, and liked the British people. Because Westminster was a long and tedious journey from their Irish bases of power, it was easy for them to lose touch with the nuances of Irish life. The introverted Redmond was sometimes insensitive to the undercurrents of Irish opinion. He and many of his colleagues did not comprehend the implications of a revived cultural nationalism or the depths of urban poverty and misery.

English and Irish "Racism"

In many ways, the new enthusiasm for Irish cultural nationalism responded to Anglo-Saxon racism. Before the late nineteenth century, British anti-Irish prejudice was rooted mostly in religion. British and Anglo-Irish Protestants and Ulster Nonconformists believed that they were superior to Catholics, who were caught in the authoritarian and superstitious clutches of "popery." With the decline of religious conviction in the British upper and middle classes, a racism implicit in sectarian arrogance became overt in a pseudo scientific ideology. Contrasts between Anglo-Saxon and Celt seemed a more rational explanation of British superiority and Irish inferiority than distinctions between Catholic and Protestant. Anglo-Saxonism was one manifestation of racial nationalism sweeping through the Western world. Gaelic or Irish-Ireland enthusiasm demonstrated that the Irish also acquired the virus.

British intellectuals and scholars drew on social Darwinism for their Anglo-Saxon racist apologia. Distinguished historians such as Edward A. Freeman, James A. Froude, William Stubbs, Goldwin Smith, and John R. Green claimed that the ancestors of the Britons of their day enshrined the concept of liberty originating in the forests of Germany in the British constitution. Scientists and social scientists measured skulls, jawbones, and other parts of the human anatomy and then ranked primates in such a way that Anglo-Saxons were on top and the Irish near the bottom, just above apes and blacks. Journalists simplified the "wisdom" of scholars and intellectuals and passed it on to readers. British politicians of all persuasions referred to the Irish question in racist terms. Disraeli and Salisbury thought the Irish so savage that they were as incapable of managing their own affairs as the Hottentots. An advanced Liberal such as Charles Dilke and even the founders of the Fabian Society, Sidney and Beatrice Webb, considered the Irish an inferior species. The Webbs thought Home Rule necessary "to depopulate the country of this detestable race."

Anglo-Saxon racism was another communication barrier between the English and the Irish. Because British Protestants believed Irish Catholics intellectually and morally inferior, they refused to listen disinterestedly to their grievances and demands for self-government. They patronized Irish Catholics as feminine or childlike in their dispositions, needing the guidance of masculine, benevolent Anglo-Saxon masters.

Racism in Britain and among the Anglicans and Nonconformists in their own country invited the Irish to reply with Celticism. Although Young Ireland in the 1840s insisted that the Irish were morally, intellectually, artistically, and spiritually superior to materialistic Anglo-Saxons, official Irish nationalism continued to reject as unimportant the sectarian or ethnic differences among the Irish population. Tenant right, Land League, and Home Rule movements kept emphasizing the common Irishness of all the people living in the country. But after the Parnell era, Irish nationalism began to assume a more racist tone.

Irish-Ireland

The cynicism stemming from the conflict between Parnellites and anti-Parnellites turned many young people from political to cultural nationalism. By diminishing Irish economic and political discontent, progressive Unionism also contributed to the revival of Irish cultural nationalism by freeing Irish energies to concentrate on cultural concerns. But the most important ingredient in the late nineteenth-century Celticism was an Anglo-Irish Protestant search for identity in a rapidly changing Ireland.

The vast majority of Anglo-Irish Protestants responded with ultra-Britishness to an advancing Irish nationalism indoctrinated with American egalitarianism and Republicanism, fueled by agrarian radicalism, and joined in alliance with the Liberals. However, two of their scholar intellectuals, Samuel Ferguson (1810–1886) and Standish O'Grady (1846–1928), thought this shortsighted. As an alternative reaction, they urged their coreligionists to find common ground with Catholics in a mutual appreciation of Ireland's Gaelic heritage. In contrast to Young Irelanders, Ferguson and O'Grady offered Irish cultural identity as a substitute for, rather than a supplement to, political nationalism. They thought that a wide appreciation for the aristocratic Gaelic tradition would sustain Protestant influence and the union by weaning Catholics away from democratic nationalism. They also expected that united in a unique cultural solidarity, Ireland would not need self-expression in Home Rule.

Ferguson and O'Grady initiated and inspired scholarly research into the Gaelic past and translations of its literature. Their efforts did not coax Anglo-Protestant Ireland out of its mental fortress into an accommodation with the majority population. And they did not distract Catholics from their goals of "the land of Ireland for the people of Ireland" and self-government. But they did reactivate cultural nationalism.

Unlike O'Grady and Ferguson, almost all of the Anglo-Irish Protestant scholars and writers they inspired were friendly to political nationalism. Douglas Hyde, the first president of the Gaelic League, and William Butler Yeats and colleagues in the literary renaissance were hostile to the British connection. Although not politically active in Home Rule, they blamed British rule for suppressing a creative, distinct, and significant culture.

Founded in 1893 by Eoin MacNeill, an Ulster Catholic scholar, and Hyde, the Gaelic League promoted the Young Ireland tenet that it took more than political sovereignty to make a nation. In its effort to emancipate Ireland from cultural Anglicization, the league was even more involved with the Irish language than was Young Ireland. Gaelic Leaguers insisted that language was more than a means of communication: It expressed cultural values and a mindset. They argued that if the Irish were to be truly free, they had to reject the English tongue as a badge of slavery and think and speak Irish.

The league reprinted ancient Gaelic literature and encouraged contemporary writing in Irish. Many members of the urban middle class, even people who never bothered to learn Irish or knew it only superficially, enrolled in the Gaelic League. A large number of its members cycled off to remote Irish-speaking districts or crossed over to the Aran Islands off the coasts of Clare and Galway to polish language skills in conversations with native speakers. They were also enthusiastic about Irish folk music and dancing.

Gaelic scholarship and the language movement inspired such a high quality of literature that at the turn of the century, little, poverty-stricken Dublin became one of the world's literary capitals. In their glorification of the simple, unsophisticated Irish peasant as a person with great folk wisdom and spiritual sensitivity while attacking the baneful materialism of Anglo-Saxon urban industrialism, writers, like Gaelic Leaguers, were in the Young Ireland tradition. In attempting to preserve the innocence of the peasant soul, they believed they were maintaining the essence of a superior Gaelic culture that would flourish again. The writers also hoped that a culturally revived and restored Ireland would serve as a messiah redeeming the world from the greed and utilitarianism of Anglo-Saxonism.

Despite its powerful impact, turn-of-the-century cultural nationalism was saturated with contradiction. The Gaelic League and Michael Cusack's Gaelic Athletic Association (1884) represented exclusivity. Fostering such "ancient" Irish sports as Gaelic football, hurling, and camogie (a version of women's field hockey), the GAA spread throughout rural and small-town Ireland. It was so intolerant of things English that participants in rugby, soccer, or field hockey games were banned or expelled from the GAA. Gaelic Leaguers also mobilized against "foreign" influences, labeling those indifferent to their ends and means as "West Britons" or "Shoneens" (little John Bulls). This xenophobia and provincialism estranged the young James Joyce from Irish-Ireland nationalism.

Within cultural nationalism, there were conflicting perceptions of literature's place. Leaders of the Gaelic League and the GAA expected writers to function as propagandists for an Irish-Ireland. Hyde also insisted that an authentic national literature must be in Irish. Writers such as Yeats, John Millington Synge, and Lady Augusta Gregory drew on the Gaelic tradition for themes and inspiration but would not abandon the flexibility of English and its wide reading audience. They were experimenting with a literature in English instructed by the Irish experience, insight, and perspective. And they insisted on the artist's duty and right to present creations in an honest way. Opposing views of the role of literature provoked two riots at the Abbey Theatre. Many nationalists in the audience expressing patriotism and an exaggerated notion of peasant virtue, believed that Synge's 1907 *Playboy of the Western World* insulted Irish peasants and women (the word *shift,* a woman's undergarment, was used) and attempted to stop its performance. Later, the play received a similar reception from Irish Americans. In 1926 some viewers of Sean O'Casey's *Plough and the Stars* complained that it defamed the Dublin working class. In both instances, Irish-Ireland nationalism defended the mob against the artist.

Although the literary renaissance occasionally scandalized and antagonized Irish-Irelanders, it strengthened Irish cultural nationalism. Audiences and critics were hostile to the pagan tones of Yeats's *Countess Cathleen,* but they applauded his *Cathleen ni Houlhihan* as the quintessential representation of the spirit of Irish nationalism. To reading and theater audiences throughout the world, Irish writers disproved the myths of Anglo-Saxon racism, demonstrating that the Irish possessed a unique and interesting cultural identity. And it was world opinion that eventually helped persuade the British that Irish genius deserved to develop and flourish in an atmosphere of political sovereignty.

From Young Ireland to the Gaelic League, cultural nationalism was intended as an alternative to Catholic nationalism, something with appeal for all the people. At first Catholic bishops and priests distrusted the nondenominational element in the cultural revival as they had in Young Ireland. They dreaded the prospect of an Irish-Ireland separated from the Catholic heritage. They came to realize, however, that they shared many of the hopes, fears, and values of Irish-Ireland proponents. Both groups worried about the impact of British culture and the American feedback on Ireland. Both wanted to isolate their country from the effects of urban industrialism. Catholic leaders exploited Irish-Ireland Anglophobia and diverted its hope for a culturally monolithic, religiously pluralistic Irish-Ireland into an essentially Catholic Ireland. They were assisted by the determination of Anglo-Irish Protestants and Scots-Irish Presbyterians to remain British. So what began as inclusive ended exclusive, increasing the cultural dimension of a mental partition that preceded one of place.

WILLIAM BUTLER YEATS, 1865–1939

William Butler Yeats was the dominant personality in the Irish Literary Revival, which perpetuated the cultural nationalism of Young Ireland and articulated it to a world opinion that pressured the British government into conceding dominion status to twenty-six Irish counties. (Courtesy of Bord Failte-Irish Tourist Board)

An Alternative to Home Rule

Irish-Ireland's emphasis on multidimensional nationalism; the generation gap between Irish party MPs and young people caught up in the mystique of Parnell, the fallen messiah, the rebel against British colonialism and Irish Catholic clericalism; and the beginnings of urban social and economic radicalism encouraged political alternatives to Home Rule. In 1898 Arthur Griffith began to present a *Sinn Féin* ("We Ourselves") program in his paper, the *United Irishman*. It synthesized (1) the arbitration courts and the proposed Council of Three Hundred of O'Connell's Repeal agitation of the 1840s; (2) C.G. Duffy's and the New Departure's suggestions that at an appropriate moment, Irish MPs withdraw from Westminster and establish a legislature in Dublin; (3) Griffith's interpretation of Austro-Hungarian history; (4) the protectionist theories of the German economist Friedrich List; and (5) the values of Irish-Ireland.

By preference, Griffith was a Republican, but he did not believe that Britain would concede total separation or that Ireland would have the strength to force it. His Sinn Féin program was a compromise between a republic and Home Rule. He proposed dual monarchy, such as Austria–Hungary, as a reasonable conclusion to the centuries-old conflict between British colonialism and Irish nationalism. As a persuasive tactic, Griffith urged passive resistance to British authority rather than the submissiveness of parliamentarism or the futility of revolution. For the future Irish nation-state, Griffith recommended cultural and economic self-sufficiency through Irish-Ireland nationalism and a protectionist economy.

In many ways Griffith was an unpleasant fellow. Imitating his hero, John Mitchel, he projected a provincial nationalism. Anti-black and anti-Semitic, Griffith had no compassion for non-Irish victims of oppression. The economic and cultural aspects of his Sinn Féin program were similarly narrow. He insisted that the writers of the renaissance should place their patriotism above their art. His plans for Irish industrial development were pro-capital and anti-labor.

Except for arranging patriotic funerals, the Irish Republican Brotherhood had been a relatively ineffective force in Irish nationalism since the rise of Parnell. Without the financing and the prodding of the Clan na Gael, it might have vanished from the Irish scene. But after the turn of the century, new leaders gave the IRB a sudden burst of energy. Thomas J. Clarke, a veteran of British prisons and a friend of John Devoy, returned to Dublin from America. His tobacco shop off Parnell Square became a focus of Republican conspiracy. Bulmer Hobson and Denis McCullough from Belfast and Sean MacDermott from Leitrim via Glasgow learned from Clarke and began to energize and discipline the IRB. Although the movement numbered only about 1,500, the membership magnified its significance by infiltrating the Gaelic League, the Gaelic Athletic Association, and Sinn Féin when it became an organization in 1905. Republicans persuaded Griffith to make the constitution of 1783, which was close to dual monarchy, his minimum demand and to keep his options open for something more.

Labor Restiveness

Throughout the nineteenth century, Irish nationalism had focused on the economic and social grievances of tenant farmers while ignoring the condition of agricultural and urban laborers. Members of the Irish working class lived in the most socially wretched cities in the United Kingdom, particularly in Dublin. Most of them inhabited the overcrowded, rat-and-vermin-infested tenements of Sean O'Casey's plays. Diets of tea, jam, and bread produced unhealthy bodies. Tuberculosis was an Irish urban as well as rural scourge, and the infant mortality rate was appalling.

In a country with little industry, few natural resources, and a low level of capital investment, urban working-class people suffered from unemployment or partial employment at low wages. Poverty, hunger, disease, and filth bred alcoholism, depression, and prostitution. Formulated in the tradition of agrarian protest and dependent on Catholic middle-class financing, the Irish party neither understood nor responded to the urban problem. Workers turned to militant labor unionism inspired by socialism.

In 1908 James Larkin, a Liverpool-born Irishman with syndicalist leanings, organized the Irish Transport Workers Union (ITWU). Another syndicalist, Edinburgh-born-and-raised James Connolly, was his chief lieutenant. Ultimately, they unionized about 10,000 workers and, through strikes, won significant concessions from Dublin employers. But in 1913, led by William Martin Murphy, a close associate of Tim Healy, proprietor of the important *Irish Independent* and the wealthiest man in Ireland, with extensive economic interests throughout the United Kingdom and the empire, the employers combined in an all-out war on the ITWU. When it struck Murphy's United Tramway Company, the employer retaliated by locking out 25,000 employees. After four months of hunger, police brutality, and the hostility of the Catholic hierarchy and clergy, Larkin had to surrender. Workers returned to their jobs on the bosses' terms.

The 1913 labor dispute revealed the frustrations and poverty of Irish urban life, exposed the shortcomings of the Irish party as a representative of working-class interests, and indicated that nationalism in Britain and Ireland was more powerful than socialism or class solidarity. During the strike and lockout, Home Rule MPs avoided the capital–labor dispute. Generally they were pro-business and frightened of Larkin's radicalism, but they despised Murphy because he and his newspaper encouraged Healy's attacks on the Irish party. As the strike dragged on, British Trade Union Congress (BTUC) support for Irish workers grew lukewarm, suggesting that it shared the establishment's anti-Irish prejudices. As a result of Murphy's victory and the inadequacy of BTUC backing, Ireland's working-class movement became more nationalist and less socialist.

After the workers returned to their jobs, Larkin left Ireland for America to raise funds for his depleted union treasury. He remained there for a number of years, organizing workers in the United States, promoting its young Communist party, and encouraging anti-British activities during World War I. In his absence, Connolly took charge of the Irish trade union movement. He created a "citizen army" to protect workers against future police brutality. More of a nationalist than Larkin, Connolly committed Irish labor and socialism to revolution on the road to a worker's republic.

Reform Under the Liberals

Despite new forces and perceptions in Irish nationalism and a growing urban social problem, the Home Rule movement at the turn of the century was far from collapse. Members of the IRB had infiltrated portions of Gaelic cultural nationalism and Sinn Féin, but Republicanism and dual monarchy had small constituencies. Gaelic Leaguers, members of the Gaelic Athletic Association, and writers of the literary renaissance did not see themselves as contradictions to Home Rule. They and the overwhelming majority of the people were Irish party constituents. More bland than in the days of Parnell, the Irish party was nevertheless an able body of politicians. It was safe as long as it continued to be effective at Westminster. The Liberal alliance continued to be both its strength and the weakness, and thus pressures external rather than internal to Irish nationalism destroyed it.

The human and financial costs of the Boer War, a steadily declining British commercial and industrial economy, and the concern that Unionists might further injure trade and manufacturing with protective tariffs resulted in a Liberal House of Commons majority of 224 in the 1906 general election. Comfortably free from the pressures of Irish nationalism, aware of its divisiveness in Britain, and determined to cater to the social and economic demands of the British electorate, Liberal leaders decided to keep Home Rule low on their list of priorities. They did, however, present one concession to Irish nationalism. In 1907 Sir Henry Campbell-Bannerman, the prime minister, offered the Irish party devolution as a step in the direction of Home Rule. He proposed an Irish Council of eighty-two elected and twenty-nine appointed representatives, financed by a generous government subsidy, to assume the responsibilities of administering existing agencies and boards. Campbell-Bannerman told Home Rule MPs that the Irish Council would provide nationalists with an opportunity to demonstrate to the British that they could govern themselves.

Redmond suspected Liberal motives, fearing that the Irish Council would be a substitute for Home Rule rather than a prelude to it. Nevertheless, he presented the offer to a national convention, which agreed with him and rejected it. Some Catholic bishops had a separate motive for asking the national convention to scorn Campbell-Bannermman's scheme. They worried that the Irish Council might lead to lay interference with Catholic education. After the convention, Redmond told the Liberals that Irish nationalism would accept nothing less than Home Rule.

Defeated in their effort to compromise and postpone Home Rule, Liberals turned to less-volatile Irish subjects, settling the university issue and improving land purchase. Arthur Balfour was a strong champion of Catholic higher education, arguing, as Sir Robert Peel once did, that university experiences and degrees would make the Irish Catholic middle class more cosmopolitan and sophisticated and thus less nationalist. In 1897 he suggested that the government finance three Irish universities: Trinity as Protestant, Queen's in Belfast as Presbyterian, and a national university, predominantly Catholic. Like Gladstone, he thought the government should not endow instruction in such controversial subjects as modern history, moral philosophy, or theology, but the individual religions could finance faculties in those areas. The Unionist leadership gave Balfour little support for his university proposal, and he never introduced it as a government measure. Later

George Wyndham wanted to create a Catholic college in Dublin University and to establish Queen's in Belfast as a predominantly Presbyterian university, but Trinity College blocked such a move.

In 1908, the Liberals, through the cooperation of the chief secretary, Augustine Birrell, and Archbishop William Walsh of Dublin, satisfied Catholic higher education demands by establishing the National University of Ireland, including the Queen's College's Cork and Galway campuses and the Jesuit University College, Dublin. The two Queen's Colleges changed their name to University Colleges Cork and Galway. Queen's College, Belfast became Queen's University, serving the needs of a mostly Presbyterian student body. A year later, the Liberals smoothed out some of the wrinkles in the Wyndham Land Act, increasing the money available for tenant loans, insisting on compulsory sale in certain circumstances, and speeding the process of peasant proprietorship.

The Liberals' Irish policy paled in comparison to their British reform legislation. During their first three years in office, they concentrated on British social and economic problems resulting from a declining industrial economy that featured unimaginative leadership, static technology, increasing foreign competition, and an ever-widening unfavorable trade balance. Because a large portion of the upper and middle classes continued to enjoy overseas investment income, workers and their families bore most of the burden of the faltering economy. Their insecurity and discontent nurtured militant, syndicalist trade unionism and provided a constituency for the new Labour party, which managed to win twenty-nine seats in 1906.

To calm the working class and to prevent its mass defection to socialism, Liberal legislation laid the foundations of the welfare state—old-age pensions, health insurance, unemployment compensation, employer's liability, and labor exchanges. This comprehensive program of social reform put great pressure on a budget already strained by heavy spending on the fleet to match German naval expenditure. Chancellor of the Exchequer David Lloyd George, once a Welsh Home Ruler, decided that the rich should pay for both national defense and social welfare. In his search for tax revenues, he borrowed ideas from Fabian socialism. The government imposed substantial duties on unearned land profits and high income taxes on wealth. It also raised inheritance taxes. In increasing revenues, Lloyd George satisfied the puritan, Nonconformist section of Liberalism by punishing vice with heavy duties on the use of beer, spirits, and tobacco. Although the Irish party disliked the negative impact of the budget on Irish distilling and brewing, it remained loyal to the alliance by voting for George's budget.

Beginning with Lord Randolph Churchill's 1886 encouragement of Orange violence against Home Rule, British Conservatives became constitutionally reckless in their efforts to defeat the Irish-Liberal alliance and social reform. In 1893 they employed the veto power of the House of Lords to defeat the second Home Rule Bill. Following their massive defeat in 1906, Arthur Balfour and other Unionist party leaders decided that the only way that they could obstruct the Liberal welfare program was to return to the House of Lords veto strategy. Given the mandate that the electorate had given the Liberals at the polls, this was a risky tactic, placing the aristocracy in the path of advancing democracy.

The House of Lords Crisis and Home Rule

In 1909 the House of Lords violated centuries of constitutional tradition by vetoing a House of Commons budget. Responding, the Liberals took the issue of the Lords to the country in general elections in January and December 1910. This first reduced the Liberal Commons margin over the Unionists to two seats; the second left the two parties even, at 272 seats apiece, placing the government under obligation to the Irish and Labour parties, who controlled the balance of power.

Obviously, the House of Lords was more popular with the public than the Liberals had anticipated, but other factors also influenced election results. Many traditional middle-class Liberals were unhappy with their party's welfare state financed by a soak-the-rich policy. And since the 1910 elections increased Labour party strength in the House of Commons to forty-two, it seemed apparent that middle-of-the-road liberalism was no more appealing to working-class radicals than to middle-class property owners. In addition, a large proportion of the lower class resented having Nonconformist, middle-class Liberals tax their pints and their smokes, the simple pleasures of the poor. No doubt, many Britons were apprehensive over German military and naval power and diplomatic arrogance. Perhaps they concluded that Unionist champions of imperialism and militarism were more likely than Liberals to conduct an aggressive foreign policy and to modernize the armed forces.

Ireland also figured in the 1910 election campaigns. Unionist politicians and newspapers warned that Home Rule would follow from a lessening of the Lords' power. Before the December election, Herbert H. Asquith, Campbell-Bannerman's successor as Liberal prime minister, promised in Dublin that Irish self-government would follow a curbing of the veto power of the peers. Without a doubt, traditional anti-Irish Catholic nativism hurt the Liberals at the polls, but the Unionist charge that the two elections failed to produce a Home Rule parliamentary majority was false. Forty-two Labour MPs gave Home Rule 314 British votes in the House of Commons, compared to 254 against (19 of the 272 Unionist MPs were from Ireland: 17 from Ulster, 2 from Trinity College). Altogether, after the December election, Home Rule had a majority of 125 in the House of Commons. Because it was a major issue in both 1910 contests, this majority was a considerable accomplishment for Irish nationalism.

When Asquith seemed reluctant to move against the Lords, Redmond gave notice that the Irish party would not vote for the budget unless the Liberals carried out their pledge to reform the upper house. Consequently, the government in February 1911 introduced and passed the Parliament Act, limiting the House of Lords' veto of a bill to three consecutive sessions or two years. King George V's message that, if necessary, he would pack the House of Lords with Liberal peers to fulfill the will of the people nudged the Unionist majority in the upper house to surrender its absolute veto power. Thanks to the pressure of Irish nationalism, in 1911 Britain took a major step toward democracy.

The Brink of Civil War

After the Parliament Act removed the last constitutional obstacle to an Irish Parliament, Asquith, in the spring of 1912, presented the third Home Rule Bill to the House of Commons. He said that because the Parliament at Westminster was swamped with more business than it could properly manage, Home Rule for Ireland was the beginning of a federal structure for the entire United Kingdom. The Liberals offered Ireland a mild measure of self-government, establishing an Irish Parliament with a democratically elected Commons and an appointed Senate. Forty-two Irish MPs—thirty-four nationalists and eight Unionists—would remain at Westminster to represent Ireland's financial and imperial interests. The British government would retain jurisdiction of the Royal Irish Constabulary for six years before turning it over to Irish control. There were other restrictions on Irish sovereignty. Britain retained management of Irish revenues, and the Dublin Parliament could not impose tariffs (a 10 percent rise in customs was permitted), conduct an independent foreign policy, or legislate matters of religion. This last limitation indicated Britain's determination to protect Ireland's non-Catholics. They received other considerations as well: Ulster was to be overrepresented in the Irish Commons, and it was expected that the crown would appoint a disproportionately large number of Protestants and Presbyterians to the Senate.

Despite its many barriers to real independence, John Redmond accepted the government's offer as a settlement of the Irish claim to self-government. He seemed to speak for the overwhelming nationalist majority. Even Sinn Féiners and Irish-Irelanders said they were content with the third Home Rule Bill. Irish party MPs could take pride in their accomplishment. They had completed the work of O'Connell and Parnell within the framework and rules of the British constitutional system. And no doubt Redmond and his colleagues realized that after Home Rule was in place, it could be renegotiated over time to expand the possibilities of the Irish Parliament.

Sir Edward Carson, Dublin barrister, MP for Trinity College, and leader of the Irish Unionist Council, and Sir James Craig, spokesman for Ulster Unionism, gave a firm no to Home Rule. They told the House of Commons that their people would always remain loyal to the union and the British constitution. They described Home Rule as a knife pointed at the heart of Ulster, insisting that it would destroy the economy and the liberties of Anglicans and Nonconformists by imposing the rule of Catholic politicians interested only in the agrarian economy and religious culture of the other three provinces.

To prove that they were not bluffing, Carson and Craig left the halls of Parliament and went to Ulster, where they obtained the signatures, some in blood, of 471,000 Unionist zealots to a "Solemn League and Covenant" to use all means which may be found necessary to defeat the present conspiracy to set up a Home Rule Parliament in Ireland. And in the event of such a Parliament being forced upon us we further solemnly pledge to refuse to accept its authority.

Carson then organized an Ulster provisional government to go into operation the day Home Rule became law. He also raised an Ulster Volunteer Army to resist the imposition of Dublin rule on the north. Craig announced that, if necessary, Ulster Protestants were ready to swear allegiance to the German kaiser in preference to the control of an Irish Catholic Parliament.

British Conservatives decided to exploit Ulster fanaticism and paranoia to destroy the Liberal government, checkmate Irish nationalism, and preserve the United Kingdom and, in their opinion, the empire. Arthur Balfour's successor as Unionist party leader, Andrew Bonar Law, had an Ulster Presbyterian heritage. He promised Ulster Unionists that his party would support their resistance to Home Rule even if it was unconstitutional and posed the menace of civil war. Seconding Bonar Law, Irish nationalism's old enemy, the *Times* of London, assured Ulster non-Catholics that they had the approval "of the whole force of the Conservative and Unionist Party."

Previous British governments had transported and jailed Irish nationalists for less defiance of the constitution than that of Carson, Craig, and Bonar Law. Asquith, however, was reluctant to prosecute British and Irish Unionist leaders when British public opinion was so split on Home Rule, especially as Europe was close to a wide-scale war. Redmond advised the prime minister not to take action against Carson and Craig because they were only bluffing and martyrdom would enhance their prestige in the eyes of their followers. And he told Irish nationalists to remain calm because "the ship of Home Rule would sail safely into port, borne on the tide of British Liberal opinion." Rationality, calmness, and decency might have been assets in most political situations, but in Ireland's relations with Britain and Ulster Unionism, they were fatal flaws. Redmond never seemed to comprehend the lunatic quality of British Unionist strategy or the vacillating mentality of British Liberals.

As Home Rule proceeded on a three-session, two-year trip through Parliament, violence became more plausible and probable. British Conservatives were so furious with Liberals for enacting the welfare state, curbing the House of Lords, and jeopardizing the United Kingdom and the empire with Home Rule that their support of Ulster unionism became more aggressive. Lord Milner, a British empire proconsul, begged Carson to commence the armed struggle. He also persuaded 2 million Britons to sign a "Solemn League and Covenant" in support of Ulster's resistance to Home Rule. F.E. Smith, the future Lord Birkenhead, outdid his party leader, Bonar Law, when he assured Carson that British Conservatives would be in his corner if the Home Rule crisis evolved into civil war. Treason under the guise of some higher law became fashionable. A.V. Dicey, the distinguished Oxford professor of constitutional law, rationalized Ulster Unionist intent to disobey an act of Parliament; Geoffrey Dawson, editor of the *Times*, propagandized Ulster defiance; Rudyard Kipling poeticized "loyal Ulster"; and Waldorf Astor and Lord Rothschild donated a great deal of money to the Ulster Volunteers.

Army generals and lesser officers, Unionist in conviction, Conservative by class and family connections, joined the conspiracy against law and order. Field Marshal Earl Roberts recommended Lieutenant General George Richardson to Carson for the position of Ulster Volunteer commander. Orangeman Sir Henry Wilson, director of military operations, revealed confidential information to Bonar Law and Carson and advised them to resist Home Rule by sabotaging a Military Operation Bill in the House of Commons. In March 1914 some 144 British officers stationed at the Curragh, County Kildare, said that they would resign their commissions rather than enforce Home Rule in Ulster. Officers in Britain expressed a similar sentiment; some threatened to offer their skills to the Ulster Volunteers.

Weighing the possibility of an Ulster Unionist insurrection, disloyalty in the army, and a war mood on the continent, cabinet members began to flinch. In 1912, when planning the Home Rule Bill, Liberal leaders did discuss the possibility of appeasing Ulster unionism with partition. They decided to keep it as a last-ditch option. In June 1912 T.G. Agar-Robartes, a Liberal MP, tried to amend the Home Rule Bill, moving that the four Protestant majority counties of Ulster—Antrim, Armagh, Down, and Londonderry—be excluded from the government's proposal. Carson and Craig voted for the amendment, believing that Home Rule could not survive without such a large portion of Ulster, but the Agar-Robartes amendment failed. In the autumn of 1913 Lord Loreborn, a prominent Liberal peer and a consistent friend of the Irish alliance, recommended a constitutional conference to settle the Irish crisis, implying that partition could be the solution. Winston Churchill, in his Liberal phase as first lord of the admiralty, suggested excluding Unionist Ulster from Home Rule because "Orange bitters and Irish whiskey will not mix." Redmond reacted with a rejection of partition and an offer to grant Ulster considerable autonomy within a Home Rule Ireland. Carson also refused partition because, as he said, Ulster Protestants and Nonconformists were selfless people trying to save all of Ireland from the political and economic disaster of Home Rule.

Aware that Ulster and British Unionists were intimidating the Liberal government, dimming the prospects for a united Home Rule Ireland, some nationalists decided on adopting Orange tactics to demonstrate to Westminster politicians that they were just as determined to fight for the Irish nation as Ulster Unionists were to fight against it. In November 1913 the Irish Republican Brotherhood took the lead in creating the Irish Volunteers, masking its role by selecting Eoin MacNeill, Celtic scholar and founding father of the Gaelic League, as Volunteer president.

At first Redmond thought the Irish Volunteers divisive and violence-prone. But after he pondered the psychologically coercive impact of Ulster defiance on the Liberal government, he decided to incorporate them into the Home Rule offensive. In April 1914 the Irish party leader began negotiations with the Volunteer command, insisting that the party control half its executive. Although IRB influences in the organization continued strong, in July the Volunteers expanded their executive committee from twenty-five to fifty, giving the Irish party 50 percent of its representation. Between January and May 1914, Volunteer membership skyrocketed from 10,000 to 100,000. After its official collaboration with the Irish party about 15,000 a week joined so that by September there were about 180,000 Volunteers. Redmond's blessing, participation, and appeal for American money increased Volunteer membership, prestige, and funding. With three unofficial armies in existence—the Ulster and Irish Volunteers and Connolly's citizen army—Ireland, like the entire United Kingdom, stood on the brink of a violent disaster.

By 1914 Asquith, always lukewarm on Home Rule, and most of the cabinet had decided on partition as an escape from the Ulster dilemma. Suddenly aware of the potential results of his irresponsible and reckless words and conduct, Bonar Law also was ready to satisfy Ulster with exclusion from the Home Rule Bill. Even Carson apparently retreated from his all-or-nothing position. He said that he would accept partition if it involved all nine Ulster counties, an unreasonable demand since five of them had Catholic majorities, and at the time seventeen Home Rule and sixteen Unionist MPs represented the province.

For obvious reasons, Redmond could not endorse a divided Ireland. At the same time, he could not repudiate the Liberal alliance and bring down the government. A general election might return a Unionist administration or lead to a coalition government, indifferent or hostile to Home Rule and independent of Irish party pressure. And it might be a long time before nationalists in the House of Commons would again hold the balance of power. With the consent of party colleagues and Ulster Catholic bishops, Redmond offered Liberals and Unionists a partition compromise: Ulster counties could vote themselves out of Home Rule for six years. In addition, he insisted on plebiscites for two Catholic nationalist majority cities, Derry and Newry in south Down. While this Liberal-approved concession was presented as an opportunity for Catholic nationalists to prove to Ulster Unionists that Irish self-government would work and to assure Home Rulers that partition was transitional rather than permanent, Redmond must have known that he had surrendered a united Ireland. Within the allotted six years a general election would take place. A probable Unionist victory in the next one would convert a temporary arrangement into a final one. The result would be a Home Rule Ireland of twenty-eight counties plus Newry and Derry and a truncated four-county Ulster as a British province. This was not a pleasing prospect for any nationalist, but it was much better than a twenty-three-county Home Rule Ireland.

Carson chose to ignore the reality of Redmond's concession. He continued to insist on a nine-county exclusion, obviously still hoping to keep the United Kingdom intact. In July 1914 George V, trying to avert civil war, asked the leaders of all parties and factions to settle the Ulster crisis in conference. Redmond, Dillon, Carson, Craig, Asquith, Lloyd George, Lord Lansdowne, and Bonar Law met from July 21 to 23 at Buckingham Palace but failed to agree on the time limit or the boundaries of partition. The government then introduced an Amending

Bill in the House of Lords calling for the temporary exclusion of the four Ulster Unionist majority counties, minus Newry and Derry, from Home Rule. But the Unionist majority in the upper house altered it to exclude permanently all of Ulster and returned it to the House of Commons. Asquith scheduled a discussion of the Amending Bill and the House of Lords' changes for July 27. Violence in Ireland delayed the government's timetable.

To deter civil war, in December 1913 the government forbade the importation of arms into Ireland. Four months later the Ulster Volunteers defied this ban by smuggling 20,000 rifles and 2 million rounds of ammunition into Larne from Germany. This bold gesture embarrassed the authorities and made the Ulster Volunteers a much more formidable force. Impressed by the Ulster Volunteers' coup, and determined to balance the intimidation factor, on July 26 the Irish Volunteers landed 900 rifles and 125,000 rounds of ammunition at Howth, a fishing village close to Dublin, and on August 1 an additional 600 rifles and 20,000 rounds of ammunition at Kilcoole, County Wicklow. They also made their purchases in Germany. Alerted by police, British soldiers, the King's Own Scottish Borderers' marched out to disarm the Volunteers returning from Howth. When they met on the Howth road, the front ranks of the Volunteers held off the soldiers with their rifle butts while their comrades disappeared into fields and byways carrying guns and bullets.

When the frustrated Borderers returned to Dublin, people on Bachelor's Walk, a narrow road along the River Liffey, taunted them. When some threw stones, a few soldiers lost control of their emotions and fired into the crowd, killing three and wounding thirty-six. The next day at Westminster, Redmond posed a reasonable question. Why, he asked, could Ulster Volunteers openly parade with loaded guns while British soldiers were attempting to disarm Irish Volunteers? Redmond's challenge forced an official inquiry into the Bachelor's Walk incident, delaying consideration of the Amending Bill. The inquiry led to scapegoat censures of the assistant commissioner of the Dublin police and the Borderers commanding officer.

The Union Temporarily Preserved by a Foreign War

Before the House of Commons could return to Home Rule, Austria declared war on Serbia, Russia mobilized, Germany declared war on Russia and France and issued an ultimatum to Belgium demanding troop passage through that small, neutral country. Perhaps Germany thought that Britain was so involved with the possibility of civil war over the Ulster crisis that it would not intervene on the continent. If so, it was wrong. On August 3 Sir Edward Grey, the foreign secretary, informed the House of Commons that Britain would honor its obligation to defend Belgium's neutrality. Redmond, without consulting his colleagues, then rose and said that the government could withdraw troops from Ireland because the Irish Volunteers would join Ulster Volunteers in defense of their common homeland. Both Unionists and Liberals rose and cheered his generosity and patriotism.

After the country's entry into World War I, Liberals attempted to pacify Ireland by settling the Home Rule issue without disturbing UK morale and unity. To please nationalists, the House of Commons passed the Home Rule Bill for the third time, placing it on the statute books, but to appease Unionists, a suspensory bill delayed its application for the war's duration.

World War I might have saved Britain from the destruction of civil war. But its politicians evaded rather than escaped the Ulster dimension of the Home Rule problem. In August 1914 Liberal, Conservative, Irish party, and Ulster Unionist MPs failed to grasp the significance of the crisis that they had passed through. When British Conservatives encouraged and cooperated with Ulster Unionist defiance of the parliamentary process and when Liberals surrendered to intimidation, they weakened the credibility of constitutional Irish nationalism. In refusing to award the Irish party the trophy of victory that it had won fairly in the parliamentary game, British politicians proved the thesis of Irish physical-force nationalism. They announced that the union was a farce, that the constitution did not apply to Ireland, and that they would only concede self-government to violence. Ulster unionism; British anti-Irish Catholic nativism, manipulated by Conservative politicians, intellectuals, and journalists; and Liberal timidity had created an Irish revolutionary situation. After 1914 the case of Irish freedom moved from the halls of Westminster to the hills, glens, and streets of Ireland. Guns and grenades, not parliamentary debates and roll calls, would determine the verdict.

8

Wars of Liberation, 1914–1921

Blood Sacrifice

Like U.S. president Woodrow Wilson, and unlike the European politicians, diplomats, generals, and admirals who created World War I, John Redmond viewed it as a contest between good and evil. He believed that German and Hapsburg authoritarianism, militarism, irresponsible imperialism, and disregard for small states menaced Western civilization. Redmond told Irish nationalists that they had an obligation to help Britain and France preserve liberal democracy and the freedom of small countries such as Belgium. He said that an Irish sacrifice for international justice would persuade Britain to concede all-Ireland Home Rule when peace came. Sinn Féiners, Irish-Irelanders, and the IRB disputed Redmond. They could not see Britain, the oppressor of Ireland, as the champion of democracy or the rights of small countries. They pleaded with Irishmen not to shed their blood or risk their lives for the power and glory of the British empire.

In August 1914 approximately 12,000 of the 180,000 Irish Volunteers refused to go along with Redmond's version of the war. The majority wing that did took the name National Volunteers. Many of its members joined the British armed forces. Dissidents continued to call themselves Irish Volunteers. Eoin MacNeill still commanded them as an unwitting front man for the IRB. MacNeill wanted to preserve the Volunteers as a strong and ready force to persuade Britain after the war that Irish nationalists were determined on United Ireland Home Rule; the IRB wanted to use them as a weapon of revolution. Patrick Pearse, IRB director of organization, barrister by profession, poet by inclination, and master of St. Enda's, a boys' school featuring instruction in Irish, was the main link between the Republican military council and the Irish Volunteers.

Pearse, who had shifted his allegiance from Home Rule to republicanism, and two of his poet friends, Joseph Mary Plunkett and Thomas MacDonagh, represented the assimilation of Catholic with Irish-Ireland. They insisted on an Ireland "Gaelic as well as free" and weaved Catholic atonement and redemption themes into a revolutionary ideology. Pearse and his associates argued for revolution as salvation rather than victory. They insisted that Ireland needed a blood sacrifice to wash away the sinful corruption of parliamentary politics and Anglo-Saxon culture. British soldiers would slaughter Irish rebels, but victory would rise like a phoenix from the ashes of defeat. Martyrs' blood would cleanse the Irish soul, and a new, stronger, purer generation of Irish youth would drive the British out and de-Anglicize the country.

Soon after Britain entered World War I, Irish Republicans in harmony with the Clan na Gael began revolutionary preparations. They decided to fight before the war on the continent concluded so as to earn a place at the peace conference. John Devoy contacted the German ambassador in Washington, who promised aid from his government for an Irish insurrection. Sir Roger Casement, an Ulster Protestant knighted for his humanitarian efforts for the British consular service in Africa and South America, went to Germany via the United States to recruit Irish prisoners of war for an Irish brigade to fight for the freedom of their own country. Irish-American nationalists, Irish POWs, and the German government did not take the English-accented Casement very seriously. Other Republican envoys had a stronger impact on Berlin and returned to Ireland with solid offers of arms and ammunition.

James Connolly was also planning revolution, but not a romantic blood sacrifice. He believed victory possible. Although there were only 200 in the citizen army, Connolly was certain that a Dublin rising would spark the entire country. According to his thinking, the British, occupied with the war in France and reluctant to destroy property in putting down an Irish insurrection, would evacuate Ireland, clearing the path for a socialist republic. To avoid competitive planning and split allegiances, the IRB in January 1916 concluded an alliance with Connolly, and he joined its Military Council.

From August 1914 to April 1916 the Irish Volunteers and the citizen army drilled in the Dublin-Wicklow mountains and held public reviews in Dublin streets. At the same time, Republicans and Sinn Féiners were pleading with Irishmen not to join the British armed forces. Their speakers and newspapers said that Irish victims of colonialism had no place in a struggle between competing forms of imperialism. They should remain at home and prepare for the coming battle for Irish freedom. Attempting to avoid another bloody incident like Bachelor's Walk, British authorities ignored the parades and maneuvers, but they did jail or deport leaders of the anti-recruiting campaign. They also shut down extremist nationalist newspapers; most of them, however, quickly reappeared under new names.

For a while Redmond's support for the war effort did not seriously damage his reputation among Irish nationalists, but the conduct of British politicians and generals gradually eroded his popularity. Lord Horatio Herbert Kitchener at the War Office permitted the Ulster Volunteers to enter the army as a separate division with their own officers and insignia, the Red Hand of Ulster. He denied a similar privilege to the National Volunteers. Kitchener's Unionist prejudices, as well as heavy Irish casualties at Gallipoli and on the western front, widened the antiwar circle in Ireland and discouraged Irish enlistments.

Continued British failures and the slaughter in France provoked extensive political and newspaper criticism of government policy. To gain popular support for the war effort, Asquith created a coalition cabinet. He invited Unionists, Labourites, and leaders of the Irish party to join. Consistent with the principles of his party, Redmond refused to participate in a British government, but Home Rule enemies Carson, Craig, and Bonar Law did enter the coalition. Its composition increased Irish nationalist distrust of the intentions and integrity of the government.

Meanwhile, the Military Council of the IRB in conjunction with the Clan na Gael selected Easter Sunday, April 23, 1916, as an appropriate day for an uprising. Germany promised military equipment. Pearse persuaded an unknowing MacNeill to summon a general review of all Volunteer units with full equipment for April 23. Plunkett and some of his friends distributed a fake document, indicating the intention of British authorities to raid the headquarters of the Irish Volunteers, the citizen army, Sinn Féin, and the Gaelic League and to arrest their leaders. This forgery, which may in fact have represented British intentions accurately, was used by the IRB to convince MacNeill and the Volunteers that they would be fighting a defensive war rather than starting a rebellion.

On Holy Thursday, Bulmer Hobson discovered the revolutionary scheme. He informed MacNeill, and they tried to prevent a futile slaughter. MacNeill insisted that the Volunteers existed to demonstrate the intensity of the Irish people's fervor for freedom and only as a revolutionary force if Britain refused postwar Home Rule. He argued that an insurrection that did not first determine British intentions and had little chance of success would be "immoral." Hobson protested that Pearse and his allies were violating the 1873 IRB Constitution. It said that a majority of the Irish people must decide the time, occasion, and appropriateness of revolution. Hobson denied that a military junta such as the Military Council spoke for the IRB membership or the Irish people.

Because Hobson was a powerful, stubborn, and persuasive personality, his old friend, Sean McDermott, pulled out a revolver and had him detained until the fighting started. Pearse and MacDonagh told MacNeill that because a German ship was on the seas bringing arms and ammunition to the Volunteers, it was too late to cancel the revolution. This argument decided MacNeill to turn the Volunteers over to the Military Council. But the next day the authorities arrested Casement on the Kerry coast after he came ashore from a German submarine to warn Volunteer leaders that German assistance would be too negligible to produce victory. Also on Good Friday, the German ship *Aud* arrived off Kerry with a supply of weapons. Confused orders and inefficiency prevented the Volunteers from unloading the cargo. While the *Aud* waited, a British warship intercepted it. To avoid the disgrace of capture, the captain scuttled his ship, sending its contents of obsolete Russian armaments, captured on the eastern front, to the depths of the Atlantic.

When MacNeill learned of Casement's capture and the fate of the *Aud* on Holy Saturday, he canceled orders for the Easter Sunday maneuvers. Knowing that they would get little support from the rest of the country but determined on their redemptive blood sacrifice, Pearse and his associates proceeded with the insurrection. Even Connolly, who once thought victory possible, must have realized the suicidal nature of the venture. But Pearse seemed to have persuaded him that some Irish nationalists had to give up their lives to restore Irish self-respect. Using the Calvary model, Connolly wrote, "Without the shedding of blood there is no redemption."

On Easter Monday morning, while most Dubliners were still enjoying the holiday season, a grim band of 1,528 rebels, including 27 women, quietly marched through the streets of the city, seizing the General Post Office and other strategic places. They almost captured Dublin Castle, the seat of British administration in Ireland. Over the General Post Office rebels hoisted a Republican tricolor—orange for the Protestant tradition, green for the Catholic, and white for the bond of love and cooperation that should exist between them. From the balcony, Pearse read a proclamation declaring an independent republic dedicated to social reform and to the civil liberties and equality of all its citizens regardless of creed.

If Pearse indoctrinated Connolly with his political theology of blood sacrifice, Connolly instructed Pearse in socialist principles. The affirmation of "the right of the people to the ownership of Ireland" was inspired by Connolly as well as James Fintan Lalor. It is ironic that while Connolly has lived in the memory and song of the Irish nation, even in the name of a Dublin railway station, his social ideology has had small impact on post-revolutionary Irish thought or action.

For six days the citizen army and the Volunteers fought the Royal Irish Constabulary, the Dublin Metropolitan Police, and the British army, quickly reinforced with men and equipment. Fighting killed 508 people (300 civilians, 132 soldiers and policemen, and 76 rebels) and wounded 2,520 (2,000 civilians, 400 soldiers and police officers, and 120 nationalists). Republicans fought with courage in a hopeless endeavor. Their enemy had superior forces and equipment. And Connolly's socialism proved naive: "Britannia's sons with their long-range guns" did not hesitate to bombard Dublin with fire and shell.

Because most of the Irish had relatives or friends fighting with the British in France, they were hostile to the Easter Week rebels as cowardly traitors. When Connolly, Pearse, and their comrades surrendered on April 29 and British soldiers herded them off to jail, Dubliners cursed, jeered, even spit on them. In denouncing the insurrection, Redmond described its participants as German dupes and reaffirmed Irish support for the war effort.

Considering the mood of Irish opinion, the government should have punished the rebels with prison, making them more pitiful than heroic. But after twenty months of slaughter on the western front, with hundreds of thousands of their young men dead or wounded and with no end in sight, the British were frustrated. They were in no mood to react to Easter Week in a calm and dispassionate manner. They wanted vengeance on Irish backstabbers. Therefore, the authorities decided not to imprison leaders of the Volunteers and citizen army as misguided fools. Instead, they turned them over to military courts for trial and punishment. Over a ten-day period, under the direction of General Sir John Maxwell, firing squads executed fifteen rebels, including Pearse, Connolly, and the other five signers of the Republican Proclamation. Although he was wounded in the post office, soldiers strapped Connolly into a chair and shot him. In addition to the executions, Brit-

ish soldiers angrily assaulted citizens in the Dublin streets. An officer murdered
F. Sheehy Skeffington, a prominent pacifist and champion of women's suffrage
with no connection to the uprising. And the authorities seized and transported
over 2,000 Sinn Féiners and Republicans, including Eoin MacNeill, many of them
completely innocent of revolutionary conspiracy, to British prisons, often without
trial. The British tried Casement for treason in England. During the proceedings,
the government released the contents of his diary, containing evidence that Casement was a promiscuous homosexual. This disclosure was designed to influence
opinion, particularly in the United States, against Easter Week Republicans. A
jury found Casement, who converted to Catholicism, guilty, and the government
executed him on August 3, 1916.

Considered in the historical context of Anglo-Irish relations, although understandable, the British reaction to an Irish insurrection while the United Kingdom
was involved in a war of survival on the continent was shortsighted. It offered
a lesson in barbarous vengeance rather than measured justice as the Irish public
reconsidered Easter Week. The "backstabbers," "dirty bowsers," and "hooligans"
became martyred heroes. People began to read and quote the poems of Pearse,
Plunkett, and MacDonagh, whose pictures, along with Connolly's, appeared in
Irish homes. British insensitivity translated blood sacrifice from poetry into reality.
As Yeats described it in his "Easter 1916" poem, "All changed, changed utterly:
a terrible beauty is born."

Shifting Irish opinion and appeals from leaders of the Irish party were factors in
a belated glimmer of reason in Britain's Irish policy. So were war considerations.
The army needed more Irish cannon fodder on the western front and help from
the United States to defeat Germany. Irish public reactions to the executions had a
negative effect on recruiting, and the Irish vote, offended by British responses to
Easter Week, was an important element in American politics, particularly with a
Democratic administration in office. Asquith assigned Lloyd George, soon to replace
him as prime minister, the task of pacifying Ireland. The "Welsh Wizard" offered
Redmond immediate Home Rule with the exclusion of six Ulster counties—Antrim,
Armagh, Derry, Down, Fermanagh, and Tyrone—until a permanent partition boundary could be determined after the war. The Irish leader was prepared to make this
major concession to the partition lobby until he discovered that Lloyd George had
promised Carson that the arrangement would be permanent.

When Lloyd George's duplicity combined with Ulster Unionist obstinacy to
wreck immediate Home Rule, the government attempted to appease Irish nationalist
opinion by releasing the internees. They returned to Ireland as heroes, especially
Eamon de Valera, the only Easter Week commandant not executed. Born in New
York, the son of an Irish mother and a Spanish-Cuban father, de Valera was raised
and educated in Ireland, became an ardent Gaelic Leaguer, taught mathematics
in a Dublin secondary school and in a teacher's training college, joined and then
left the IRB, and enlisted in the Volunteers. On Easter Monday he commanded
the Volunteer force in Boland's Flour Mill. For the duration of the insurrection

it successfully prevented British reinforcements landing at Bray from reaching Dublin. Some historians have said that de Valera's U.S. citizenship spared his life in 1916. But his survival owed more to the British realization that the executions were counterproductive than to his birth in the United States.

In 1917 the Volunteers took over Sinn Féin and used it as a political front to hamper British army recruiting and to defeat the Irish party. By the end of the war, Sinn Féiners had won six by-elections but refused to sit in the British Parliament. Changing Irish politics should have instructed the British that the Irish party no longer controlled nationalist opinion and that the next general election would present a completely new Irish situation.

After entering the war in April 1917, the United States advised the British that the enthusiasm of its contribution would be related to an improvement in Irish affairs. As prime minister, Lloyd George once more approached Redmond, offering immediate Home Rule with the permanent exclusion of the four Ulster Unionist counties plus Fermanagh and Tyrone. The Irish leader said no. The most he was prepared to concede was the 1914 compromise: temporary exclusion of Ulster counties that decided by plebiscite to remain outside the jurisdiction of a Dublin Parliament. And as in 1914, he insisted that the cities of Derry and Newry be treated separately from their counties. This offer was unsatisfactory to Carson, Craig, and the British Unionists in the coalition government. To relieve the stalemate, Redmond suggested to Lloyd George the convening of an Irish convention, including all interested parties—Home Rulers, Unionists, and Sinn Féiners—to work out mutually satisfactory terms for Irish self-government. The prime minister agreed to the suggestion and told Redmond to proceed.

The Irish Convention met in Dublin from July 1917 to April 1918. Sinn Féin refused an invitation to participate, and Ulster Unionists obstructed rather than contributed to conciliation. Accepting the inevitability of some sort of Home Rule, southern Unionists were more open-minded, asking only that Westminster continue supervising customs, excises, and defenses. Eager to cooperate, Redmond accepted those conditions. In so doing, he alienated a significant portion of the nationalist community, particularly Catholic bishops.

A month before the convention adjourned in failure, an exhausted and disillusioned Redmond died after what seemed a routine gallbladder operation. He did not have to witness the destruction of a party he had served so long and well. John Dillon replaced him as party chair, to face the impossible task of attempting to save Home Rule nationalism in the wake of Easter Week.

At the close of 1917, with Russia out of the war and German strength concentrated on the western front, Britain was unsure of how long it would take the United States to fully mobilize its manpower, and Lloyd George and his colleagues decided to draft Irishmen. When Parliament authorized conscription for Ireland in April 1918, Dillon led the Irish party out of the House of Commons and joined Sinn Féin, trade unionists, and the Catholic hierarchy in a united nationalist front against forced military service. It increased Republican respectability, speeded the rebuilding of the Volunteers, and goaded Britain into more coercion. On the flimsiest charges, including trumped-up accusations of collaborating with the Germans, officials deported and arrested some Sinn Féiners (including de Valera) and closed down a number of Republican newspapers. But when the war ended on November 11, 1918, the government still had not enforced conscription in Ireland.

The Anglo-Irish War

The post-Armistice general election in December 1918 gave a substantial parliamentary majority to Lloyd George's Unionist-dominated coalition government over Labour and Asquith Liberals. In Ireland, however, Sinn Féin won seventy-three seats to only six for the Irish party and twenty-six for the Unionists. Except for the two Trinity College seats, all of the Unionist victories were in Ulster. Only two Irish party candidates—Captain William Redmond, John's son, and Joseph Devlin from Belfast—won in direct contests with Sinn Féiners. In an East Mayo confrontation between the leaders of Home Rule and republicanism, de Valera defeated Dillon by an almost two-to-one margin. Sinn Féin success owed much to the pre-election Representation of the People Act, which extended the franchise to include all men over 21 and women over 30, expanding the number of Irish voters from 701,475 in 1910 to 1,936,673. Because the Irish party in contested constituencies actually increased its vote, it seems that previous voters and their wives stayed with Home Rule while younger people declared for Sinn Féin.

Victorious Sinn Féiners refused to enter the British Parliament. Instead, they assembled at the Mansion House in Dublin as Dáil Éireann, the legislative expression of the Irish Republic. It established arbitration courts (shades of O'Connell) as an alternative to British justice, an Industrial Disputes Board to mediate labor-management conflicts, and a Land Bank to provide land purchase loans. It also sent delegates to the Versailles Peace Conference to obtain international recognition of the Irish Republic. They made little impression on Anglophile Woodrow Wilson. Despite the piety of his Fourteen Points, he did not think Ireland met his requirements for national self-determination.

In February 1919 two members of the Sinn Féin executive committee, Michael Collins and Harry Boland, arranged de Valera's escape from Lincoln Gaol in England. On his return to Ireland, the Dáil elected him its president. In June de Valera left for the United States to solicit funds for and acceptance of the Irish Republic. Arthur Griffith, who in 1917 had relinquished the Sinn Féin presidency to de Valera, served as acting leader of the Dáil in his absence. Although de Valera managed to collect a considerable amount of money during his tour of the United States, he did not persuade Democratic or Republican politicians to add planks recognizing the Irish Republic to their 1920 national convention platforms. And he had personality clashes with such strong Clan na Gael leaders as John Devoy and Judge Daniel Cohalan. Many clan members were more interested in preserving Irish power in American politics than in liberating Ireland. Devoy and Cohalan thought de Valera too conciliatory toward British interests. They resented his willingness to have Ireland assume a subordinate geographic sphere-of-interest position to Britain, similar to the one Cuba had with the United States.

While de Valera was having American problems, Collins emerged as the strongman of the Sinn Féin executive committee. He was minister of finance, but his real power came from his role as leader of the IRB and adjutant general and Volunteer director of organization. Collins resisted Dáil control of the IRB, which he kept independent of the Volunteers. Cathal Brugha, minister of defense and Volunteer chief of staff, resented the existence of a secret army free from Dáil supervision. No doubt jealously played a role in the frequent clashes between the two. Collins's handsomeness and dashing personality, his brilliant intelligence network and operations, and his daring evasions of capture made him the Scarlet Pimpernel of Irish republicanism. His glamour overshadowed Brugha's solid but less colorful contributions.

The connection of the Dáil with the Volunteers and the IRB became more critical in January 1919 when Sinn Féin's passive resistance to British authority evolved into a guerrilla war of liberation. Dressed as civilians, members of the Irish Republican Army (IRA), the new name for the Volunteers, ambushed military lorries, captured arms, assassinated suspected spies and informers, and shot soldiers and policemen. They concentrated their efforts on the paramilitary Royal Irish Constabulary (RIC), destroying barracks, seizing weapons, and killing constables. Even before the Anglo-Irish war began, events in Ireland demoralized and depleted the RIC. The IRA completed its destruction. Many constables resigned out of either fear or reluctance to fight against their own flesh and blood. The RIC collapse turned over large sections of the country to the IRA. Although Lloyd George and other British government ministers described IRA tactics as murder, a guerrilla approach was the only practical strategy for a small nation at war with a great power.

Britain met terrorism with counterterrorism, recruiting ex–World War I servicemen, often sadists or psychologically scarred combat veterans bored with civilian life, to reinforce the diminishing RIC. Their uniforms of dark green caps and khaki pants gave them the name Black and Tans. Later the government enlisted ex-army officers as RIC auxiliaries. Tans and auxiliaries often tortured and sometimes murdered IRA prisoners, and they looted and burned towns, demolishing a section of Cork. But compared to some later armies of occupation, including the U.S. Army in Vietnam and Iraq, British atrocities were relatively restricted. Even the Tans were reluctant to molest women.

In responding to Irish republicanism, the British were confounded by their own World War I propaganda on rights and self-determination for small countries. As coauthors of the peace treaties, they had dismembered the German, Austro-Hungarian, and Turkish empires. This resulted in a plethora of Arab and Slavic states. During the Anglo-Irish conflict, world opinion began to ask whether the British empire was any more sacred than those it had defeated. Were the Irish, the people of the literary renaissance and the leaders of Catholic America, less deserving of independence than Arabs, Czechs, Slovaks, Croats, Serbs, or Poles?

Since Britain refused to accept the Sinn Féin election victory as a mandate for an Irish Republic, its leaders insisted that they were engaged not in a war but in a police action to suppress illegal terror and to restore law and order. This distinction restricted the amount of force they could apply in Ireland. They were trying to contain rather than annihilate Republicans, hoping to coerce them into negotiations that would lead to a settlement short of an Irish Republic.

If the IRA was a courageous and troublesome foe, British and world opinion was an even more difficult challenge for the British government. Irish propaganda was more persuasive than the British variety was. It successfully exploited postwar anti-imperialism. Influential voices from all over the world regarded Ireland as a gallant little nation standing up to a bully. Black and Tan and auxiliary tactics damaged Britain's reputation as a civilized power, even shocking large and important sections of British opinion. During the early stages of the Anglo-Irish war, most Britons were indifferent to events in Ireland. But Irish propagandists and British journalists turned apathy into concern. Labour, Liberal, even a few Conservative MPs; Anglican, Catholic, and Nonconformist clergymen; journalists; trade unionists; businessmen; university professors; distinguished literati; and some members of the aristocracy criticized government Irish policy. Many joined the Peace with Ireland Council, demanding an end to British barbarism and accommodation with Irish nationalism. Council members argued that while concessions to the Irish might weaken the fabric of the empire and the Commonwealth, the risk was preferable to the erosion of Britain's image throughout the civilized world. In addition to mounting British criticism of the government's approach to Ireland, Commonwealth leaders pressured Lloyd George to come to terms with Irish nationalism.

End of a War, Start of a Nation

"We are all Home Rulers today," said the *Times* in March 1919. Unfortunately, British politicians and their constituents failed to realize that the 1914 failure to award the Irish party its properly earned constitutional victory and Easter Week and its aftermath had escalated the demand of Irish nationalism beyond Home Rule. But in 1920 Lloyd George returned to it as his solution to the Irish crisis. Parliament passed a bill creating Home Rule parliaments for the six Ulster counties of Antrim, Armagh, Derry, Down, Fermanagh, and Tyrone and for the other twenty-six. It also included a Council of Ireland to administer mutual services between north and south and to function as a bridge of reconciliation and eventual unity between them. The bill retained Nationalist and Unionist MPs at Westminster.

Although Ulster Unionists had rejected Home Rule for all of Ireland, they seized it for themselves as an opportunity to create "a Protestant nation for a Protestant people." In the south, Sinn Féin took advantage of the elections for a Dublin Parliament to demonstrate to Britain and the world that Irish opinion remained

Republican. So the Anglo-Irish war continued with its ambushes, assassinations, burnings, lootings, torture, night raids, curfews, and general atmosphere of violence and terror. Republicans added another weapon to focus attention on their determination when Terence MacSwiney, lord mayor of Cork, died in October 1920 of a hunger strike in Brixton Prison. The anti-British chorus of world opinion swelled to the point that Lloyd George was forced to negotiate with Sinn Féin. On July 11, 1922, a state of truce, preliminary to negotiations, began between Britain and Irish Republicans. In the thirty months of the Anglo-Irish war, the IRA had killed 230 soldiers and policemen and wounded 369; British military and police forces had killed 752 and wounded 866 members of the IRA. Republicans may have suffered the most casualties, but they won the propaganda war that brought their enemy to the settlement table.

During July talks in London and in subsequent correspondence, Lloyd George offered de Valera dominion status with the following reservations: Irish nationalists would have to accept partition, maintain free trade with Britain, contribute to the British war debt, limit the size of their army in conformity with the British military establishment, permit the continued existence of British air and naval bases in their country, and allow the British armed forces to recruit in Ireland. Although the prime minister warned that if Republicans rejected his offer they could expect all-out war, de Valera said no. He did, however, indicate that he was not a doctrinaire Republican and said that he would submit the British proposal for Dáil discussion.

The Dáil agreed with de Valera that dominion status was inadequate, but Lloyd George kept communications open. He scheduled, and de Valera agreed to, an October treaty conference in London. In a still puzzling and controversial decision, de Valera decided not to attend. Did he think a republic was impossible to achieve? Did he send others who would have to take the blame for failure? There are other possible explanations. Perhaps he thought that since he and Lloyd George were at loggerheads, other Republicans would be more persuasive. Or did he believe that he would be more effective in Dublin than in London? There he could restrain hotheaded, no-compromise Republicans, and he could control the tempo of the London negotiations. Because the Irish envoys would have to refer all offers back to Dublin for discussion and advisement, they would be less likely to cave in to the pressure of operating in enemy territory. Whatever his reasons, de Valera stayed home while Collins, Griffith, George Gavan Duffy, Eamon Duggan, and Robert Barton went to London. Barton's cousin, English-born Robert Erskine Childers, accompanied the delegation as its secretary. Author of the classic spy-adventure novel *The Riddle of the Sands,* Childers and his American wife, Molly Osgood, had in July 1914 smuggled guns into Howth on their yacht, the *Asgard.* In World War I he served in the British navy and earned the Distinguished Service Cross. During the Anglo-Irish war, Childers was a member of the Dáil and minister for propaganda. As a dedicated Republican, he served as de Valera's London watchdog. The Irish envoys arrived for discussions with vague instructions. As plenipotentiaries, they had the authority to negotiate and conclude a treaty with Britain, but at the same time they carried orders not to sign anything without first consulting the Dáil cabinet.

In London, unsophisticated Sinn Féiners negotiated with tough and tested politicians skilled in all the nuances of pressure diplomacy: Lloyd George, Austen Chamberlain, Lord Birkenhead, and Winston Churchill. And they were caught in the middle between British party politics and Republican fanaticism in Ireland. Lloyd George's coalition government was dominated by anti-Irish Unionists. They would not tolerate too generous an offer to Sinn Féin.

The prime minister resubmitted his proposal for conditional dominion status. If they had accepted it without partition, Collins, Griffith, and their colleagues would have had him in a quandary. Instead of concentrating on the divided-Ireland issue, they made a serious tactical blunder by focusing on their abstract, almost metaphysical objection to taking an oath of allegiance to the British crown. Coalition Conservatives were loyal to Northern Ireland Unionists, but British public opinion would not have tolerated a resumption of the war with Ireland over partition. By contrast, Britons were as passionately devoted to the symbols of monarchy and empire as Sinn Féin was to the tokens of republicanism. They insisted that Ireland remain in association with Britain through mutual allegiance to the crown.

When the British insisted on the oath of allegiance, the Irish suggested an alternative arrangement, external association. This plan, conceived by de Valera, proposed that the Irish Republic recognize the crown as head of an association of states comprising the British Commonwealth. After the conclusion of World War II Britain accepted external association in the Commonwealth for the republics of India and Pakistan, but in 1921 such a concept was too *avant-garde* for Lloyd George and company. But instead of a flat no to de Valera, they offered an oath of allegiance that would place primary loyalty to Ireland rather than the crown.

Frustrated by stalemated negotiations, Lloyd George tried a two-pronged blitz on the weary Irish delegation. He split the Northern Ireland and oath of allegiance issues, concentrating first on partition, where his position was the weakest. He told Irish envoys that he could not persuade Ulster Anglicans and Presbyterians or British Conservatives in the coalition to accept a united Ireland and that any effort to do so would return Anglo-Irish relations to where they were in 1912. Lloyd George then got Griffith to agree to a post-treaty Boundary Commission to redefine the border between the two Irelands on the basis of residential preferences. He suggested that the Boundary Commission would shrink Northern Ireland to a small enclave around Belfast, and he predicted that its geographic and economic nonviability and heavy British taxes would lead to a united Ireland.

After evading the shoals of partition, Lloyd George returned to the dominion offer. In early December 1921 the Irish envoys presented it to the Dáil. Led by Cathal Brugha and Austin Stack, Republican extremists rejected the modified oath of allegiance to the crown. De Valera told the envoys to return to London and negotiate a treaty on the principle of external association. They did so, but Lloyd George bluntly told them to either accept dominion status or prepare for war against the might of the British empire. Griffith found the British offer compatible with his original dual-monarchy Sinn Féin program. Collins knew that just before the truce, the IRA had reached the point of exhaustion and that the cessation of hostilities had further eroded the Irish will to return to the inconvenience and hardship of war. Since he believed that Ireland could not resist unrestricted British military power and was convinced that dominion status, even with its reservations, was a major British concession and a firm foundation on which to build complete Irish sovereignty, Collins joined Griffith in accepting Lloyd George's terms. They persuaded their colleagues, except Childers, to join them. With little enthusiasm and many doubts, on December 6, 1921, the Irish envoys signed the treaty establishing a twenty-six-county Irish Free State as a dominion within the British Commonwealth.

In early January 1922 the Dáil debated the treaty in the Senate chamber of University College, Dublin. In leading the opposition, de Valera insisted that it betrayed the republic and perpetuated British colonialism in Ireland. Collins replied that the Free State was a considerable improvement on Home Rule. He said that the Irish people could expand on dominion status; it was a beginning, not an end. After a long and increasingly bitter verbal battle that barely touched on partition, the Dáil ratified the treaty, 64 to 57. A defeated de Valera resigned as president of the Dáil. The pro-treaty majority elected Griffith as his successor. Within a few weeks, British officials began to relinquish the instruments of government and to depart from their oldest colony, a country that they had occupied for almost 800 years.

From the distance of time and influenced by the contemporary situation in Northern Ireland, some historians have argued that Easter Week and the Anglo-Irish war have not justified the human sacrifice involved. Revisionists argue that if they had never happened, a post–World War I British government would have put a Home Rule Ireland into operation and that it could have evolved into a dominion, even a republic. They say that even though revolutionary nationalism provided a shortcut to national sovereignty, it left the country divided and established and sanctified the cult of the gunman that has afflicted constitutional government in Ireland ever since. But in all fairness to the Sinn Féin envoys in London, it must be remembered that the treaty only confirmed the psychological, cultural, religious, and physical reality of two Irelands. In light of the Anglican and Nonconformist sectarianism and British loyalism of Ulster unionism and the Catholic roots and the post-1880 Gaelic emphasis and pretensions in Irish nationalism, a divided Ireland was close to inevitable. However, the revisionists are probably right when they maintain that the post–World War I attitudes of British opinion and the changing natures of the empire and Commonwealth promised Home Rule for Ireland and its development into something more for most of the country.

Revisionist conjectures ignore the importance of myth and legend in the making of a nation. Like the American Revolution, the Irish versions provided heroes and examples of sacrifice and courage that helped sustain and inspire a people in times of difficulty. Because patriots died for independence, it became more precious to Irish citizens. Despite the ifs and might-have-beens of revisionism, Easter Week, the Anglo-Irish war, and the treaty creating the Free State altered Irish, British, and, to a certain extent, world history. As the first victim of imperialism and colonialism to wage a successful twentieth-century war of liberation, Ireland inspired similar efforts in other places. And post-treaty Ireland continued to be a relevant experiment in national development. Britain and the world watched to see if the Irish had the patience, fortitude, and skills to convert nationalist ideology and tradition into a stable economic, social, and political community.

Part II

From Free State to Republic

Thomas E. Hachey

9

The Irish Free State, 1922–1932

A Reluctant Dominion

Establishing the New State

In the debate over the treaty that would create the new Irish Free State, the Sinn Féin assembly probably confirmed the view of those in Britain who had always believed that the Irish were unsuited for self-government. Men and women who had endured months and years of adversity together while fighting the common foe of English rule were seen shouting abuse at one another during the so-called treaty debate in the Dáil. Ultimately, the treaty was ratified by the narrow margin of 64 to 57, and that divisive schism within the Irish nationalist movement actually foreshadowed what were to become permanent political alignments. The divisions that separated the treaty party (Cumann na nGaedhael from 1923 to 1933 and Fine Gael thereafter) from the anti-treaty party (which retained the name Sinn Féin until 1926, when de Valera founded Fianna Fáil) were not temporary disagreements. Their differences have endured to the present day.

Eamon de Valera resigned the presidency of the Dáil on January 9, 1922, and the following day Arthur Griffith was elected in his place and nominated a new cabinet. Doctrinaire Republicans promptly joined de Valera, who then permanently withdrew from the Dáil, leaving that assembly to its slim majority of troubled survivors. The anti-treaty people, now in political exile, continued to insist that an Irish Republic had been declared in 1916, that it had been ratified in 1919, and that every member of the Dáil had sworn allegiance to it in 1921. The republic was inviolable, went the argument, and not only was it treason to attempt to disestablish it, but it was also beyond the competence of anyone—even a majority in the Dáil—to do so.

These were not the best of times in which to launch the first attempt at Irish self-government in nearly 800 years. Military barracks and arms depots were being quickly taken over by local IRA forces as soon as the British evacuated them, but whether those forces were in fact loyal to the supporters of the Free State or to the fancied republic was anyone's guess. The IRA had never given more than nominal allegiance to the Dáil, and it had often acted in defiance of its own leadership. What direction the army might take seemed uncertain, but the danger that it posed to democratic governance was without question. The IRA was now better armed than ever before, and many young recruits had taken their place at the side of veteran gunmen, now local folk heroes, whose ill-disguised impatience with any government authority did not bode well. It was fortunate for Michael Collins that the secret Irish Republican Brotherhood, which pervaded a large part of the IRA, was still very much under his control. This gave Collins the loyal organizational network he needed to rally support for the Free State within the IRA, and it provided, even for Collins, the justification for believing that the establishment of the Free State was but a temporary and transitional step toward the ultimate goal of a republic. This reasoning helped Collins and his senior military officer, Richard Mulcahy, to win over about half the IRA in support of the treaty. These men were then armed, given uniforms, and organized into what became the Free State Army. The uneasy relations between the new army and the anti-treaty forces, who often occupied different premises in the same towns throughout the countryside, were further complicated by the fact that so many men on both sides had been close comrades a short time earlier.

One of the more persistent myths about this period in Irish history has been the widely accepted belief that Eamon de Valera was to blame for the civil war that began in 1922. But the responsibility was not his. Perhaps his anti-treaty attitude did help to provide a focus for the opponents of the Free State, but anti-treaty members within the IRA looked to their military leaders, to men like Liam Lynch, Ernie O'Malley, and Sean Moylan, rather than to de Valera. If anything, de Valera spent considerable energy attempting to negotiate a political compromise with the new leaders of Dáil Éireann, even though he did warn that he would do everything in his power "to see [that] this established Republic is not disestablished."

In April 1922 a group of anti-treaty officers occupied the Four Courts, a government building in the heart of Dublin. It was located just a few hundred yards down the road from where Irish blood had first been spilled by British guns at Bachelor's Walk on the eve of World War I. This time, however, both the rebels and the authorities were Irish. Collins tried for two months to negotiate a peaceful withdrawal from the Four Courts. Then, on June 22, Field Marshall Sir Henry Wilson was assassinated on his own doorstep in London by men who were apprehended and identified as members of the IRA. A furious Prime Minister Lloyd George wrote Michael Collins demanding action against the Four Courts occupants whom the British believed were responsible. The irony is that the assassins not only had no orders from the anti-treaty IRA leadership, but they may quite possibly have been acting on a still-unrescinded order that Collins himself had issued while the Anglo-Irish war was in progress.

Contributing to the sense of urgency in this situation was the fact that the time was fast approaching when a general election would have to be held. Under the provisions of the treaty, a new parliament was to be elected for the purpose of hammering out a constitution for the Irish Free State. The treaty required at minimum the ratification of a document that specifically acknowledged dominion status, and it mandated that this be done before the end of 1922. As tensions heightened,

Lloyd George recalled home General Sir Neville Macready and instructed him to prepare for an assault on the Four Courts. Neither Macready nor Lloyd George really preferred that course of action, however, as they feared it might have the effect of uniting the pro-treaty and anti-treaty groups in Ireland against their old nemesis, the British. Meanwhile, the deputy chief of staff of the pro-treaty army was kidnapped by men from the Four Courts garrison. Just what their objective was is unclear, but the immediate consequence was a challenge that Collins could not afford to ignore. He decided that the insurgents, headed by Rory O'Connor, would have to be flushed from their quarters, and he accepted the loan of British military artillery, repeatedly offered earlier by Colonial Secretary Winston Churchill, to complete the task.

The attack on the Four Courts went on for two days until the flames so consumed the building that the garrison was compelled to surrender. Many regard this event as the beginning of the civil war, but in truth the country had been drifting in that direction for several months. What it did do, of course, was polarize the conflict, whereupon the political opponents of the treaty promptly joined the military types in an atmosphere of increasing violence. Many of the leading figures in the old Sinn Féin republic, such as Cathal Brugha, Austen Stack, Countess Markievicz, and Eamon de Valera, quickly volunteered for service in the anti-treaty army, now popularly known as the Irregulars. At the outset of hostilities, there were a few battles in central Dublin that the Free State forces won without much difficulty, but the conflict soon gave way to guerrilla warfare in the hills and bogs. During the ten-month-long civil war that followed, the Free State army drove the Irregulars from one strong point after another without ever being able to render the knockout blow. As is often true of civil wars, the most enduring cost of the hostilities for the country was in the enmities that were produced and then perpetuated by the tactics employed by both sides. No fewer than seventy-seven captured Irregulars were put to death during the struggle as evidence of the Free State's determination to reestablish its authority.

Although the provisional government eventually "won" the civil war, at least in the sense that the Irregulars were compelled to cease and desist in their armed resistance after May 1923, the peace was obtained at an incredibly heavy price. More than 600 people lost their lives, and 3,000 others were wounded. The cost for the Dublin government in putting down the rebellion was almost 20 million pounds, money that might have been put to productive use in restoring Irish agriculture, industry, and social services. Moreover, the violence had taken a heavy toll on Irish leadership. On August 12, 1922, Arthur Griffith, president of the provisional Free State government, worn out by the tension and fatigue from which he had been suffering since the treaty negotiations, died of a cerebral hemorrhage at the age of fifty. Ten days later, Michael Collins, commander in chief of the Free State army, was killed in an ambush while on an inspection tour of his military postings in West Cork. He was struck down by a ricochet in a gun battle at Béal na mBláth, a spot within walking distance of his birthplace, only two months before his thirty-second birthday. Thus in less than a fortnight the Free State had lost its chief architects and principal signatories to the Anglo-Irish Treaty.

Despite these setbacks, the Dublin government continued its relentless campaign against the Irregulars. William Cosgrave succeeded Griffith as president, and he, together with Kevin O'Higgins, the minister of home affairs, and Richard Mulcahy, minister of defense, attempted to fill the leadership vacuum created by the death of Collins. A different temper now guided the Dublin government. While Collins had been inclined to view the civil war as a tragic conflict between former comrades, Cosgrave and O'Higgins perceived it as a clash between civil law and anarchy. In October, special emergency powers were given to the army for the purpose of conducting military courts and imposing the death penalty for a wide range of offenses, including the unauthorized possession of arms. By the end of 1922 no fewer than 12,000 people had been interned. Meanwhile, Erskine Childers, Rory O'Connor, Liam Mellows, and other heroes of the Irish War for Independence, now Irregulars and prisoners of war, were executed by Irish government authorities. The new state would show no mercy to those who continued to threaten its existence.

On December 6, 1922 (the first anniversary of the treaty), the provisional government was dissolved and the Irish Free State formally came into being. A few months earlier, de Valera had been elected by Irregular political sympathizers as president of the true Irish Republic, and it was expected that he would lead a government in exile. But the Irregular fighting forces ignored de Valera's attempts to negotiate an armistice and followed instead their uncompromising combat leader, Liam Lynch. When Lynch was killed in action on April 10, however, de Valera persuaded the fallen commandant's more amenable successor, Frank Aiken, to terminate hostilities. De Valera then tried to secure a ceasefire with Dublin on favorable terms, but when the government refused to consider any of his proposals, he issued this proclamation to his followers on May 24:

> Soldiers of the Republic, Legion of the Rearguard: The Republic can no longer be defended successfully by your arms. Further sacrifice of life would now be vain and continuance of the struggle in arms unwise in the national interest and prejudicial to the future of our cause. Military victory must be allowed to rest for the moment with those who have destroyed the Republic.

What is perhaps most remarkable about this sudden cessation of hostilities, after ten months of vicious attacks and reprisals, is that it was not accompanied by any joint negotiations or formal exchanges between the combatants. There were no peace talks, no agreed terms, and no surrender. The Republican Irregulars simply stopped fighting, hid their arms, and went "on the run" as fugitives from justice. There was no declared amnesty, nor was there any surrender of principle. The republic may have suffered a reversal, but in the eyes of its supporters, it was still the only legitimate form of government for the Irish people. And it was precisely this legacy of dissent and animosity that would prove most difficult of all for the

Free State government to eradicate. The bitterness caused by the civil war had pitted family against family and had left indelible scars on the new state.

There was no spirit of triumph, no glee over having vanquished the enemy among the Free State ministers who now sought to bring back an atmosphere of normalcy within the country. The provisional government, which had taken over from the British, was in a precarious enough economic situation before the outbreak of civil war. Conditions thereafter were considerably worse. Thousands of acres of land were lying uncultivated, and unemployment and poverty were widespread. The systematic destruction of vital links in the railway system by the Irregulars, for example, was but one of the factors that made economic recovery immeasurably more difficult than it might otherwise have been in the absence of an internecine struggle. Indeed, the promise of great achievement, which had inspired so many Irish nationalists in the 1919–1921 Irish War for Independence, now gave way to intense frustration and demoralizing cynicism.

Aside from the legacy of hatred and bitterness the civil war also had an immutable impact on the configuration of Irish party politics, which is unique to that country and bears no resemblance to the right/left, conservative/socialist divide so characteristic of British and European politics throughout this century. Indeed, for more than a generation the civil war would contribute to the unnatural polarization around the treaty issue, with the resulting consequence that social and economic considerations suffered from inattention and neglect. And within that divisive and enduring dialogue over the treaty, Free Staters might be seen as reasonable men pragmatically attempting to create a viable political community while, by contrast, Republicans might appear as simple-minded fanatics without regard for political necessity or reality.

There were, however, treaty opponents who embraced republicanism in response to what they perceived as the betrayal by the Free State government of the sacred policies embraced in the democratic program that had been unanimously ratified in 1919 by the first Dáil. That document, which among other things, had declared that "all rights to private property must be subordinated to the public right and welfare," had been a hastily contrived expedient by Sinn Féin nationalists to win the favor and support of the tiny Labour and Socialist followings. Most of the nationalist leadership espoused more bourgeois interests and, not surprisingly, this came as a profound disappointment to those on the political left in 1923. For these true believers in a new social order for Ireland, the Free State represented a counterrevolutionary cabal that had deserted the people in exchange for the support of the Catholic, clerical, landowner, shopkeeper, and Protestant Unionist classes. There could be no reconciliation with people who were so antithetical to the vision of men like James Connolly, and the socialists remained a minority within a minority as they joined the Republicans in political exile. But it would be more than a generation later before this left wing of the advanced nationalist movement would come to the fore.

Perhaps the most compelling problem to confront the new state was not any of these internal ideological issues, however, but rather that of the Northern Ireland question. The subject of partition had been totally eclipsed by the dominion versus republic arguments during the Dáil debate on the treaty, but during the civil war the Republicans succeeded in making the division of Ireland a political controversy once again. What seemed to give the dispute a special sense of urgency was the overt Protestant oppression of Catholic nationalists in Northern Ireland. Indeed, the campaign of Protestant violence in that region would extend, intermittently, until 1935, during which time hundreds would be killed and thousands more wounded, almost all of them Catholic. For the unrepentant Republicans, who had just lost the civil war, the pogroms in the north were indisputable evidence of Britain's continuing imperialism in Ireland, as well as dramatic proof of the unfinished business of Irish nationalism.

During the treaty negotiations, it will be recalled, British Prime Minister Lloyd George had persuaded the Irish delegation to accept what he characterized as the necessary but temporary exclusion of the six Ulster counties from the new dominion. He promised that if the north refused to form part of a united Ireland, a Boundary Commission would be created to determine the frontiers between the two regions. Therefore, although Article 12 of the treaty contained a proviso permitting Northern Ireland to opt out of the anticipated union, Lloyd George led both Griffith and Collins to expect that the Boundary Commission appointed by the London government would so drastically reduce the size of the Ulster region as to make it economically unfeasible to remain apart. At least that was the tacit, if unwritten, understanding in 1921. Who could tell, then, that by the end of the next year, both Griffith and Collins would be dead and Lloyd George would be displaced as Britain's prime minister?

Northern Ireland exercised its right under Article 12 and, on December 7, 1922, opted out of a united Ireland. William Cosgrave, the new head of government in the Free State, was just then preoccupied with the problem of consolidating his government in the twenty-six counties and with suppressing the civil war insurgency. Meanwhile, the new British Conservative prime minister, Andrew Bonar Law, was forced to resign within the year due to ill health. He was succeeded by Stanley Baldwin, a man who keenly distrusted Lloyd George and who could be expected to find suspect any agreement that the latter might have entered into. And Baldwin himself was out of office for a time in 1923, when Ramsay MacDonald assumed the premiership of a short-lived Labour government. Baldwin returned to power in 1924, but it is hardly surprising, given the political instability in England during the early 1920s, that scant attention was paid to the Northern Ireland question for several years.

Indeed, it was not until October 1924 that Cosgrave and Baldwin got around to establishing the repeatedly postponed Boundary Commission under the neutral chairmanship of Justice Richard Feetham of the South African Supreme Court. J.R. Fisher, a prominent Northern Unionist, was nominated by the British government to represent Northern Ireland, and Eoin MacNeill, the Free State minister of education who hailed from a Catholic family in Ulster's County Antrim, was selected to be Dublin's representative. For most of 1925 the commission met with individuals and groups on both sides of the border, and took testimony and collected evidence without ever indicating what action was in fact contemplated. Then, in early November 1925, the *Morning Post,* a British newspaper, leaked a story that caused an instant sensation and led to Eoin MacNeill's resignation from the commission. According to the *Morning Post,* a ruling was imminent that would leave the frontier much as before except that an important section of County Donegal, in the Free State, would be given over to Northern Ireland.

No one doubted the integrity of Eoin MacNeill, or the loyalty of that celebrated patriot, but even he could scarcely escape the wrath of his indignant colleagues in the Dáil. And it was before that assembly that MacNeill stood and explained how he had foolishly agreed in principle to a joint report of the commission before knowing what it was going to contain. He did so, he said, in the mistaken belief that Judge Feetham shared his interpretation of Article 12, and he resigned when he found out otherwise, since he could not possibly subscribe to the report about to be issued.

MacNeill's resignation from the commission did not preclude his two fellow members of that body from publishing their findings, and that possibility caused great consternation and anxiety throughout the Free State government—for good reason. The publication of the Boundary Commission report would, according to the Judicial Committee of the Privy Council, give it the force of law. Eoin MacNeill resigned in disgrace from the Executive Council, and for a time it seemed possible that the entire Cosgrave government would fall.

It was in this atmosphere of crisis, then, that an Irish delegation traveled on November 28 to London, where it met with both British and Northern Ireland representatives. The price that the Irish had to pay to prevent the promulgation of the commission's report was adherence to a tripartite agreement signed in London on December 3, 1925. Under its terms, the Free State accepted the existing frontier of Northern Ireland and in return, Britain absolved both the Dublin and Belfast governments of their obligations to the British debt. Moreover, the Council of Ireland, which had been established under the provisions of the 1920 Government of Ireland Act as a conduit through which to promote Irish unity, was eliminated. The abolition of the council was no real tragedy, since it had never functioned anyway, and the expressed intent of the tripartite agreement, calling for direct negotiations between the two Irelands over matters of mutual concern, was doubtless a more rational structure for any future negotiations between north and south. Yet the distrust and suspicion with which each community viewed the other made the prospects for constructive dialogue extremely remote.

What the Boundary Commission scandal did, despite the fact that the report itself was suppressed until 1969, was to heighten anxieties that were already intense within the Free State owing to a crisis within the army at about the same time. In March 1924 the government decided to reduce the size of the Free State army, which had expanded to 60,000 men because of the civil war situation. The demobilization was to involve almost 2,000 officers and over 35,000 men. That order was keenly resented by many veteran soldiers who had fought in defense of the treaty more out of loyalty to the memory of Michael Collins and to his vision of an eventual republic than to any Free State leader or principle. To be sure, a number of these old IRA members knew no trade other than soldiering, and they were neither favorably disposed nor well equipped to assume civilian jobs. The response from some of these malcontents was an ultimatum, dated March 6, 1924, signed by two officers, Liam Tobin and C.F. Dalton, that was dispatched to the government.

Even in the chaotic days of post-revolutionary Ireland, this was a startling development. The ultimatum demanded (1) an immediate end to demobilization; (2) the removal of the army's internal controlling body, namely the Army Council; and (3) some guarantee of the government's intention to achieve an Irish Republic. The Free State government responded quickly, arresting all of the document's signatories and appointing General Eoin O'Duffy, the commissioner of the civic guards (the police), as commandant of the army. Kevin O'Higgins, who assumed full responsibility for the government during the incapacitating illness of President Cosgrave at this time, sought to minimize the damage to the state with an approach that reflected firmness and impartiality. He promised an inquiry into army administration and assured that a number of deserting officers who had refused to return to their posts, following the government's initial sanctions, would be judged to have simply "retired" from the army. Last, O'Higgins promised to ensure the implementation of an army service pension scheme.

The so-called army mutiny was short-lived, but the threat it represented to the life of the young state cannot be overestimated. Kevin O'Higgins and his Executive Council colleagues redressed what they felt to be genuine grievances, but they insisted on the resignation of three senior officers and were about to make the same demand of General Richard Mulcahy, the minister of defense, who was also implicated, when he resigned of his own accord. The question of who possessed ultimate control in the state, the civil authorities or the army, was decisively resolved. As O'Higgins himself remarked, "Those who take the pay and wear the uniform of the state, be they soldiers or police, must be non-political servants of the state."

Despite the civil war of 1922–1923, and the army mutiny and Boundary Commission crises of 1924–1925, the Free State had survived—but it was still endangered. In March 1926 the government concluded with Britain the so-called ultimate financial agreement, which became the occasion of yet another political emergency for the Cosgrave government. The sense of that agreement had been confirmed by the Irish Free State as early as 1923, when it committed Dublin to pay the British government the land annuities that were owed due to the land legislation of the late nineteenth and early twentieth centuries. In addition, the Free State acknowledged responsibility for the payment of certain Royal Irish Constabulary pensions. The total cost of these twin obligations was approximately 5 million pounds a year. Even in the best of times the agreement would have been controversial, all the more so because it had not been submitted for parliamentary approval. Cosgrave may have felt that he had no choice but to honor his government's earlier pledge, but his political enemies were quick to exploit the dissatisfaction that most people felt over this pact with the British.

That same month, the Sinn Féin party organization met to discuss a new departure in basic strategy. Ever since 1922 the anti-treaty Republicans, calling themselves the Sinn Féin party, had boycotted participation in the Dáil because of the oath to the crown that members were obliged to take upon admission to that assembly. Party leader Eamon de Valera, however, declared his readiness to discuss joining the Dáil now that a full convention of the IRA, on November 25, had formally withdrawn its allegiance to him as president of that still-revered abstraction, the Irish Republic. To IRA militants, the Sinn Féin leader had not been vigorous enough in advancing the day when partition might be ended by force. De Valera's response was to urge Sinn Féin, at its March meeting, to enter the Dáil in parliamentary opposition to the hated Cumann na nGaedhael (Community of Irishmen) party then in power. The motion generated a furious debate in which Sinn Féin purists made it abundantly clear that many within the party were still opposed to legitimizing the "usurper" legislature through association with true Republicans like themselves. Thus repudiated by Sinn Féin, as he had been previously by the IRA, de Valera broke with his old comrades and launched a new party only two months later, which he named Fianna Fáil ("warriors of Fál," the term *Fál* being a poetic symbol for Ireland). Most of de Valera's more moderate Sinn Féin associates joined him, as did other admirers from outside that party. It was an auspicious turn of events.

Republicanism was scarcely dead in Ireland. Despite their recent military defeat and their subsequent suppression by the law, Republicans had made an impressive showing at the time of the first general election under the new Irish Free State constitution in August 1923. Cumann na nGaedhael won 63 of the 153 seats in the Dáil, but the Sinn Féin Republicans secured 44 seats and over 27 percent of the popular vote. Yet de Valera and his colleagues steadfastly refused to enter a Dáil that they had repudiated. Fianna Fáil, therefore, expressed a new willingness to participate in democratic opposition, but the question of the oath remained an obstacle. Whether or not it could be overcome was a question that would not take long to resolve. The next general election was due to be held in 1927.

The timing of the electoral contest did not favor Cosgrave's government. Not only had it just concluded the highly unpopular financial agreement with Britain, but the government had also introduced a new public safety act in its uncompromising quest to impose law and order on a still-turbulent society. The act provided for powers of detention and suspension of habeas corpus in response to the successive IRA attacks against police barracks in late 1926. And almost as if to add insult to injury, the government alienated a diverse and vocal constituency with the Intoxicating Liquor Act, the purpose of which was to reduce the number of licensed pubs and to limit the hours during which they could operate.

Fianna Fáil, of course, sought to fan the flames of discontent. The new party accused its opponents of being pro-British and attacked what were said to be the government's ruinous economic policies. If elected to power, Fianna Fáil promised to remove the oath, dismantle the treaty, withhold the land annuities, protect the small farmer, foster manufacturing industries, and extend social services.

As it happened, the real winners of the June 1927 campaign were a multiplicity of small parties. Cumann na nGaedhael dropped from the 63 seats it had won in 1923 to 47, while Fianna Fáil's 44 seats represented no gain over the Sinn Féin position in 1923. But Labour took 22 seats; Farmers 11; National League 8; Sinn Féin 5; and Independent Republicans 2. In addition to these parties, which suggested that the proportional representation system of election was destined to fragment political alignments in Ireland, 14 independent deputies were elected.

For the first time it was possible for Fianna Fáil to seize control of the government, assuming that it acted in coalition with a few of the minor parties. Given the charged emotions on all sides, it is difficult to say whether there could have been a peaceful transfer of power, with the preservation of democratic government, at that moment in 1927. A crisis was averted, however, when de Valera and his followers were denied admission to the Dáil after they refused to take the obligatory oath. Without Fianna Fáil to contend with, Cosgrave again formed a government with support from farmers and independents. Any hope that political tranquility might follow after Cosgrave had been given a new lease in office was quickly dashed two weeks later, on July 10, with the assassination of Kevin O'Higgins.

Perhaps no person since Michael Collins had had so commanding a presence in the Irish government. He was, at the age of thirty-five, the most forceful and dynamic member of the cabinet, and many Republicans saw him as their real nemesis far more than they did Cosgrave. O'Higgins's power in the new government was evident from the fact that he had held three portfolios; that of vice-president, minister of justice, and minister of external affairs. No one admitted responsibility for his killing, and some Republican leaders, like de Valera, condemned it in the strongest possible terms. All the same, the government responded with the passage of the harshest public safety act to date (ultimately repealed in December 1928), which authorized severe penalties for membership in specifically proscribed organizations, granted the police extreme latitude in any search that they might conduct, and established a special court that was empowered to impose the death sentence or life imprisonment for unlawful possession of firearms.

Events within the Dáil were no less dramatic. An electoral amendment act was passed that henceforth would require every candidate for the Dáil and Seanad (or Senate, the less-important upper house of the Irish Parliament), upon nomination, to sign an affidavit that he or she would take the oath, if elected. Failure to do so would disqualify the person from his or her seat. The purpose of such legislation, of course, was to put an end to the abstentionist policy of Fianna Fáil. De Valera and his followers were suddenly confronted with the need to choose between giving up all meaningful political action and taking the oath and entering the Dáil. For a man who had spent from August 1923 to July 1924 in jail primarily because he had sought to substitute a republic for the Free State, Eamon de Valera was not easily reconciled to taking the hated oath simply to gain admission to a parliament that he regarded as illegal. But on this occasion he permitted his political pragmatism to prevail over his lofty idealism and, on August 10, 1927, he took the oath and led his party into the Dáil. Yet even then de Valera, whose reputation for semantic distinctions was well deserved, insisted that the oath was an empty formula that could be taken by Fianna Fáil members "without being involved, or without involving their nation, in obligations of loyalty to the English Crown."

In the long term, Fianna Fáil's entry into the Dáil would prove a significant development if only because that action compelled the second-largest party in the state to accept a fully responsible role in the parliamentary system. It also helped to ensure peaceful changes of administration in the future. But the immediate consequence was to threaten Cosgrave's political survival, particularly when Labour deputies joined with Fianna Fáil in a vote of no confidence in the government. Balloting on that motion resulted in a tie, and the government was able to prevail only because the chairman could, and did, cast a tie-breaking vote. The margin of victory, however, was much too close for Cosgrave to govern effectively, and he called for a general election, the second within a year, in September 1927.

The political issues remained unchanged, but the response of the electorate had the effect of restructuring the Dáil membership. Hardest hit were the smaller parties. The National League was almost wiped out, as it lost 6 of its 8 seats, and Sinn Féin representation disappeared entirely. Correspondingly, the Farmers fell from 11 seats to 6, while Labour, suffering from internal strife between moderates and extremists, lost 9. The beneficiaries of these losses were the two big parties: Cumann na nGaedhael won 67 seats and Fianna Fáil 57. Some interpreted the results as voter disenchantment with the power maneuvering of smaller parties. Others saw it as an expressed preference by the electorate for the stability of a two-party system over the uncertainties of proportional representation if left unchecked. Whatever their thinking, the Irish had succeeded in bringing accountability into the affairs of government through the established parliamentary means of a legitimate oppositional party. Fianna Fáil promptly began establishing a constituency organization second to none throughout the Free State, and in 1931 de Valera founded the *Irish Press* as the party newspaper. It would soon boast a circulation of 100,000, which was proof enough, if any was needed, that a new political force was emerging.

Irish Economic, Cultural, and Religious Life in the 1920s and Early 1930s

Against the backdrop of political uncertainty, life in the Irish Free State was anything but the utopia some revolutionary idealists might have expected. The country was without any important natural resources, or at least none that were known or could be easily retrieved during the 1920s. Partition had deprived the Free State of the only industrially developed portion of the island, and the civil war had squandered funds that might otherwise have been used to help build the economy.

Men like D.P. Moran and Arthur Griffith had once preached the doctrine of a self-sufficient Ireland achieved through protective tariffs and subsidies to industry and agriculture. Free State politicians, however, soon realized the necessity of making theories conform to reality, given the reciprocal responsibilities and trade concessions that dominion status implied. Moreover, the Commonwealth notwithstanding, the plain fact was that geography and history had integrated Ireland into the British economy, and Dublin had little choice but to remain a part of the latter's economic complex. Britain was the natural market for Irish agriculture, and over 90 percent of all Irish trade was with the United Kingdom. Hence any attempt to impose tariffs that would protect Irish industries could be met by British reprisals against Irish agriculture, with potentially devastating consequences for the Free State.

As it was, Irish agriculture was floundering in a state of inertia by the time the War for Independence ended in 1921. Part of the problem may have been attributable to the residues of the landlord system, which had debilitated the energies of the Irish farmer. More significant was the static condition that pervaded agricultural life in Ireland. While other countries during the late nineteenth and early twentieth centuries had been applying technology to agriculture and thereby increasing food production substantially, the yield from Irish farms improved only marginally. It was not until 1927 that the government established the Agricultural Credit Corporation for the purpose of making loans to farmers who needed overall improvements. And although reforms of this kind did in fact halt the pace of the economic recession that had plagued Ireland in the early 1920s, progress was still retarded by instinctively conservative farmers, who resisted experimentation and seemed content with subsistence production levels. The halcyon days of agricultural prosperity, which were as much a boon to the merchant as to the farmer in an earlier time, were now but distant memories.

Nor were things much better among the domestic industries, which were often woefully inefficient. People employed in industrial jobs frequently earned less than their counterparts in the United Kingdom, though the cost of living was roughly the same in the two countries. Even when counting partial and temporary jobs in Ireland, the unemployment rate was about 6 percent through most of the 1920s. People in rural regions fled to the cities, and others sought new lives in the United Kingdom and abroad. Emigration therefore persisted as a demoralizing dimension in Irish life. And although it did have the effect of functioning as a safety valve, draining off social, economic, and political discontent, emigration also deprived the country of much of its youth, talent, intelligence, ambition, and energy.

There were some exceptions to the otherwise dismal economic malaise. A sugar beet factory was developed in Carlow, and it became in time an important national industry. An even greater enterprise was the state-sponsored Shannon Scheme for providing electricity by harnessing the flow of the country's longest river at a juncture just a few miles outside Limerick. German engineers and Irish workers completed this project, and the Free State government established the Electricity Supply Board in 1927, just two years before the Shannon Scheme was put in operation. Nothing before or since has had such a profound impact on the social and economic development of Ireland, especially in the rural areas and farming communities. Even fairly populated regions, such as Sligo, Kilkenny, Tralee, and Athlone, had had no electricity until the 1920s, and in Dublin itself no more than one in every three homes was serviced by this marvelous new energy. Modernization was taking place in Ireland, even if the pace sometimes seemed imperceptible.

What did not change in post-treaty Ireland was the dominant influence Catholicism continued to have on Irish mores, values, and culture. Bishops and priests had been involved in nationalist issues since the days of O'Connell, and before, but that fact did not make their influence welcome to intellectuals or to members of the literati after independence. Indeed, most of the important Irish writers have characterized Catholicism as a negative force in Irish life. Unlike the upper-class Anglo-Irish Protestants of the literary renaissance, the majority of post-revolutionary Irish writers were from working-class or lower-middle-class Catholic families. Nearly all of them had participated to some degree in the cultural and revolutionary nationalist movements. They were idealists whose sympathies reflected their class origins and hence placed them apart from the ascendancy writers, who, like the Catholic hierarchy, tended to be conservative on social issues.

Although the Irish Free State's constitution was that of a secular state, it has been said that this may have been more the consequence of what the British would require rather than to what the Irish might aspire. Affairs of state, in any event, were not very long administered in any purely secular spirit. The Catholic hierarchy, it should be remembered, had supported the treaty and had excommunicated those who opposed it in the civil war. The government therefore appeared to be composed of "better Catholics" than its opponents, and some ministers and deputies encouraged this image of themselves. A law preventing divorce was passed in 1925; and although there is no evidence that the bishops had requested the legislation, it was congenial to them all the same, and it further strengthened the church-state alliance. For some in the new state's tiny Protestant minority, which was perhaps less than 7 percent of the total population, the divorce law confirmed the old fears of those who had equated Home Rule with "Rome rule." And to other Protestants, it was a betrayal of the constitution, which had stressed freedom of conscience and religion and, unlike the later constitution of 1937, had recognized no special position for the Catholic Church. But Protestants remained generally passive, even as the divorce law was succeeded by further sectarian legislation against contraception. Nor were there many audible protests from this minority community when the Dáil approved the Irish Censorship of Publications Act of 1929 for the purpose of excluding "immoral and obscene" literature. Acquiescence did not mean approval, however, and most Protestants balanced their guarded criticisms with expressions of support for the government precisely because they believed that to do otherwise might help the Republican cause, which to them represented a still greater threat to position and property.

Despite their unchallenged authority among the laity and their indisputable influence on the government, some Catholic bishops still worried during the 1920s that the moral fabric of society was unraveling in an era of rapidly developing mass media. Their concern was misplaced, for the great majority of the faithful would continue to be loyal adherents of a very pietistic, devotional Catholicism until the 1960s. Ireland's Catholic population simply was not terribly receptive to the increasingly libertarian climate that had pervaded other postwar Western societies. And the reasons for this are attributable not only to the power of the Church but also to the fact that Irish Catholicism was ideally adapted to the Irish social reality of the time. The regularized rites and practices of the faithful had helped, in the period after the famine, to engender a sense of national identity. The devotional exercises became for many Irish men and women an external expression of the differences that set them apart from other inhabitants of the British Isles. It served the needs of a nascent Irish nationalism, therefore, at a moment when the Irish language and culture of the past were in rapid decline.

However, the essentially democratic nature of the Irish Free State is evident from the way in which the Anglo-Irish Protestants have been treated. They have retained their civil rights, they continue to own a percentage of the national wealth that is hugely disproportionate to their numbers, and they are still prominent in cultural and political affairs. Such tolerance and liberalism had not been automatically assumed by the Church of Ireland and a delegation of that denomination visited with Michael Collins on May 12, 1922, to inquire whether the Protestant minority would be permitted to live in the twenty-six counties. Collins's firm assurance that they were welcome to remain and would have the protection of the new state must have been reassuring to those petitioners. The promise, in any event, was fully honored in the years thereafter.

Critics have argued that Catholic triumphalism became, all the same, a hallmark of the Irish Free State and that the 1922 Irish constitution, which insisted on the separation of church and state, was itself an illustration of how actual practice could differ from abstract theory. But successive centuries of British repression of and discrimination against Irish Catholics make it hardly surprising that there was a certain sense of Irish triumphalism. Moreover, those who would deride that spirit would do well to recall that it was precisely that kind of prejudice and discrimination, of an anti-Catholic variety, that became the given condition of the portion of the island that was to remain a part of the United Kingdom. And as for constitutional theory and practice, it might be noted that Irish legislation concerning divorce, birth control, and abortion was more representative of democratic public opinion than it was of clerical politicking. The bishops were indeed conservative, even reactionary in some instances, but there was also a xenophobic hostility toward the outside influences of modernism within Irish society that derived equally from the Gaelic and Irish-Ireland movements.

The Gaelic language and the Irish-Ireland ideology inspired enthusiasm, dedication, and a sense of purpose to the liberation movement. Cumann na nGaedhael leaders implemented Patrick Pearse's proclaimed objective to make "Ireland Gaelic as well as free." And although only a small percentage of the Irish population could speak Irish in 1922, the Free State constitution established it as the "national language." Yet this commitment to cultural orthodoxy by Cosgrave's party made good political sense. On the one hand, enthusiastic support of the language revival would dispute the presumption of Republicans that they were the sole custodians of true nationalism. On the other, two key ministers of these years, Ernest Blythe (of finance) and Eoin MacNeill (of education, until the end of 1925), were avid enthusiasts of the cause. In addition, Richard Mulcahy, who for a time served as minister of defense, was chairman of the Gaeltacht Commission of 1925. It was the purpose of the commission to preserve the Gaeltacht—the Irish-speaking districts of Waterford, Cork, Kerry, Galway, Mayo, and Donegal—as an inspiration and source of instruction for the rest of the country. Indeed, the commission pronounced it a national duty "to uphold and foster the Irish language, the central and most distinctive feature of the tradition which is Irish nationality."

A strategy for the linguistic transformation of the Free State was undertaken by the government in the following way. The compulsory teaching of Irish was to be adopted by the National University, with the ultimate objective of extending the requirement to the secondary and elementary school levels as soon as it became practical to do so. In the meantime, proficiency in the Irish language was required of all civil servants and members of the army and police force (An Garda Síochána). Preference was to be given, for example, to native speakers hired by the government, and it was decreed that Irish be used in official business, during Dáil debates, and for legal proceedings whenever possible. The language was a fixture in the school curriculum as early as 1928, and it became a requirement for all certificate examinations by 1934. Indeed, the necessity for students to earn a pass in Irish before becoming eligible for the school-leaving certificate (diploma) would persist until 1973.

It was an ambitious but unrealistic scheme. The custodians and evangelicals of the Gaeltacht Commission mistakenly assumed that popular support for their program could be obtained through government-sponsored prizes, bonuses, and scholarships. They also failed to recognize that the hereditary education patterns of Gaeltacht people were quite foreign to the secondary and postsecondary school programs that were intended to open new careers for these native speakers. Last, very few people outside the schools could or would speak Irish. There was therefore no reinforcement in the community at large for what children spent almost half their school time acquiring painfully in the classroom. The futility of the language revival was conceded in the Department of Education report of 1929, which read in part:

> As far as the general use of Irish is concerned, little progress seems to have been made in the last ten years. It appears to be true that very few pupils speak Irish outside school hours, and a still smaller number can be still classified as Irish speakers a few years

after leaving school. . . . English is the language of their sports and pastimes and of the means of earning their livelihood, while Irish remains a school subject closely allied to lessons and examinations. Under such circumstances it is inevitable that a very considerable part of the work done by the schools must fail to bear fruit.

Neither this report nor any of the similar testimony that was given over the next several years had the slightest effect on the government, which continued, undaunted, to strive for the unachievable. Cumann na nGaedheal was displaced from power in 1932, but the new government had its own zealots. Indeed, Thomas Derrig, minister of education from 1932 through 1948, was obsessed with the campaign for Gaelicization. When elementary school teachers complained to him in 1934 that the time given to compulsory Irish was impoverishing primary education, Derrig responded by *reducing* the teaching time available for English, mathematics, and science in order to allow for a greater concentration on Irish. But it was all to no avail. English remains today the spoken language and means of communication for most Irish citizens, and people continue to leave the Gaeltacht and settle in English-speaking places in Ireland and the United Kingdom. Nevertheless, the Irish-Ireland movement continues as a powerful lobby. Its supporters contend that Irish independence requires cultural integrity as well as political sovereignty. And although the Irish people have continued to resist using the Irish language, a majority of them still piously pays lip service to the Irish-Ireland ideal. However irrational such behavior may appear to an outsider, most Irish citizens justify that ambivalence as a reasonable compromise between the deference that they feel is owed to the quest for national identity and the conformity that they believe is essential for surviving in a non-Gaelic world.

Sean O'Faolain, an Irish novelist and critic whose nationalist credentials were impeccable, carried out a brave and desperate campaign some years later in his journal, *The Bell*, in which he wrote: "The sum of our [Irish] local history is that long before 1900 we had become part and parcel of the general world process—with a distinct English pigmentation." And other intellectuals, who were otherwise friendly to the Irish-language movement, have argued that it has reinforced the thinking that divides Catholics in the south from Protestants in the north. They insist that Irish-Ireland represents an exclusive, Catholic, provincial, puritanical, and culturally anti-intellectual and isolationist perspective. If, therefore, the Anglo-Irish had been guilty of a dismissive contemptuousness toward Irish nationalism that reflected an offensive blend of insecurity and class snobbery, Irish-language fanatics had responded in kind by proposing a theory of Irish nationality that denied full spiritual assimilation with the Irish nation to the Anglo-Irishman with his English manner and Protestant faith.

Hence it was not the deprivation of civil rights or the appropriation of private property that precipitated the exodus of many Protestants from the twenty-six counties upon the establishment of the Irish Free State. There was none of the panic, for example, that years later would accompany the departure of French *pieds noirs* from North Africa. The guarantees that Collins had promised to Protestants were respected and enforced by the Cosgrave government. No fewer than twenty-four Protestants, including sixteen who were former Unionists, were appointed to the Senate by Cosgrave and his colleagues. Despite these gestures of reassurance, however, Protestants still continued to leave. Political oppression may not have been a concern of theirs, but cultural intolerance decidedly was.

Anglo-Irish anxieties were perhaps inevitable in any event. Before the partition of the country in 1920, that minority had taken comfort in the knowledge that Protestants comprised one-quarter of the population of the entire island. In the new Irish state, however, they totaled slightly more than 7 percent. And the sense of isolation was still more intense in Connaught and Munster, where the Protestants accounted for only 2.6 and 3.6 percent, respectively, of the population. The emotional state of Anglo-Ireland was reflected in a number of novels that appeared in the 1920s and early 1930s that employed the Big House as the prism through which successive authors portrayed the socially disintegrated world of the Protestant ascendancy. Edith Somerville's *Big House of Inver* (1925) and Elizabeth Bowen's *Lost September* (1929) are typical of this genre, employing the metaphor of the emptiness of spaces in the house, contrasting it with the space between the house, the landscape, and society, in order to describe the emotional isolation of the Anglo-Irish community. In the period between 1911 and 1926, the Protestant population in the twenty-six southern counties declined by about one-third as an ever-increasing number of Protestant professional men, civil servants, and small farmers moved to different parts of the United Kingdom. Some of these people probably left because of the violence during the insurgency years, but a good number of them moved because of the cultural and intellectual climate. The closing of the Maunsel publishing company in 1926 must have seemed symbolic to those who recalled how that firm had once published the works of many writers associated with the literary renaissance. P.L. Dickinson's book, *The Dublin of Yesterday* (1929), conveys the sense of bitterness and betrayal that Anglo-Irish men and women took with them into exile and how they truly believed that the Ireland they had known was no longer hospitable to their kind.

The Irish Constitution: Blueprint for Democracy at Home and Equality Abroad

Irish nationalists who were charged with the task of constructing a government in 1922 may have felt a bit alien themselves in the circumstances. As Professor Donal McCartney reminds us, none of their dreams had been fulfilled. Neither the Gaelic League's Irish-speaking nation, nor Yeats' literacy-conscious people, nor Redmond's home rule for a united Ireland, nor Connolly's worker's democracy, nor Griffith's economically self-sufficient dual monarchy, nor de Valera's and Collins's republic. What they had instead was a truncated twenty-six-county domain with imposed liabilities, such as land annuity payments and occupied naval ports, which no other British dominion had been forced to endure. Compelled to accept

Commonwealth membership, the Irish proceeded to draft a constitution that both fulfilled the conditions of the treaty and permitted the new state a notably amended version of the Westminster model of government.

Adopting a written constitution was in itself a marked departure from the British example. Other differences included electing the lower house of parliament through a system of proportional representation; a formal Bill of Rights; initiative and referendum; and extern ministers chosen for their skills in political, economic, and cultural matters. Except for the Bill of Rights, these innovative departures from the Westminster model were intended to make the Irish parliament more responsive to the electorate and less susceptible to the corruptive influence of vested interests. In practice, however, initiative and referendum soon retreated before the power of parliamentary majorities, and the experiment of extern ministers proved short-lived. Even proportional representation, which was intended to redress the antidemocratic tendencies associated with traditional party politics, failed to survive in any meaningful form. Initially, that system had encouraged a variety of political organizations, but the treaty controversy and the civil war polarized Irish politics around two major factions. Consequently, party considerations dominated the Irish parliamentary process as they did throughout the English-speaking world.

Differences between the Irish and British forms of government were nevertheless rather unremarkable, aside from the innovations just noted. The Irish equivalent of the British cabinet was called the Executive Council, and the prime minister was described as the president of that council. The Oireachtas (Parliament) contained two chambers: The Dáil Éireann and the Seanad Éireann (Senate), whose relations were broadly comparable to those between the British House of Commons and House of Lords.

The Dáil, or lower house, was therefore predominant, while the Senate, or upper house, could suspend legislation for nine months, suggest amendments to bills, and initiate legislation in certain areas. Members of the Dáil, numbering 153, were elected by universal adult suffrage under the proportional representation (single transferable vote) method of voting. The Senate had sixty members, half of whom were appointed by the president of the Executive Council, the other half elected by the Dáil. Presiding nominally over this government was the governor general, who represented the British crown.

From 1922 to 1932, William T. Cosgrave, leader of the pro-treaty Cumann na nGaedheal party, served as president of the Executive Council. He had become head of government quite by accident and had none of the charisma of Collins or the magnetism of de Valera. Personally unambitious and politically unspectacular, he nonetheless was an honest, intelligent, and efficient administrator who deserves much of the credit for placing the new state on solid political and institutional foundations. Cosgrave's government created a police force, preserved the integrity of the civil service, reorganized local government, put down the incipient 1924 army mutiny, and stabilized the economy. Social services suffered, unemployment continued unabated, and the flow of emigration went unchecked, but Cosgrave's conservative fiscal programs had the support of the pro-treaty constituency of businessmen and large farmers, and the health of the Irish economy earned for it good credit and investment ratings from bankers and financiers. Cumann na nGaedhael succeeded in maintaining the political momentum on the domestic front until 1927, when a combination of unpopular policies and organizational deficiencies began to jeopardize the party's control over a restive electorate.

Yet it was not on the domestic front but in Commonwealth and foreign relations that Cumann na nGaedhael enjoyed its most significant and enduring triumphs. After being denied a republic and being compelled to enter the Commonwealth as a British dominion, the subsequent performance of the Free State within the confines of that organization made Ireland something of a Trojan horse. It must be remembered, of course, that the Irish-led campaign for dominion sovereignty during the postwar decade was not exclusively Dublin-orchestrated. The other dominions, after all, had grown greatly in power and self-confidence as the result of the war, and this was bound to reflect itself sooner or later in constitutional advance. But led by Kevin O'Higgins, Patrick McGilligan, and Desmond Fitzgerald, the Irish were the best-briefed and most articulate delegates attending the imperial conferences of the 1920s and 1930s. Their leadership, often shared by Canada and South Africa, helped to produce substantive changes in the concept and operation of the Commonwealth. The British Parliament abandoned any claim to legislate henceforth for the dominions, and members of the Commonwealth no longer had to abide by treaties that Britain negotiated bilaterally with foreign powers. These momentous reforms, which helped to untangle the confused constitutional anomalies that existed between Great Britain and the Commonwealth of Nations, led ultimately to the passage of the Statute of Westminster by the imperial Parliament on December 11, 1931. That ruling defined dominion status as a free association of sovereign and equal states united in common allegiance to the same monarch. The statute was later described as having "put the goblet of freedom into Ireland's hands, to be drained at her discretion."

Outside the Commonwealth and in the forum of world affairs, Cosgrave's government deported itself with an independence indicative of the latent Republican ambitions that Dublin's ministers hardly sought to disguise. The Free State, for example, joined the League of Nations in 1923, much to London's disapproval, and then proceeded in 1924 to register the Anglo-Irish Treaty with that body despite protests from the British, who regarded dominion relations as an internal matter for the Commonwealth. Dublin further insisted on having separate diplomatic representation abroad and moved thereafter to appoint Irish ambassadors to the United States, Canada, France, Italy, and the Vatican. Acting more like nationals of a sovereign nation than a dominion, Free State citizens traveled abroad on Irish passports. And although those instruments bore the seal and signature of the British king, the irony was that Britain was now conceding the main essentials of de Valera's proposed external association, which London had emphatically refused to consider in 1921.

Republicans, however, remained unimpressed with these successes of Free State diplomats and continued to concentrate on the symbols of British influence in Ireland rather than the reality of Irish sovereignty. As one might expect, this was especially true of the IRA, which had become, for all intents and purposes, a military organization committed to the establishment of a republic that embraced all thirty-two counties of Ireland. A part of that organization espoused left-wing political views that were inimical to the ruling bourgeois interests of Cumann na nGaedhael. They took their inspiration from James Connolly and exploited the discontent felt by many over such issues as unemployment, poverty, and the payment of land annuities. What may seem more surprising was the fact that the newly minted parliamentary republicans, Fianna Fáil, were equally disdainful of the Free State's gains. Instead of acknowledging that the Cosgrave government had begun to use the treaty as "the freedom to achieve freedom," as Collins had promised, de Valera and his colleagues continued to castigate their opponents as heretics, traitors, and usurpers. Irish majority opinion was deemed irrelevant by these ideologues, who judged that the people had "no right to surrender their independence at the ballot box . . . no right to do wrong." Quite naturally, perhaps, some degree of political posturing was behind this rhetoric by Fianna Fáil spokesmen, who knew that the government was in trouble and were determined to make the most of it.

Cosgrave and his colleagues were caught in an economic and political morass that was both international and local. A severe economic depression caused financial dislocation the world over, especially between 1929 and 1931. The Wall Street Crash of 1929 had resonating echoes in Ireland as elsewhere. These took many forms, including reduced remittances home from the emigrants in America and a sharp decline in the export of cattle and dairy products. Factories closed, and investment in Ireland nearly halted as the unemployed population soared from 20,000 to 30,000 between 1929 and 1932.

While the internationally generated economic crisis was still at its height, the Cosgrave government was suddenly confronted with a domestic security threat more lethal to the survival of the state than fiscal default. It began with Ireland's own version of the red scare, which, in retrospect, was of small consequence compared with the incipient militancy of several other IRA groups that had a fearsome potential for violence and destruction. The radicalization of left-wing elements of the IRA by men like Peadar O'Donnell and Seán MacBride led to a new organization in 1931, Saor Éire, whose professed purpose was the overthrow of capitalism and the formation of a workers' and farmers' revolutionary republic. Denounced as Marxist by the Cosgrave government, it was suppressed only a few months after its inception even though most of Saor Éire's members were more likely socialists than communists. The latter did not emerge as a party until 1933 and failed persistently thereafter to have any influence on Irish public opinion. Typical of the more dangerous revolutionary groups was the Comhairle na Poblachta (Central Council of the Republic), which engaged in crimes of violence and intimidation, particularly against jury members sitting in judgment of Republican defendants.

To meet these threats, the Cosgrave government, in the face of bitter opposition from Fianna Fáil in the Dáil, passed legislation that banned, in addition to Saor Éire, the IRA and ten other organizations.

Outrages like the murder of a Garda (police) superintendent in Tipperary during March 1931 convinced Cumann na nGaedheal that drastic countermeasures were necessary, but the party leadership knew that it was also entering a political minefield. Accordingly, they set about, as they had in 1922, obtaining advance episcopal endorsement for what they intended. The bishops were no less sensitive to political nuances, however, and they now perceived Fianna Fáil as a more moderate Republican alternative to anything that had existed eight years before. Mindful that this party had a reasonable chance of soon coming to power, the hierarchy muted its denunciation of IRA radical organizations. Cosgrave's party therefore took the brunt of criticisms that inevitably grew out of the government's rather draconian Constitution Bill (Amendment No. 17). It provided for a military tribunal of five members with the power to punish political crime by use of the death penalty, if necessary, with appeal only to the Executive Council. And the council itself was given authority to declare associations unlawful without reference to the Dáil. Finally, the police were given wide powers of arrest and detention. The severity and comprehensiveness of these rather totalitarian methods shocked many people more than the comparatively isolated IRA atrocities, and the tide of public opinion began to flow against the government.

Against this backdrop, the most important election in Free State history was about to take place. The Dáil was not legally obligated to call for a general election until October 1932, but Cosgrave decided for his own reasons to hold a snap election in February of that year. His motives may have been influenced by the impending International Eucharistic Congress scheduled for Dublin at the end of June and by the Imperial Economic Conference slated for Ottawa in late July and early August. The president of the Executive Council hoped to obtain, if at all possible, a positive expression of public support prior to appearing before either of these two groups. And he hoped that an early election might help distract attention from criticisms of his repression of groups threatening public disorder.

Fianna Fáil already had put together a remarkably efficient political machine. The energies and the enthusiasm of the voluntary workers, whose allegiance to de Valera was intense, formed a vital ingredient in the party's success. De Valera did not conduct a strident campaign, and he cunningly avoided using hyperbolic attacks against his opponents that might alienate undecided voters. Instead, he enticed the electorate with the pledge that, if elected, he would abolish the oath and other offensive features of the 1921 treaty. He also appealed to the farmers by declaring that under his administration, land annuities would no longer be paid to Britain but would instead be retained in the state treasury for domestic use. With a platform that promised something for nearly everybody, de Valera committed Fianna Fáil to a vigorous program of economic self-sufficiency that was calculated to win the favor of agricultural and industrial interests.

Cumann na nGaedhael responded by stressing its achievements in safeguarding the institutions of the state. That theme, however, failed to give the momentum to Cosgrave's party, which then turned to the desperate tactics of a smear campaign. Patrick McGilligan, for instance, publicly suggested a Bolshevik influence in the ranks of the Republicans, and Richard Mulcahy proclaimed that Marxists were behind de Valera's quest for power. Advertising posters appeared everywhere warning that a vote for Fianna Fáil was a vote for IRA violence and communist stooges.

When the election results were tallied, Fianna Fáil emerged as the largest single party with 72 seats as against 57 for Cumann na nGaedhael. Nevertheless, there were also 11 Independents, 7 Labour, 2 Independent Labour, and 4 Farmers to be taken into account. De Valera was able to fashion a bloc of 79 supporters, while Cosgrave could summon only 74 at best. William Cosgrave was thus compelled to step down, and de Valera became the leader of the new government. Few people would have expected the transition of power in this decade-young democracy to follow so peacefully and uneventfully. Fewer still, given the narrowness of victory, could possibly have imagined that a sixteen-year dynasty had just been inaugurated.

10

The de Valera Era, 1932–1959

Continuity and Change in Irish Life

Dismantling the Treaty and Supplanting the Free State

The name Eamon de Valera can evoke to this day a strong and spontaneous response throughout most parts of Ireland. And the sentiment conveyed in that response will vary from unswerving loyalty and unmeasured devotion, on the one hand, to profound bitterness and hostility, on the other. Such has been the legacy of this man, who, upon coming to power in 1932, had already been a nationally prominent figure for over fifteen years. Yet he was to embark upon a career as head of government for twenty of the Irish state's first thirty-seven years of existence, whereupon he would become head of state (Uachtarán) for another fourteen years. His towering presence, like that of O'Connell and Parnell before him, so dominated the life of the nation that it is not inappropriate to view this period in the making of modern Ireland as the "age of de Valera."

This new era began as William Cosgrave's came to an end. Cosgrave had labored effectively for ten years to extend the frontiers of dominion sovereignty, but he had done so in strict accordance with the spirit of the Anglo-Irish Treaty, and true to the letter of the Commonwealth agreements that culminated in the 1931 Statute of Westminster. Fianna Fáil was now in power, however, and if there were some signs of anxiety among that party's opponents in the Dáil, the feeling of apprehension in London was almost palpable. De Valera was interested neither in defining dominion status nor in refashioning Commonwealth relationships. He made it abundantly clear, upon taking office, that his ultimate aim was an Irish Republic that would be in association with the British Commonwealth of Nations and would recognize the British monarch as head of that association. Indeed, that affirmation prompted Prime Minister Ramsay MacDonald to respond immediately with the creation of an Irish Situation Committee for the specific purpose of monitoring the activities of the de Valera government and remediating any differences with it. The committee included a number of cabinet ministers and senior civil servants, and it met on a regular basis from 1932 to 1938, when the Anglo-Irish Agreements were concluded. That high-level and sustained scrutiny of the Dublin government by London is indicative of just how important the Irish Free State was to British interests.

EAMON DE VALERA, 1882–1976

Eamon de Valera was the dominant personality in post-treaty Ireland. During his many years as taoiseach he altered the treaty and led Ireland on the road from Free State to republic. His neutrality policy during World War II was the ultimate test of Irish independence. (Courtesy of the National Library of Ireland)

Eamon de Valera began his promised attack on the provisions of the 1921 Anglo-Irish Treaty within days of assuming office in March 1932. His immediate targets were the oath of allegiance to the crown, which he desired to have removed completely from the constitution, and the suspension of land annuity payments to the United Kingdom. Those annuities were annual payments of about 3 million pounds made by Irish farmers in repayment of money lent to them under the Land Purchase Acts of 1891–1909. Beginning in 1923, the annuities had been transmitted each half-year by the Free State government to the British National Debt commissioners. A subsequent agreement negotiated with Britain in 1925 obligated the Dublin government to pay 250,000 pounds per annum, over a period of sixty years, as compensation for property damage in Ireland between 1919 and 1925. De Valera believed that these obligations were contractually invalid because they had never been ratified by the Dáil. He further insisted that the annuities represented a contingent liability for a share of the United Kingdom's public debt, a responsibility for which the British, in 1925, had agreed not to hold the Irish accountable. Efforts to resolve this difference between the two governments broke down in June 1932. The British responded by promptly imposing duties of 20 percent on Irish cattle and on Irish agricultural exports to the United Kingdom for the purpose of recovering the revenue owed to the exchequer by the Irish Free State. Dublin retaliated by imposing tariffs of its own on imports from Britain, and a trade war ensued that escalated in the months and years that followed until a negotiated settlement was eventually reached in 1938.

On the subject of the oath of allegiance, de Valera was equally assertive. He declared it a relic of medievalism and an intolerable burden that the Irish people would no longer endure. J.H. Thomas, secretary of state for the dominions, was appalled by the suggestion that the oath was no longer obligatory because of a general election and a change of government in the Irish Free State. De Valera remained unimpressed by this expression of moral outrage from London, and his bill to remove the oath was ratified in the Dáil in May 1932. It was not until a year later, however, that the bill became law, owing to the fact that the Senate sought to amend and then to delay its implementation. Meanwhile, another general election was held in January 1933. Fianna Fáil proceeded to capture half the seats in the Dáil and, with the support of eight Labour members, now enjoyed a working majority of sixteen. Therefore, when de Valera returned to the attack in the new year, it was from a position of increased strength, and the bill to remove the oath quickly passed a third reading in the Dáil and came before the Senate. Under the law, the upper house now could do no more than retard the bill's progress for sixty days, after which, on May 2, 1933, it became law. Dominions secretary J.H. Thomas, famously described de Valera as "the Spanish onion in the Irish stew," loudly protested that the withholding of the annuities, together with the removal of the oath, represented nothing less than a full-scale assault on the entire 1921 Anglo-Irish Treaty settlement.

As the trade war intensified and the dispute over the unpaid annuities continued, de Valera launched yet another attack against the treaty with a campaign of calculated affronts against the office of governor general. The incumbent, James MacNeill, had had a distinguished career in the Indian civil service and had served, for a time, as high commissioner for the Irish Free State in London. Appointed during the Cosgrave administration in 1928, Governor General MacNeill found himself excluded from nearly all official functions after de Valera took control of the government. That may have demoralized MacNeill, but it did not dispose of him, and de Valera thereupon exercised his right to ask the king for the governor general's dismissal. With that accomplished, de Valera sought and obtained the appointment of Donald Buckley as MacNeill's successor. Buckley was a country shopkeeper, an Irish-language enthusiast, and a Fianna Fáil loyalist. The fact that he had no particular credentials to recommend him for the office of governor general was perhaps what de Valera found most attractive about his appointment. In any case, Buckley refused to move into the official residence and instead made his home the simple Dublin suburban house provided to him by the Irish government. He never appeared at public functions and restricted his official role to that of signing acts of Parliament until the office of governor general, which de Valera had succeeded in reducing to ridicule, was abolished in 1937.

Still more controversial was the new Irish government's view of appeals to the Judicial Committee of the Privy Council. The 1921 treaty contained no specific guarantee for this provision, but that instrument had defined the relationship between the Irish Free State and the United Kingdom all the same as being essentially modeled after the Canadian example. Insofar as Canada in 1921 did not possess the right to abolish by legislation the right of appeal to the Privy Council, it seemed to follow that the Irish Free State did not have it either. But even as early as 1922, Free State leaders had insisted that the model Ireland would follow in this regard would be that of South Africa, not Canada, in which only exceptional Irish court cases involving international issues could be appealed to London. Dominions secretary J.H. Thomas reacted with astonished indignation to the 1933 Free State Act abolishing the appeal to the Privy Council. The progressive elimination of the crown and imperial Parliament from the constitution was, he warned, all part of an ill-disguised plan aimed at the establishment of an all-Ireland republic that would be associated only tangentially with the British Commonwealth. And that, of course, went contrary to the principle of free association under the crown agreed to at the imperial conference of 1926 and, therefore, was unacceptable to King George V's government. Thomas also emphasized that the Irish Free State enjoyed all the privileges that derived from Commonwealth status, and he reminded Dublin that these privileges entailed responsibilities.

Because the dominions secretary had implied that the Irish Free State could not reasonably expect to have it both ways, de Valera immediately asked whether the Free State would be released from its responsibilities if it were willing to forgo the privileges. He also wondered whether London was prepared to accept Ireland's right "to exist as a distinct and independent nation" and if the British contemplated making war on the Irish people if they chose to sever their connection with the Commonwealth. The dominions secretary's reply reflected his sense of exasperation as he rejected de Valera's view that the 1921 Anglo-Irish Treaty had imposed dominion status upon the Irish Free State. His majesty's government therefore had no need to respond to so hypothetical a question based on a fallacious understanding of history. Thomas concluded his rejoinder by remarking that Ireland's free intercourse on equal terms with other members of the Commonwealth, together with the guarantees affirmed in the Statute of Westminster, constituted the most obvious proof of the fact of Irish freedom.

Indeed it did, as events made clear shortly after the Irish unilaterally abrogated the appeal procedure. In June 1935 the Judicial Committee of the Privy Council considered, on appeal, a test case intended to resolve whether Irish legislation abolishing the appeal was valid. The finding of the Judicial Committee was that the Irish Free State Parliament, as a direct consequence of the Statute of Westminster, did in fact possess the necessary power to repudiate the provisions of the 1921 Anglo-Irish Treaty. That judgment effectively cut the ground from under the British government's feet by rendering Dublin's initiative legally unimpeachable. Disheartened by this unexpected reversal, British attorney general Sir Thomas Inskip scornfully remarked that a legal power did not confer a moral right and that some obligations other than legal obligations had to be binding.

From the British viewpoint, one can perhaps understand the bewilderment and frustration felt in London over the apparent contradictions of Free State policy. Cosgrave, after all, had declared in 1931 that his government regarded the 1921 Anglo-Irish Treaty as a mutually binding agreement. Without that affirmation, it is doubtful that the Statute of Westminster would have been ratified so readily by the House of Commons. Both the British government and Cosgrave, who was now the opposition leader in the Dáil Éireann, accused de Valera of acting dishonorably. Fianna Fáil, quite naturally, viewed the matter from an entirely different perspective. Members of that party had never regarded the treaty settlement as either just or honorable, nor did they accept as normal the Dublin government's subsequent relationship with the United Kingdom and the Commonwealth, since that relationship had been adopted by the Dáil Éireann under duress.

Meanwhile, de Valera lost no time in further demonstrating the independence of action that the Judicial Committee of the Privy Council had conceded was Dublin's right under the Statute of Westminster. Under his leadership in 1935, the Dáil passed the Irish Nationality and Citizenship Act and the Aliens Act. What the first of these laws did was to define Irish citizenship so that it allowed for reciprocal citizenship between the Free State and other countries. It also repudiated the view that Irish citizens were British subjects, which occasioned yet another angry response from the dominions secretary. The second of these laws, the Aliens Act, added insult to injury by declaring that British subjects in the Free State were aliens. Yet insofar as British subjects were exempted from the actual application of the law by an Executive Council decree, the Aliens (Exemption) Order, the London government chose not to lodge any official protest. There could be, however, no doubt about what de Valera really intended by insisting on external association with the Commonwealth, rather than membership in it, and by arguing for reciprocal citizenship in preference to shared citizenship. In an address before the Dáil only a few months earlier, in November 1934, the Irish premier had asserted that the language of his recommended legislation would require no change if the whole of Ireland were declared an independent republic the following day. It was an accurate enough statement, given the implications of the Free State's constitutional initiatives since 1932, but it did nothing to assuage the anxious concerns of officials in London.

Throughout this period of political difficulty, the economic war between the two countries persisted. Punitive and protectionist trade policies were having a ruinous effect on the Free State economy. Irish agricultural exports, the majority of which went to Britain, fell from 35 million pounds in 1929 to just under 14 million pounds in 1935. And the cattle industry, the very lifeblood of the country's economy, was threatened with collapse. Although the economic war provided an opportunity for pursuing de Valera's cherished ambition of economic self-sufficiency, as increased tillage and expanded industrialization were undertaken, the effort proved less than successful. Even allowing for the complicating effects of the general collapse of world agriculture prices at this time, the reduced income of Irish farmers was directly attributable to British tariffs. Moreover, the economically depressed agricultural community's reduced purchasing power had a direct impact on the growth of domestic industries. Lenin once observed that facts are stubborn, and it was an incontrovertible fact that Irish exports were utterly reliant on the British market. A diligent but costly campaign by de Valera to find alternate markets for Irish products, in which subsidies and bounties were paid irrespective of profit or loss, failed cataclysmically. Six years of trial and error resulted in only a modest redirection of the Irish export trade. For example, in 1929 only 6 percent of the Irish Free State's exports went to countries other than Britain; by 1935 that figure had increased to only 7 percent. One object lesson that some Irishmen drew from this experience was that, regardless of the political relationship between the United Kingdom and the Irish Free State, the latter simply was in no position to endure the cost of economic insularity.

Although British ministers could and did find alternate sources of foodstuffs, the United Kingdom was seriously affected by the precipitous decline in its trade with the Irish Free State. As 1934 drew to a close, it became increasingly clear that some movement toward mediation would be in the best interests of both countries. The United Kingdom could preach about the principle of treaty obligations and the Irish Free State might aspire to the ideal of national self-sufficiency, but the economic lessons of this unfortunate experience could not be ignored indefinitely.

Under the terms of the so-called coal-cattle pact, which took effect at the beginning of 1935, the British quotas on Irish cattle imports were raised a third in return for a promise by the Free State that it would purchase all its coal from the United Kingdom. The compromise was gratefully accepted by both sides for very good reasons. The Irish cattle industry was in a state of critical decline, and the British coal market in Ireland was in peril of being lost forever. Irish representatives were already in Germany and Poland negotiating for coal and, had this undertaking resulted in a trade agreement, Irish furnaces would have had to be converted at considerable expense to accommodate a different type of coal. Such a conversion, once made, could not have been easily reversed. At stake was a British monopoly that in 1935 involved millions of tons of coal exports to the Free State per year. Following the implementation of the coal-cattle pact, the Irish Situation Committee, which had met twenty-two times from its inception in 1932 until this point in early 1935, did not convene again until May 1936. This long absence by British ministers serving on the committee was not indicative of any *détente* in Anglo-Irish relations but reflected instead the fact that London's attention was now increasingly preoccupied by other, perhaps more compelling, international concerns.

Throughout the months of May through December 1936, the Irish Situation Committee resumed its meetings in an atmosphere of special urgency. What particularly alarmed committee members were reports that de Valera was at work on a new constitution for the Free State and that he intended in the process to eliminate the crown entirely from Irish domestic affairs while recognizing the king simply for external purposes. Malcolm MacDonald, who had succeeded J.H. Thomas as dominions secretary, warned his British colleagues on May 12 that any constitution of this kind would end all hope of keeping the Free State within the empire. In a memorandum titled "Relations with the Irish Free State," MacDonald insisted that reconciliation between the London and Dublin governments was essential for preventing the further weakening of the moral authority of the British Commonwealth in world affairs. He affirmed, however, that any satisfactory settlement would require strict adherence to two fundamental principles. First, the Dublin government would be obligated to recognize the constitutional position of the king in both the internal and external affairs of the Irish Free State. Second, a united Ireland could not be established without the consent of northern as well as southern Ireland. In return, as part of a comprehensive Anglo-Irish agreement, the British government would consent to the abolition of the office of governor general and to the substitution of some other formula, possibly including one in which the king himself might perform the functions of the crown in the Irish Free State. Other concessions included the promise of ending the economic war and a British declaration affirming that the Free State was responsible for its own destiny.

What MacDonald intended was to remind de Valera that although membership in the Commonwealth was entirely voluntary and not compulsory, any departure from that body could make the Free State a foreign country whose citizens would then be aliens anywhere in the empire. But Attorney General Sir Donald Somervell was troubled by some of the language in the MacDonald memorandum, particularly with regard to the imprecision of Irish allegiance to the crown, and the secretary of state for India objected on the ground that any renunciation of force by Britain would make for an unfortunate precedent with regard to the empire. Complicating matters still further was the fact that other committee members, such as Sir Thomas Inskip, minister of defense, and Walter Elliot, minister of agriculture, either supported elements of the MacDonald proposal or actually favored still-greater concessions. Moreover, it was known that some of the dominions, notably Canada and South Africa, had no objections to de Valera's suggested plan for external association. Even as the committee wrestled with the problem of how best to respond to any new constitutional challenge from de Valera, events once more overtook the British government.

The abdication crisis of December 1936 caught the committee completely off-guard and provided Eamon de Valera with a welcome occasion to implement his particular concept of Commonwealth association. Because Edward VIII had removed himself from the throne before de Valera had the opportunity to remove him from the Irish constitution, the Irish premier promptly undertook to ensure that the king's successor, George VI, would represent a new reality in Anglo-Irish relations. On December 10, 1936, members of the Dáil were summoned by telegram to meet at 3 P.M. the following day for the purpose of considering, in connection with the proposed Act of Abdication, which would require action by all dominion legislatures, two specific amendments to the Irish constitution. The two bills that the Irish premier introduced were swiftly characterized by the *Times* of London as a revival of Document No. 2, which de Valera had put forth nearly fifteen years earlier as an alternative to the Anglo-Irish Treaty. The first bill was designed to remove the crown from the constitution of Saorstát Éireann, while the second recognized the crown for the purposes of external relations, so long as other members of the Commonwealth continued to recognize it as "the symbol of their cooperation."

Opposition members in the Dáil denounced the proposed legislation on the grounds that it changed the functions of kingship rather than providing for the abdication of King Edward. De Valera was also attacked for not having consulted with opposition party leaders on an important matter involving constitutional change. John A. Costello, who had served as William Cosgrave's attorney general during the last six years of the preceding Irish government, proclaimed that the new legislation would violate the Free State's pledge to the dominions that had helped "the Irish people to achieve their freedom in the Imperial Conferences of 1926, 1929 and 1930."

What the debate really involved was a difference over symbolic interpretation between the Cumann na nGaedhael, the Centre party, and the Independents, on the one side, and Fianna Fáil and its Labour allies, on the other. The opposition accused the government of pursuing ambivalent and contradictory policies in its simultaneous embrace of republicanism and Commonwealth ties. If the state was already sovereign—and both the government and the opposition agreed that it was—the proposed bills could not possibly increase the power of the Saorstát Éireann. They would, however, constitute a clear breach of the 1921 Anglo-Irish Treaty and violate the Commonwealth principle of association in which the crown was explicitly recognized as an integral part of the state. Opposition spokesmen in the Dáil, like Richard Mulcahy and Desmond Fitzgerald, noted that the Constitution Amendment Bill removed the king from the constitution but not from the state and that neither of the two bills dealt with the abdication of King Edward. De Valera conceded the validity of the latter argument, and on December 12 he introduced into the second bill an amendment that did in fact deal with Edward's abdication. But another amendment endorsed the interpretive issue on which Cosgrave's and de Valera's followers could not agree: In it the Irish premier described the crown in the words accepted by the nations of the Commonwealth—"as the symbol of their free association"—rather than, in the words employed by the bill—"the symbol of their cooperation."

When the Constitution (Amendment) Bill was voted on in the Dáil on December 11, it passed, by a vote of 79 to 54. In reporting these proceedings, the *Times* noted that the governor general's last act was thus to sign the bill that abolished his own office. In fact, the bill left the office of governor general in existence for the time being but rendered it functionless. The adoption of a new constitution a few months later formally abolished the office. A far more significant measure was the Executive (External Relations) Bill, which the Dáil ratified on December 12 with the amended phrasing intact. Aside from effectively clearing the way for the Constitution of 1937, the bill allotted to the crown a narrowly defined place and limited functions in the external field. So long as the Free State was associated

> with the following nations, that is to say, Australia, Canada, Great Britain, New Zealand, and South Africa, and so long as the King recognized by those nations as the symbol of their cooperation continues to act on behalf of each of those nations (on the advice of the several governments thereof) for the purposes of the appointment of diplomatic and consular representation and the conclusion of international agreements, the King so recognized may, and is hereby authorized to, act on behalf of Saorstat Éireann for the like purposes as and when advised by the Executive Council so to do.

Throughout the hectic months of 1936 and early 1937, Eamon de Valera devoted a good part of his time and energy to the task of crafting a new constitution for the Irish Free State. And although he did consult with different interest groups within the Irish community, notably with members of the Roman Catholic hierarchy, the constitution of 1937 was very much de Valera's personal creation. It began with a preamble reasonably suited to a confessional state:

> In the name of the Most Holy Trinity, from Whom is all authority and to Whom, as our final end, all actions, both men and States must be referred, We, the people of Éire, Humbly acknowledging all our obligations to our Divine Lord, Jesus Christ, Who sustained our fathers through centuries of trial, . . . Do hereby adopt, enact, and give to ourselves this Constitution.

But the new constitution also reflected a Republican spirit that dated back to Wolfe Tone, whose enthusiasm for the social contract and for revolutionary France had never been shared by the Irish Catholic hierarchy. Unlike the constitution of 1922, which embraced the conflicting constitutional doctrines of the British monarchical system and Irish republicanism, the 1937 document clearly affirmed the concept of popular sovereignty. It was, however, a sovereignty that was to be exercised with a full awareness that ultimate authority derives from God. To this extent, the Irish constitution of 1937 sought to reconcile the notion of an inalienable popular sovereignty with the medieval concept of a theocratic state.

There was no reference in the new constitution to either the king or the Commonwealth. Also absent was the term *republic,* because de Valera was of the belief that such a usage could be employed only if the state had jurisdiction over the whole of Ireland. To do otherwise, he thought, would be to dishonor the martyrs of 1916 who had died for an all-Ireland republic. The name of the state was to be Éire or, in the English language, Ireland. The national territory was defined as "the whole island of Ireland, its islands and the territorial seas" but, pending the reintegration of Northern Ireland, the laws of the state would apply only to the Irish Free State area. The head of state was to be a popularly elected president whose essential duties were more formal than functional. A *taoiseach,* or prime minister, would head the government, with powers and prerogatives substantially stronger than those of the president of the Executive Council under the old constitution. Despite opposition from the pro-Commonwealth Cumann na nGaedhael party, now called Fine Gael, and from the Labour party, which would have preferred a unequivocally Republican proclamation, the new constitution was approved by the Dáil on June 14, 1937, and then voted on by the electorate in a referendum that was held in conjunction with the general election conducted on July 1. Approved by a vote of 685,105 to 526,945, the constitution automatically came into force on December 29, 1937.

Even before the endorsement of the constitution by the Irish electorate, the British government had anxiously sought to anticipate the constitutional implications for the Commonwealth relationship. At a meeting of the Irish Situation Committee on June 9, which was chaired by the new prime minister, Neville Chamberlain, Dominions secretary Malcolm MacDonald advised his colleagues that they were faced with a "choice of evils." It was difficult, MacDonald conceded, to reconcile the language of the Irish constitution with the 1926 imperial conference agreement on being "united by common allegiance to the crown." It would not be inappropriate, therefore, to declare that the Free State had put itself outside the Commonwealth. But to do so, MacDonald warned, would only emphasize the division of Ireland, destroy the hope of all future settlements, leave an unfriendly country at Britain's flank, and strain London's relations with America while at the same time give encouragement to republicans in South Africa and to enemies abroad. The committee reached no agreement that day regarding the proper British response to this latest and most significant constitutional challenge from Dublin, but the general disposition clearly favored the cautious and conciliatory approach recommended by MacDonald.

The Anglo-Irish Agreements of 1938

Hence the Irish Free State, renamed Éire in the new constitution of 1937, became a republic in everything but name. Britain was confronted with the choice of either accepting de Valera's unilateral changes or expelling Éire from the Commonwealth. If Britain chose the latter course, there was a good prospect that some of the dominions would not follow Britain's lead in rejecting Éire and the unity of the Commonwealth would be shattered, along with much of its influence in the world. A public acceptance of external association, however, could further encourage the already awakened national aspirations of India and other British colonies and create a nightmare for the constitutional theory of the Commonwealth. The British answer was a masterpiece of political pragmatism: London chose to ignore, at least publicly, the implications of the new constitution and to maintain the fiction that Éire was still part of the Commonwealth.

De Valera decided not to challenge this British pretense, and his restraint made possible a negotiated settlement, the following year, of the six-year trade war first caused by Dublin's refusal to pay the land annuities that had been previously promised to the London government. Of course, reasons other than de Valera's tempered approach help explain the ready willingness of the British to seek such an accord. Neville Chamberlain and Malcolm MacDonald, respectively, had replaced Stanley Baldwin and J.H. Thomas in the offices of prime minister and dominions secretary. London's new leadership clearly placed a higher premium on achieving goodwill with Dublin than it did on enforcing treaty obligations, an attitude no doubt then encouraged by Adolf Hitler's increasing bellicosity. Indeed, even the British military chiefs agreed that it would be better to give up the Irish ports that de Valera wanted than to alienate the Irish at a time of such international uncertainty.

In January 1938, therefore, delegations led by Eamon de Valera and Neville Chamberlain began conferring in London. From the outset, de Valera's objectives were the abolition of partition, the transfer to Irish control of the treaty ports, and an end to duties that were crippling Irish exports. For his part, Chamberlain hoped to extract a defense agreement with the Irish in return for any British concessions. Negotiations almost reached an impasse, however, when de Valera insisted that London abolish partition in order to end Unionist discrimination against the nationalist minority. The unification of the country, he promised, would give the British the next best thing to a defensive alliance. It would, he said, ensure that the country would not be used as a base of attack against Britain. But Chamberlain was adamant in maintaining that there could be no question of London's putting pressure on Belfast, particularly because his majesty's government had pledged repeatedly never to allow the status of Northern Ireland to change until a majority of its population so approved. Because de Valera never truly grasped the complexity of the Ulster Unionist issue, either then or later, it is not surprising that he acted as though partition were a problem that the British could resolve at will. He did, however, reluctantly conclude that a solution to the Northern Ireland question was not imminent, and he quickly shifted the focus of discussions to goals that were more obtainable.

The Anglo-Irish Agreements were finally signed on April 25, 1938, and were published the following day. Under the provisions of the first of these, Articles 6 and 7 of the Anglo-Irish Treaty of 1921 were abrogated. British control over the dockyard port at Berehaven and the harbor defenses in and aviation facilities near Berehaven, Queenstown (Cobh), and Lough Swilley was terminated. The second agreement effectively ended the economic war: The British dropped their demand for land annuity payments in return for an Irish payment of 10 million pounds against an initial claim of 104 million. And a third agreement provided for a trade pact under which the British market was to be opened again to Irish cattle and foodstuffs. Furthermore, Irish manufacturers could sell their products in the United Kingdom with few restrictions, while Ireland agreed only to review existing tariffs. Allowance was made for certain British goods to be given duty-free access in the Irish market, and Irish industries not yet "fully established" would continue to be given protection.

When assessing the significance of the 1938 Anglo-Irish Agreements, some historians have given more attention to the return of the so-called treaty ports than to the economic implications of the settlement. And that is perhaps entirely understandable. It was, after all, Britain's handing back of the ports that gave Dublin true independence of action and made neutrality achievable. And it was the later implementation of that policy that confirmed the reality of Irish sovereignty.

For Eamon de Valera, the agreements were a personal triumph. His enhanced popularity with the electorate was evident in the 1938 general election, when Fianna Fáil more than recovered the losses it had sustained in the 1937 election and was given an overall majority once more. The political leader of the anti-treaty forces had achieved a new respectability in Ireland, where his dismantling of the treaty was widely acclaimed, as well as in Britain, where it was more accepted than applauded.

In 1938, however, it was neither the fear of an invasion from Nazi Germany nor the constitutional evolution from dominion to sovereign status that most concerned the majority of people in Ireland. It was the continuing state of the national economy, which, in the opinion of some, had been grievously damaged by de Valera's handling of the trade war. What the agreements might ultimately have produced in economic terms is difficult to determine with any certitude since World War II intervened before any clear trends could be discerned. The apparent beneficiaries of the new trade pacts included Ireland's livestock producers, who stood to gain greater access to British markets. But London had made this concession in return for the promise that British industrial products would be given better access to the Irish market. Therefore, the taunts by opposition members in the Dáil who accused Fianna Fáil of moving toward free trade and of modifying its proclaimed policy of industrial protection had some justification.

To understand how dramatic this break with the hallowed Fianna Fáil principle of self-sufficiency was, it is necessary to recall the almost evangelical zeal of that party's economic nationalism. Ever since first taking office in 1932, de Valera had relentlessly promoted the creation and success of native industries that were to be protected by rigid tariff walls. True freedom, he insisted, was more than political liberty; it also meant independence from foreign economic subjugation. Sean Lemass, de Valera's chief lieutenant in industrial affairs, fought an unequal battle against the ravages of world depression and a debilitating trade war while attempting to make Fianna Fáil's policy of economic self-sufficiency a reality. Unemployment, however, remained a serious problem, and emigration in the 1930s almost equaled that of the 1920s. But some notable gains were also made. Unemployment benefits were both extended and increased, as were old-age pensions, and beginning in 1934 pension provisions were introduced for widows and orphans. Perhaps most dramatic of all was the ambitious program of slum clearance and new urban housing construction that the Irish government vigorously pursued.

Why, then, did de Valera depart from his basic economic creed in the 1938 agreements? The fact is that the money needed to finance his social programs was no longer obtainable. Worse yet was the fact that the economy's failure was to some extent due to the government's protectionist policies. Severe quota restrictions on imports, together with high tariff barriers, had permitted many new firms to establish virtual monopolies in the Irish market. The result was that it was not foreign producers but Irish consumers who ended up paying higher prices for poor-quality goods in order to subsidize the new native industries. Pervasive profiteering and rampant inefficiency provoked a sense of public discontent throughout the state. For this reason, therefore, Sean Lemass gave new purpose to the agreements, which were now used to prod Irish industries into becoming efficient and competitive. The Irish-Ireland quest for self-sufficiency was thus slowly but surely discarded from Fianna Fáil's ideological baggage, although no party leader would publicly admit to this for some years to come.

Social and Political Unrest in the 1930s

Otherwise, however, there were not many departures from the orthodoxy of Fianna Fáil's often parochial nationalist vision. Irish-language promoters and Irish traditional music enthusiasts enjoyed the patronage of official government support, but music and art that reflected any hint of cosmopolitan standards met with suspicion or derision. An almost farcical air of prudery and a repressive spirit of anti-intellectualism characterized the cultural landscape of the 1930s in Ireland under Fianna Fáil. There was, for example, official criticism at this time of certain paintings on exhibit in Dublin's National Gallery because they featured nudes. And more than 1,200 books and some 140 periodicals were banned by the Censorship Board between 1930 and 1939. Irish writers like Liam O'Flaherty and Frank O'Connor decried these attacks on artistic expression, to no avail. Sean O'Faoláin expressed his own protest with the 1938 publication of what many believe to be his finest work, *The King of the Beggars*. In it he argued that Gaelic Ireland had died in the eighteenth century because that culture had grown weak by clinging to aristocracy and hierarchy in a world that was gravitating toward democracy. O'Faoláin dismissed the romantic vision of Irish-Irelanders, who thought in terms of ancient Celtic sagas, like Cuchulain, instead of taking their inspiration from a far more relevant model, namely, O'Connell. Modern Ireland, declared O'Faoláin, was conscious of the liberal democratic tradition that it had inherited from the Great

Liberator, and it would remain an English-speaking nation in which the differing roles of church and state were subtly but irrevocably defined.

For some Irish intellectuals, like Professor James Hogan of University College, Cork, and Professor Michael Tierney, a former Cumann na nGaedhael TD (deputy member of the Dáil) and professor of Greek at University College, Dublin, such remarks were nothing less than cultural heresy. They rebuked O'Faoláin for characterizing Irish society as mediocre, occasionally neurotic, and generally disenchanted with life in the new state. Nor were such critics any more likely to find other Irish short-story writers of the 1930s and 1940s, like Frank O'Connor or Mary Lavin, any less offensive because these authors also attacked the frugal but virtuous paradise that Gaelic purists evoked as the ideal social reality for Ireland.

Hogan and Tierney were, of course, concerned with issues that went far beyond literary criticism. They were representative of a whole sociopolitical movement in Ireland whose ideological roots were grounded in the vocational ideas on social organization that were first articulated by Pope Leo XIII in his *Rerum Novarum* encyclical of 1891 and subsequently reaffirmed by Pius XI in his *Quadrageismo Anno* encyclical of 1931. Central to the beliefs of these Irish conservative activists of the 1930s was the view that both capitalism and communism were incapable of addressing the crisis then confronting European civilization. What was needed instead, they believed, was a new vocationalist order in which men and women would organize into guilds or corporations that reflected their respective vocations and professions. Government would hence reflect this vocationalist organization of society and thereby promote social harmony by reducing the conflicts between classes and eventually between states. The idea of a corporate state appealed to right-wing nationalistic movements throughout Europe in the 1930s, and Ireland was no exception. These corporate state supporters were invariably critical of democracy for its leniency and permissiveness and were hostile toward all forms of socialism, especially communism. In Ireland, however, their propensity for conservatism and authoritarianism was further characterized by rigid Catholicism. Similarities could be found, therefore, but also differences, between the Blueshirts in Ireland, the Blackshirts in Mussolini's Italy, and the Brownshirts in Hitler's Germany.

The Blueshirts were symbolic of the profound tensions threatening democratic institutions in the Irish state at this time. The group began as a response to the increased activities of the IRA following de Valera's accession to power and was known initially as the Army Comrades Association (ACA). Consisting largely of ex-officers and soldiers of the Free State army, the ACA soon grew to a membership of 20,000. In February 1933 General Eoin O'Duffy was dismissed from his post as commissioner of the Civic Guards (police), and he promptly assumed the leadership of the ACA, which had begun to adopt as its uniform a blue shirt. O'Duffy changed the name of the ACA, calling it the National Guard, although the popular name for his following remained the Blueshirts. Eamon de Valera was quick to restrict parades and public demonstrations by this paramilitary organization, which, though unarmed, was perceived as a public menace. Perhaps the most surprising development in the brief two-year period of Blueshirt militancy was its alliance with W.T. Cosgrave, the leader of Cumann na nGaedhael, which had just reorganized to help form the new Fine Gael party. The Blueshirts were welcomed initially by Fine Gael politicians as protectors against the harassing tactics of IRA hooligans, but O'Duffy's men often broke the law themselves, and they ultimately became a political liability for the Fine Gael party. That fact was brought home most dramatically in 1934, when Fine Gael won only 6 out of 23 local elections, a result that at least partly reflected the disenchantment of farmers over the Blueshirts' failure to alleviate the costs of the economic war as they had promised. By mid-1934, scarcely two years from its inception, the Blueshirt movement was already in eclipse and about to pass from the political scene in Ireland.

Because O'Duffy was sympathetic to the corporatist ideas of the Italian Fascists, it is tempting to perceive the Blueshirts as indicative of a certain amount of Irish support for that ideology. Indeed, that impression is reinforced by the fact that O'Duffy and 700 of his supporters sailed to Spain in 1936 for the purpose of fighting on the side of General Francisco Franco in the Spanish civil war. In fact, however, the appeal of the Blueshirt movement had far more to do with local Irish political conditions than with any Irish desire to imitate European Fascists. Blueshirtism, therefore, was a peculiarly Irish phenomenon that did not espouse the antidemocratic beliefs of continental totalitarian movements.

Eamon de Valera successfully met the challenge to his government from the political right by preventing the Blueshirts from holding uniformed parades and by defeating their candidates at the polls. But the threat from the political left, namely, the IRA, proved a good deal more formidable. At first it appeared that Fianna Fáil, upon coming to power in 1932, was about to reconcile its differences with the IRA and form a cordial alliance with it. IRA prisoners were released from the jails, the organization's weekly newspaper, *An Phoblacht*, was permitted to operate once again, and the order outlawing the IRA was allowed to lapse. None of this, of course, converted any of the irreconcilable Republicans to constitutional methods, but the IRA was muted in its criticism of Fianna Fáil so long as there was a more obnoxious enemy, the Blueshirts, with which to contend. By the end of 1934, however, *An Phoblacht* was attacking de Valera with a vehemence that it had once reserved for Fine Gael and the Blueshirts. What angered the IRA was the tendency of Fianna Fáil to represent symbolic changes, such as an end to the oath or the abolition of the post of governor general, as meaningful steps toward an Irish Republic. Radical nationalists demanded instead an immediate break with the British empire and the quick establishment of a thirty-two-county socialist republic.

IRA violence intensified in 1935, resulting in some bloodshed and death. De Valera was compelled to revive the military tribunal that he had suspended upon first taking office, and he called out against the IRA the special police that he had once used against the Blueshirts. In June 1936 the IRA was again proclaimed an illegal body, and its chief of staff was imprisoned. For a time, at least, it appeared as though de Valera had neutralized yet another paramilitary threat to the Irish state. But events soon proved otherwise.

To Sean MacBride, a former IRA chief of staff, and many of his colleagues, the 1937 constitution was an attempt to legitimize the betrayal of their sacred republic. And the 1938 Anglo-Irish Agreements provoked them still more. If de Valera had hoped that the return of the British-held ports would mollify the militant Republicans, he was wrong. The IRA condemned the agreements for having failed to deal with partition, seeing it as a further proof of the fact that only direct action could reunite the country. Shortly thereafter, British customs stations along the border came under IRA attack, and several were destroyed.

An IRA ultimatum was sent to British foreign secretary Lord Halifax on January 12, 1939, demanding the withdrawal within four days of all British forces, civil and military, from Irish soil. Failure to comply would have immediate consequences. The IRA neither expected nor received any response, and it soon implemented an intensive bombing campaign throughout England in the hope that it would reignite an Anglo-Irish conflict and focus world attention on the partition issue. Initially conceived as a careful strategy of sabotage against factories, communications, and power installations, it became instead an indiscriminate attack on harmless civilian targets, with bombs being placed in mailboxes, public lavatories, and suitcases in railway depots. During the first six months of 1939 there were over 120 such incidents, leaving one person dead and fifty-five others wounded. Then came the most violent attack, the detonation of a bomb in a crowded street in Coventry, which killed five people and injured seventy others.

If nothing else, the IRA succeeded in outraging British public opinion. Two men were hanged for their part in the Coventry explosions, and in virtually every instance IRA men were given stiff sentences whenever apprehended and found guilty. Meanwhile, Irishmen living in Britain who had been born in Ireland were compelled to register with the police or, in some cases, were sent back to their native land. No hostility was directed toward Dublin, however, as most English people recognized that de Valera was as much opposed as they were to IRA violence. Indeed, the Dáil passed the Offences Against the State Act in June 1939, providing for the internment of prisoners without trial. That was followed by the Treason Act, which authorized the death penalty for acts of treason. And in January 1940 the Emergency Powers Act was passed, under which the Curragh internment camp, just west of Dublin, was opened for IRA detainees. These measures broke the back of the IRA, but they did not cripple that organization, which now regarded Fianna Fáil with almost the same loathing as it did the British. The years between 1940 and 1944 were the harshest times ever endured by the IRA, as detainees experienced extended imprisonment, hunger strikes, and even execution. Suppressed by the Irish government and divided by its own factionalism, the IRA was now a small and enfeebled group that had no choice but to go underground for an indefinite period. So long as the island remained partitioned and the goal of an indivisible republic remained unfulfilled, however, the phoenix-like IRA would rise again if the time came for a new generation to take up the sacred cause.

Irish Neutrality and World War II

It was the prospect of war and not Republican militancy in 1939 that began to erode the new cordiality in Anglo-Irish relations resulting from the agreements of the previous year. Tensions heightened, for example, when it appeared for a time that the British government might include Northern Ireland in a military conscription bill. Parliament's decision in May to exclude Northern Ireland from the bill helped to avoid a crisis, because a violent nationalist reaction on both sides of the border would otherwise have ensued. But relations between London and Dublin became strained all the same on September 1 when the Dáil enacted legislation affirming Ireland's neutrality after the German invasion of Poland. De Valera had previously and publicly declared that he would never permit the use of Éire as a base for enemy attacks on Great Britain; but he had also affirmed that Éire's cooperation with British military forces was inconceivable while Ireland remained partitioned. Despite frequent pronouncements of this kind by the Irish leader, London reacted with astonishment when de Valera remained firmly committed to neutrality even after Britain entered the war on September 3.

Partition was a real and legitimate concern of the Éire government, but de Valera also manipulated the issue for his own purposes. Throughout the war, for example, he repeatedly complained that England, not Ulster Unionists, occupied a part of Ireland. It was a clever stratagem, particularly when directed toward the significant number of Irish Americans who, especially after Pearl Harbor, were unreservedly committed to participation on the Allied side. These people often did not fully understand the partition issue, but for many of them it somehow made Irish neutrality seem more justifiable.

There was never any likelihood, however, that de Valera would join the British war effort even if London did agree to end the partition of Ireland. When emissaries from the London government offered to negotiate that eventual prospect with Dublin in the summer of 1940, they found de Valera pessimistically resigned to a Nazi victory in the war and resolutely determined not to abandon his policy of neutrality. In fact, de Valera had good reason to doubt that the British were prepared to compel the entry of Irish Protestant Unionists into an Irish state.

Partition may have been a useful pretext for de Valera in propagandizing a rationale for neutrality to people abroad, but there should be no mistaking the fact that neutrality was supported by virtually every constituency in the twenty-six counties. The real reason that the overwhelming majority of Irish citizens favored that policy was that they could see no purpose being served by exposing their defenseless country to the ravages of a war that was not of their making. Moreover, many of them knew that Éire's entering the conflict on the side of Britain would provoke Republican extremists to engage in a relentless campaign of sabotage and guerrilla warfare. The real irony of the partition pretext is the fact that it was the availability of Northern ports to Britain that induced the London government to accept the loss of Éire's harbors and thereby respect the claim of Irish neutrality.

Precisely how much the denial of the treaty ports actually cost Britain in terms of vessels sunk by German U-boats is difficult, if not impossible, to estimate. But it should be remembered that the Germans had cracked the Royal Navy's secret code in 1936, a security breach that was not entirely remedied until 1943. Indeed, by that time the British would become far less aggressive in their representations to the Éire government on the subject of the ports, for two reasons. First, experience in the early and critical years of the war had shown that the Irish ports simply were not as vital as was previously assumed; second, underscoring the wisdom of de Valera's policy, Britain did not have the capability to defend Éire effectively if that country became involved in the war. Later publication of British government records revealed that the cabinet was confidentially informed of these realities by people from the appropriate ministries. London nevertheless continued to make a public issue of the dangers posed by the loss of the Irish ports, all of which suggests that de Valera was not alone in propagandizing for foreign consumption.

Irish neutrality did not prevent individual Irish citizens from contributing to the British war effort. More than 100,000 of them worked in British munitions factories, providing the Irish with needed employment while also compensating for Britain's manpower shortages that resulted from wartime conscription. Another 60,000 Irishmen volunteered for the British armed forces, 40,000 of whom crossed the border to enlist in Belfast. If Prime Minister de Valera had wished to prevent Éire citizens from joining the Royal Army, Navy, or Air Force, he could have followed the example of other neutral countries by passing a foreign enlistment act making it an offense, punishable by the loss of all civil rights, to join the fighting services of any of the belligerent powers. He did nothing of the kind, and all through the war Irishmen were at liberty to join the British forces. The fact that they did so in comparatively large numbers caused de Valera no notable concern, although he undoubtedly would have preferred that the enlistments not include men on active duty in the Irish army who deserted in order to fight for Britain. At the end of 1945 it was admitted in the Dáil Éireann that some 4,000 of the Irish army, about 10 percent of its total force, had deserted during the war to join British units combating the Axis powers.

Irish neutrality was decidedly tilted in favor of Britain in many ways. For example, Dublin continued to supply London with crucially important meteorological reports. Two strategically located wireless direction-finding stations at Malin Head on the northern tip of County Donegal cooperated with British ships and aircraft. Irish security authorities informed their English counterparts about the activities of all aliens, particularly Germans, in Éire. The de Valera government also agreed to prohibit commercial lighting in coastal areas north of Dublin that could have been used to guide German bombers bound for Belfast. Finally, the Irish permitted the use of their territory for the installation of a British radar station to track German submarines.

None of this mollified Winston Churchill, who had replaced Neville Chamberlain as British prime minister after the fall of France in June 1940. Churchill had helped to negotiate the Anglo-Irish Treaty of 1921, and he took very personally Eamon de Valera's role in unilaterally dismantling it. The personal antipathy between the two men was only compounded by Éire's proclamation of neutrality, which Churchill viewed as an illegal act by a Commonwealth nation, and by de Valera's refusal to grant the British access to the treaty ports. Churchill was prepared on more than one occasion to order the seizure of the ports. He was dissuaded by the military chiefs of staff, who warned that Irish resistance would make the cost of such a seizure greater than any gain, and by cabinet colleagues, who predicted that other dominions would denounce such an act. Even as the tide of war turned against the Germans and the threat to British security substantially diminished, Churchill still fumed about the ignominy of Irish neutrality. In November 1943, noting that Éire had been excluded from a forthcoming food conference sponsored by the United Nations, Churchill told Foreign Secretary Anthony Eden, "Southern Ireland is a neutral and this is the moment to make her feel her isolation and the shameful position she will occupy at the peace."

By the following year, as the war was approaching its dramatic climax, both Washington and London became exceedingly anxious about the possibility that the Irish might endanger Allied security. The U.S. minister to Éire, David Gray, recommended that the Irish government be asked to close the Axis legations in Dublin lest they somehow compromise the D-day preparations then under way. With Churchill's encouragement and support, therefore, President Franklin Roosevelt sent de Valera a formal request on February 21, 1944. This communication, which is often referred to as the "American note" in accounts of this period, called for the Irish government to take appropriate steps to effect the recall of German and Japanese representatives in Ireland because of the opportunity they afforded for highly organized espionage at a critical juncture in the war. De Valera replied that his government had done all it could to prevent espionage against the Allies, and it could not and would not do more.

What de Valera found particularly objectionable about the American note was Roosevelt's contention that the Irish government, in spite of its declaration of friendly neutrality, had in fact pursued a policy that operated in favor of the Axis. It seems reasonable to conclude that the German government would not have shared that view. German airmen who bailed out or were shot down over Éire were interned for the duration of the war, whereas nearly all captured British servicemen were returned to their units. Furthermore, the Irish government compelled the German minister, Dr. Edward Hempel, to surrender his wireless transmitter during the war and denied Berlin's 1940 request to add two additional members to its five-man delegation in Dublin. For its part, the German government refused to accept Éire's newly appointed minister to Berlin without the usual letters of credence, which, in the existing circumstances, still needed to be signed by the British king. King George VI could hardly be expected to accredit a minister to a power with which he was at war, with the consequence that Éire's Berlin legation was left to the supervision of a chargé d'affaires, William Warnock. And when the legation premises in the

Drakestrasse were demolished by an RAF bomb in 1943, Warnock was offered no other facilities, whereupon he transferred the legation's business to a stud farm outside Berlin owned by an Irishman. There was therefore little cordiality, and still less cooperation, between the governments of Dublin and Berlin. And although there was admittedly a certain amount of German espionage, particularly in the early years of the war when some spies did parachute into Éire, it never got very far, thanks largely to an efficient Irish Secret Service and a vigilant Home Defense Force. By any fair standard of judgment, Roosevelt's contention that Irish neutrality operated in favor of the Axis was simply misinformed.

De Valera provoked another storm of protest in Britain and in the United States on May 2, 1945, when he called on the German minister to express condolences upon the death of Adolf Hitler. Éire's secretary of external affairs, Joseph Walshe, who accompanied de Valera for the ceremonial visit, was apprehensive about the wisdom of that gesture because he anticipated what world reaction would be. But the Irish prime minister had paid a similar visit to the U.S. minister in Dublin upon the death of President Roosevelt a few weeks earlier, and he thought that it was only correct diplomatic procedure to be consistent in such matters.

De Valera's visit to Hempel took place just when the full horror of Buchenwald and other Nazi extermination camps was being revealed, and even those who had otherwise been sympathetic to Éire's neutrality joined in denouncing the Irish prime minister for his diplomatic courtesy on the occasion of Hitler's death. Ironically enough, it was Churchill who helped restore de Valera's popularity, at least among his countrymen in Éire. In his May 13 victory speech, Churchill bitterly attacked his nemesis:

> Had it not been for the loyalty and friendship of Northern Ireland we should have been forced to come to close quarters with Mr. de Valera . . . [and] though at times it would have been quite easy and quite natural, we left the Dublin government to frolic with the Germans . . . and the Japanese . . . to their hearts content.

De Valera waited four days before responding, and the moderate, statesman-like tone of his address gave the Irish prime minister a psychological and moral advantage. Churchill had admitted that he would have justified violating Ireland's neutrality if Britain's necessity had so required. This was an unfortunate remark with the Nazi example so recent, and de Valera took full advantage of it by asking whether the prime minister intended to say that if Britain's necessity became sufficiently great, other people's rights would not matter. But then de Valera went on to say,

> Mr. Churchill is proud of Britain's stand alone, after France had fallen and before America entered the war. Could he not find in his heart the generosity to acknowledge that there is a small nation that stood alone, not for one year or two, but for several hundred years against aggression . . . a small nation that could never be got to accept defeat and has never surrendered her soul?

The British representative to Éire, Sir John Maffey, advised London of the spontaneous change in the national mood in Ireland. "After de Valera's call on Hempel," Maffey wrote, "the public mind had been too stunned to react quickly, but overnight there came the collapse of the Reich and with the sudden end of censorship there came the atrocity stories and pictures of the concentration camps." To many Irishmen, de Valera's condolences to the Reich had seemed morally reprehensible, and a sense of disgust had emerged amid the growing belief that ideals had been sacrificed for symbols. But Churchill's inflammatory remarks had allowed the Irish prime minister to regain his lost prestige.

Indeed, the truth of Maffey's observation was eloquently demonstrated by R.M. Smyllie a short time later in an article for *Foreign Affairs*. Smyllie was the editor of the *Irish Times*, which was associated with both the diminishing Anglo-Irish ascendancy and ex-servicemen with pro-Unionist sympathies who regarded de Valera's ideal of a rural, frugal, self-sufficient Gaelic Ireland with much distaste. But Smyllie spoke for many Irishmen of different creeds and politics when he wrote:

> Neutrality, almost by definition, is something negative; but Mr. de Valera raised it to the dignity of a national principle, largely because he wanted to be able to prove to the world at large that, after more than seven hundred years of subjection to England, the 26 counties of Southern Ireland at last were really free.

Irish Life and Politics During the Emergency

Behind the edifice of neutrality, life in Ireland from September 1939 to May 1945 was profoundly influenced by what the Irish referred to rather quaintly as "the emergency." An outbreak of hoof-and-mouth disease in 1941 decimated livestock throughout the country, and crops suffered from a scarcity of needed fertilizers. The government did sponsor the compulsory growing of wheat, but it was insufficient to offset other export losses. Finance ministers also kept a ceiling on salaries in order to check inflation as costs continued to rise and the standard of living fell. Sugar, tea, and fuel were all rationed almost from the outset of hostilities, with bread and other staples added to that list by 1942. Gas and electricity were nearly always in short supply, and coal was replaced by native peat, or turf, for most home heating. Transportation, particularly the railway system, was hard hit because machinery of all kinds was difficult to obtain and maintain. Compounding the problems of the Irish economy was the fact that the heavy fall in industrial production and the hard times suffered by the farming community contributed to record unemployment and increased emigration, mostly to Britain. It was in these dire circumstances that de Valera tapped Sean Lemass in 1940 to head the newly created Department of Supplies. Though successful in planning and providing for the country's most essential needs, efforts of this kind never raised the economy above the subsistence level.

Ireland in the early 1940s is sometimes described as culturally isolated and economically destitute. But these were not new dimensions of Irish life; they had been central to the country's experience since independence in 1922. If anything, the period of the emergency provided an opportunity for national introspection and self-evaluation. The Gaelic revival movement, for instance, was called into question by teachers who saw it as irrelevant in the face of the unabated emigration from rural areas. The future of the Gaelic revival, therefore, would be found not in the Gaeltacht (Irish-speaking regions, principally in the south and west) but, rather, in urban settings, where the philosophical underpinnings of the movement could be explored by sophisticated intellectuals. It was, indeed, an evolution different from the one Douglas Hyde projected when he founded the Gaelic League.

Throughout the emergency Sean O'Faoláin remained a vocal critic of Irish laws and institutions. He said of wartime Ireland, "Life is so isolated now that it is no longer being pollinated by germinating ideas windborne from anywhere." But O'Faoláin's remarkable periodical, *The Bell*, which he founded in 1940 and edited until 1946, contributed richly to the literary landscape of this era. *The Bell* was published each month in an edition of 3,000 copies and contained the writings of both new and established authors. Moreover, O'Faoláin used the journal to editorialize against some of his old adversaries, including the Censorship Board and the Gaelic revival. Again and again, he condemned the provincialism and prudery that he saw in the cultural and aesthetic standards of Irish society. *The Bell* helped to promote the ideals of rational reflection and social analysis without which postwar Ireland would have been less well prepared to meet the challenge of social modernization.

There were changes as well in the fortunes of the respective Irish political parties during the period of the emergency. Fianna Fáil succeeded in greatly expanding its base of support by attracting business and property interests, which had heretofore been alienated by the party's populist focus. But de Valera's repression of Republican extremists, together with the modification of his more radical policies, won him supporters from some merchants, strong farmers, and Anglo-Irish families. He was also able to use the almost universally popular policy of neutrality to good party advantage in the election of 1943, when Fianna Fáil's slogan was "Don't change horses in midstream."

The war years, however, were disastrous for Fine Gael. Its brief flirtation in the early 1930s with the quasi-Fascist Blueshirt movement continued to haunt the party well into the 1940s. And the popular response to de Valera's role in the Anglo-Irish Agreements of 1938 did not help either. Fine Gael was confronted with a major dilemma at the outbreak of war. A decision to support neutrality would effectively repudiate the party's pro-Commonwealth position, but to do otherwise would be contrary to the wishes of the vast majority of the Irish people. Fine Gael elected to support the national policy, which resulted in the resignation of its deputy leader, James Dillon. The 1943 election represented a serious defeat in which the party lost thirteen seats and, in 1944, the Fine Gael leader, W.T. Cosgrave, retired from political life.

While Fine Gael appeared to be in serious decline, the parliamentary Labour

SEAN O'FAOLAIN, 1900–1991

Sean O'Faolain was the most important intellectual force in post-treaty Ireland. As novelist, short-story writer, literary critic, biographer, political commentator, and editor he served as the liberal conscience of Irish nationalism. (Courtesy of the Irish Tourist Board)

party made a surprising advance in the election of 1943. Labour, benefiting from public disaffection with wartime shortages, increased its strength in the Dáil from nine to seventeen seats. In an election the following year, however, Labour was badly split by an internecine struggle between the moderate followers of William O'Brien and the militants led by James Larkin. As a result, Labour won only twelve seats in 1944, and even these were divided between rival factions.

A new party, Clann na Talmhan (Children of the Land), which represented essentially a farming constituency, emerged in the election of 1943. It was reflective of the general unhappiness among small farmers with Fianna Fáil's lack of farming progress, particularly in the western counties. The party won ten seats in the 1943 election but never exercised much influence in the Dáil due to its political inexperience and to programs that had only regional interest. Clann na Talmhan had only seven seats after the election of 1948, but those were enough to win representation that year in the first interparty government. Thereafter, the party fell into permanent obscurity, but its very presence in the mid-1940s was a signal of Fianna Fáil's vulnerability.

That was not, however, the popular image of the governing party. De Valera won a strong overall majority in the election of May 1944 thanks to the split in the Labour party, the weakening of Fine Gael after Cosgrave's retirement, and the public outcry against the American note and the challenge that it represented to Irish neutrality. Indeed, Fianna Fáil appeared to be solidly entrenched as the governing party for many years to come when the war ended in 1945. Even the party's 1945 candidate for the largely ceremonial post of president, Seán T. O'Ceallaigh, won a decisive victory at the polls. Yet for a party in power, the outlook in the immediate postwar years was not promising. Imports were up, exports were down, and wages continued to be repressed by government action. Not only was there no end to the wartime restrictions and shortages, but the weather also contrived to deal the Irish economy a devastating blow. The summer of 1946 was exceptionally wet, reducing grain production and leading to bread rationing, and the severe winter of 1947, which crippled much of western Europe, caused major dislocations in Irish industry and transport. Fianna Fáil responded in 1947 with increased taxation in order to finance higher food subsidies, and that legislation contributed to a growing sentiment of discontent and frustration.

These increasingly depressed circumstances produced a political reaction that found expression in the emergence of yet another new party, Clann na Poblachta (Children of the Republic). The thrust of this movement was in the direction of social and economic reform, with a special emphasis on the Republican ambitions that Fianna Fáil had first articulated upon coming to power in 1932. The Clann na Poblachta also had a popular leader in Seán MacBride, the son of Irish actress Maud Gonne and John MacBride, an executed martyr in the Easter Rising. Many contemporary observers believed that this new party was destined to dethrone Fianna Fáil, particularly after a few by-election triumphs in 1947. De Valera decided not to allow MacBride's followers an opportunity to consolidate a national organization and hence called for an early election in February 1948.

The Irish Republic, 1948–1959

Fianna Fáil won the battle but lost the war with this strategy. Clann candidates gained only ten seats while Fianna Fáil, although losing its overall majority, was still by far the largest single party (68 seats out of 147). Fine Gael increased its strength but marginally, from 30 to 31 seats, with the remaining Dáil contests won by Labour,

Clann na Talmhan, and Independent candidates. So profound was the desire to oust Fianna Fáil after its sixteen years in power that these ideologically disparate parties actually succeeded in forming the coalition needed to drive de Valera from office. The post of prime minister (taoiseach) went to a distinguished Fine Gael lawyer, John A. Costello, who had served as attorney general in the Cumann na nGaedhael government of yesteryear. The Fine Gael party also claimed the ministries of finance, defense, justice, agriculture, and industry and commerce. Labour ministers were given the portfolios of *tánaiste* (deputy premier), local government, and posts and telegraphs. The Ministry of Lands and Fisheries went to Clann na Talmhan. Finally, the new party, Clann na Poblachta, was given the respective ministries of external affairs and health. It was an improbable alliance that nonetheless managed to remain in office for three years, around the average length of time for most Irish governments since independence. Numerous reasons account for the unexpected success of the coalition, not least among them Costello's skill as a chairman and the concern shared by all parties that de Valera might return to power.

Innovative programs were begun, including a land rehabilitation project to bring some 4 million acres back into production and an industrial development authority for the purpose of promoting and coordinating industrial expansion. New housing construction was vigorously undertaken, and national health programs were improved. Critical to the success of most of these programs, however, were the funds received from the European Recovery Program (ERP; the Marshall Plan), in which Ireland had begun participation under Fianna Fáil in 1947. By 1950, the ERP had provided grants and loans totaling $150 million all of which represented desperately needed capital investment even if it did cause subsequent problems with inflation.

It was perhaps inevitable that some action favoring the declaration of a republic would be forthcoming, given Clann na Poblachta's preoccupation with that subject and the coalition's dependence on Clann's ten votes in the Dáil. The initiative to repeal the 1936 External Relations Act, which had defined an ambiguous relationship with Britain and the Commonwealth, came quite naturally from Sean MacBride. But the proposal was genuinely supported by Taoiseach. Costello, who was well aware of how the goal of a republic had divided Irishmen since the civil war, believed a resolution to that question would take the gun out of Irish politics. For the leader of Fine Gael, which was popularly seen as the pro-Commonwealth party, this was a statesmanlike view. There has been some controversy among historians over whether the Irish cabinet had agreed to repeal the External Relations Act before Costello's announcement to that effect in September 1948 while on a tour of Canada. It now seems reasonably clear that this was a deliberative decision reached collectively beforehand. The taoiseach, however, astounded the London government when he replied in the affirmative to a news reporter who asked whether the proposed act required Dublin's secession from the Commonwealth.

In November 1948 the Republic of Ireland Bill was introduced in the Dáil. The preamble explained that the status of a republic would permit the Irish president, rather than the British sovereign, to exercise executive powers or functions in connection with the state's external relations. Costello said, in the course of the debate on the bill, that the republic would put an end to the generations of alienation in Irish politics and that it would strengthen, not weaken, relations with Britain and the Commonwealth. In reply to the objection that this step would make the goal of ending partition more difficult than before, Costello held that Northern Ireland had seemed unmoved in any case by Éire's earlier restraint. The bill ultimately passed through all the stages, and it was agreed that the republic would be formally established on the symbolic date of Easter Monday 1949.

British prime minister Clement Attlee complained that he had not been given notice of the Irish government's intentions, and indeed he had not. But Attlee reciprocated the discourtesy later in 1949 at the time when the imperial Parliament passed the Ireland Act, recognizing the change in Ireland's constitutional status. Without consulting Dublin, the British added a proviso that Northern Ireland would never be detached from the United Kingdom without the consent of the Northern Ireland legislature. That, of course, angered the Irish government, but this so-called guarantee to the Unionist majority in Ulster was destined to cause much regret also for future British ministers. Meanwhile, however, the most remarkable development in these events of 1949 is that the Irish demanded, and the British conceded, all the privileges that Commonwealth membership had previously afforded. Indeed, the arrangement gave new meaning to the phrase "special relationship," which is sometimes used to describe Anglo-American ties but in fact is a more appropriate description for Anglo-Irish relations since 1949.

Attlee's government was no less keen than its predecessor had been to preserve the essential links of Commonwealth, but Labour ministers were perhaps more pragmatic and less sentimental when pursuing that objective. Attempts by London to draw Éire back into a closer Commonwealth relationship were unavailing precisely because the trend in Irish politics was clearly in the other direction. Nevertheless, postwar shortages and rationing in Britain prompted the Labour government to appreciate the value of Éire as a source of food and labor and as a market for British goods. It was becoming painfully apparent that the continuation of Commonwealth trade preferences to Éire was likely to be at least as beneficial to Britain as it was to Éire.

British cabinet minutes and other documents on London's policy toward Éire between 1945 and 1949 reveal sharp differences of opinion within the Labour leadership. Herbert Morrison, Ernest Bevin, and Harold Wilson, among others, deeply resented Dublin's repeal of the External Relations Act and believed that the end of Éire's membership in the Commonwealth also ended reciprocal citizenship rights and imperial preferences. Unlike Churchill, their objections did not relate to any romantic concerns about the sanctity of the empire but to the more materialistic issue of Britain's trade relations with other nations. Even ministers who sought accommodation with the Irish, like Lord Addison and Philip Noel-Baker, did so without any apparent affection for the Irish or for the merits of the Irish viewpoint.

London's response to the 1948 Republic of Ireland Act was initially hostile. Realizing that it was no longer possible to perpetuate the fiction that Éire had not left the Commonwealth in 1937, the British suggested to Dublin that there would be serious implications involving nationality questions and trade preferences if Ireland were to become a foreign country in relation to the Commonwealth. The dominions, however, already worried about the negative impact that punitive measures of any kind might have on their own constituents of Irish descent, demanded that London find some way of protecting the Irish from the consequences of their own action. Even members of Attlee's own Labour party who represented urban constituencies with a large Irish vote spoke openly of the need for Britain to do something. London's response was decidedly innovative. Under the terms of the Ireland Act of 1949, the Westminster Parliament accorded the Republic of Ireland a "non-foreign" status that insulated the Irish in the two areas where they were most vulnerable—citizenship and trade.

The retention of Commonwealth trade preferences for Ireland was important, but so was the question of Irish citizenship, which de Valera had attempted to resolve earlier with the Irish Nationality Act of 1935. But London and Dublin had never shared a common interpretation of that particular law—and not until the British Nationality Act of 1948, which was mutually agreed on by both countries, was the question put to rest. The effect of the 1948 law was that citizens of Éire, though no longer British subjects, would, when in Britain, be treated as if they were British subjects—a concession of enormous importance for the many Irish men and women living and working in Britain. Reciprocity was accorded to British subjects who, when in Ireland, would be accorded the same treatment as Irish citizens. What is sometimes overlooked, however, is the fact that there was a very real distinction in the way each country perceived this non-alien status. British subjects in Éire could not vote, hold public office, or work in the government service of Éire, whereas Éire citizens in Britain could do all of these.

Hence the British Nationality Act acknowledged Éire's symbolic need for a separate citizenship without changing its practical effects on individuals. The Republic of Ireland Act created in law what had been in fact true since the External Relations Act was passed in 1936: Éire had been a sovereign independent republic and not really a participating member of the Commonwealth since that date. Finally, the Ireland Act also recognized the desire of the Éire government to manifest its independence from the United Kingdom and that of the Northern Ireland government to maintain its independence from Éire. British policy toward partition never changed: If the northern and southern Irish wished to unite into a single political entity, no obstacle would be put in their way; but no British government, not even a Labour government with a large parliamentary majority, could surrender a part of the United Kingdom against its wishes.

Domestically, the pivotal event in the history of the Costello coalition government was the "mother-and-child scheme" crisis. Dr. Noel Browne, Clann na Poblachta minister of health, had made impressive strides in improving the quantity and quality of Irish health care. A former victim of tuberculosis himself, Browne labored diligently to institute a comprehensive program of X-ray diagnosis, increased and improved sanitarium facilities, and routine vaccinations for schoolchildren in what proved to be a highly successful war on that disease. He was also interested in lowering the high infant mortality rate in Ireland.

In 1951 the coalition presented to the Dáil a bill sponsored by Browne that called for a national prenatal and postpartum health program. It specifically provided for, among other things, maternity treatment and medical attention for children up to the age of sixteen free of charge and without a means test. The Irish Medical Association quickly denounced the scheme as a step toward socialized medicine and further objected that it would interfere with the doctor-patient relationship. Catholic bishops joined in the attack, claiming that the right to provide for the health of children belongs to the parents, not the state. These clerics were especially opposed to the proposal that local medical officers instruct women and girls in sex education, a proposal that might well lead to birth control and abortion. Browne then went to considerable lengths to ensure that the program would in no way be in conflict with Catholic teaching. The bishops were unmoved, however, and Costello informed Browne that the government could not endorse a program that the bishops found objectionable. But Browne stood his ground until he was told to resign by his own party chief, Sean MacBride. The controversy became a national scandal when Browne then released the correspondence on the affair to the press. Lamenting the loss of the talented and dedicated cabinet minister and physician, *The Irish Times* remarked: "The most serious revelation however is that the Roman Catholic Church would seem to be the effective government of this country."

Browne's removal from office and the abandonment of his proposed scheme were no more the exclusive consequence of episcopal politics than was Parnell's repudiation in 1891. Some members of the hierarchy, particularly Archbishop John McQuaid of Dublin, admittedly did engage in questionable pressure tactics. But there were other reasons for Browne's defeat, such as the opposition of the Irish Medical Association and the growing estrangement between Browne and some of his colleagues who doubted that the scheme was financially viable. Nevertheless, people resented the intrusion of the bishops and priests in what they considered essentially a secular matter. The coalition government fell because of defections resulting from Browne's departure from office. Fianna Fáil then returned to power and, after negotiating mutually acceptable terms with the hierarchy, de Valera won passage of a health act that retained much of Browne's original proposal. Perhaps the most salutary effect of this first church-state crisis since independence was that it was also the last one. The bishops were quick to realize that although the populace still respected their moral authority in what were truly episcopal affairs, the Irish would not permit a clerical veto over the proper functioning of liberal democracy.

Fianna Fáil foundered as a minority government from 1951 to 1954, whereupon de Valera was forced to call another general election. The result of the balloting was that Costello headed a second coalition administration. But the 1950s were a dismal economic period irrespective of which party was in power as inflation, increased taxation, and trade imbalances continued to hound Costello as they had de Valera. Perhaps the most noteworthy event came in 1955, when the Soviet Union, in a compensatory deal worked out with the West, agreed not to veto Ireland's admission to the United Nations as it had before. The Dublin government, which had previously refused to join the North Atlantic Treaty Organization (NATO) so long as partition existed and Britain remained a NATO member, made clear that UN membership represented no departure from the Irish policy of neutrality.

This was also a time of IRA resurgence. A new generation of young nationalists had grown up in a country that had been insulated not only from war but also from prosperity and hope. The 1949 declaration of the republic had still left a truncated country, and the boredom and frustration of a stagnant economy caused much discontent. The IRA leadership, strengthened with fresh recruits, began a Northern campaign in the closing months of 1956. When raids were subsequently conducted against police barracks across the border in Northern Ireland, Taoiseach John Costello responded by pledging the full resources of the state to halt the campaign of violence. That provoked Sean MacBride to renounce the government and to take the tiny Clann na Poblachta party out of the ruling coalition because Costello offered no alternative of his own for ending partition. Beset by political defections and economic decline, the government fell, only to be replaced by a resurgent Fianna Fáil, which won seventy-eight seats and thereby held a comfortable overall majority of ten. This 1957 election was to inaugurate yet another sixteen-year reign for Fianna Fáil. And although de Valera had been returned once more as taoiseach, he stepped down two years later, in 1959, to become his party's successful candidate for president of the republic.

This marked the end of a remarkable era in Irish politics. De Valera was now seventy-seven years old and nearly blind, but he was destined to have two presidential terms. He was reelected in 1966 and served with distinction in his nonpolitical and ceremonial post until 1973 when, at the age of ninety-one, he retired to private life. Although he lived another two years, into his ninety-third year, and died on August 29, 1975, the age of de Valera in Irish politics effectively had ended in 1959.

11

Modern Ireland, 1959–1998

Adjusting to a European Future

Abandoning Economic Self-Sufficiency

Sean Lemass succeeded de Valera in 1959 as the new parliamentary leader of Fianna Fáil and as taoiseach. He came to power at a time when a new generation of voters was obviously bored with the old quarrels between the veterans of the treaty debate and the civil war. These people aspired to a lifestyle then being enjoyed by an increasing number of Americans and Europeans. They wanted to join the mainstream of Western culture and to enjoy the comforts and luxuries that were derived from modern-day technology.

Lemass responded to these new aspirations. Abandoning the self-reliance of Sinn Féin's economic nationalism and de Valera's frugal-comfort idealism, T.K. Whitaker, secretary to the minister of finance, began a campaign to lure foreign investment to the Irish economy. Some of the strategies employed were: offers of tax exemption, land and financial grants for factory location and construction, and an emphasis on the availability of cheap labor. Companies from all over the Western world and Japan accepted the generous Irish offer and set up factories and plants, which, in time, diminished unemployment and drastically reduced the tide of emigration.

Between 1959 and 1966, therefore, Lemass presided over a miniature industrial revolution as foreign investment increased substantially and Irish exports expanded dramatically. In 1961 the Dublin government sought to obtain membership in the European Economic Community (EEC) but allowed the application to lapse when French president Charles de Gaulle vetoed British entry in 1963. So dependent were Irish producers on the British market that it made no sense for Ireland to join the EEC if Britain were kept out. By 1971, however, the British and Irish were again debating the merits of EEC membership in terms of what was now seen as their "European destiny." In Ireland, that resurrected the old arguments regarding Irish-Ireland and Irish economic self-sufficiency, but now that British entry was assured, proponents of membership warned against the dangers of being excluded from the powerful and prosperous European trading bloc. A national referendum was held in 1972 during which four out of every five voters favored joining the EEC. Ireland subsequently became a member on January 1, 1973.

Dublin, of course, had begun moving away from the shelter of tariff walls into wider trade structures almost a decade earlier. The Irish had participated in the Kennedy Round of trade negotiations under the General Agreement on Tariffs and Trade that resulted in general tariff reductions and had, in December 1965, entered into a free trade agreement with Britain. This pact represented a major breakthrough in which London abolished virtually all restrictions on Irish imports in return for a dismantling of tariff barriers on British goods and an end to tax incentives and subsidies for foreign investors over a period of fifteen years. Membership in the EEC, however, did not bring the immediate profits expected earlier by the farming community. The Irish economic boom, like that of the rest of the West in the 1970s, crashed on the rock of inflation. Hardest hit were the poor, whose wages simply did not keep pace with price increases. Even tourism, which had emerged in the 1960s as Ireland's most important economic activity after agriculture, suffered from the oil embargo by the Organization of Petroleum Exporting Countries (OPEC) in 1973 and the general decline in the world economy. Without the generous incentives of earlier years, and disenchanted by the lack of energy and initiative among some members of the Irish labor force, foreign industries began closing plants by the late 1970s and early 1980s. Ireland, a society that already had the fastest-growing population under the age of thirty in Western Europe, witnessed once again the frustration of high unemployment and the sorrow of involuntary emigration. Making matters more difficult was the fact that one popular option for earlier emigrants, settling in America, was no longer readily available because of the quotas established by Congress in the 1960s for all foreign nationals seeking admission to the United States. Many Irish citizens came to America anyway, ostensibly as visitors, and remained as illegal aliens. The plight of these people in the late 1980s, and continuing to the present day as economic conditions have waxed and waned, represents a persistent problem in relations between Dublin and Washington.

Irish foreign policy has always accommodated itself to shifting economic, cultural, and social winds. After being admitted to the United Nations in 1955, Ireland was capably represented by articulate diplomats who condemned imperialism and who often acted as spokesmen for third world victims of Western colonialism. Irish envoys, like Conor Cruise O'Brien, believed that the history of their own country made them the natural allies of oppressed and disenfranchised people. Their conduct at the United Nations often infuriated Catholic bishops in Ireland and in the United States, for instance, Ireland's initial willingness to consider the membership of Communist China in that world organization. But the increasing interdependence of Irish trade with that of the West led inevitably to more cautious positions, as demonstrated by the Irish vote against the admission of mainland China to the United Nations in 1962. Indeed, Minister for External Affairs Liam Cosgrave made it abundantly clear that Ireland's opposition to imperialism did not extend to national liberation movements that were either Soviet-inspired or otherwise incompatible with progressive Western positions. Indicative of that sentiment is the fact that of the forty-four roll call votes taken in the eleventh plenary session of the General

Assembly, a period during which Cosgrave held the external affairs post, thirty-nine of those cast by Ireland coincided with those of Britain and the United States. What was often insufficiently appreciated by some officials in London and Washington, of course, was the fact that Western interests could sometimes be better served by an Ireland that had influence with third world countries precisely because of its nonalignment in the world arena. Reflective of this reality was the popularity and effectiveness of Irish soldiers on UN peacekeeping missions over a period of three decades in the Middle East, Congo, Cyprus, and elsewhere.

New Challenges and Opportunities

Perhaps the boldest initiatives undertaken by Fianna Fáil taoiseach Sean Lemass were his meetings with the reformist Prime Minister Terence O'Neill of Northern Ireland, first in Belfast and later in Dublin, during January and February 1965. It marked the first time that any head of government from the south had held official talks with his northern counterpart on Irish soil. For a time it appeared that the meetings might help to normalize relations between the two governments and lead to increased cross-border cooperation. But in 1966, the celebrations to mark the fiftieth anniversary of the 1916 uprising were used in the north by nationalist and Unionist extremists alike as an occasion for resuming intercommunal tensions. Lemass retired from office later that year and was succeeded by Jack Lynch, who also met with O'Neill in a second round of shuttle summitry between Belfast and Dublin during December 1967 and January 1968. By that time, however, the civil rights agitation in Northern Ireland had begun to imperil O'Neill's political fate and to reduce the prospects for any further progress in north-south discussions.

Jack Lynch led Fianna Fáil to a triumphant victory in the general election of 1969. Yet gaining a majority of seats in the Dáil did not mean that the party was spared serious challenges. A somewhat self-inflicted Fianna Fáil crisis was Lynch's May 1970 firing of two of his senior ministers, Charles Haughey and Neal Blaney, who were later arrested on charges of conspiring to import arms and ammunition for the IRA into Northern Ireland. A third minister, Kevin Boland, resigned in sympathy. Haughey and Blaney were subsequently acquitted of the charges, and Haughey later went on to become the leader of the Fianna Fáil party and taoiseach of the Republic. But the incident illustrates how corrosive the Ulster question had become for the political environment of the Irish state.

Dissatisfaction over the government's Northern Ireland policy, or lack thereof, may have been part of the reason the electorate turned against Fianna Fáil in the general election of March 1973, but inflation and rising prices were also the cause of much unhappiness. After sixteen years in power, there developed against Fianna Fáil the same sentiment as had been evident in the 1948 election: the desire for change for its own sake. In any event, Fine Gael and Labour were able to agree on a fourteen-point program that carried them to power. Fine Gael leader Liam

Cosgrave and Labour leader Brendan Corish then became taoiseach and tánaiste in yet another attempt at coalition government.

Despite the failure of various British attempts to devise a power-sharing plan for Unionists and nationalists in Ulster, the tenor of Anglo-Irish relations improved during the early years of Prime Minister Liam Cosgrave's term in office. Indicative of the ecumenical spirit of the time was the popularity of President Erskine Hamilton Childers, a Protestant, whose appeal for sectarian harmony and moderation struck a responsive chord within the republic. Childers, a peace-loving man who died in November 1974, would have been appalled and dismayed by the July 21, 1976, assassination in Dublin of British ambassador Christopher Ewart-Biggs and by the bombing of a Dublin courthouse a few weeks later. Despite denials of responsibility by the "Official" and "Provisional" branches of the IRA (OIRA and PIRA), the government of the Irish Republic promptly declared a state of emergency. The Dáil then introduced two bills that increased the powers of the Garda Síochána in combating IRA activities and provided more severe penalties for membership in the IRA and other subversive organizations.

The coalition government of Fine Gael and Labour had been in office for over four years when Cosgrave called for an election in 1977. Fianna Fáil, led by former Taoiseach Jack Lynch, campaigned against taxation programs, poor employment prospects, and the growing crime rate. The party also promised to abolish the automobile tax and to increase the level of tax-free earnings. It was a platform that appealed to the electorate; Fianna Fáil won 84 of the 148 seats in the Dáil, and Lynch's new government took office in July 1977.

The February 1978 budget completed the implementation of the campaign promises that Fianna Fáil had made before the election, and the republic, for a short time anyway, appeared to be enjoying an economic boom. But soon the spiraling cost of housing and trade union demands for substantial wage increases prompted the Lynch government to issue a green paper calling for a curb on public expenditure and greater restraint in wage demands. The Irish Congress of Trade Unions and the government took to issuing charges against each other as the economy began to deteriorate.

An economic challenge of another kind confronted Dublin when pressure mounted within the Irish Republic to join the European Monetary System (EMS). Mindful that bank interest charges and the earnings from Irish trade with the continent were affected by British industrial difficulties and, occasionally, by the political needs of the British government, Irish public opinion strongly favored entry into the EMS. After five years of beneficial EEC membership, many Irish nationals could see little reason why their agriculture-based economy should be conditioned by the notably different problems and interests of the United Kingdom. Thus in the closing weeks of 1978 the republic made its historic bid to "break with sterling." The actual transition, however, was delayed when the EMS members failed to produce the 650 million pounds in grants over five years that Ireland required. In March 1979 the long-awaited break between the Irish and British currencies was accompanied by a decline in the Irish pound to an exchange rate of 88 pence sterling by midsummer. A strike by postal workers also deprived the country of mail collections and deliveries for five months, and the international oil crisis caused severe gasoline shortages throughout the republic. Contrasting markedly with the problems and tensions of the year was the national euphoria that greeted the visit of Pope John Paul II at the end of September 1979. At least 300,000 people attended the appearances of His Holiness at Drogheda, Galway, Limerick, and the Marian shrine at Knock in County Mayo. An estimated 1.3 million attended a mass celebrated by the pontiff in Dublin's Phoenix Park.

Virtually everyone was surprised by Prime Minister Jack Lynch's sudden resignation on December 5, 1979, and the quick succession of Charles Haughey as taoiseach and leader of Fianna Fáil. Haughey began his term in office by appealing for national understanding of the country's economic ills. An agreement was reached in October between the government, the unions, and the employers for a 15 percent pay increase over fifteen months. Meanwhile, Haughey and British prime minister Margaret Thatcher paid each other official visits in London and Dublin, and relations between the two countries became unexpectedly cordial in the first year of the new taoiseach's term. In the autumn of 1980, Brian Friel's play *Translations* began its Dublin run and was hailed by some critics as the finest Irish drama in a generation. The theme of the play, a culture clash between Irish and English attitudes in nineteenth-century Donegal, had a special significance for everyone who had endured the Northern Ireland tensions of the 1970s.

Unionist alarm in Ulster over the reported discussions between London and Dublin induced Thatcher to reaffirm Britain's resolve that the people of Northern Ireland not be compelled to join the republic against their will. The reaction in the south to that affirmation, combined with Dublin's deteriorating economy, did not favor Charles Haughey, who chose the spring of 1981 to call for a general election. Fianna Fáil's substantial majority was converted into a minority of 78 seats in the new 166-seat Dáil (which had been expanded to reflect the population increase of the 1970s), and Fine Gael won 65 seats in that balloting. That was far short of a majority, but Fine Gael was able to forge a coalition with the Labour party and four independent deputies. Fine Gael leader Dr. Garret FitzGerald, who took office June 30, brought to the premiership a reputation for integrity and competence as one of the country's leading economists. FitzGerald soon embarked on a crusade for constitutional reform within the republic, the purpose of which was to delete the elements of the republic's constitution that Northern Protestants found distressing. At issue were factors encompassing family law, especially the prohibition against divorce in the republic, and nationalist aspirations, such as the claim to jurisdiction over "the whole island of Ireland." Opposition in the Dáil to these initiatives was vocal and spontaneous, but that did not prevent FitzGerald from paying a call to 10 Downing Street in November. After their meeting, the British and Irish prime ministers announced the creation of an intergovernmental council to advise both governments on matters of common concern.

By any standard, 1982 was a momentous year in the political life of the Irish Republic. On January 27 the Fine Gael coalition government fell after an independent deputy refused to support a budget proposal to tax clothing and footwear. In the general election that followed, neither major party gained a majority, but Fianna Fáil was able to come to power when smaller groups, such as the Socialist Workers' party, gave it their support. Accordingly, Charles Haughey was returned to office as taoiseach on March 9. Haughey was soon involved in a dispute with the United Kingdom over EEC agricultural policy, and he later rejected a London proposal for a new assembly in Northern Ireland. What outraged the British most, however, was the Irish government's response to what London regarded as Argentine aggression in the Falkland Islands (called the Malvinas by Argentina). Dublin appealed to the UN Security Council to end hostilities in the South Atlantic and, together with Italy, subsequently refused to renew EEC sanctions against Argentina.

Anglo-Irish relations, which earlier had been strained by London's tough stance in 1981 toward the hunger strikers in Northern Ireland, were aggravated still further by the occasion of Prime Minister Haughey's 1982 visit with President Ronald Reagan at the White House on St. Patrick's Day. After inviting the president to pay an official visit to Ireland, Haughey publicly called on the United States to encourage Britain to take a more positive attitude toward Irish unity. Reagan remained diplomatically noncommittal while Margaret Thatcher silently fumed in London.

But 1982 was also the year in which Ireland celebrated the centenaries of the birth of its most distinguished writer, James Joyce, and statesman, Eamon de Valera. There was also much jubilation throughout the country when the Irish rugby team won the Triple Crown for the first time since 1949, defeating Scotland 21–12. And in late November, Radio Telefís Éireann (RTÉ; Irish television) and FR3 (a French channel) began transmitting the first episodes of the jointly produced television version of Thomas Flanagan's novel *The Year of the French.*

Economic woes and a ministerial scandal involving the resignation of the attorney general led to a vote of no confidence in the Haughey government on November 4, thus requiring a third general election in less than eighteen months. In the subsequent balloting, Fianna Fáil won 75 seats in the Dáil, but Fine Gael picked up 70 and, together with Labour's 16, was able to form a coalition on a program of national recovery. It was not the economy that now challenged Taoiseach Garret FitzGerald, but the issue of abortion. Mother Teresa of Calcutta had addressed a capacity crowd in Dublin's national stadium during the month of August, lending her support to those opposed to abortion. Both Fine Gael and Fianna Fáil were strongly pressured into supporting a constitutional amendment that would outlaw abortion in the republic, but FitzGerald wished to have it worded in such a way as to avoid offending the Protestant community. Fianna Fáil insisted on more categorical language, and thanks to some Fine Gael defections, the Fianna Fáil version prevailed in the Dáil and was subsequently put to the people in a referendum. Meanwhile, the Irish Labour party condemned the amendment, and many academics, professional people, feminist leaders, and various other groups, including some who opposed abortion but saw no virtue in prohibiting it in the constitution, formed a vocal opposition. It was all to no avail, however, for the eighth amendment to the Irish constitution carried in the referendum, held September 7, 1983, by a wide margin (841,233 votes to 416,136). It reads:

> The state acknowledges the right to life of the unborn, and with due regard to the equal right to life of the mother, guarantees in its laws to respect, and as far as practicable, by its laws to defend and vindicate that right.

This was a personal rebuff for FitzGerald, who had previously announced that he would vote against the amendment. Reaction among Ulster Protestant leaders, as he had expected, was sharply critical. Yet for a year that began with a January scandal involving the unauthorized telephone bugging of certain journalists and politicians, which led to the resignation of the Garda commissioner, even the divisive issue of Northern Ireland might have been a welcome distraction from the taoiseach's domestic woes. In March 1983 the Irish government, for the first time in its history, boycotted New York's St. Patrick's Day parade to protest the appointment of a pro-IRA activist as grand marshal of that event.

Social and Political Responses to the New Realities

This was also a time of profound social change in the republic, as indicated by the new militancy toward the Northern question and the debate over abortion and other moral issues. Still, for all its problems, life in Ireland had become notably better than it had been for generations. To be sure, the changes in Irish society in the last decades of the twentieth century were nothing less than revolutionary. Television was clearly a catalyst in this transformation. Viewers in Dublin were receiving BBC transmissions as early as 1953, and Irish newspapers soon began publishing that network's program schedule for the convenience of subscribers. RTÉ, which began broadcasting in 1962, gave further impetus to the interest in the new medium, and by the mid-1960s the slightly less than 700,000 households in the republic owned about 350,000 sets. By that time a good number of viewers could also access the two principal British channels, ITV and BBC, in addition to RTÉ. Anglo-American values and lifestyles, wholly alien to the traditional values fostered heretofore by both church and state in Ireland, began to have an effect on Irish viewers.

Cinema censorship was made considerably more liberal after the establishment of the Films Appeal Board in 1964. Three years later the Censorship of Publications Act limited to twelve years the period for which a book might be banned. Although the prohibition could be renewed at the end of that time, the effect of the act was to release 5,000 suppressed titles at a single stroke. Nudity in magazines or on the stage encountered greater difficulty, but there too the earlier restraints gave way by the late 1970s and 1980s. Contraception and other issues of sexual morality were now as likely to be discussed on talk shows in Dublin as they were in London. The inhibitions of a more parochial era were gradually being worn away.

The 1960s, 1970s, and 1980s also entailed sweeping change in the Roman Catholic Church in Ireland. Pope John XXIII and the Second Vatican Council set in motion a revolution of change no less significant than the one that accompanied the changes in Irish cultural and social mores. Some of the changes were liturgical, as in the instance of Latin being replaced by the vernacular, and in the discontinuance of Lenten and Eucharistic fasts and abstention from meat on Fridays. Other changes were ecumenical, allowing for joint religious services with Protestants and for attendance at non-Catholic weddings and funerals. The surrender of so much traditional authority may have been consistent with the societal changes of the day, but it also had an impact on new religious vocations in Ireland. Despite the growth in overall population during this period, the number of seminarians studying for the priesthood fell more than 50 percent between 1959 and 1972. Some of this, of course, may have been due to more increased socioeconomic mobility than to uncertainty over changes in the Church, but the effect was to diminish religious vocations in a nation that had once sent missionaries to virtually every part of the world. A Catholic ethos still pervaded the country, however, despite the appearance there of greater secularization, as in the hierarchy's removal in 1970 of the ban prohibiting Catholics from sending their children to Trinity College, Dublin, under pain of excommunication, or the 1972 national referendum that removed the special status of the Church (Article 44) from the constitution.

In June 1984 U.S. president Ronald Reagan visited Ireland. He was, at that time, only the second foreign guest ever (President John Kennedy being the first, in 1963) to be given the honor of addressing a joint session of the Irish Parliament. In his remarks, Reagan reviewed East-West relations but also took note of the violence in Northern Ireland and condemned terrorism. The Kennedy and Reagan visits, however, were not comparable other than the parliamentary address. While Kennedy, who was universally popular throughout Ireland, had generated a devotional fervor approaching that of a religious pilgrimage, Reagan's visit was marred by public protests against U.S. foreign policy and a boycott by some faculty and students on the occasion of his receiving an honorary degree at University College, Galway.

The following year, inflation in Ireland fell to one of the lowest levels in Europe, but the means by which that was accomplished—price controls—resulted in record unemployment. FitzGerald's efforts to guide the Irish economy away from the shoals of recession was further handicapped by declining international demand for microchips, which prompted several foreign manufacturers to leave Ireland. Equally debilitating was the cost of foreign borrowing, which continued to expend resources that might otherwise have funded investment in the republic. This was also the year when social activists confronted the Roman Catholic Church once more, this time in support of a limited liberalization of the law on the availability of contraceptives. The archbishop of Dublin, Dr. Kevin McNamara, denounced this move, as well as the attempt by activists to remove the constitutional ban on divorce. African famine relief, however, was a cause that engendered little dissent in Ireland, and Dublin rock star Bob Geldof conceived and led the Live Aid concert, in which the republic made the biggest financial contribution relative to population (8 million Irish punts from a population of 3.5 million) of any country in the world.

Perhaps the greatest accomplishment of this particular FitzGerald administration was the Anglo-Irish Agreement of November 1985 (discussed in Chapter 12). The popularity of the Fine Gael government, together with the difficulties then being encountered by Fianna Fáil, gave the impression that FitzGerald would be reelected easily in the next balloting, which could be held no later than the autumn of 1987. Moreover, the defection of some Fianna Fáil Dáil members to the newly founded party by the right-wing Progressive Democrats seemed to suggest the imminent decline of Charles Haughey's political party. Garret FitzGerald, however, was the unlikely savior of Fianna Fáil owing to his persistent attempts to liberalize the laws and the constitution to make them more suitable to a modern pluralistic society.

It was FitzGerald's coalition partner, the Labour party, that actually precipitated the sudden change in the political climate. Labour had been urging the removal of the constitutional ban on divorce for some time, and FitzGerald thought the moment propitious because he mistakenly read public opinion as having swung in favor of the reform. The government therefore proposed an amendment to the constitution that allowed divorce if a marriage had irretrievably failed for at least five years. Protestant churches endorsed the proposed bill, but Roman Catholic bishops said that the experience of divorce laws in other countries counseled against emulating that example. Some priests and conservative laymen went still further and warned that divorce would subvert the rights of the spouse and children of the first marriage, in addition to complicating the operation of traditional inheritance laws. A referendum was held June 6, 1986, in which nearly 60 percent of the electorate voted, of which 64 percent rejected the amendment. It was another setback for FitzGerald and another cause for concern throughout the Protestant community on both sides of the border.

Charles Haughey and Fianna Fáil captured control of the twenty-fifth Dáil in a general election on February 17, 1987, in which 76 percent of the electorate voted. Fianna Fáil won a commanding 81 seats, Fine Gael captured only 51, and the remaining seats were divided among the Progressive Democrats (14), Labour (12), the Worker's party (4), Independents (3), and the Democratic Sociality party (1). On October 9, 1987, Haughey announced the most dramatic domestic initiative in many years: the Program for National Recovery. Designed to put Ireland's economy back on a path of long-term and sustained growth, the plan was a product of several months of negotiation among the Dublin government, the Irish Congress of Trade Unions, the Confederation of Irish Industry, the Construction Industry Federation, and the farming organizations. One major objective of the plan was the creation of no fewer than 20,000 additional jobs by 1998.

Haughey's blueprint for an economic miracle also involved the toughest program cuts in public expenditures that Ireland had had in thirty years. Indeed, the government's retrenchment proved harsher than anything imagined in the proposal that had driven Fine Gael from power in early 1987. Some of Fianna Fáil's traditional constituencies, such as workers in the health, education, and the construction industries, had been among the areas hardest hit. The taoiseach's nonpartisan approach left Alan Dukes, who succeeded to the leadership of Fine Gael after FitzGerald's resignation, with no choice but to support the government. To do otherwise would have made the opposition party appear uncommitted to solving the nation's financial problems.

But even the challenges of a worsening economy and the controversy provoked by the issues of contraception and divorce could not entirely eclipse the conflict in the north in the national consciousness. It continued unabated, despite the cautious attempt for Anglo-Irish *glasnost* after the accord at Hillsborough Castle in 1985. The mindless bombing deaths of eleven civilians in November 1987 at a Remembrance Day service in Enniskillen provoked such intense feelings of guilt and disgust that few protested the infringement of civil liberties when some several thousand homes in the republic were raided by Irish authorities, in cooperation with Northern Ireland police in the hunt for those engaged in cross-border incursions.

Ireland Confronts Modernity

The late 1980s and 1990s proved a period of enormous change for the Republic of Ireland. In 1988, a decidedly sober mood pervaded the country. Ireland was troubled by violence, poverty, and fading confidence in the future. None of this, of course, was intrinsically new to the Irish experience, but rapidly increasing urbanization altered the nation's economic and social landscape, and changed the nature of its traditional problems. The poverty that Ireland now experienced was no longer primarily a result of its traditional rural setting. Nor did Ireland experience the same urban poverty that had given rise to the movement of Jim Larkin and others like him in the earlier part of the century. Instead, Ireland was at the time confronting the experience of urban unemployment, drug-related crime, and the attendant consequences that have long plagued modern European and American societies.

By the late 1980s, fully 50 percent of the Irish population resided in Dublin and its environs. The traditional landscape of "dear, dirty Dublin" became nearly unrecognizable as gentrification transformed much of the city center, while working-class suburbs, which possessed all the charm of American public housing projects, grew up around the city's edges, particularly to the north. Typical examples were the tower blocks and terrace houses of Ballymun that have been immortalized in the novels of Roddy Doyle and in such films as *The Commitments* and *The Snapper.*

The north side of the Liffey remained home to Dublin's working class. Although this area was traditionally regarded as more blue-collar than the bourgeois south side, the fact remains that the north side and the ever-expanding suburbs had to cope with growing social and economic problems, and indeed continue to be the scenes of increasing crime and violence. Overcrowding and unemployment produced crime, family instability, and drug dependence on a scale unexpected for many who thought that Irish life would somehow escape these contemporary social problems. In fact, a good deal of Dublin's disorder related to heroin and cocaine use.

Urbanization also contributed much to the sense of doubt and uncertainty that fell upon Ireland in the late 1980s. Because a majority of the country's population was born after 1960, some social and economic dislocation was inevitable as that generation came of age. Compounding the problem in Ireland was that maturation of this generation coincided with the negative consequences of unemployment, a fading economy, and urbanization, all of which contributed to a growing crisis of confidence, especially among the young, over the future of the country.

Meanwhile, the absence of appropriate economic opportunities in rural Ireland helped spark urban migration. Ireland's embrace of the economic policies and opportunities afforded by its membership in the European Community (EC) had, at least initially, positively influenced the modernization of agriculture and the improvement of the general standard of rural living. Indeed, in the 1980s, the revered Irish family farm appeared to be a stronger institution than it had been before the arrival of the EC. While modernization had improved the economic prospects of rural Ireland during the 1970s, it had also created an economic situation in which the country's agricultural base could no longer provide employment for the bulk of the rural populace. In and of itself, that situation hardly represented anything new. Rural areas had long been the country's principal source of emigration. The difference in the late 1980s, and in fact much of the 1990s, lay in the fact that the younger generation, which could find no place for itself in rural Ireland, was better-educated and more easily adjusted to life away from the farm. It was also true that the young were not as willing to desert their native land as were earlier generations. Thus the migration of rural school-leavers to the urban areas of Dublin, Cork, Galway, and other cities reflected a desire to find an economic niche without following the traditional path of overseas emigration.

Because this ascendant generation recognized that rural Ireland could not provide a livelihood for them, they sought refuge in the cities. Unfortunately, the arrival of those young people in the urban centers coincided with a period of severe economic recession. So, while many sought their fortune in their own country, even the best educated among them discovered that there was little need for their skills. Meanwhile, those with still fewer qualifications soon discovered that Dublin and other urban areas offered little more opportunity than did their native villages. For them, life in the city generally meant a life on the dole in a bleak suburb or in a crumbling working-class neighborhood.

The chronic unemployment that had generally plagued Ireland since independence in 1922 reached particularly high levels in the late 1980s. Cuts in government spending decreased the size of the public workforce at a time when a global recession was also leading to job losses in the private sector.

Nor, as previously noted, was emigration as attractive or as feasible an option as in earlier days. Britain, the United States, and Australia—Ireland's traditional outlets for those seeking a better life—were experiencing economic difficulties of their own. Moreover, the U.S. policy of limiting immigration further exacerbated the problem. However, both Britain and the United States still attracted sizable numbers of Irish immigrants. Although as many as 50,000 illegal Irish immigrants were in New England alone during the late 1980s, the days when the United States could or would absorb the majority of Ireland's excess population seemed to be over.

If the Irish urban scene seemed especially bleak during the late 1980s, the Irish made a concerted attempt to address their fiscal problems in the 1990s. Although the unemployment rate remained high in both rural and urban areas, efforts to improve the cities themselves proceeded apace. In 1991, for example, Dublin celebrated its millennium, and the major renovations that accompanied that celebration helped to transform a part of the central city for its many visitors. Employment schemes also lessened somewhat the despair of working-class youth, while the government, albeit belatedly, recognized the severity of the drug problem in urban Ireland and endeavored to address it.

Perhaps even more important was the sense that the Irish people's view of themselves had changed over that decade, as the urbanization of the country had led to differing views on society, religion, and politics. Modern Ireland and the monolithic conservatism and economic self-sufficiency to which de Valera aspired share little resemblance. Rather, the combination of the relative prosperity of the 1960s and 1970s with the parallel population increase created a younger generation that was demographically large and well-educated and far more cosmopolitan than their parents' generation. With such a substantial a number of them living in urban areas, these youths tended to drift away from the traditional emphasis on hearth and home. More open to differing lifestyles, they found the lack of "progress" in traditional Ireland frustrating and backward. Many of them supported politicians and social developments that reflected their own attitudes and, indeed, often disparaged the traditional Ireland from which they came.

These changing social attitudes became evident in political developments during the 1990s. Although the Irish had to contend with a political system dogged by scandal and reactionary politicians, positive signs of change emerged. Perhaps the most important was the 1991 election of Mary Robinson as president of the republic. The presidency has traditionally been a largely ceremonial office and had usually been seen as a sinecure for politicians well past their prime. Robinson, a Labour party member and barrister who made her reputation as an advocate for women's rights, was never expected to win office. Indeed, her election can be attributed to the opportunity provided by the bickering between the two major political parties during the campaign. Having won the presidency, however, Robinson remade it in her own image. Although constitutionally barred from speaking out or participating in political matters, she established herself as the most respected and trusted figure in Irish government. In her travels throughout the country, she reached out to the dispossessed among Ireland's citizens and gave them hope of a better day. She was especially appealing to the young, who saw in her the embodiment of the change that they believed was necessary for their nation. In a nonpolitical but highly effective manner, she established a dialogue with women in Northern Ireland and effectively supporting peacemaking efforts in that province. On the international stage, President Robinson assumed a role as the representative of all that is positive and good about Ireland. Irish Americans in particular developed a genuine respect and affection for her. It was perhaps one of the most encouraging indications of Ireland's changing sense of self that Mary Robinson became the most popular figure in the country during her tenure in office.

The Old Boy Network of Irish Politics

Yet, on the political front, change did not come as easily. Politics remained the province of a "good-old-boy" system of government. From 1987 to 1992, Charles Haughey of Fianna Fáil served as taoiseach. Haughey represented old-style Irish politics in the extreme. With a career often highlighted by controversy and scandal, Haughey had the effect of dividing the country along personal lines. People tended to be for or against him rather than for or against his party's positions. Haughey's business dealings, as well as his involvement in nationalist activities in Northern Ireland, contributed to the perception, at least on the part of some, that he was not an entirely trustworthy figure.

Nonetheless, his term as taoiseach did contribute economic benefits to the country. Haughey made large-scale cuts in public spending in an effort to reduce the public debt, a courageous if highly unpopular move. He managed to win the support of organized labor, and, to almost everyone's surprise, he succeeded in reversing the downward slide of the Irish economy.

Before long, however, Haughey was once again engulfed in scandal. A series of business deals in 1991 had taxed the country's patience with its flamboyant leader. Then, in 1992, his own colleagues in Fianna Fáil turned on him. His party's coalition partners, the Progressive Democrats, threatened to bring down the government if Haughey did not resign. Finally, when it became clear to him that his support in Fianna Fáil was diminishing, Haughey did just that.

The period that followed illustrated the extent of Ireland's new mood. Emboldened by the election of Mary Robinson, people appeared anxious for change. Although Haughey was succeeded by his former finance minister, Albert Reynolds, similarities between the two were relatively few. A businessman who had made a fortune, Reynolds was nonetheless a simple, decent man, quite unlike the flashy Haughey. The early days of the Reynolds administration continued many of Haughey's economic policies, but were also devoted to restoring faith in the integrity of government.

By autumn 1992, Reynolds too was in the glare of unpleasant political wrangling, and, in November, he called a general election after his government fell. Both of the traditional political parties lost 10 to 20 percent of their seats in the

Dáil Éireann, while the Labour party doubled its representation. Fianna Fáil and Fine Gael each retained large blocs of seats, but not enough for either to form a government without Labour's assistance.

The election also brought into greater prominence the popular Labour leader Dick Spring. Born in 1950, Spring enjoyed popular support among younger voters. He had served as deputy prime minister and had been an active opponent of Haughey, especially during the final days of the latter's term as taoiseach. Now Spring found himself in a position in which he could determine the shape of the next government. After long negotiations, Labour finally agreed to form a coalition government with Fianna Fáil. In exchange, Albert Reynolds stayed on as prime minister, while Spring himself became deputy prime minister and foreign minister.

For two years, Spring and the policies of the coalition drew praise from all sides. In particular, Spring was given major credit for advances in the Northern Ireland peace process, including the ceasefire of August 1994. Yet the coalition government's proposed reform program, which was popular with the people but not with the Dáil, foundered. Several of the more substantial elements of the program—including better housing, an ethics in government bill, and fairer taxation—failed to be enacted into law.

Church-State Relations in the 1990s

Issues of church-state separation continued to plague the new government as they had the old. In 1992, Ireland faced one of its most difficult political-religious controversies. The nation as a whole had always maintained a solid opposition to abortion. Legislation even forbids the dispensing of information about abortion availability in other countries. Although some pro-choice groups have tried to overturn the ban on information about abortion, and although hundreds of women each year cross the Irish Sea to obtain abortions in Britain, the nation's leaders and the public in general have taken an unyielding anti-abortion stance. Despite criticism, Ireland had, as previously noted, even gone so far as to enshrine its opposition to abortion in its constitution.

It was in 1992 that a controversy arose that no one had anticipated and that forced the Irish to revisit the issue of abortion that had been made constitutionally illegal by the referendum of September 1983. The catalyst this time was the incendiary account of a fourteen-year-old girl who had been raped by a family friend and found herself pregnant. She could have done as many Irish women do each year and gone quietly to England for an abortion. Instead, her parents, who wished to see her rapist prosecuted, asked permission to bring fetal tissue back from England in order to establish paternity and thus identify the rapist. When the news of the request became public, the girl and her plight became a cause célèbre, while identifying or prosecuting the rapist became a minor concern. Instead, the Irish courts, media, and people seemed to focus their attention on preventing the abortion. In order to do so, the courts ruled that the girl could not leave Ireland.

International outrage erupted. The EC argued that the Irish courts could not impede Irish citizens' right to travel freely. Women's rights organizations expressed their horror. The Church came down squarely on the side of those who wished simply to prevent the abortion by whatever means. The girl herself, largely lost in the tumult, threatened suicide. Ultimately, the Irish High Court ruled that the girl could travel to England but evaded the issue of freedom of travel in general; instead, it used the girl's mental instability and threats of suicide as a rationale for allowing her to go to England. It never addressed the issue of the rape or the abortion. For most people in Ireland, irrespective of their position on the abortion issue, the decision was no decision at all. To the more progressive elements of the Irish voting population, it seemed once again that the Church had dictated to the state.

The always potentially troublesome issue of the relationship between the Church and the Irish state arose again, even if indirectly, in the political crisis of 1994. The coalition government, led by Albert Reynolds of Fianna Fáil, was generally admired for its efforts at political reform and its contribution to the cessation of hostilities in Northern Ireland, but it faced a serious scandal at home. In spite of accusations that the attorney general had delayed for many months the extradition to Northern Ireland of a Catholic priest charged with sexual abuse of minors, Reynolds named the attorney general to the High Court. Furthermore, he did so in full knowledge of the attorney general's equivocation with regard to the extradition issue. Once again it seemed that a member of the government had placed the image of the Church above the public good. Eventually, the priest was extradited, but Reynolds had made a serious blunder. In November 1994 he was forced to resign. Many worried that, without his leadership, the peace process in the north might unravel. That did not happen, and Reynolds's successor, John Bruton of Fine Gael, showed himself both willing and able to continue the work of peacemaking.

The Church's influence on the Irish state persisted, however, and it continued to be a source of no little frustration to those who desire the modernization of the Irish Republic. In mid-1995, the Irish government threw the full weight of its support behind a referendum that would end Ireland's status as the only member of the EC to forbid civil divorce. A similar referendum had failed to achieve a majority of the votes in the late 1980s. In the hope of avoiding a repeat of that outcome, the government sought to anticipate and to respond to concerns related to the proposed legislation. Such concerns as inheritance, child support, and spousal support were addressed in that referendum. The Church itself took no stand, though private organizations arose to speak for the Church and Irish conservatives. The proposed solution was hardly radical. Four years of separation would be necessary before a divorce would be granted.

Initially, it appeared that the referendum would pass handily. As many as 70 percent of the voters at one time expressed support for it. As referendum day grew closer, however, opposition to the divorce bill intensified. When the polling was finally conducted in November 1995, the referendum passed by less than 1 percent of the vote. Indeed, the vote was so close that opponents filed appeals, albeit unsuccessfully, to stop its implementation. Yet—though change in Ireland seemed to move at a glacial pace—both the Church and state were consistently prodded by the writers and custodians of the country's culture.

Irish Catholicism and Irish-Ireland: Cultural Identities in Transition

Catholicism continued to be a dominant force in post-treaty Ireland, influencing values, mores, and culture. Connections between church and state, and politicians and bishops, were often so close that some observers, even well into the 1980s, described the country as a theocracy. Many writers, usually Catholic, criticized this alliance as a threat to liberal democracy, intellectual and artistic creativity, individual choice, and a healthy social environment, the lack of which, they believed, only encouraged emigration. Masters of the short story Frank O'Connor and Sean O'Faolain led the crusade to separate church and state and to bring their country into the twentieth century. Their Cork City mentor, Daniel Corkery, an Irish-Ireland nationalist, and a writer of considerable talent, imbued them with his vision of what Ireland should be and encouraged their writing vocations. As a model, he recommended Russian over British literature.

Although O'Faolain and O'Connor had both participated in the Anglo-Irish war, and were Republicans in the civil war that followed, they were disappointed that the struggle for freedom ended in a culturally depressing and oppressive Ireland, rather than the intellectually creative and dynamic Ireland they had fought and hoped for. O'Connor and O'Faolain blamed much of the stagnant character of Irish life and its cultural isolation on the close linkage between religion and politics. They also protested what they perceived as an excessive, Irish, puritanical version of Catholicism, which often resulted in laughable, but sad, censorship of books and movies.

Disillusion represented the theme of post-revolutionary Irish literature. Writers observed and evaluated their country of the 1920s, 1930s, 1940s, and 1950s, bitterly decrying its frozen economy, poverty, and emigration. They also lamented the inertia of people who stayed at home, the power and profit motives of priests, politicians, businessmen, and societal resistance to economic progress and artistic freedom. They charged that the shift in governance from London to Dublin had changed little for the better, and some things for the worse.

Writers specifically blamed the Catholic Church for a failed revolution, pointing to bishops and priests as the nucleus of a coalition standing in the way of meaningful change, demoralizing the nation, and preventing its adjustment to the modern world. In *Innishfallen Fare Thee Well,* Sean O'Casey referred to the Catholic seminary at Maynooth as "the brain, the body, the nerve and the tissue of the land, controlling two-thirds of the country, influencing it all." In *The Bell,* a journal he first edited, O'Faolain described Maynooth as a second parliament that dominated the Dáil in Dublin, and too often public opinion. The Church, they said, exploited its religious influence over a devout laity, and dictated political, social, and economic policy to politicians. O'Faolain and other writers insisted that Catholic authoritarianism, anti-intellectualism, and puritanism helped enslave and paralyze intellect and imagination. And because the Irish literati continued to impress a world audience, their view of Ireland became a widely accepted portrait of their country.

Catholic power was indisputably an Irish reality. Historical connections had limited national and religious identities. The leadership roles of many bishops and priests, who helped agitate for Catholic emancipation, repeal of the union, tenant rights, and Home Rule alliances between church and state, had provided the clergy with control of education. And the deep piety of the 95 percent Catholic majority rendered the hierarchy, priests, nuns, and religious brothers much prestige and respect. Their virtual monopoly over the educational system, much public discourse, and publications affected laws and customs. Politicians legislated Catholic morality on such minor issues as drinking hours and dancehall licenses, and on major ones such as divorce, family planning, and health. Certainly, Irish legal and political systems did not leave much room for private conscience and morality.

Religious and Irish-Ireland dimensions of Irish nationalism contributed to the thrust of Catholic power. Because the ideology of Irish nationalism attempted to avoid conflict with Anglo-Protestant interests by deemphasizing the economic and social aspects that once were key issues of the Irish question, Irish Catholic viewpoints filled the vacuum. With the support of a pious laity, bishops, and priests sought to have papal encyclicals, neo-Thomistic philosophy, and moral theology shape the national conscience. In their effort to de-Anglicize their country, cultural nationalists insisted on an Irish-Ireland. Catholic leaders twisted the hope for a unique, intellectual, Gaelic Ireland into a unique, holy, Catholic Ireland, converting Irish-Ireland's condemnation of shallow, materialistic, and alien West-Britainism into a campaign against secularism, liberalism, and socialism.

If links between Irish and Catholic identities made it difficult for nationalism to develop social and economic agendas essential to twentieth-century needs, it also limited Church responses to the realities of the outside world. In the period under discussion, Catholicism in Ireland was more conservative in theology, philosophy, liturgy, sociology and moral preaching than it was in most parts of the West. Hispanic Catholics, for example, took religious dogma much less seriously than did their Irish counterparts.

Critics, however, who referred to the country as a "theocracy" inaccurately described post-treaty Ireland. "Catholic confessional state" is more appropriate. Irish nationalism, after all, embraced a liberal-democratic as well as a Catholic tradition. Catholic influence was only effective when harmonized with the climate and goals of nationalist opinion. Frequently, bishops and priests suffered defeat or were compelled to retreat when their ambitions contradicted nationalism's liberal-democratic spirit and other goals. Anglo-Irish Protestants retained their civil liberties. They continued to own much of the country's property and businesses, remained prominent in cultural affairs, and furnished Ireland with two presidents.

But, although the Irish constitution insisted on separation of church and state, it was easier to define in theory than it was to put into practice, especially in a nation of deeply religious people. Most important matters of legislation had moral as well as political, social, cultural, and economic considerations. Both the friends and enemies of divorce, contraception, and abortion would admit that these issues had moral implications. Irish laws that prohibited rights and practices permitted in other countries represented in Ireland democratic public opinion more than they did clericalism.

Irish-Ireland was less controversial than Catholic Ireland, but at the same time provoked considerable discussion and criticism. Moreover, Irish-Ireland ideology contributed enthusiasm, dedication, idealism, and a sense of purpose to the liberation movement. In the first (1963) edition of his autobiography (*Viva Moi*), Sean O'Faolain described how Irish-Ireland enthusiasm created a sense of community among young idealists like himself:

> Irish became our runic language. It made us comrades in a secret society. We sought and made friendships, some of them to last forever, like conspirators in a state of high exaltation, merely by using Irish words.

Post-treaty leaders actively sought to make Ireland Irish as well as free. A considerable sum of money was spent to preserve the Gaeltacht, the Irish-speaking areas in Waterford, Cork, Kerry, Galway, Mayo, and Donegal, as an inspiration and model for the rest of the country. Although only about 17 percent of the population in 1922 spoke Irish as a first language, the Free State constitution designated it as the "national language." In order to make that claim real rather than just an aspiration, the Irish government required civil servants, soldiers, and policemen (Garda Siochána) to be proficient in the language. It also recognized Irish as an official language for Dáil debates and legal proceedings and required elementary and secondary schools to teach in Irish. But recruiting a sufficient number of teachers competent in Gaelic hampered the early efforts to revive the language. In time, government-sponsored prizes, bonuses, and scholarships helped remedy some of this shortage. Until 1973, Irish language training was given increasing emphasis, making it necessary to earn a pass in order to be eligible for a leaving certificate.

Despite these efforts, English persisted as the means of communication for most citizens, and Gaeltacht residents continued to leave and settle in the English-speaking areas throughout Ireland, the United Kingdom, and North America. Nonetheless, Irish-Irelanders remained a powerful lobby, insisting that independence required cultural as well as political sovereignty. And while people generally continued to resist the use of spoken Irish, a majority continued to piously embrace the Irish-Ireland ideal.

Some language movement foes protested that compulsory Irish lowered educational quality. They argued that the time and money invested in teaching Irish would be better spent in improving English language skills, and promoting vocational instruction. Parents of potential emigrants wanted their children to have the tools to survive and advance in Britain, Canada, Australia, or the United States. Others insisted that the language movement smacked of elitism. While successive Irish governments poured money into Gaeltacht regions, other impoverished areas such as Leitrim, Monaghan, and Cavan received little official attention or concern. And complaints were leveled about how preferences were sometimes shown to readers and speakers of Irish in civil service appointments that discriminated against other qualified candidates.

Many intellectuals, including friends of the language, argued that insistence on an Irish-Ireland as well as a Catholic Ireland reinforced a partition dividing Catholics in the south from those Protestants in the north who continued to cherish British historical and cultural traditions. They maintained that Irish-Ireland represented an exclusive, Catholic, provincial, puritanical, culturally anti-intellectual and iso-lationist perspective. While Sean O'Faolain in the previously noted *Viva Moi* paid tribute to Irish-Ireland's contributions to the freedom campaign, he admitted that it no longer expressed national hopes or values: "The language that once spoke to a teeming life, and which is already speaking to fewer and fewer, will then only speak to ghosts, the language of the dead." By 1958, a Swiss philologist could already write in a publication of the Dublin Institute of Advanced Studies, "we are dealing with the ruins of a language," and report that Irish was vernacular only in pockets of Mayo, Connemeara, Dingle, and Donegal. English was infiltrating even the Aran Islands. "So the old life dies, the old symbols wither away, and I and my like who warmed our hands at the fires of the past are torn in two as we stand on the side of the bridge and look back in anguish at the Ireland beyond it."

Mervyn Wall's satire also served as an effective weapon against Irish and Catho-lic Ireland enthusiasts, especially his two Fursey novels. Evicted from his monas-tery because of a speech impediment that made it impossible for him to exorcize his cell of evil spirits, Fursey travels through medieval Ireland accompanied by witches and other satanic creatures. Bishops and politicians whom he encounters are stupid lummoxes, obviously examples of their twentieth-century counterparts. Wall's *Leaves for the Burning* offers yet another excellent fictional look at prevail-ing ignorance in mid-twentieth-century Ireland. Once a Catholic, Austin Clark writes poetry that is often a bitter complaint against his former religion. Parodies of Irish culture of the 1940s and 1950s appeared on stage, as well as in books. For example, Louis D'Alton's 1953 Abbey Theatre play, *This Other Eden,* was hugely popular and enjoyed an exceptionally long run.

Subsequently, the situation for both Catholic and Irish-Ireland changed. The republic's cultural and religious landscapes changed for several reasons. Mem-bership in the United Nations (1955) and the EEC (1973) had done much to end isolation and increase cosmopolitanism, as did tax breaks for international firms that made Ireland increasingly urban and industrial. Tourism, television, travel, and the cinema opened Irish eyes and whetted appetites for things in the outside world, just as did the return to Ireland of emigrants from Britain and the United States. In

1970, John Montague, a talented poet, wrote: "Puritan Ireland is dead and gone, a myth of O'Connor and O'Faolain." Of course, O'Faolain and O'Connor had also contributed to the demise of Puritan Ireland. For years after Ireland entered the United Nations, its representatives often took pride in their role as champions of small and third world nations. But after the country joined the EEC, their focus became decidedly European.

While the use of Irish inspired some excellent prose and poetry, and was considered by many symbolic of a unique cultural identity, it remained a secondary language of communication, spoken fluently by very few. In the 1970s, the Irish language disappeared as a civil service requirement. And, after the beginnings of turbulence in Northern Ireland, a number of leaders in the republic sought to court Ulster Protestants. Realizing that a continuing emphasis on the republic as Catholic and Irish-Ireland dimmed long-held aspirations for a united Ireland, they attempted to demonstrate that northern Unionists need not fear becoming part of an open society.

Toning down the significance of Irish-Ireland was but one example of this strategy. Another was the 1972 referendum that removed Article 44 from the Irish constitution, which had given Catholicism a special status in the state. Ireland was rapidly becoming a secular society. In 1973, for example, Ireland's Supreme Court decided that bans on contraceptives were illegal, compelling the Dáil to reach the same conclusion. Subsequent legislation banning divorce was often as much an economic decision as a moral judgment. Many women feared that if their husbands could divorce them they would fall into poverty after their ex-husbands remarried. But husbands and wives did separate and often found new companions, while others divorced in Britain. Boats to England also carried an increasing number of young Irish women bound for abortion clinics. Still a third significant social change involved women: No longer were they expected to be humble housewives. Rather, an ever-increasing number of them were well educated, and many secured professional and business vocations. The successive elections in the 1990s of Mary Robinson and Mary McAleese as president of the Republic of Ireland have been more than symbolic of the very real extension of Irish women's influence and power in the country.

Certainly, the Ireland that appeared so static and unchanging during the first six decades of the twentieth century no longer exists at the beginning of the twenty-first century, particularly in its rural, Catholic, and Irish-Ireland self-image. It has now blended with general mid-Atlantic culture, adding an Irish twist. Indeed, the Irish experience has been particularly notable for its remarkable resilience. Having endured the famine, the land wars, the war for independence, the bleak frugal comfort of the de Valera era, the isolation of wartime neutrality, and the failed experiment of economic self-sufficiency, the nation finally achieved the promise of a higher standard of living after gaining membership in the EEC. But throughout this long odyssey no Dublin government has been able to ignore the haunting issue of Northern Ireland. From the start of "The Troubles" in 1968 to the 1998 agreement, it was the one issue for which no solution appeared imminent.

12

The Northern Specter, 1920–1998

A Continuing Crisis in the Conflict of Cultures

Early Background to the Modern "Troubles"

From its inception, Northern Ireland made little sense as a geographic entity (it covers an area of 5,276 square miles, only slightly more than the state of Connecticut) or as a cultural community. During the 1912–1914 Home Rule crisis, British politicians decided that if nationalist demands and unionist anxieties were to be eased their most feasible option was to partition Ireland. These ministers had concluded that it would be unjust to place a 25 percent Protestant minority in an Ireland controlled by a 75 percent Catholic majority. Instead they passed the 1920 Government of Ireland Act, which not only partitioned the country but also created a six-county northern state in which a 33 percent Catholic minority was placed under the domination of a 66 percent Protestant majority.

London had never intended to include only counties with Unionist majorities, Tyrone and Fermanagh were made a part of the new state of Northern Ireland despite their nationalist majorities for two reasons: It was hoped that an area large enough to make the north economically and politically viable would help pacify the Protestant Unionists and that the security provided by the latter's two-to-one majority over the Catholic nationalists would produce a tolerant government that would seek to conciliate and integrate the minority. Both hopes proved ill-founded. Ulster Unionists had never asked for Home Rule and ultimately accepted it only because it was preferable to a united Ireland. For their part, the Catholic minority in Northern Ireland was committed to the values and destiny of Irish nationalism.

Both sides are therefore to blame for the early failure of the Ulster experiment. Catholics simply did not reconcile themselves to permanent inclusion in a remnant of the United Kingdom and felt betrayed by their exclusion from the long-awaited Irish nation. Their militancy against the local Parliament at Stormont, just outside Belfast, gave even moderate Unionists little encouragement for believing that cooperation with Catholic nationalists was at all possible. The schism between the two communities was not helped by Sir James Craig, the first prime minister of Northern Ireland, who then proceeded to announce that the partitioned state would be a Protestant nation for a Protestant people. Whether the outcome would have been different had the Catholic minority shown itself capable of functioning as a loyal parliamentary opposition is difficult to say, but there is no denying that Northern Ireland adopted statutes and policies that quickly relegated Catholics to second-class citizenship.

Prime Minister Craig sought and obtained British permission to scrap the proportional-representation features of the Better Government of Ireland Bill. And his successor, Sir Basil Brooke, once advised Protestants not to employ Catholics as one way of driving them out of Northern Ireland. Moreover, while the Westminster and Stormont franchises were, theoretically, both based on democratic British election practices, Catholics in Northern Ireland were routinely denied fair representation in local government through gerrymandering, household suffrage, and plural votes for business property. The consequence was that even in places where they formed a majority, Catholics did not control county, town, or urban councils. In Londonderry, for instance, Catholics constituted a two-thirds majority of the population, but there were twelve Protestants and eight Catholics on the city council. This absence of local influence was even more damaging to Catholic interests than was their minority position at Stormont because it was the local government authorities who allocated jobs, housing, and social welfare.

Because politics in Northern Ireland have been rooted in sectarian distinctions rather than in attitudes toward social and economic issues, representative democracy by majority rule proved unworkable. From 1920 to 1972, Northern Ireland functioned as a one-party state. The vast majority of Protestants have been uncritically and unreservedly loyal to a Unionist party under the dictates of the Orange Lodges. In its economic development programs, the Stormont government routinely ignored the Catholic districts west of the Bann River, resulting in chronic Catholic unemployment of close to 40 percent throughout that area.

Northern Ireland Catholics had good reason to believe that they were victims of an authoritarian system. In addition to the overwhelmingly Protestant Royal Ulster Constabulary (RUC), the Stormont government created the armed and exclusively Protestant B-Special force to supplement the regular police. To Catholics, oppressed by B-Special arrogance, brutality, and bigotry, these sectarian paramilitary enforcers of law and order were the Gestapo of the Orange police state. The work of the RUC and the B-Specials benefited from Britain's Special Powers Act, which permitted authorities to arrest and imprison suspected nationalist enemies of the state without ordinary legal procedures and to detain them in jail for an indefinite period without trial.

Inferior educational opportunities plus government and employer discrimination policies meant that Catholics carried the largest burden of poverty in the region, but it was not an exclusively Catholic condition. In rural Northern Ireland, Protestants owned most of the best lowland farms while, more often, Catholics eked out a hazardous existence in the rocky hill country. But most Protestant farmers were by no means affluent. And a post–World War II decline in the shipbuilding and linen industries made Northern Ireland the most economically depressed portion of the United Kingdom, with an unemployment rate that victimized Catholics and Protestants alike.

Irish Republicans with socialist leanings insisted that Northern Ireland was an example of capitalist divide-and-conquer tactics. They said that men of wealth and property encouraged and manipulated sectarian rivalries to prevent working-class solidarity, leaving the rich in control of the economic and political structures. This was a reasonably plausible interpretation of the situation. Sectarian conflict did help preserve poverty-ridden Northern Ireland as the most conservative portion of the United Kingdom. Protestant farmers and urban workers did follow and support the leadership of the ultraright Unionist party, and "no-popery" has often made it possible for politicians to distract the Protestant proletariat from pressing economic and social problems. It is an interesting paradox: British welfare state policies have eased the political burdens of reactionary Ulster unionism.

Despite the rationalism of the socialist perspective, bigotry in the north defies reasonable explanations. The loyalty of the Protestant masses was more than the product of capitalist manipulation. Like poor whites who despised poor blacks in the United States, Ulster Protestants received a psychological lift from believing that they were superior to Catholics. And lower-class Protestants appeared to be even more bigoted than their upper- and middle-class coreligionists.

Protestant xenophobia was often expressed in racist rhetoric. They referred to Catholics as "pope heads," "bloody Micks," and "Fenians." Many Protestants warned their children against associating with Catholics because they were inherently treacherous, violent, dirty, and lazy. Catholics were said to breed like rabbits on orders from their priests so that they would outnumber Protestants at the polls. It was a claim that struck some Protestants as credible, especially after the 1981 census reported that the population ratio between the two communities was then 60 to 40 percent, rather than the 66 to 34 percent of six decades earlier.

Anti-Catholicism in Ulster reflected fear as much as ignorance, a function of the old siege mentality. After almost four centuries in Ireland, Protestants still felt like strangers in the land, convinced that the native Catholic Irish were bent on revenge. And they had little confidence in the staying power of the British when things got tough. For these reasons they translated their fear of Catholic vengeance, and doubts about British fortitude, into years of brutal oppression, which Catholics often answered with violent resistance.

Protestant anxieties were not entirely without merit. The reality of Catholic power in the south, and the institutionalization of Irish-Ireland nationalism in the constitutions of both the Free State and the republic have contributed to the cultural and religious dimensions of partition. Moreover, World War II played a significant part in defining the separate identities of north and south. To the nationalist inhabitants of the twenty-six counties in the Irish Free State, the neutrality of their country was a statement of sovereignty. Going it alone from 1939 to 1945 gave Irish nationalists a psychological boost and confidence in the durability of the state that they had created. To Ulster Unionists, the neutrality of Irish nationalists was an unconscionable tribute to the forces of totalitarianism that threatened the survival of the United Kingdom. World War II divided the historical experiences of the two Irelands, emphasizing the Irishness of the south while accentuating the Britishness of the north. Some Northern Ireland Protestants even today are attracted by a "no-popery" nativism that is no longer fashionable in Britain, and the nationalism of Catholics is often more intense in the north than it is in the south. Ulster Catholics cling to myths, legends, and memories of revolutionary heroes that are quickly fading in the increasingly Europeanized Ireland of the south. Because of the close connection between Irish nationalism and the literary muse, the northern troubles have inspired much literary talent, energy, and production in the Ulster Catholic community, perhaps even more than in the republic. Seamus Heaney, John Montague, Brian Moore, Patrick Boyle, Benedict Kiely, Seamus Deane, and Brian Friel are some outstanding examples of the northern Catholic genius. Surprisingly, for all its advantages in education, wealth, and opportunity, the Northern Ireland Protestant community has not come close to matching the literary contributions of a people that it considers inferior. One Protestant writer, Maurice Leitch, forlornly describes his own kind as "An ugly race . . . No poet will ever sing for them—of them."

More Catholics in the north expressed frustration in violence rather than in literature. Many of them joined the IRA in terrorist attacks on symbols of British authority. Some Northern Ireland Catholics were so bitter about their condition and partition that they hoped and prayed for a German victory in World War II as a prelude to a united Ireland. In Brian Moore's novel *The Emperor of Ice Cream,* Burke, a middle-class Catholic solicitor in Belfast, tells his son, "When it comes to grinding down minorities, the German jackboot isn't half as hard as the heel of John Bull." And there was Gallagher, the working-class Catholic from the Falls Road. He and his neighbor "considered it a point of honor to leave a light shining in the upstairs window at night in case any German bombers might come over the city." Gallagher had once been a member of the IRA but lost confidence in it: "He put his money on Hitler. When Hitler won the war Ireland would be whole again, thirty-two counties, free and clear." Burke and Gallagher did not change their minds about the Nazis until a bombing raid on Belfast destroyed the home of the former and the family of the latter.

After World War II, many Catholics realized that neither the oratory of politicians in the republic nor IRA terrorism would unite the two Irelands. They also understood that the British Labour government's welfare state program could improve the condition of their existence. A 1944 British education act provided scholarships for Northern Ireland Catholics to attend university. An increasing segment of Catholic opinion, particularly among the expanding middle class, decided that first-class citizenship in Northern Ireland was a more practical objective than a united Ireland. This shift in attitude, and the good work of police forces on both sides of the border, resulted in the failure of the IRA's 1956–1962 terrorist campaign, forcing militant Republicans to reevaluate their strategy. For all practical purposes, the IRA ceased functioning for a time in Northern Ireland after 1962.

Friendly contacts in 1965 between the prime ministers of Northern Ireland and the Irish Republic suggested that the Ulster question was moving from hate-provoking rhetoric and violence to negotiation and conciliation. In his 1966 book, *Ireland Since the Rising,* Tim Pat Coogan, an influential Irish journalist, predicted that while serious problems of sectarian discrimination still existed in Northern Ireland, conversations between northern and southern leaders would:

> Have healthy repercussions on the relationships between Protestants and Catholics on both sides of the border. . . . The new spirit discernible in so many quarters is more representative of the future character of the North than the present evidence of gerrymandering and discrimination.

The Northern Ireland Civil Rights Movement

The process of slow but gradual change in Northern Ireland came to an abrupt halt in 1968. Civil rights agitation in other parts of the world, particularly in the United States, inspired Northern Ireland Catholics. In 1967 the Northern Ireland Civil Rights Association started as a coalition effort to achieve equal citizenship, rights, and opportunities for all residents of Northern Ireland. Catholic middle-class moderates joined with socialists, Republicans, Protestant liberals, and the People's Democracy, a group seeking an Irish Worker's Republic that included Bernadette Devlin and Eamon McCann. They marched through the streets singing the song of the American civil rights movement, "We Shall Overcome." The RUC, B-Specials, and Protestant mobs harassed and beat them. Television cameras brought life behind the "Orange curtain" to the attention of British and world opinion, creating a wave of international sympathy for the oppressed Catholic minority in Northern Ireland.

Encouraged by Prime Minister Harold Wilson's Labour government in Britain, Northern Ireland prime minister Terence O'Neill cautiously weighed the situation and decided to take a few small steps in the direction of civil rights and social justice. But fanatics in the Orange Order, including the Reverend Ian Paisley, the leading "no-popery" demagogue, and ambitious politicians like William Craig, shouted, "No surrender!" Frightened by the frenzy of majority Protestant opinion, O'Neill lost his nerve, equivocated, procrastinated, and finally resigned from office. His successor, James Chichester-Clark, promised early reform. After moving too slowly for the determined Catholics, and too fast for defiant Protestants, he also resigned, turning power over to Brian Faulkner, a somewhat flexible Unionist.

After 1969, the older issues of partition and a united Ireland re-emerged from the shadows to reduce the importance of civil rights. Orange extremists resumed their hate-filled rhetoric and taunting sectarian parades; the RUC (reorganized as the Police Service of Northern Ireland in 2001) and B-Specials (abolished in October 1969) acted as partisan Protestant armies rather than as police forces; timid Stormont and Westminster politicians and impatient Catholic radicals, socialists, and Republicans combined to transform confrontational protest tactics into a condition of civil war. Encouraged by police apathy, and sometimes support, Protestant mobs forced Derry and Belfast Catholics to retreat to barricaded ghettos. During the civil rights phase of the Ulster crisis, the IRA kept a low profile, promoting civil liberties as a strategy to mobilize and radicalize Catholic ghetto communities. In 1969 Protestant violence revived the IRA as a Catholic defense force, and Catholics welcomed IRA protection. And the Irish in Britain and America supplied them with money to purchase weapons.

At the very time when the IRA emerged again as a paramilitary force, it split into "Official" and "Provisional" wings. Members of the Official wing interpreted the Northern Ireland situation in a Marxist context. They aspired to an all-Ireland socialist republic as the ultimate solution to their conflict. Until a truce was reached with the British army in 1974, Officials directed their violence against British authority, carefully avoiding attacks on Irish Protestants. Members of the Provisional wing, however, were indiscriminate in their terrorism, killing Protestant civilians as well as British soldiers, and also claimed to be socialists, but not Marxists. Despite their proletarian slogans, Provisionals represented the traditional Republican thesis that violence is the only way to convince the British to depart Northern Ireland and unite the country. They proposed a nine-county Ulster regional legislature subordinate to an all-Ireland Parliament, which, they contended, would satisfactorily fulfill Ulster Catholic nationalist hopes for a united Ireland as well as accommodate Ulster Protestant Unionist demands for regional autonomy. Those early objectives were not frequently articulated as the Troubles wore on, and Marxists came to dominate both the Provo leadership and the Irish National Liberation Army, a militant group that broke away from the Officials.

In August 1969, after weeks of violence in Derry and Belfast, the British government sent troops to Northern Ireland to keep the peace. At first Catholics welcomed them as protectors, but within a few months the IRA and the soldiers were at war. Permanent good relations between the Catholic community and the British army were almost impossible to sustain. Because the army was a law-and-order extension of the Protestant Unionist state, it could not function as a neutral agency. Soldiers disarmed Catholics but permitted Protestant extremists to keep their weapons. The presence and conduct of the army only served to support the IRA contention that the conflict in the north was but a renewal of the Anglo-Irish war.

On August 9, 1971, acting on the orders of the Faulkner regime, the army aided the police in seizing and interning 342 people who were alleged to be members of, or sympathizers with, the Provisional and Official IRA groups. Yet the Protestant extremists who were the first to instigate violence in the region were spared internment. By mid-December the authorities had apprehended over 1,500 suspects (934 were quickly released), virtually all of them Catholic. Instead of calming the situation, these detentions intensified minority bitterness, bringing the inhabitants of the Catholic ghettos solidly behind the IRA. While Republicans vigorously protested the existence of Long Kesh and other internment camps, and the torture that went on in them, they were a boon for IRA propaganda, providing examples of British injustice and cruelty in Ireland. After these events, Catholic opinion turned decisively against coming to terms with Stormont: Extremists demanded a united Ireland; moderates would accept nothing less than the end of the Northern Ireland state as established in 1920.

On Sunday, January 30, 1972, British paratroopers gunned down thirteen Derry Catholics who were participating in a protest demonstration. "Bloody Sunday," as it became known, further fanaticized Catholic nationalist opinion and dealt a death-blow to Stormont. In March 1972 the British Conservative government suspended the authority of the Northern Ireland government for a year and placed the territory under direct rule from Westminster. It promised a quick and satisfactory solution to the Northern Ireland crisis. William Whitelaw, who went to Belfast as British secretary of state for Northern Ireland, did appear to have a keener sense of the Irish milieu and was able to communicate with both Protestant and Catholic camps.

When the blood-soaked streets of Derry and Belfast shattered southern optimism concerning the situation in Northern Ireland, politicians in the republic expressed sympathy and concern for Northern Ireland Catholics and pledged traditional nationalist commitments to a united Ireland. The Fianna Fáil government sent frequent protests to Westminster concerning the harsh treatment of Northern Ireland Catholics, unsuccessfully tried to get the United Nations to mediate the crisis, and established refugee camps and hostels for Catholic refugees who had fled Protestant violence in the north. Official Irish government response to the northern situation went beyond protest when it said the republic could not stand idly by if the Stormont regime or Protestant mobs continued to menace the Catholic minority with acts of brutality.

As people in the Irish Republic discussed Northern Ireland during the 1980s in their homes or pubs, some often expressed empathy for the IRA as the heirs of Easter Week and the Anglo-Irish war. Other than spontaneous reactions to outrages like Bloody Sunday, however, Irish opinion remained generally calm and often ambiguous on the subject of events in Northern Ireland. Even today only a small percentage of voters in the republic support Sinn Féin candidates in elections. As Conor Cruise O'Brien affirmed in *States of Ireland* (1973), there was a deep concern at the time that the virus of violence in Northern Ireland might destroy liberal democracy in the republic. Many members of the business community were frightened that the turbulence in Northern Ireland could discourage potential investors in Irish industry, just as they were also concerned about scaring off prospective tourists from Britain and the United States. More than a few citizens of the republic frankly conceded that they did not understand Ulster people, Protestant or Catholic. They thought of them as a breed apart, with their own regional personality, presenting difficult if not insurmountable religious, economic, and cultural problems of assimilation for a united Ireland.

Attempts at Power-Sharing and Devolution

In March 1973, the British government presented its solution to the Northern Irish problems in a white paper, *Northern Ireland Constitutional Proposals*. The white paper rejected majority rule and proposed power-sharing as the alternative. It also proposed an eighty-member assembly elected by proportional representation and an executive committee with Catholic representation. Britain refused to give the new government the authority or stature that had been accorded earlier to Stormont and specifically reserved police and judicial powers for Westminster. In addition to establishing new power-sharing political institutions, the white paper guaranteed Catholic civil rights in voting, local government, jobs, housing, and education. It also constructed a potential bridge to Irish unity by suggesting a Council of Ireland composed of British, Irish, and Northern Irish representatives to discuss problems of mutual interest and concern. Britain thereby gave notice of its implicit acqui-escence in the principle of a united Ireland if accomplished through negotiations and with the consent of public opinion on both sides of the border.

Led by Ian Paisley and James Craig, extreme Unionists denounced the white paper as a betrayal of Ulster Protestants and a major step in the direction of a united Catholic Ireland. Paisley said that he preferred complete integration into the United Kingdom to the existence of a power-sharing puppet legislature. The IRA also rejected the white paper, arguing that it perpetuated the British presence in Ulster. Ignoring those dissenting expressions, Whitelaw began implementing the white paper. In this he had the support of Faulkner's moderate Ulster Unionist Party (UUP) and the Social Democratic and Labour Party (SDLP), a socialist, nationalist parliamentary constituency that enjoyed more support in the Catholic community than did the IRA. The Alliance party, a nonsectarian coalition of moderates, also agreed to give the British proposal an opportunity to work.

In June 1973, elections were held for the Northern Ireland Assembly that resulted in giving Faulkner's UUP 23 seats; SDLP 19; Unofficial Unionists 10; Democratic Unionists 9; Alliance 8; Vanguard 6; West Belfast Loyalists 2; and Northern Ireland Labour 1. Five months later a coalition formed an Executive Committee of eleven seats, held by six members from the UUP, one from the Alliance party, and four representing SDLP. Faulkner became chair and Gerry Fitt, the SDLP leader, was appointed as his deputy.

Representatives of the British, Irish, and Northern Ireland governments met in December 1973 at Sunningdale, England. After four days of discussion they agreed to establish a Council of Ireland with a fourteen-member ministry, equally divided between representatives of the Irish Republic and Northern Ireland, and a Consulta-tive Assembly to which citizens of both Irelands would be elected proportionately. The Sunningdale conference also recommended that the Irish Republic recognize British sovereignty over Northern Ireland as long as a regional majority preferred to remain in the United Kingdom and urged the British government to agree to implement Irish unity as soon as that objective represented a Northern Ireland con-sensus. In March 1974 the republic's taoiseach, Liam Cosgrave, responded to the Sunningdale recommendation by recognizing Northern Ireland as British territory until its citizens, in a democratic election, indicated another preference.

Public opinion in Britain and in the Irish Republic was confident that the white paper and Sunningdale would pacify Northern Ireland and bring Ireland closer to national unity. But the new arrangement was doomed from the start. Consensus, not documents, produces stability, and the white paper and the Sunningdale agreements did not represent the will of the majority in Northern Ireland. While many Ulster Catholics were ready to compromise on their grievances and aspirations, the vast majority of Protestants disliked power-sharing and hated the Council of Ireland.

While politicians talked in the assembly, terrorist bombings, murders, assassinations, and deliberately incited fires convulsed Northern Ireland, with a variety of Protestant paramilitary organizations competing with the Provisional IRA as instruments of violence. By the spring of 1974, over 1,000 people had died from shootings, bombings, and fires; three years later the figure approached 1,500. Protestant terror gangs assassinated Catholics in all parts of Northern Ireland and extended their campaign of intimidation to the south. On May 17, 1974, bombs killed five people in Monaghan and twenty-three in Dublin and wounded hundreds of others. During 1975, the IRA transported terror to Britain using arson, bombing, and assassination in efforts to coerce the London government's withdrawal from Ulster.

Beginning in the spring of 1974, Protestant extremists opened a determined and coordinated offensive against the white paper program, concentrating primarily on the Council of Ireland. On May 15, the Protestant Ulster Workers Council, with the support of ultra-Unionist politicians and paramilitary terrorist groups, like Vanguard and the Ulster Defense Association, began a general strike, insisting on the termination of the Council of Ireland. Merlyn Rees, the British Labour party secretary of state for Northern Ireland, refused to negotiate with the strike leaders. Within a few days Northern Ireland experienced a severe economic crisis involving shortages of food, electrical power, and other basic necessities. Responding to strike coercion, and to the urgent requests of its moderate Unionist ally in the coalition, the SDLP reluctantly agreed to the suspension of the Council of Ireland for four years. Sensing victory, Protestant extremists escalated their demands. They insisted on the resignation of the Executive Committee and the assembly and called for new elections, obviously expecting the restoration of Protestant ascendancy.

The nationalist SDLP responded by demanding that the British government take action to preserve power-sharing. On May 24, after insisting that he would preserve law, order, and the constitution in Northern Ireland, Prime Minister Harold Wilson sent 500 more soldiers into the region, bringing British troop strength there to a total of 16,500. In the early morning hours of May 26, the military occupied electrical power plants and some gas stations, but the British Labour government had moved too late. Soldiers lacked the competence to operate the power plants, and the British show of strength only solidified Protestant opinion—both urban and rural—against the Faulknerite-SDLP-Alliance party coalition. Finally, Faulkner and his moderate Unionist colleagues resigned from the Executive Committee, destroying the power-sharing experiment. Britain then suspended the Executive Committee and the assembly for four years and returned Northern Ireland to the jurisdiction of Westminster.

But London persisted in seeking a possible solution. Only a few weeks later, in July 1974, the British government offered another white paper solution to the Northern Ireland problem. It called for a convention to meet for the purpose of producing a consensus constitution based on the principle of power-sharing. Elections for the convention gave the ultra-Unionist factions 40 out of 78 seats. During the summer of 1975 the convention prepared recommendations for presentation to the British government. Although the ultra-Unionist camp was split between Paisley and Craig, the latter was willing to make some concession to power-sharing. The convention submitted a report in November that insisted on a return to majority rule and an end to British government interference with the right of Protestant unionists to control the destiny of Northern Ireland. Britain quickly rejected that bid to restore Protestant ascendancy. Northern Ireland remained under the authority of Westminster, and violence continued as before.

Sometimes a tragic event had the unexpected consequence of inciting a widespread reaction. On August 10, 1976, for example, three young children walking with their mother were killed by an IRA car that crashed after the driver was shot dead in a gun battle. In Ulster that day, thirty-seven different shooting incidents took place, in addition to twenty bomb attacks and nineteen car hijackings. But the deaths of these innocent children inspired a group of Protestant and Catholic women, led by Mrs. Betty Williams and Miss Mairead Corrigan, the children's aunt, to form a movement they called Peace People and to invite women everywhere to join in a campaign against violence. Ten thousand women, including a fair number of Protestants, attended a peace rally in Andersontown on August 14, 1976, despite death threats from the IRA. That demonstration served notice to the world that the perpetrators of violence in Northern Ireland were a small minority and that most people there yearned for peace. A little more than a year later, on December 10, 1977, the Nobel Peace Prize was awarded to the peace movement's cofounders, Williams and Corrigan.

The highlight of that year for Ulster, however, proved to be the queen's Silver Jubilee visit in August. The IRA made a concerted effort to force the visit to be cancelled by threats of bombing and civil disorder, but the queen followed her appointed schedule, under heavy security, without hindrance. In September, U.S. president Jimmy Carter responded to pressure from Irish Americans by making a guarded statement on Northern Ireland in which he endorsed power-sharing as a solution and offered industrial investments as an incentive for peace. Neither Unionist nor British leaders evinced much interest in Carter's cautiously phrased remarks.

During 1978, as the level of violence in Northern Ireland began to decline for a time, the IRA initiated a propaganda campaign for the restoration of "special category" status for terrorists serving prison sentences. More than 300 IRA prisoners declined to wear prison uniforms and thus naked, except for their blankets, proceeded to deface their cells with urine and feces, creating a health hazard for themselves and the prison staff. IRA propagandists attempted to represent the outrageous conditions in the H-Block of the Maze Prison as the deliberate policy of the state authorities, but the London government rejected such claims as nonsense and sternly warned that there would be no compromise with the men who had gone "on the blanket" and defied prison regulations. Later, on November 26, the deputy governor of the Maze in charge of the H-Block was shot dead at his home in Belfast.

Failing to move London by its propaganda efforts, the IRA turned in 1979 to violence against British dignitaries. On March 22, the British ambassador to the Netherlands, Sir Richard Sykes, was shot dead at The Hague and, on March 30, MP Airey Neave was killed by a bomb in the members' parking lot at the House of Commons. Public outrage in Britain was almost unrestrained when on August 27, the earl of Mountbatten, a member of the royal family, was killed in a boat by an IRA bomb while on vacation at his home near Mullaghmore in the Irish Republic. Moreover, eighteen British soldiers were killed at Narrow Water Castle, County Down, that same day by land mines detonated from across the border. Prime Minister Margaret Thatcher flew to Belfast and visited troops on the border. At a meeting with Thatcher after the Mountbatten funeral, Irish prime minister Jack Lynch pledged Dublin's cooperation in future border security.

Throughout much of 1980 a good deal of time and attention were spent on a British-sponsored interparty conference on Northern Ireland that included the Reverend Ian Paisley's Democratic Unionist party, the largely Roman Catholic SDLP, and the moderate, largely Protestant, Alliance party. The purpose of the conference was to explore possible common ground for a future constitution. On July 2, the London government published a "discussion paper" that ruled out any return to a simple majority administration for Ulster and recommended instead an assembly of eight members elected by proportional representation. The proposal also included a power-sharing formula, which was viewed suspiciously by Protestants and Catholics alike. British patience was growing thin, as shown by a December poll published in the *Sunday Times,* showing that substantially more than half the respondents welcomed an end to the union.

On March 1, 1981, Provisional IRA prisoner Bobby Sands began a fast to protest British rule in Northern Ireland and the nonpolitical status of nationalist prisoners in the H-Block. The fast became an IRA publicity coup when Sands was put forward as a candidate for Parliament after the death of Frank Maguire, the Independent MP for Fermanagh and South Tyrone. The Catholic SDLP was afraid to contest the seat, and Sands defeated former Unionist cabinet minister Harry West by a vote of 30,492 to 29,046. It was a stunning propaganda victory for the IRA, which promptly claimed that Sands's victory had destroyed the British myth that the Irish "freedom fighters" were not supported by the majority of Catholics. After Sands died on May 5, following a sixty-six-day fast, serious disorder broke out in the nationalist areas of Belfast as the polarization between Catholics and Protestants became still more intense. Ten other prisoners subsequently died on hunger strikes, the last on August 20, and each death was followed by outbreaks of violence.

The New Ireland Forum and the Anglo-Irish Accord

Renewed efforts to find an acceptable form of devolved government for Northern Ireland began again in 1982. On February 17 the British government proposed a seventy-eight-member assembly, elected by proportional representation. A Northern Ireland assembly bill was given royal assent on July 23, and elections were duly held on October 20. All the major parties in the province contested the election. The SDLP did so, however, on the understanding that it was not prepared to take any seats that it won. Only the Ulster Unionists, the Democratic Unionist party, the Alliance party, and two other independent Unionists, totaling 58 of the 78 members elected, took their seats when the assembly met for the first time on November 11. The SDLP, which had won only 14 seats, due in part to an unusually heavy Sinn Féin turnout at the polls, argued that there was no point in its participation since the main assembly parties had excluded the prospect of power-sharing. Instead, the SDLP called for the government of the Irish Republic to set up a Council for a New Ireland that might study acceptable forms of government for the whole island and prepare the way for all-Ireland institutions. The New Ireland Forum, which first met in Dublin in May 1983, was a response to that appeal. The forum suggested three different possible options: first, a unitary state with pluralist constitutional guarantees for all; second, a federal solution in which north and south would be separate units under one central government, but each with rigid guarantees of religious liberty and each with its own laws on such matters as contraception and divorce; and last, dual sovereignty, with Dublin and London sharing authority in the north. The Forum received over 300 submissions and heard oral presentations from 31 individuals and groups. Despite the fact that British prime minister Thatcher rejected the alternatives for Northern Ireland that were proposed by the forum, SDLP leader John Hume hailed the event as "an extraordinary day in the history of our island. . . . Things cannot be the same again."

There was also cause for concern, as the Sinn Féin electoral victories after the hunger strikes had illustrated: Fear that the Catholic minority in the north might be won over by the IRA prompted the British and Irish governments to join in a bold 1985 plan for breaking the cycle of violence and despair in Northern Ireland. Meeting at Hillsborough Castle in County Down, Prime Minister Margaret Thatcher and Taoiseach Garret FitzGerald signed, on November 15, what has come to be known as the Hillsborough Agreement, or the Anglo-Irish Accord. With that document the Irish Republic formally recognized the right of the northern provinces to remain within the United Kingdom for as long as a majority of its citizens so desired. The agreement also provided for an intergovernmental conference, serviced by a secretariat located at Maryfield outside Belfast, to provide a framework for regular meetings between the two governments at both the ministerial and official levels. This conference enabled the Irish government to advance views and proposals on a range of political, security, and legal matters, thus reflecting and representing the concerns of the minority in the north. Finally, the agreement endorsed the

Westminster policy of seeking devolution on a basis that would secure widespread acceptance throughout the communities.

The SDLP enthusiastically backed the agreement and expressed the hope that various social and political reforms would follow. A more cautious note was struck by the Alliance party, which expressed reservations about the new arrangements, especially with respect to the lack of consultation with local parties. But that party said it would suspend judgment in order to allow time to see if the agreement would bring benefits to the communities. Nationalist and Unionist militants were more openly critical. Sinn Féin opposed the new understanding because it accepted partition and promised valueless reforms. Almost as predictably, the Official Unionist party and the Democratic Unionist party both opposed it because it permitted a foreign state, the Irish Republic, to have a voice in the affairs of Northern Ireland.

It was, to be sure, a remarkably subtle and sophisticated agreement, and the Unionists were correct in their assumption that it could eventually compromise the position of Northern Ireland within the United Kingdom. Specifically, the amount of power that the Irish government might be able to exercise in Northern Ireland was, by definition, in inverse proportion to the amount of power conferred on a devolved government in Belfast. Yet the condition that Britain had set for the reestablishment of any devolved government in Northern Ireland was, quite simply, the power-sharing formula that Unionist politicians had consistently rejected since 1974.

The impact of the accord on the Unionist majority in Northern Ireland was nothing less than traumatic. Public demonstrations, confrontations with the police, and sporadic violence all broke out as outraged loyalists expressed their sense of shock and fury over what they perceived as Thatcher's "treachery." Then, on December 17, 1985, all fifteen Unionist MPs resigned their seats at Westminster in protest over the Hillsborough Agreement.

Not to be deterred, Dublin and London proceeded to implement the November 15 understanding in a timely fashion. The measure was ratified in the Dáil, 88 to 75, and, interestingly, it passed the House of Commons by an overwhelming majority of 473 to 47. The agreement then automatically came into force on November 29, and the first meeting of the Anglo-Irish Intergovernmental Conference subsequently took place at Stormont Castle on December 11. As 1985 drew to a close, the number of people killed in the province as a result of political violence totaled fifty-five, down from sixty-four the previous year. But the IRA and the splinter Irish National Liberation Army (INLA) had begun to focus on members of the security forces, resulting in the deaths of no fewer than twenty-three members of the RUC. Another notable feature of deaths during 1985 was the high number of Catholics who were killed by IRA or INLA terrorists because of even casual or benign contact with security forces, as in instances of craftsmen involved in the construction of police stations.

The Northern Irish cultural, national, and sectarian conflict has many obvious parallels with the Israeli-Palestinian confrontations and guerrilla escapades, but also many differences. One cannot, for example, imagine an Israeli or a Palestinian becoming a hero, however briefly, to very many people among those warring communities. Yet that is exactly what happened in Northern Ireland, where sports can, and occasionally does, eclipse politics. Barry McGuigan, the "Clones Cyclone," won the world featherweight boxing championship in June 1985, just as Dennis Taylor had won the world snooker championship a few weeks earlier, in April. Their respective achievements were a source of great pride to nearly all Ulster inhabitants, irrespective of denominational affiliation. Music was yet another shared experience, particularly among Northern Ireland teenagers, Protestants and Catholics alike, who often wore the same sweatshirts featuring Irish rock musicians, like Bob Geldof, or Irish rock bands, like U2.

But at the outset of 1986, the spirit in Northern Ireland was anything but ecumenical. The IRA's response to Sinn Féin reversals at the polls was to intensify the terror. Radicalism was increasingly evident among Unionists too, whereupon newly emergent leaders, like Peter Robinson, appeared to be only slightly less dogmatic than the Reverend Ian Paisley. In June 1986, however, the assembly was dissolved, and London made it clear that the future of Northern Ireland self-governance was directly linked to the intergovernmental conference. The joint British and Irish staffs met regularly at the secretariat outside Belfast even as the destructive conflict continued unabated. Sixty-two deaths resulted from political violence, seven more than the previous year. And new categories were targeted: for instance, an unusually high number of loyalist assaults against both Catholic homes and the homes of policemen of either faith who were seen as upholding government policies resulting from the agreement.

In the general election of 1987, thirteen of Northern Ireland's seventeen seats in the Westminster Parliament were won by Unionist parties, three by the SDLP, and one seat, West Belfast, by Sinn Féin. The so-called McBride Principles, a strategy advanced by Irish statesman Sean McBride for a boycott of all commercial investment in the north because of discrimination against the minority population, was a particularly divisive issue given the 17.6 percent unemployment in the province, compared with 9.5 percent in the rest of the United Kingdom. London responded in September 1987 with a revised guide to religious equality of opportunity in employment for the government's frankly ineffective Fair Employment Agency.

Anglo-Irish relations began to wear thin in January 1988, when the Thatcher government announced that it would not, for reasons of national security, prosecute a group of officers in the RUC who were involved in a shoot-to-kill policy in 1982 and 1983. That drew loud protests from Dublin, and it angered Irish taoiseach Charles Haughey. The official inquiry into the case has never been published. Haughey met with Thatcher in mid-February to demand that the report be made public and that the implicated officers be brought to trial. Thatcher's rejection of Haughey's request appeared all the more callous, when that same month an explosive new book appeared. Titled *Stalker,* it was written by now-retired deputy chief constable John Stalker of the Greater Manchester police force, who was placed in charge of the RUC probe in 1984 but was dismissed two years later. Stalker writes that he was fired because he had implicated RUC officers and found that at least eleven policemen were involved in a conspiracy to subvert justice.

Dublin was further outraged in late January 1988 by a British appeals court's decision to uphold the convictions of six men, all Ulster Catholics, who had previously been sentenced to life imprisonment for two terrorist bombings in Birmingham in 1974. The defendants had argued that their confessions had been coerced. Moreover, new evidence had emerged that cast doubt on their guilt. Then, in February, a Roman Catholic Ulsterman, Aidan McAnespie, was mistakenly shot and fatally wounded as he passed through a security checkpoint in Northern Ireland. Haughey ordered an independent investigation of the case on Dublin's side of the border when it was learned that McAnespie, who had done low-level electioneering for Sinn Féin, had been harassed at the same checkpoint on earlier occasions. An infuriated Thatcher then publicly declared that Dublin had no right to inquire into "matters north of the border." Her response was cheered by Unionists, and it put in doubt the future effectiveness of the Hillsborough Agreement. It was, after all, critically dependent on a successful improvement of relations not only between the security forces and Catholics in Northern Ireland but also between the republic and the north in cross-border monitoring of the IRA. The full implications of this pact were perhaps only dimly understood even by some British and Irish citizens, given that the arrangements it contained were virtually unprecedented. Under the agreement, Northern Ireland was unique in international law. Although the region remains part of the United Kingdom, the accord conferred on two distinctly separate governments the legal right, underscored by a treaty registered with the United Nations, to determine jointly specific issues that touch on the essence of how sovereignty is exercised in it. Little wonder, therefore, that these distinctions have often escaped the attention, or interest, of many Irish Americans.

Irish-American Familiarity with the Ulster Issue

Irish America was far less responsive to the strife in Northern Ireland during the 1970s than it had been to the cause of nationalist Ireland only fifty years earlier. One reason is that a large part of this American community was now two generations removed from any direct experience with Irish life. Another is that most Irish Americans were descendants of immigrants from the west and south of Ireland and had little familiarity with the traditions of Ulster's communal schisms. It may even be argued that Irish Americans had, as a group, become too assimilated in the United States to think much about events in Ireland, despite pervasive contemporary interest in ethnic identity. As Oscar Handlin and other immigration historians have observed, organizations like the Sons of St. Patrick and the Sons of Italy have no counterpart in Europe. Nationalist sentiment may be the force that holds such groups together, but their real purpose is to ease the transition of immigrants into American life. They help compensate for a sense of individual weakness by asserting group strength. Contrary to the contention of their critics, such organizations did not create "hyphenated Americans"; they served to smooth away the hyphen. They promoted adjustment to American ways and the adoption of American ideals, rather than retard them. By the 1970s, millions of second-, third-, and fourth-generation Irish Americans had moved well away from the initial period of immigrant anxiety and adjustment. As Americans, they had the security to view the Ulster problem from an emotional distance. Former U.S. ambassador to Ireland William V. Shannon believed that for Irish Americans to "enter fully into the passions that convulse Northern Ireland would require a journey into the past that they are reluctant to make. They are too involved with the American present and future."

However, another constituency within the Irish-American community had perceived the Ulster crisis in an entirely different way: comparatively recent Irish immigrants, who provided the hard-core support for the IRA in the United States. Like past Irish-American nationalism, the response of Irish immigrants to the events in Northern Ireland communicated the bitterness they felt about the impoverished Ireland they had left, as well as their sense of insecurity in America. And because IRA supporters held the Irish government responsible for the economic conditions that forced them to emigrate, they denounced it as a puppet of British imperialism and remained unmoved when Irish officials pleaded with Americans not to assist IRA activities. Indeed, the Irish immigrant support for the IRA often reflected dissatisfaction with their position in the United States. They did not share the values and attitudes of the American-born Irish or participate in their middle-class standing or respectability. The situation in Northern Ireland afforded them the means of expressing their own identity in an increasingly ethnic-conscious America. Yet their attitude was strangely incompatible with their strong law-and-order stance on American issues. They refused, for example, to recognize the obvious similarities between black America and Catholic Northern Ireland. They deliberately ignored the socialist pronouncements of the contemporary IRA and terrorist political organizations in other parts of the world.

Irish-born Irish Americans are not nearly as numerous as they were at the time of the Irish War for Independence. For example, there were some 4 million such immigrants in 1919, compared with fewer than 300,000 in 1969. Yet this immigrant community, particularly in the Eastern states of Massachusetts, New York, New Jersey, and Pennsylvania, provided much of the militant thrust behind Irish America's support for the IRA. These people were often driven by blind hatred and had no faith in British power-sharing proposals or in any rational political compromise. They had no interest in any minority rights guarantee by the United Kingdom, the United States, or the United Nations. They believed that the IRA's objective of a sovereign and united Ireland that included all thirty-two counties was historically justified and had to be accomplished by force of arms. Their perception of Ireland was often simplistic and uninformed.

IRA Propaganda in America and the Problem of Perception for Britain

But Irish republicanism nonetheless was often given a wider and more sympathetic hearing in the United States during the 1970s than the relative size or illiberal views of the Irish immigrant community would seem to warrant. One reason was the carefully calculated tone of the Irish Republican campaign in America. As Maria McGuire relates in her memoir *To Take Arms,* Provisional IRA fund-raisers were instructed to make copious references to the martyrs of 1916 and 1919–1922. They were also advised to promote anti-British sentiment by recalling the potato famine and the Black and Tans, but were cautioned against saying anything praiseworthy about socialism or anything critical of the Catholic Church. American television was another reason a disproportionate amount of attention was given to the Northern Ireland issue in the United States. At the 1981 funeral of hunger striker Bobby Sands, correspondent Neil Hickey reported that the IRA ensured that American television crews were afforded fully equipped scaffolding on which to mount their cameras. Viewers in the United States were thereby treated to the dramatic spectacle of hooded Provisional IRA members at the gravesite firing volleys of salute toward an overcast sky. The image conveyed on the television screen was that of a noble tribute to an honored martyr of a rightful cause.

This problem of perception became a major obstacle for the British to overcome when explaining their own position in Northern Ireland to American audiences. In condemning the atrocities and in suppressing the terrorism of the Provisional IRA, London failed to capitalize on the fact that the IRA platform called for the overthrow of government authorities on both sides of the border and for a socialist program involving the nationalization of banks and industries throughout Ireland. Instead, the members of the Provisional IRA were permitted to characterize the IRA campaign as a holy war, perhaps even the final chapter in the age-old struggle between Celt and Anglo-Saxon. The frequently conservative social thinking of many Irish Americans has, as a result, given way to the romantic idealism deliberately and effectively cultivated by IRA disinformation. Once again, as happened during the 1919–1921 war for Irish independence, Irish republicanism bested Britain in the propaganda war for American public opinion. Only gradually did some Irish Americans become more discriminating in their assessment of IRA claims.

Indeed, the terrorist image that became synonymous with the Provisional IRA during the late 1970s was the single most important reason for the merely modest success that the IRA enjoyed in winning widespread American support for its cause. Neither the IRA's stridently Anglophobic rhetoric nor its patently socialist manifestos have alienated people in the United States as much as did that organization's identification with violence and killing. And that general sense of revulsion was also shared by some Irish Americans. Appearing before a 1972 congressional subcommittee hearing on conditions in Northern Ireland, New York City resident and writer Jimmy Breslin recounted his own experiences in Ulster and condemned people who collected funds in Manhattan taverns for the purpose of purchasing weapons for the IRA. Breslin remarked:

> The idea of raising money on Second Avenue to buy guns so that an 18-year-old in Derry can kill an 18-year-old British soldier, a soldier from Manchester who knows nothing of the reasons for the fight he is in, this notion to me is sickening.

NORAID and the American Connection with Ulster

One of the major conduits for smuggling arms from the United States to Northern Ireland during the height of the Troubles was the Northern Aid Committee. Popularly known as NORAID, the organization was founded in 1970 by Michael Flannery and two other IRA veterans of the 1919–1922 period. NORAID publicity director Martin Galvin, an attorney with the New York Sanitation Department, once claimed that the organization had ninety-two chapters in seventy American cities and that the total membership was about 5,000. Headquartered in a drab second-floor office on Broadway in upper Manhattan, sandwiched between a funeral parlor and a bank branch, NORAID did not give the appearance of being an ominous organization that supplied illicit weapons to terrorists abroad. Moreover, NORAID officials always insisted that the funds raised by their organization, estimated by Martin Galvin to be $300,000 a year, were used mostly to support the families of IRA members interned by British authorities. But American intelligence sources estimated in 1975 that only 25 percent of that money was spent for such purposes, while fully 75 percent was used for the purchase of weapons and munitions.

U.S. citizens, including Irish Americans, did not have to depend on the judgment of their government alone in evaluating NORAID's complicity in providing weapons to the IRA. Indeed, four successive Irish prime ministers made the same charge. Liam Cosgrave told a joint session of Congress that aid to "relief" organizations such as NORAID did not help resolve the problem of Ulster. Jack Lynch warned American contributors to NORAID that their money, rather than going for the support of widows and orphans, was in fact used to *create* widows and orphans. Garret FitzGerald similarly condemned such American aid to the IRA, and Charles Haughey went still further, declaring, "There is clear and conclusive evidence available to the government . . . and other sources that NORAID has provided support for the campaign of violence."

Such remarks as these prompted former New York Council president Paul O'Dwyer, a NORAID attorney, to decry the growing rift between the Irish and Irish Americans. O'Dwyer, a distinguished member of the Democratic Party in New York, was a native of County Mayo and was representative of that community of Irish-born Americans who identify with the Democratic tradition in American politics, but with the republican tradition in Irish politics. Yet as Irish cabinet minister Conor Cruise O'Brien observed in a 1976 speech before an American Chamber of Commerce meeting in Dublin, the republican tradition in Ireland had set itself above democracy. And in direct response to O'Dwyer, O'Brien denied that any rift existed between the Irish and Irish Americans. "I do believe," he added, "that a minority of Irish republicans are interested in trying to produce such a rift, and to intimidate the Irish people with the idea that they cannot afford such a rift."

Throughout the 1970s and early 1980s, courts in the United States and Canada tried a number of NORAID officials on weapons charges. Some received suspended sentences; others were jailed. Michael Flannery and four codefendants, however, were acquitted by a New York court in November 1982 when the government failed to prove that they had deliberately sought to export arms without the necessary official permit. Organizers of the 1983 St. Patrick's Day parade in New York then selected Flannery as the parade's grand marshal, which resulted in public denunciations of that decision by leading Irish-American politicians. NORAID was also condemned by the U.S. Bureau of Alcohol, Tobacco, and Firearms, which, together with other federal agencies, helped to secure the indictments of those who were transporting guns into Northern Ireland.

As more NORAID members were jailed on weapons charges and as that organization became publicly linked with the Provisional IRA, another group, calling itself the Irish National Caucus, assumed a more prominent role among Americans concerned over the course of events in Ulster. The caucus, first formed in 1974, had as its purpose to make the violations of human rights in Ulster a moral issue for all Americans. By 1979 no fewer than 130 members of Congress had signed on with the caucus-sponsored Ad Hoc Committee for Irish Affairs, under the chairmanship of Representative Mario Biaggi (D-NY). An open schism developed between Irish National Caucus director Father Sean McManus and NORAID leader Michael Flannery when the caucus proposed hosting a "peace forum" in Washington, DC, to which members of both the Ulster Defence Association and the IRA would be invited. Nothing came of the plan and, aside from providing further evidence of the divisions within the Irish-American community over the subject of Northern Ireland, the Irish question remained as much on the periphery of American politics as it had been for more than fifty years.

Concern and Constraint in Confronting the Ulster Crisis

Irish-American politicians gradually came to appreciate the complexity of the Northern Ireland problem after making a few missteps while promoting the ever-controversial aspirations of Irish nationalism. In 1971, for example, Senator Edward Kennedy (D-MA) somewhat impulsively called for Britain's immediate withdrawal from Ireland and declared that those Protestants who could not accept a united Ireland "should be given a decent opportunity to go back to Britain." By 1973 Kennedy was affirming that Protestants had to have an equal role with Catholics, but he continued to insist that the unification of Ireland under the jurisdiction of Dublin was the only sensible solution to the Ulster crisis. Ultimately, in 1977, in response to appeals privately communicated from Garret FitzGerald, John Hume, and others, Kennedy and Senator Daniel Patrick Moynihan (D-NY), together with Governor of New York Hugh Carey, a Democrat, and House Speaker Thomas "Tip" O'Neill (D-MA), issued a St. Patrick's Day statement that condemned the IRA as the real obstacle to peace in Northern Ireland. It was these same Irish-American leaders, popularly referred to as "the Four Horsemen," who persuaded President Jimmy Carter to make his August 1977 offer of U.S. help toward a solution for Ulster. Specifically, the president promised to encourage substantial American investment in Northern Ireland, provided a settlement could be reached between the Protestant and Catholic communities.

Kennedy and his colleagues became increasingly frustrated over the next two years when none of the principal parties took any real initiative toward reconciliation in Ulster. Meanwhile, successive human rights investigations continued to condemn police brutality in Northern Ireland. The Four Horsemen accordingly issued another St. Patrick's Day statement in 1979, which, reflecting their keen sense of betrayal, blamed British insensitivity rather than IRA terrorism as the principal cause for the continuing strife in Northern Ireland. That contention was promptly dismissed as naive by British Labour leader Shirley Williams, while a subsequent statement by these Irish-American leaders calling for British withdrawal from Northern Ireland was ridiculed as reckless and irresponsible by Irish Labour leader Conor Cruise O'Brien.

Nevertheless, the Four Horsemen, together with President Carter, succeeded in impressing upon London the importance of the American dimension to the Irish problem when considering any future resolution to the Northern Ireland conflict. British prime minister Margaret Thatcher reflected this change when she gave the *New York Times,* but not a single British newspaper, an exclusive interview on her proposal for devolution of political power in Ulster one week before announcing it publicly.

But while subsequent power-sharing proposals advanced by the British government had the effect of tempering the criticism of some members of Congress and governors, who beginning in 1981, acted as a group known as "the Friends of Ireland," the devolution schemes were sharply rejected by militant Irish American groups who demanded Irish unity. The latter were not interested in the achievement of civil rights for all citizens of a Northern Ireland that remained within the United Kingdom. Rather, they supported the IRA call for the overthrow of British authority in Ulster and for the unification of Ireland. The majority of Irish Americans, however, were increasingly disinclined to heed appeals from the IRA as that organization's true character became better known. On March 1, 1981, for instance (the same day that Bobby Sands began his hunger strike), the *New York Times Magazine* featured a story on international terrorism, and its depiction of the IRA was illustrative of the kind of journalistic commentary on Northern Ireland that was gaining wider currency among American readers. One excerpt reads:

The IRA has come a long way since its early days of dependence on the United States. Fundraising is mostly done at home nowadays, by means of protection rackets, brothels, massage parlors and bank stickups. And the incoming hardware is largely Soviet-made. It took only a few years to make the transformation with the help of the international terror network.

On March 1, 1988, exactly seven years from the date of the *New York Times Magazine* article, the Associated Press carried a story that addressed the same reality. According to the AP, more than 100 tons of weaponry had been clandestinely shipped to Ireland from Libya. What worried authorities in both London and Dublin about this particular instance of arms smuggling from terrorist suppliers were reports that the shipments contained Soviet-made SAM-7 antiaircraft missiles. If true, the IRA would have possessed a fearsome new potential for escalating the violence in Northern Ireland.

Perhaps, therefore, it was not only their assimilation into the mainstream of American society that distanced most Irish Americans from the cause of Irish republicanism. Disillusionment with the nature and methods of the contemporary IRA almost certainly was an equally restraining factor for these well-educated and sophisticated ethnics. John Breecher, a correspondent for *Newsweek*, made this generational difference rather poignantly in a May 1981 article. Beecher recalled that when three Irish nationalists in British custody starved themselves to death in 1920, fully 100,000 angry Irish Americans filled Boston Common. In May 1981, when IRA hunger striker Bobby Sands died similarly in yet another act of protest, barely 100 people demonstrated outside the home of the British consul-general in Boston. Although that numerical disparity did not necessarily represent the true nature of Irish-American concern for the Northern Ireland problem in the 1980s, it did serve to underscore an essential difficulty for this ethnic community. Irish Americans discovered that they supported an ideal, the unification of Ireland, which was the professed goal of an organization that they increasingly came to regard as morally abhorrent. That was the dilemma confronting thoughtful Irish Americans, and it accounts, to a large extent, for the diminishment of their traditional enthusiasm for the romantic aspirations of nationalist Ireland.

13

Ireland into the Twenty-First Century

This chapter, despite its title, commences in the 1990s because that decade represented a truly seismic change in the Irish experience. It was a prelude to a new century, a new millennium, and, arguably, a new Ireland. If anyone living in Ireland in 1800 had been somehow able to return there in 1900, he would have found little significant change. Similarly, a resident of rural or urban Ireland in 1955, north or south, would have detected few notable differences with the Ireland of 1925. But the quick and profound shift in economic, sociocultural, political or constitutional, religious, and sectarian developments during this truly transformational era in both the Republic of Ireland and Northern Ireland seemed to place all of Irish society in a "fast forward" mode by contrast with the often-laconic pace of yesteryear.

The republic, in particular, embraced the global economy and a European identity that brought unprecedented affluence, an end to compulsory emigration, the liberalization of social mores, and a pervasive cynicism toward Church authority. It also brought a dramatic increase in serious crime, escalating drug use, and, in some instances, a notable decline in personal integrity and public values. In Northern Ireland, criminal activity had long prevailed owing to the mafia-like world in which paramilitary organizations across the sectarian divide combated one another while simultaneously preying upon defenseless coreligionists in destitute working-class neighborhoods. But even in that cold home for liberal democracy, enormous changes typified life in the 1990s. An agreement for a power-sharing assembly at Stormont was concluded in 1998, but few hearts were altered as more "peace walls" dividing nationalist from Unionist communities had been erected after 1994 than before. Militant Republicans remained unhappy about the failure to achieve a united Ireland, while dissident Unionists resented reforms targeting the north's police service and justice system. Education continued in a separate but equal school system despite rare experiments with "integrated" primary- and secondary-level institutions. Perhaps the most salutary outcome of the agreement for a large number of Unionists was the reduction in their paranoid fear that London would betray them and secretly agree to having the north placed under Dublin's jurisdiction. But the public commitment of both the British and Irish governments to honor the expressed wish of the majority of the north's population altered the psychological, if not the sociological, outlook of individual political moderates who, collectively, might represent the best long-term prospect for peace and reconciliation in that troubled province.

The Genesis of the Peace Process

Some historians cite the Anglo-Irish Accord in 1985 as having established the foundation for the Good Friday Agreement of 1998. That is a credible premise, but in those intervening thirteen years it often appeared that prospects for any peaceful resolution were nil. British prime minister Margaret Thatcher had deeply alienated Republican and nationalist constituencies in the north by her hard and unsympathetic handling of the IRA hunger strikers in the early 1980s. She no doubt felt similarly aggrieved when, in October 1984, the IRA exploded a bomb at the Conservative party conference in Brighton that nearly killed her. But Thatcher was prodded into pursuing Northern Ireland peace negotiations with the Haughey government in Dublin by none other than her good friend, President Ronald Reagan. In retrospect it appears that Reagan, who no doubt would have welcomed any reconciliation of the Ulster conflict, was motivated primarily by a desire to mollify House Speaker Thomas (Tip) O'Neill, whose support Reagan sought in defense of his Nicaragua policy. Taoiseach Garrett FitzGerald also petitioned the prime minister to help produce a venue through which the London and Dublin governments might jointly defuse sectarian conflict in the north at a time when Sinn Féin was making electoral gains in the European Parliament. It was a valid concern that prompted Thatcher to agree to an accord she really did not support with much enthusiasm.

One outcome, as noted earlier, of November 1985 accord was that the Irish government gained a permanent presence in the north with monitoring offices located at Maryfield in County Down. Ireland, in turn, formally acknowledged the legitimacy of Northern Ireland as an integral part of the United Kingdom. In the aftermath of the accord, however, nothing proceeded as first anticipated. John Hume had expected that his own constituency, the SDLP, would reach an early agreement with the Unionists after Dublin had revoked the territorial claim to the northern state that had been enshrined in the Irish constitution since its adoption in 1937. And the British believed that Sinn Féin would experience a sharp drop in electoral appeal. Neither proved true because the Unionists blamed the SDLP for supporting an agreement Unionists found demeaning, while Sinn Féin suffered only a negligible decline in the general election of May 1987. But even if things did not happen quite the way London had expected, it is interesting to note just how dramatically events over the next ten or more years would be determined by changes in the leadership of three different countries.

In 1987, after the general election in which Fianna Fáil displaced Fine Gael with yet another coalition government, Charles Haughey assumed power at a time when Ireland's economy was deteriorating. Nearly a quarter-million people were unemployed, a situation that was compounded by a national debt that far exceeded the country's gross national product. Haughey brokered a novel social partnership between employers and unions, resulting in wage moderation and enhanced stability within the labor movement. The taoiseach also discarded his own party's long opposition to the Single European Act in order to improve Ireland's access to structured funds, with beneficial results. It was against this backdrop of high stakes economic juggling, and much social unrest, that Haughey began secretive efforts to reignite the peace process in Northern Ireland.

Father Alec Reid, a Redemptorist priest from Tipperary, then based in West Belfast, was a seemingly unlikely—but critical—liaison between the Dublin government and the leadership of Sinn Féin and the SDLP. Father Reid had labored quietly, but persistently, for meaningful reconciliation in the pursuit of peace, refusing to be deterred even by the callous massacre of innocent bystanders in the November 1987 IRA bombing of a Remembrance Day ceremony in Enniskillen. This was the same Father Reid who had earlier caught Haughey's attention after he produced a written proposal for dialogue between rival nationalist groups. To this day some uncertainty remains as to exactly what role Reid played in those early and tentative efforts to initiate a peace process, but most specialists on the topic of "The Troubles" share the consensus view that the publicity-shy priest proved a critical catalyst who was generally trusted by all parties. Reid arranged for discussion venues with the London government through the British Northern Ireland office, and with the Dublin government through Haughey's personal representative, Martin Mansergh. What is especially remarkable about these behind-the-scenes deliberations is how principal figures like Charles Haughey and John Hume were not always fully aware of the many occasions on which Sinn Féin was in direct discussions with British government representatives. With so many competing, and often mutually exclusive, channels of negotiation, involving parties with distinctly different agendas, it is a wonder that any peace process survived, let alone prevailed, during so perilous an incubation.

When neither the British government sponsored round-table talks between constitutional parties in the north nor London's secret negotiations with Sinn Féin yielded any notable progress, Hume sought Haughey's support for a joint Anglo-Irish declaration to identify agreed principles that would help define any eventual settlement. Hume also approached Gerry Adams in the hope that Sinn Féin would endorse a shared nationalist position with SDLP, acknowledging how any fundamental change in the exercise of sovereignty over Northern Ireland would be dependent upon the consent of its residents. Sinn Féin initially opposed this approach, in the belief that it provided Unionists with a veto over Irish unification, but ultimately agreed for strategic reasons. Leadership changes offered the prospect of new opportunities. John Major had succeeded Margaret Thatcher as British prime minister in November 1990 when she lost her leadership battle in the Conservative party; Charles Haughey was forced from office in February 1992, to be succeeded by Albert Reynolds as the new Fianna Fáil taoiseach; and William Jefferson Clinton was elected as the next president of the United States in November 1992. Neither Major nor Reynolds possessed the charismatic profile of their predecessors, and Clinton, an unknown quantity in international politics, yielded in January 1994 to those asking him to authorize a visa for Adams to travel to the United States, despite the rejection of an earlier application in April 1993. From Sinn Féin's vantage point, little stood to be lost and potentially much to be gained in agreeing to a Hume-Adams declaration that made republicanism appear amenable to consensual change in the political setting.

But Major and Reynolds proved far more confident and assertive in their leadership on the Northern Irish question than Sinn Féin might have anticipated. On July 4, 1993, Adams drew much attention by his interview with a journalist in which he affirmed that Republicans might be favorably disposed to consider some sort of "joint authority" in the north as a step toward ending partition. British officials, seeking to reassure Ulster Unionists that no governance scheme was being clandestinely discussed, declared once again that any change in the constitutional status of Northern Ireland would require the approval of a majority of its population.

However, on November 2, 1993, a London newspaper broke the story that, despite all denials to the contrary, the British government had in fact been engaged in secret discussions with Sinn Féin and the IRA for three years. That disclosure quickly prompted a major damage control effort by officials in Whitehall, who were desperately anxious to allay Unionist displeasure. The outcome of that debacle was the December 15, 1993, release of the Downing Street Declaration, made jointly by Major and Reynolds. In it, Major explicitly declared that Great Britain would accept the democratically expressed wishes of the people of Northern Ireland as to whether they wished to remain in the United Kingdom or to form a new relationship with the Irish Republic. Correspondingly, Reynolds affirmed that the republic would recognize and respect whichever choice was embraced by the majority of the people in that province. Neither Sinn Féin nor the more militant Unionists were pleased with that joint declaration, but for different reasons.

What the document made unequivocally clear was that official British policy made approval by a majority in the north an absolute prerequisite for any future Irish unity. And despite Reynolds's earlier inclination to view Unionist consent as simply desirable, rather than essential, Dublin did not in any way resist acceptance of the British condition. That concession was influenced in large measure by a growing realization within the Irish government that the country's economy simply could not afford to pay for Irish unity. It was a realistic assessment. By the 1990s Britain, in order to provide Northern Ireland with the same services and benefits to which all other members of the United Kingdom were entitled, was then subsidizing Northern Ireland at a cost of several billion pounds annually.

Even the IRA seemed to recognize that an impasse had been reached. Reynolds had warned that Dublin's patience was wearing thin. Several leaders in the SDLP, who had earlier followed Hume's leadership in seeking some negotiated settlement with the militant nationalists, openly expressed similar frustration. Regardless of whether such pronouncements had any direct effect, the IRA announced on August 31, 1994, that it was ordering a complete cessation of military operations.

Meanwhile, the Irish government, which had participated in helping to promote the ceasefire, actively sought to enroll Britain's cooperation in establishing some intergovernmental procedures regarding the steps needed to assure that Northern Ireland might be given a viable and reassuring plan for its political future.

It was at this juncture that the peace process became almost irretrievably derailed. Throughout the protracted series of Hume-Adams secret contacts with both the British and Irish governments, the expectation of northern nationalists had been that Britain would help press for Irish unity obtained under some "joint authority" in the near term. But no such concession was ever proffered by London and, in late 1994, pervasive rumors about secret Anglo-Irish negotiations created an apprehensive environment. The two governments next decided to issue a Joint Framework Document intended to allay Unionist and nationalist misgivings. Naturally, the text was the product of compromise and contained language that encouraged Republicans to believe that the achievement of Irish unity was close, if not imminent, while simultaneously assuring Unionists of a permanent future within the United Kingdom. It was a tactic that David Lloyd George had used with some success in 1921, but ambiguity provided no refuge on this occasion. Once more, newspaper leaks helped to scuttle any hope of consensus. In January 1995, *The Times* published an early draft of the proposed Framework Document, which alarmed Unionists with its references to "cross-border" institutions so much that Prime Minister Major quickly attached several dozen amendments to the declaration that was officially published in February. Those provisions angered Republicans who had hoped for a commitment to some early British withdrawal from Northern Ireland, just as it infuriated Unionists when it was discovered that the Irish government still had not agreed to remove the language in its constitution claiming jurisdiction over Northern Ireland.

This situation did not augur well for the prospect of an impending advance in the so-called peace process. The hope for all-party talks appeared remote as Unionists angrily recalled how the Downing Street Declaration had pledged to allow Sinn Féin a place at the table only after that party disavowed the politics of violence and surrendered its weapons. Both the Dublin and London governments had, after all, subscribed to that condition. Meanwhile, there continued to be key leadership changes in different political parties. Ulster Unionist party leader James Molyneaux had been so compromised by the appearance of ineptitude that in September 1995 he was replaced by David Trimble, who was seen as a more aggressive, if not a more inflexible, leader. Nine months earlier Albert Reynolds had been displaced as taoiseach after he uncompromisingly insisted on the appointment of Attorney General Harry Whelehan as president of the High Court despite his lack of judicial experience. The nomination proved politically fatal for Reynolds when, as discussed in Chapter 11, it was discovered that, during Whelehan's tenure, the attorney general's office had delayed the processing of an extradition warrant for a pedophile priest. A Fine Gael coalition government, with John Bruton as taoiseach, came to power in December 1994, and it was left to this able and conciliatory new

Irish leader to approve nearly all of John Major's amendments to the Framework Declaration.

With no reason to believe that anything was likely to change in the prevailing political environment, the IRA unilaterally abandoned its self-imposed cease-fire and, on February 9, 1996, detonated an explosive device in the underground garage of a six-story building near Canary Wharf in South London. Because the explosion took place at seven o'clock in the evening, only two people lost their lives in the blast. But the building and immediate environs were destroyed, at a cost of approximately 100 million pounds, and some of London's more coveted commercial real estate was heavily damaged. It was a clear signal that the militants were not going to allow themselves to be marginalized while the Anglo-Irish negotiators deliberated about the conditions under which the IRA might be given a place at the negotiating table. It was also a cleverly calculated move as the Republican political arm, Sinn Féin, was now prepared to await the British general election in May 1997, in which Tony Blair and his Labour party were expected to triumph. And Sinn Féin correctly anticipated that this new leadership would be more receptive to at least some Republican demands. In July the IRA restored its cease-fire in the wake of Blair's landslide victory. Shortly thereafter Republican militants were admitted to the negotiating table, thus undermining the Downing Street Declaration precondition that they make a permanent pledge not to resort to violence.

A month after Blair's electoral victory, the Irish Republic also had a general election in which Fianna Fáil was returned to power under the leadership of a new taoiseach, Bertie Ahern. It was the arrival of Prime Minister Blair and Taoiseach Ahern that facilitated the consummation of a peace process that had already been given unexpected but substantial impetus by the Clinton administration. Sinn Féin had welcomed the American involvement in the belief that it too would help advance nationalist interests over those of Unionists. That proved a miscalculation, as the political agenda was now being driven in ways that no one could entirely predict or control.

Bruce Morrison, a U.S. representative (D-CT) who led a fact-finding mission to Northern Ireland in September 1993, was but one of many Irish-American politicians and lobbyists who urged President Clinton to become directly involved in the Ulster conflict. While campaigning for the presidency in New York a year earlier Clinton had hinted that he might favor sending a peace envoy to that troubled region. U.S. policy under previous administrations had consistently accepted that Northern Ireland issues were the domestic concerns of the United Kingdom alone. However, the Downing Street Declaration (DSD) of December 1993 illustrated how the Ulster Unionists, together with the Irish and British governments, had participated in what were unprecedented collaborative deliberations. President Clinton hailed the DSD and saw it as an invitation for all interested parties to help advance the peace process. His decision, however, to authorize a travel visa to the United States for Gerry Adams in January 1994 went contrary to the counsel given him by British officials in London, as well as by their diplomatic representatives in Washington, each of whom deemed that authorization "inappropriate."

It was not the first time that a U.S. president had strained the "special relationship" that had been so strongly anchored by the Anglo-American alliance during World War II. Indeed, Dwight D. Eisenhower had perturbed and perplexed the British government over the Suez situation in 1956, while Reagan had once incensed Margaret Thatcher when he failed to inform her about his rescue mission to the British Commonwealth island of Grenada in 1983. But Northern Ireland was neither a colonial outpost nor some distant Commonwealth territory but, rather, an integral part of the United Kingdom. As Timothy Lynch reminds us in his book *Turf War: The Clinton Administration and Northern Ireland,* Clinton turned to Anthony Lake and the National Security Council in formulating his policies toward that region because his own secretary of state, Warren Christopher, subscribed to the standard State Department position that the north was intrinsically and exclusively a British issue.

At a February 1, 1994, press conference Clinton explained that he had approved a limited travel visa for Adams in the belief that doing so could have a constructive effect in advancing the peace process. He did so on the advice of the U.S. ambassador to Ireland, Jean Kennedy Smith, who, like her brother, Senator Edward Kennedy, had been originally hesitant about supporting the visa application. Both were convinced to endorse the Adams visa by their conversations with SDLP leader John Hume, himself a late convert to the idea, Taoiseach Albert Reynolds, Irish journalist and friend Tim Pat Coogan, and the shadowy priest Alec Reid.

Adams's February 1994 visit to New York was followed by a second visa in September with the hope, as Hume had suggested, that respectability would make it far more difficult for Sinn Féin to condone future violence. But a still more unusual Clinton initiative was his appointment of former U.S. senator George Mitchell as special adviser to the president and secretary of state for economic initiatives in Northern Ireland. Mitchell began his tenure in January 1995 and gradually won the confidence of a substantial number of people in both the Unionist and nationalist communities. Together with Harri Holkeri, the former prime minister of Finland, and John de Chastelain, a retired Canadian general, Mitchell was chosen as a cochair of the plenary sessions for the all-party talks that contributed so significantly to the Good Friday Agreement of 1998. SDLP leader John Hume and UUP leader David Trimble , representing the largest nationalist and Unionist constituencies, received the 1998 Nobel Peace Prize for their respective roles in the peace process. The Reverend Ian Paisley, leader of the Democratic Unionist party (DUP), and Gerry Adams of Sinn Féin also accepted the agreement although both were unhappy with different provisions it contained.

Sinn Féin took exception to the mandate requiring the IRA to decommission all weapons by 2000. In fact, it did not do so and remained noncompliant with the agreement until 2005, when the IRA finally consented to destroy weapons under the supervision of the appointed international monitoring body. Moreover, Sinn Féin was compelled to acknowledge the democratic legitimacy of partition, a status it had fought for thirty years to destroy. Unionists, however, were forced to accept the equally unpalatable concessions of power-sharing and cross-border cooperation. Both sides managed to leverage their losses. Cross-border institutions were limited at the outset to such less controversial areas as inland waterways, food safety, special programs of the European Union, and the Irish and Ulster Scots languages. Left for future resolution were protocols relating to policing arrangements, arms decommissioning, and demilitarization. Republicans prevailed in obtaining the release of nearly all paramilitary prisoners as specifically provided for in the agreement.

It was, as Francis Carroll cogently details in his book *The American Presence in Ulster,* an incredible achievement and a historic settlement that finally allowed the people of Northern Ireland the right to determine their own political future. Self-government was restored to the province for the first time since 1972, with nationalists finally agreeing to participate fully. But in the wake of three decades of systematic terror and indiscriminate violence, it was no surprise that malcontents persisted in resisting the new framework of government. Dissident Republican groups, like the "Real IRA," were soon engaged in setting off bombs in towns like Newry and Banbridge, while the Orange Order attempted to defy the Parade Commission's refusal to permit marches through the Catholic neighborhood along Garvaghy Road. But these fringe groups constituted a small minority. The agreement was endorsed by no less than 96 percent of those who voted on the referendum in the republic. And while Catholics in the north supported it by a similar margin, only 55 percent of Protestants in that province did so in the referendum.

The text of the Good Friday Agreement is particularly noteworthy for its paradoxical combinations of precision and vagueness as all sides had attempted to employ language that benefited their own objectives while blunting that of others. When the concept of "power-sharing" was first proposed at the outset of the peace process, it had been thought of as a structural formula for isolating the extremes (e.g., Paisley's DUP and Adams's Sinn Féin). But in a few short years these two parties would displace the moderate Unionists (UUP) and moderate nationalists (SDLP) leaving the same Good Friday instrument as the venue through which these often diametrically opposed parties are required to function.

Under the terms of the agreement, ratified by all Northern Ireland political parties and the governments of Great Britain and the Republic of Ireland on Good Friday, April 10, 1998, a Legislative Assembly was established. On June 25, 108 people were elected as members of the Legislative Assembly (MLAs), with six individuals representing each of Northern Ireland's Westminster constituencies. An Executive Committee and ministers for ten government departments are drawn from the ranks of the MLAs, in proportion to party strength. Ministers and their departments are accountable to the assembly, which has full legislative authority for all "transferred matters," such as education, health, and agriculture. Areas identified as "reserved matters," for example, policing and criminal law, were initially kept within the remit of the British secretary of state for Northern Ireland, while "excepted matters" involving defense, taxation, and foreign policy were permanently retained by the Westminster Parliament.

Despite or because of this closely structured governing model, whose closest example of executive function is that of Switzerland, the assembly did not work as effectively as had been hoped. Members often became confrontational in their deliberations owing to the entrenched interethnic competition between unionism and nationalism. Even the uncertainty over Northern Ireland's constitutional status had a polarizing effect. People were conditioned to think of themselves as belonging to competing communities and perceived issues in zero-sum terms; anything deemed a success for one side was by definition a loss for the other. By 2001 opinion polls reflected mainly Unionist unhappiness with the agreement and, by 2005, a more comprehensive survey showed that only 30 percent of the Northern Ireland population believed that the pact had benefited all sides equally.

One of the continuing deterrents to effective governance was the inability to control the paramilitary organizations. The IRA had consented to a cease-fire in 1994, but that commitment essentially applied to the state, economic targets, and members of the opposing community. That left untouched a whole range of criminal activities, such as training narcoterrorists in Colombia, gun smuggling from the Florida Keys and, in 2004, the Belfast bank robbery, which was the largest of its kind in the history of the United Kingdom. Later, when the IRA eventually agreed to the total decommissioning of its weapons in 2005, loyalists protested the refusal of the IRA to allow photographing the destruction of those weapons. That objection had been swiftly rejected by Republicans, who saw it as an attempt to humiliate rather than elucidate. The Independent Monitoring Commission (IMC), chaired by Canadian General John de Chastelain (ret.), did subsequently confirm the IRA's essential compliance, and that concession was eventually matched by the main loyalist paramilitary groups, the Ulster Defence Association (UDA) and the Ulster Volunteer Force (UVF). On June 12, 2009, the UVF destroyed its entire weapons stocks under the supervision of the disarmament body, and the UDA surrendered a large part of its own arsenal with the promise to hand over the balance of its weapons in the months to follow. However, splinter groups on both sides refused to participate. One consequence of that resistant attitude among both loyalist and IRA renegade dissidents toward the decommissioning of weapons is that paramilitary influence remained intact in a number of areas, particularly in working-class neighborhoods. And it is in these economically depressed areas that organized crime is so prevalent that its revenues total an estimated 10 percent of Northern Ireland's gross domestic product.

After the "Stormontgate" spying scandal of 2002, in which police raided the offices of MLAs at Stormont, the nineteen-month Good Friday power-sharing experiment was suspended. The Irish government criticized British authorities for what is believed to be a premature rush to judgment about Sinn Féin's complicity in a spy scandal. But two years later, in 2004, the IRA was condemned by both London and Dublin for the theft of 40 million pounds from the Northern Bank headquarters in Belfast.

Many Unionists now expressed the view that even if the IRA disarmed and disbanded, power-sharing with Sinn Féin was no longer an acceptable option. It was at this juncture that the IRA released a statement on July 20, 2005, promising again to abandon all illegal activity. Both the British and Irish governments responded with the hope that all criminality would now end and that democratic governance might yet prove possible. After protracted and often-difficult negotiations between the now-dominant Sinn Féin and DUP, together with their Anglo-Irish sponsors, the assembly was reconvened in May 2007 with Ian Paisley (DUP) as first minister and Martin McGuiness (Sinn Féin) as deputy first minister. Paisley retired a few months later and was succeeded by Peter Robinson. It was an improbable leadership for the new assembly that would have been inconceivable only few years earlier, but the parties now seemed aware that this might indeed be their last opportunity. Both Prime Minister Blair and Taoiseach Ahern had provided increased funding to buttress the north's economy. The time had come for the parties in the north to demonstrate their willingness to make effective self-government a reality.

Decade of the Celtic Tiger

The signing of the Good Friday Agreement in 1998 was not the significant event for the north that year; it was also the year in which the Irish Republic, experiencing the birth of a ten-year period of phenomenal economic growth, was dubbed the "Celtic Tiger." Unemployment rates tumbled, and the GNP growth rate reached an unprecedented 11 percent. Much of that growth was attributable to substantial foreign investment, especially in the information technology and pharmaceutical industries. Firms were initially attracted to Ireland by a combination of generous tax breaks, moderate labor costs, an English-speaking workforce, and the proximity of the continental European market, for which Ireland was well positioned to serve as a gateway.

As early as 1999, Ireland became one of the original twelve European countries to commit to a single European currency. The euro entered circulation on January 1, 2002, replacing the punt in Ireland. Symbolically, the retirement of the punt in a certain sense closed the door on the economic hardships dating back to the 1922 establishment of the state. For a country whose fight for independence had been as much about symbols as it was about literal freedom, this was a significant move. While their forebears had gone to war with a distinctively Irish currency and postage numbered among their long list of demands, the Irish of the twenty-first century were focused on the pragmatic benefits of a globally competitive currency. By abandoning coins and bills that were particular to the nation-state, another nail was driven into the coffin of de Valera's Ireland.

For Ireland, modernization has been tantamount to globalization or, more accurately, "Europeanization." By joining the European Economic and Monetary Union in 1999, Ireland made a symbolic as well as an economic shift, as noted above, particularly in light of the fact that Britain opted not to join the eurozone but remain instead on the sterling standard. It was the first time Ireland had associated with continental Europe without Britain, and this act of sovereign independence was quickly apparent in the country's enhanced power relating to European social and governing issues, as well as in economic policy. Ireland had, by that action, become more firmly rooted in European society.

As a direct consequence of Ireland's popular democratic processes, that small nation wielded notable power and influence within the EU during the decade after 1998. Ireland is the only European country constitutionally bound to hold a nation-wide referendum on policy changes. In 2001, the Irish population exerted its direct influence over the European community at large when the country became the only EU member-state to reject the Nice treaty, which had been designed to expand the union to include ten new member-states. The referendum on that treaty, held in June 2001, was placed on the same ballot with two critically sensitive Irish social issues: the removal of capital punishment from the Irish constitution and the strengthening of Ireland's involvement with the International Criminal Court. Historically low poll numbers allowed the approval of both measures. But to the grave disappointment of the sitting Fianna Fáil government, the Nice treaty was firmly rejected amid fear of involvement in the trend toward growing militarization in Europe and a likely dilution of Irish influence in the EU's existing structure. To those familiar with the evolution of Irish politics and attitudes over the course of the twentieth century, that rejection served as a reminder of Ireland's penchant for autonomy and conservatism in its relationships with the outside world. Although Ireland's negative stance was also a response to other considerations, the vote may also have suggested a latent sense of xenophobia. A year later, however, the same treaty was voted on in a second referendum, and this time it passed by a narrow margin, thus granting admission to the EU for ten new member-states. Ironically, as the incumbent holder of the European presidency (each member holds the office for a six-month term), it was the Republic of Ireland that hosted the welcome ceremonies at Dublin Castle that included the ten countries newly admitted to the EU through the Nice treaty of 2004.

History repeated itself in June 2008 when Ireland became the only EU member to reject the Lisbon treaty, this time as the sole dissenter among twenty-seven member-states, rather than the fifteen in 2001. This treaty was intended to streamline the EU's policies regarding taxation, defense, the executive council, and other issues. Alarms were raised in Ireland about threats that the treaty's policies might pose to Irish business prospects and to Irish neutrality. It is important to recall that in the summer of 2008 the country's economy was sliding into an ever-deepening recession and the U.S.-led wars in Afghanistan and Iraq were still being waged with no end in sight. Both taxation and neutrality were sensitive issues with the electorate. Moreover, one of the treaty's proposals entailed trimming the European Commission, thereby diluting each member-state's influence; critics who led the campaign in Ireland against the treaty's ratification claimed that the country's influence would be reduced by 60 percent. Taoiseach Bertie Ahern's own coalition government was not in full agreement on the merits of the treaty, as Fianna Fáil and the Progressive Democrats favored it, while their Green party partners were sharply divided.

It is difficult to determine whether the negative vote in the national polling was in response to the hyperbolic and apocalyptic projections regarding the consequences for Ireland if the treaty were approved. The *Irish Times* survey on voter responses found that the most troubling reservation for a large percentage of respondents in fact had been their inability to understand the degree to which Irish interests would be affected. Most people understood that as the EU grew, each of the member-states would inevitably hold less influence. A federation of twenty-seven countries by its very nature cannot cater to the specific needs or policies of each individual member. But in order to function effectively, the EU required an efficient system that was not saddled with bureaucratic complexities. The latter was the message the Dublin government relentlessly conveyed to the Irish people in every possible forum in the months after the failed referendum. There can be little doubt that the Irish electorate was strongly motivated by a desire not to lose access to potential EU economic support at a time when the national economy was in such dire straits. The second referendum on the Lisbon Treaty was held on October 2, 2009. Having been previously rejected by 53 percent of Irish voters, that second referendum decisively endorsed the treaty with 67 percent of the ballots cast. It was a significant moment in Irish history, as it was also for the EU. Had Ireland voted negatively a second time it would have effectively killed the treaty. Two weeks later, on October 16, the Irish president, Mary McAleese, signed the document that was then formally deposited in Rome.

As the Irish Republic contended with the membership realities of the EU, its elected representatives to that body made repeated overtures to fortify Ireland's traditions and cultural past within the context of a new European identity. They further sought to ensure that the identity of the EU, a cultural patchwork of all its member-states, also reflected Ireland's distinctive heritage. As the new century commenced, the president of Ireland, Mary McAleese, announced her government's intention to install Irish as a working EU language. This initiative contrasted sharply with the spirit Ireland demonstrated in the 1970s, when the government declined to request the recognition of Irish by any broader European constituency. During those thirty intervening years, the nation had acquired a confident sense of its place in the international community. In June 2005 the EU endorsed McAleese's initiative by officially recognizing Irish as a working language; in January 2007 that recognition was officially enacted.

In reality, this recognition simply will amount to increased paperwork because the likelihood of the EU's actually conducting its work in Irish is minimal. But the formal endorsement of Irish could have a salutary impact on the language movement at home. In the republic the language is in a peculiar state of flux, as the number of Gaeltacht speakers continues to decline while the number of speakers from metropolitan areas increases. More intriguingly, nonnative English speakers comprise one of the most proactive groups seeking to learn Irish. That phenomenon is explained in part by immigrants, particularly those with small children, who are seeking better ways to integrate into Irish society. Irish immersion schools are attractive to these parents because their children are less apt to be socially isolated in an environment in which the language is new and challenging for all the students. Moreover, by learning the language these differing ethnic families are enabled to grasp a core element of Irish identity that remains elusive to the majority of Irish-born citizens.

The impact of immigration for modern Irish society cannot be overestimated. Since 1997 a tidal wave of immigrants has arrived in Ireland, primarily from Eastern Europe—Poland and Lithuania, in particular—and northern Africa. In the wake of this reverse-migration trend in the Irish experience, the indigenous population has had to adapt to diversity and to a genuine sense of multiculturalism for the first time. Unsurprisingly, this adaptation process has had its triumphs and challenges as the previously insulated and overwhelmingly homogeneous society has had to embark on a course in cultural sensitivity, tolerance, and acceptance.

On balance the Irish have done remarkably well in learning to grapple with and embrace a multiethnic society in a short time, unlike the decades or centuries other societies have had to assimilate immigrants from diverse cultural backgrounds. One example of the "growing pains" in cultural sensitivity that this experience has entailed for Ireland took place in August 2007, when the police (Garda Síochána) in Cork announced that they would not permit a Sikh man to wear his turban while carrying out his duties as a member of the Garda reserve. Less controversial was the preference of some women for wearing hijab in public, a practice that elicited more curiosity than criticism.

A new Ireland is rapidly emerging in the twenty-first century. Rotemi Adebari, who fled Nigeria in 2000 and applied for asylum in Ireland on the grounds of religious persecution, was elected a city councilor for Portlaoise, County Laois, in 2004. Three years later, with the help of an unlikely alliance between Fine Gael and Sinn Féin, he was elected mayor of Portlaoise—the first black person to hold that office in the republic. Also in 2007, the Central Statistics Office officially confirmed that Ireland had the fastest-growing population in the EU. Insofar as the country's birth rate had been in steady decline during the last quarter of the twentieth century, the announcement underscored the significance of immigrants in a demographically changing Irish Republic.

Old-Age Politics in a New-Age Nation

Since 1926 Fianna Fáil had predominated in Irish politics thanks, in large measure, to the powerful personalities and capabilities of such leaders as Eamon de Valera, Sean Lemass, and Jack Lynch. Other Fianna Fáil taoiseachs, like Charles Haughey and Albert Reynolds, had made important contributions; but either through corruption and scandal, or due to political missteps, both men had also hurt their party's standing. Bertie Ahern, who succeeded Reynolds in April 1997 at the age of forty-five, was the youngest taoiseach in Ireland's history. He would also prove one of the most enduring, serving three successive terms in office. When he resigned eleven years later, in May 2008, he had served longer than any previous Irish head of government except Eamon de Valera.

Bertie Ahern had been raised in working-class Dublin, the child of staunchly Republican parents, and had studied to be an accountant at University College Dublin. In many respects, Ahern was representative of the "new" Ireland that was emerging in the late 1990s. He was the first taoiseach to separate from his wife and live openly with another woman. He nonetheless considered himself a practicing Catholic, cheekily telling the media that he preferred Bass Ale to Guinness, but that he gave up said Bass every year for Lent. It was this cafeteria approach to Catholicism that had become more commonplace as Ireland transitioned into the twenty-first century. And in this respect Ahern typified what some regarded as the modern Irish man.

Fianna Fáil continued to endure public disgrace from the past abuses of its party leadership. In 1999 a report credited to a former tánaiste, Mary Harney, was made public and revealed a secret list of 120 account holders in the Ansbacher scheme on the Cayman Islands, in which former taoiseach Charles Haughey had been prominently associated. And the Flood Tribunal of 1999–2000 fed still further scandal, when it was discovered that a former Fianna Fáil government press secretary and political lobbyist, Frank Dunlop, admitted having accepted enormous amounts of money from councilors, thereby opening a virtual floodgate of details concerning numerous politicians who had accepted considerable sums of money from land developers. Sensitivity to public outrage over serial acts of corruption was at a heightened pitch when the venerable and widely respected former taoiseach, Jack Lynch, passed away in 1999. Traditionally, former heads of government had been eulogized by whoever held that office at the moment. But Bertie Ahern was not invited to deliver the eulogy. Rather, that honor was extended to Desmond O'Malley, in a deliberate slight. O'Malley had defected from Fianna Fáil in 1985 in order to found the Progressive Democrats, and his selection highlighted the Fianna Fáil's party fissures. It seems likely that the rebuff was directed not toward Ahern personally but, rather, against the political party to which Lynch had dedicated the better part of his career, but with which he had increasingly disagreed.

While Fianna Fáil suffered from disclosures about past and possibly ongoing improprieties, and even indictable activities, Ahern's reputation was less damaged. Many believed that he had acquitted himself effectively in the Northern Ireland peace process and appeared to have guided the nation's economy, occasional bumps notwithstanding, with generally satisfactory results. By contrast, Sinn Féin experienced a somewhat qualified revival at the opening of the twenty-first century. That party's linkage with the IRA compromised its efforts in the eyes of officials in Dublin, London, and Washington. Nonetheless it not only survived as a viable political entity but also displaced the SDLP in a few short years as the majority nationalist party in the north. Sinn Féin perceives itself as a national party and continues to cultivate a following south of the border. It is currently the only all-

Ireland political party. Although its overall election returns in the south are slim when compared to that of the heavier-hitting parties, its presence on the ballots of both the republic and Northern Ireland suggests that Sinn Féin's appeal may yet resonate among the electorate and usher in unexpected political paradigms in the wake of any dramatic development involving either the economy or some critical national interest.

Mary McAleese represents one of Fianna Fáil's triumphs. The Queen's University law professor was the party's presidential candidate when Mary Robinson resigned from office in 1997. McAleese was born and reared in north Belfast and is the first Irish head of state to hail from Northern Ireland. Already in the fifth year of her second seven-year term of office, McAleese is a woman who has held that position for just under two decades, a development that would have been inconceivable only a generation ago. Most important, she had made an important contribution to the peace process, as she has urged her own nationalist community to seek understanding and reconciliation with the Unionist community. That she could and did make that plea despite the fact that two close friends had been murdered on the day of her Belfast wedding because they were Catholic, or that her deaf brother was nearly beaten to death for the same reason, gave her instant credibility in her appeal for greater understanding and forgiveness in Ulster's sectarian society. In the republic, where McAleese has lived since the 1970s, she is sometimes perceived as less tolerant of the secularization of Irish culture. But she unhesitatingly condemned the clergy's sexual abuse revealed in the "Ryan Report" in June 2009, saying, "We are no longer paralyzed by false deference," and predicted that clerics shown to be guilty would be punished.

Another indication of how dramatically attitudes and beliefs are changing in the new century became evident when the abortion issue emerged once again. While abortion remains illegal in Ireland in most circumstances, the electorate's refusal in March 2002 to approve the government's effort to tighten anti-abortion legislation reflected a notable unwillingness to adopt additional restrictions. Then, in May 2007, the generational shift in perspective again came to the forefront when the High Court ruled *against* the Health Service Executive (HSE) in its decision to prevent a seventeen-year-old from traveling to Britain for an abortion. The teenager, who was four months pregnant and under the care and guidance of social workers, had learned via ultrasound that the fetus had anencephaly, a condition in which the head and a majority of the brain fail to develop, and thus would never survive. According to Ireland's current laws, notably reinforced by a 1992 court precedent, a woman is entitled to termination only if her life is at risk. But in a vague loophole of the law, that definition of risk includes suicidal tendencies. The HSE attempted to define "Miss D," as the girl became known to the courts, into this suicidal exclusion in order to avoid public controversy. But Miss D refused to admit that which was not true, and consequently the case went to the High Court.

It is a clear indicator of the times in Ireland that the court assessed Miss D's case not as an abortion issue but, rather, as a simple breach of her freedom to travel. Justice Liam McKechnie criticized the HSE and ruled that neither was there an impediment on Miss D's right to travel for any reason nor was there any law requiring her to seek permission from the courts. Her business outside the state was her own. The HSE easily accepted the court's decision and told the press that it had merely been seeking to comply with what it understood to be the intent of the law. Unlike the case some fifteen years earlier, the outcome of Miss D's travail received comparatively little media attention.

What was most remarkable about these deliberations was the total absence of any reference to the position on abortion of the Roman Catholic Church. In previous iterations of this debate, the Church and its perspective played heavily in the secular discussion and eventual judgment. That neither the Church's teachings nor the "moral question" at hand were emphasized in these proceedings is telling. The de-Catholicization of Irish legislation became increasingly more pronounced through two landmark legal developments in 2007. In a pivotal case, the High Court ruled in favor of Dr. Lydia Foy, a transgender woman who had been born male but who had been attempting for ten years to obtain a new birth certificate listing her as a female. The court determined that the state was in breach of Article 8 of the European Convention on Human Rights in denying Dr. Foy this recognition. Soon the government moved to recognize same-sex partnerships legally and socially. Although both of these developments were driven by EU conventions and pressure, their extraordinary departure from the conservative social values that defined twentieth-century Ireland is further evidence of the progressive advance taking place in the secularization of the country.

Popular Culture in the New Ireland

Irish popular culture in the early twenty-first century provides further evidence of Ireland's movement in a direction away from the Church. The internationally successful 2007 Irish film *Once* contains virtually no mention of the Church. Rather, the film focuses on the secular and multicultural issues facing the "new Ireland" of today. Sensitively addressing a set of modern social realities, the most prominent being that of immigration, within the context of a bittersweet Dublin romance set to an inspired original soundtrack, the producers explicitly omit the Church from the context of the characters' lives. In what is a perhaps starker contrast to the Ireland presented in *Once,* another immensely popular though disturbing film, *Garage,* is set in rural Ireland but does not even hint at the presence of the Church. Rather, it depicts a social vacuum that in many ways seems purposeful, indicating the now empty space where the Church and its representatives once featured heavily. The film follows Josie, a simple garage caretaker, in his struggle to find acceptance in the only town he has ever called home in the Irish midlands. Without guidance or support, Josie is left to flounder and eventually suffers both social and physical demise as a result of this isolation. In nearly any film of an earlier generation, the Church and the clergy would have played a prominent role in this town and in

Josie's life. The absence of this formerly stalwart social pillar is striking.

In 1999 Gay Byrne, the iconic host of the "Late Late Show," retired after a thirty-seven-year run. The show had served as a crucial social forum for many of the controversial discussions of the day, ranging from contraception, abortion, and the women's liberation movement to Northern Ireland and "The Troubles." Byrne played a prominent role in Ireland's massive social transformations during the second half of the twentieth century by virtue of his producer's willingness to risk disagreement, debate, and backlash. The show's format was based on hot-topic guests whose presence often guaranteed a verbal storm from the television audience. In bringing these guests and their arguments into this public setting, the "Late Late Show" producers and, by extension, Gay Byrne, modernized Irish media and, arguably, the Irish social dialectic. Byrne's retirement on the eve of the new century and the new millennium could be regarded as the close of a chapter that had helped pioneer the development of a new sociocultural ethos. Whereas thirty-seven years earlier many in Ireland had been outraged by public discussion and hence quasi-validation of such previously repressed subjects as contraception, one now witnessed a vastly less inhibited disposition to engage in taboo topics without fear of censorial consequences. Byrne set the standard for such successors as Pat Kenny, who next hosted the "Late Late Show" for ten years, and Ryan Turbridy who was chosen in May 2009 to succeed Kenny. Turbridy, like those who succeeded Jack Paar, Johnny Carson, or Jay Leno on the "Tonight Show" in America, anchored his own RTÉ show—"Turbridy Tonight"—before his appointment. And like his U.S. counterparts, he brings a structure and style that differs from that of Byrne or Kenny. But the legacy left by the latter two would not be diminished; Irish television had been changed profoundly and permanently.

As Ireland moved into the twenty-first century, adopting new mores and developing new social structures at seemingly warp speed, vestiges of its twentieth-century past faded slowly away or nestled into nostalgic niches within the new culture. Both chronologically and socioculturally, the turn of the century was the end of an era, as the lasting traces of the old society confronted a new population—literally as well as figuratively, due to the huge immigration numbers—and new expectations.

Education: Liberating or Limiting?

Some people in the Irish Republic who see themselves as liberal and progressive occasionally comment on how the north is hopelessly fated never to break out of its self-inflicted sectarian dead zone. They say that Catholics and Protestants attend separate schools, which exacerbate tensions and compound old myths and prejudices. Neither community, these disapproving critics note, evince much enthusiasm for Ulster's experimental integrated schools that some had hoped would eventually produce a shared sense of identity. But people in the south who live in glass houses should be the last to cast stones. Over 90 percent of Irish primary schools in the republic are operated by the Catholic Church. These schools, like all others, are funded by the Department of Education. In recent years a massive increase in immigrants, involving people of all colors and creeds, has affected already over-crowded schools, with escalating consequences for the educational system.

Catholic parents in Ireland have first claim to enroll their children in most of the schools throughout the republic. But when Catholic children are given perfectly legal preferential treatment in areas where overcrowding is widespread, the result inevitably leads to schools where the majority of the students are of white, Irish descent. In many places, the children without a baptismal certificate are relegated to alternative ad hoc emergency accommodations. Unlike the American South, where segregation was intentionally designed as separate but equal (the U.S. Supreme Court later ruled that "separate educational facilities are inherently unequal"), the educational system in Ireland is leading to a growing number of segregated and unequal schools that were never intended as such. The Irish constitution guaran-tees an education for every child, but the 2007 experience in Balbriggan, County Dublin, is instructive. Approximately fifty students without baptismal certificates were unable to enroll in that town's established school, and the alternative site provided them was inevitably separate and decidedly unequal.

Church officials are mindful that they can ill afford to remain passive in the resolution of this dilemma. They claim to have "no desire" to be the sole education provider in the country and announced a plan to sell or lease land to the Department of Education so as to allow for the construction of nondenominational schools in areas that need them. What this response suggests, of course, is that there may be a long learning curve for some in understanding the full implications of the fast approaching end to Ireland's homogeneous culture.

The Celtic Tiger and Cultural Change

Despite the political, episcopal, and sociocultural problems that Ireland encountered at the turn of the century, it was generally an upbeat and optimistic economic period in the life of the republic. David McWilliams, the Irish economist and investment banker who became a best-selling author and talk-show host ("The Big Bite"), published a book in 2005 titled *The Pope's Children: The Irish Economic Triumph and the Rise of Ireland's New Elite* that is a witty, irreverent portrayal of the eco-nomic miracle that propelled Ireland from centuries of deprivation to a nation that in 2005 was enjoying one of the highest living standards in the world. The title seizes upon what McWilliams views as the ironic coincidence of the baby boom of the 1970s, which peaked nine months to the day after Pope John Paul II's historic visit to Dublin. McWilliams depicts his fellow compatriots of the new century in a less than flattering light. The "Pope's Children," he contends, are the most hedonistic, status-conscious, and decadent Irish generation ever. They are seen as having abandoned their Catholic birthright, nationalism, and limited expectations in exchange for the new Irish dream of instant gratification, material possessions, and endless possibility. Although entertainingly anecdotal and humorous, if not always accurate, McWilliams does capture the scope of Ireland's transformation when describing the typical boutique restaurant in Dublin where the menu is French, the diligent workers are Slav, the cheap credit is German, the easy capital is American, and the big spenders are Irish. But there is no hyperbole in his contention that tiny Ireland received more direct American investment in 2005 than all of China, a point that the then–U.S. ambassador to Ireland, James Kenny, often asserted when asked about Washington's commitment to Irish economic growth.

What was so remarkable about the decade of the Celtic Tiger (ca. 1998–2008), however, was not the rapidity with which Ireland was catapulted from a mediocre economy to a nation with one of the highest living standards in the world, but indeed how quickly that bubble burst and confidence collapsed following the U.S., and then the global, recession that began in 2007. And not everyone enjoyed even that brief encounter with affluence. Tens of thousands of poor throughout Ireland did not prosper from the economic miracle. Just how rapid that decline was is noted below, but it suffices to say that the McWilliams book of 2005 was woefully out of date in terms of describing the "new Ireland" less than three years after it was published.

Many examples could be cited to illustrate the infectious nature of the new spirit of confidence inspired by the Celtic Tiger economy during its brief duration. Among them certainly are the Irish government's decision in 2006 to reestablish the military parade honoring the participants of the 1916 Rising. That annual commemoration had been abandoned by the Fine Gael-Labour government in 1973, when it seemed inappropriate to give special attention to the physical force movement that had achieved national liberation from Westminster, and Irish nationalist guerrillas were waging an armed campaign in the British province of Northern Ireland. Every Irish government since 1973 had followed suit in sustaining that suspension. Why, then, resurrect that commemorative celebration in 2006 on the Rising's ninetieth anniversary, an anniversary not commonly observed? It was a question many asked themselves, and the ceremony held on Easter Monday 2006 generated passionate feelings and protracted arguments throughout the country between Republican sympathizers and anti-militarists or Irish neutrality advocates. The parade involved 2,500 active and veteran members of the Irish army, navy, and air corps, all of whom marched through Dublin city center to the accompaniment of brass bands, the rumble of tanks, and the roar of military aircraft. At the General Post Office, headquarters for the rebels who led that Rising, President Mary McAleese and Taoiseach Bertie Ahern participated in a wreath-laying ceremony.

Perhaps the most compelling reason for this commemoration, even more than the economy, was the timing. The Good Friday Agreement of 1998 and the 2005 IRA pledge to lay down their arms provided the Dublin government with a welcome opportunity to reclaim a part of the nation's heritage that illegal paramilitary forces had seized for themselves. Many in Ireland still view the rebels of the 1916 Rising as martyrs to the cause of Irish independence and as the founding fathers of the Irish Republic. Others regard those rebels as treacherous insurgents whose actions enjoyed little support and resulted in a civil war that led to even greater loss of life. The government clearly wished to align itself with the former. But it also did so in 2006 because it could afford to economically. Ireland in 2006 was both confident and prosperous. That mood would soon fade.

Irish Neutrality in the Twenty-First Century

One enduring fixture of Irish foreign policy has been its commitment to neutrality, whether under a Fianna Fáil or a Fine Gael government, or in times of adversity or prosperity. It was no different when Ireland rejected the Lisbon treaty in June 2008 because of many concerns, not least of which was neutrality. That repudiation came one month after Bertie Ahern had resigned as taoiseach and was succeeded by his finance minister , Brian Cowen. The Lisbon treaty would have authorized the fourth constitutional revamp of the EU since 1991, providing for a full-time president and foreign minister, and the strengthening of the European Parliament. All the other twenty-six members ratified the document, but Ireland's veto threw the EU into a constitutional limbo until Dublin was provided assurances that Irish tax policy, abortion curbs, and *neutrality* would be protected as EU power expanded. In return for such concessions, Brian Cowen promised to do all he could to obtain a "yes" vote in that subsequent referendum.

Neutrality evolved over the past fifty years as an integral part of the trinity of Irish identity, along with the Catholic Church and the Irish language. And given the recent slippage in the nation's adherence to the latter two, there often appears to be a determined effort to ensure neutrality as indivisible with Irish identity. Former taoiseach Garret FitzGerald has written that Ireland should have been a member of NATO from the outset and need have no misgivings about participating in the collective defense of the EU. Professor Patrick Keatinge agreed, saying that the Irish government's willingness to send troops to Bosnia to operate under the command of the demonized NATO simply denied Ireland the benefits that could accrue from participation in the Partnership for Peace. Eamon de Valera did proclaim a policy of Irish neutrality during World War II, but even his critics will concede that de Valera had little choice given Ireland's defensive posture, and that in any case he pursued what might be described as a pro-Allied neutrality during that conflict. After the war on occasion Dublin appeared more than willing to exchange membership in NATO for an end to partition in Northern Ireland. Such an equivocal approach did not reflect any deep philosophical commitment to the concept of neutrality, as Irish spokesmen often insist; and it helps explain why some scholars have described the policy as simply "a vehicle for the assertion of independence, a commitment to non-belligerence, and a piece of comforting inertia."

Brian Linehan, currently Cowen's finance minister, was once asked during a Dáil debate if he could help clarify the essential nature of Irish neutrality. Serving as foreign minister at the time, Linehan replied: "We are neutral in a military sense but are not neutral in a political sense. That is the net position." That answer may indeed have represented a meaningful distinction to the Dublin government, but it did not alter how Ireland was perceived by others in the international community. Among so-called nonaligned nations, for example, Ireland's profession of neutrality made little impact. In a 1979 survey of the Organization of African Unity and Arab League members, not a single one identified Ireland as neutral or nonaligned, as, for example, some 33 percent did with regard to Austria.

On January 19, 2009, U.S. ambassador to Ireland Thomas Foley in an open letter to the *Irish Times* commended the Irish on their characteristic magnanimity on behalf of the disadvantaged and their caring attitude toward people in general. But he wondered whether Ireland's continued adherence to a policy of neutrality was in sync with Ireland's culture and temperament. For reasons that were abundantly understandable at the time, he said, Ireland chose not to enter into an alliance with Britain during World War II. That was not a decision based on culture or ideology; it was merely circumstantial. But circumstances have changed while Ireland's long-term policy of neutrality persists. Foley acknowledged that some interpreted neutrality as pacifism, which he believed had even less precedent in the Irish historical experience. "Small countries benefit most from alliances," the ambassador opined.

Clearly that is not a view shared by many Irish political leaders in any of the major parties. No matter how inconsistent Ireland's concept of neutrality is with the future direction of the EU, it seems safe to predict that the Irish will prevail in retaining their own definition within that community of nations.

Economic Collapse and the Prospect of an Uncertain Future

Bertie Ahern, the taoiseach who enjoyed a charmed political life as the second-longest-serving Irish head of government, encountered difficulties of his own as early as the turn of the century and before, owing to what critics referred to as his Haughey connection and unorthodox personal financial affairs. It is true that Ahern was seen by some as a bagman for Haughey, having brought in large donations for the party, particularly from businessmen whose firms had benefited from Fianna Fáil policies. Haughey had once described Ahern as "the best, the most skillful, the most devious and the most cunning." But he bitterly condemned his protégé later, most particularly on the occasion of Ahern's role in the Good Friday Agreement, to which Haughey was staunchly opposed. The affable Ahern was skilled at negotiating deals with union leaders and with his Progressive Democrat coalition partners. Despite a heavy north Dublin accent, occasional spoonerisms, and other public-speaking gaffes, together with a public extramarital liaison, the taoiseach continued to prevail over his detractors in the Dáil and in the press. Indeed, even as the October 7, 2007, issue of the *Sunday Independent* reported that while 56 percent of respondents in a poll expressed no confidence in the future of Ireland's increasingly wobbly economy, a plurality of them still favored Bertie Ahern, though rejecting Fianna Fáil. As a columnist in the *Sunday Times* of the same date reported, voters were not particularly troubled by the disclosure that some 300,000 euros were unaccounted for in his personal financial statement. Columnist Sarah Carey explained, "the breakdown of a marriage provides a significant motivation to hide money." With his legal separation concluded in 1993, people generally did not find it surprising that Ahern might wish to hide assets from a spouse who could lay claim to them. By May 2008 too many different pressures combined and Ahern had no choice but to yield the leadership to his appointed successor, Brian Cowen. And his timing could not have been better.

It is no coincidence that Ireland was one of the first European countries to benefit from the information technology (IT) bubble of the late 1990s nor that it was one of the nations that gained most from the increased centralization of the European economy. Overseas investment and the large-scale arrival of foreign nationals helped shape new opportunities in the Irish financial industry and greatly bolstered the Irish economy as early as 1997–1998. Ireland reaped considerable benefits during the decade that followed as a result of this cash infusion. However, Ireland's fortunes also became, to a notable degree, dependent upon the success of overseas economies, particularly that of the United States. As America faced an increasingly questionable financial future in 2007 and 2008, Ireland's economic confidence and prospects also faltered. In September 2008 the credit market in the United States swiftly collapsed and the repercussions were soon visible in Ireland. It is true that most of Europe soon followed suit, but Ireland's financial world was so intrinsically dependent on the U.S. economy that the fiscal collapse quickly eclipsed Treasury failures on either side of the Atlantic.

Compounding the precipitous recessionary decline in Ireland was the fact that the traditional "safety valve" of emigration was no longer a dependable counter balance. In the decade leading up to 2007–2008, Ireland had been an appealing destination for immigrant workers from eastern Europe and Africa who were lured by welcome employment and lifestyle opportunities. Many Irish citizens who had emigrated during leaner economic times in the 1980s and early 1990s now returned home. Ireland's GNP, projected to fall by 14 percent over between 2008 and 2010, will give the country the dubious honor of holding a record that previously be-longed to Finland. When that nation's GNP fell by 11 percent between 1990 and 1993 after the collapse of the Soviet Union, it deprived the Finns of their principal market. But Ireland's collapse was still more precipitous as it went from being the fastest-growing economy in the developed world to having the worst recession in that same cohort of nations. Ireland's prestigious Economic and Social Research Institute (ESRI) forecasts unemployment of 17 percent by late 2010. Because Irish-owned firms do 80 percent of their foreign business with Britain, where the value of the pound has fallen 20 percent since 2007, it is perhaps to be expected that the Irish economy may well shrink by double digits after 2010.

In March 2007 Ireland was "slammed" by a European Commission report for having the poorest broadband service in western Europe. It should have served as a stark reminder that while the country had made significant social and technological advancements, it had done so very quickly and still had significant catching up to do. Four years earlier, Garret FitzGerald, the former taoiseach and respected economist, attempted to sound that same alarm for the country when he warned:

> The achievement of the EU level of GNP does *not* mean, however, that average Irish living standards in the broadest sense have now attained EU levels. Because Ireland's infrastructure—roads, public transport, hospitals, schools, etc.—still largely reflect inadequacies untouched from the pre-1990 period, when Ireland was 40% poorer than all its neighbors, a huge programme of public investment is required in order to expand and modernize these inadequate facilities—and will continue to be required for perhaps ten to fifteen years.

Taoiseach Brian Cowen discovered the fragility of the Celtic Tiger almost immediately upon taking office. Within months of his succession to leadership, the property slowdown was painfully apparent, including the catastrophic effect it would have on government tax revenues. And it was not only in the construction sector that the economy was faring badly. The manufacturing industry was also losing hundreds of jobs weekly as Ireland's diminished competitiveness after the boom sent multinationals scurrying elsewhere. Then the banks went into crisis, resulting in a critical flight of public finances as the gap between revenue and spending began to grow exponentially. The situation became so serious that Cowen's government proposed, in October 2008, a budget containing radical measures with which to heal the bleeding by trimming state spending. These included an attempt to tax people over the age of seventy for their own health care if they were deemed capable of doing so by some "means formula," as well as slightly increasing class sizes in schools. Public reaction was spontaneous and hostile as marches were organized and mass demonstrations were held in the streets.

Initially, people had seemed willing to allow Cowen some time to remedy the financial problem he was thought to have inherited. He appeared as precisely the sort of government leader that the times required. Unlike Bertie Ahern, he had a gruff, no-nonsense demeanor, the courage to share with the electorate that which was and was not possible to achieve, and a reputation for financial expertise. But public patience evaporated quickly as it was soon recalled that it was Cowen himself who had served as finance minister at a time when contractors were building five times as many houses in Ireland, proportional to population, as they were in other European countries that were also experiencing a property boom. The billions of euros lent by Irish banks to land and property speculators, in transactions now toxic, totaled a considerably higher sum proportionately than the loans in other countries, including Britain and the United States. Meanwhile, state spending was allowed to soar, paid for largely by sales taxes on houses. When the property market collapsed, resulting in a price fall of 50 percent from the high point in many areas, so did tax revenues.

The situation grew even more ominous as the Irish government found itself having to take responsibility for the mistakes of private bankers. In September

2008, Ireland sought to shore up confidence in its banks by offering a government guarantee on their liabilities, leaving taxpayers to cover the risk of *potential* losses in excess of twice the country's GDP, a figure roughly equivalent to $30 trillion were it in the United States. Economists in Ireland engaged in many of the same debates that their counterparts did in America, whose economy had fallen into a serious recession of its own. The argument some made was that the government should temporarily nationalize the banks, as was in fact done with the huge Anglo-Irish Bank, rather than recapitalize them with an infusion of millions more euros for which taxpayers would assume responsibility. Many financial specialists expressed the view that Ireland's only hope was for an "exported" recovery, if and when the rest of the world's economy bounced back.

Just when it appeared that the situation could not possibly get worse, it did. In May 2009, President Barack Obama announced a plan to compel American companies to have their overseas profits taxed at home. According to U.S. estimates, Ireland collected nearly $3.3 billion in taxes from American multinationals in 2008. If compelled to pay U.S. taxes on their revenue, these companies would almost certainly be forced to close their Irish operations. Some 100,000 desperately needed jobs in Ireland are directly linked to the 580 American companies that earn more than 70 percent of the revenue tracked by the Irish Industrial Development Authority. An additional 200,000 "downstream jobs" are also said to be associated with those American companies. The Obama administration identified Ireland as one of three countries that are sources of nearly one-third of all American overseas corporate profits , the other two being Bermuda and the Netherlands. The Dublin-based American Chamber of Commerce Tax Committee disclosed that U.S. firms report 8.3 billion euros of products and services from Ireland annually and contribute approximately 13 billion euros in expenditure to the Irish economy by way of payrolls and goods and services spent in their operation. Tánaiste Mary Coughlin responded to the president's announcement, saying that the Dublin government would be monitoring the situation as Obama's tax plans are deliberated upon in Congress, a likely agenda item in 2010. Coughlin attempted to put a reassuring face on the glum news with the remark that Ireland had some "very fine" lobbyists in Washington. Senior politicians from both American political parties have expressed reservations about the president's proposal, so its passage is by no means assured at the time of this writing.

Meanwhile, the ESRI predicted not only that the Celtic Tiger was gone but that it would never return. Specialists at this prestigious Irish think tank concluded that even if the world economy soon stabilized, permitting an annual growth rate in Ireland of 5 percent between 2011 and 2015, the country almost certainly would suffer a permanent 10 percent drop in economic output. ESRI economist John FitzGerald warned that Ireland's recovery will be dependent on the Dublin government's sticking to a policy of higher taxes and reduced spending.

Even in these times of severe financial plight, Ireland's humorists indulged in self-deprecating and ghoulish retorts about the country's return to business as usual, joking that Ireland could now rediscover its traditional identity in the comfort zone of economic difficulty. Amid the doom and gloom, Irish society continued to confront old challenges of earlier decades with mixed results. In 2006, the government launched a new twenty-year strategy to create a bilingual Irish-English society. But the number of Irish speakers has continued to dwindle, and despite the infusion of resources during the more affluent early Celtic Tiger years, the Gaeltacht areas have not experienced any notable growth other than the stately vacation homes built in more prosperous years. Many such residences are occupied for limited periods, creating, a hundred years after the Land Act, a homegrown version of the absentee landlord in rural Ireland. The 2005 Ferns Report regarding Dr. Brendan Comisky, the Bishop of Ferns, and his failure to expel Father Sean Fortune, a pedophile priest, in an effort to handle the matter internally, resulted in yet another backlash against the Church when the Ferns Report regarding Fortune's victims was converted into a widely viewed documentary. A year later, the editor of the *Irish Theological Quarterly* published a book called *The End of Irish Catholicism?* Although hopeful about the Church's potential to reclaim a place in modern Irish society, the author examines the relevance of the Church in the early twenty-first century and asks whether Ireland can still be considered a Catholic country.

The decline of Catholicism's influence in Ireland was attributable in part to the expansion of secularism, Ireland's merger with the rest of Europe, and, most decisively, the profound loss of respect from lay people toward the clergy. Initially, Ireland did not react as negatively to Pope Paul's 1968 encyclical *Humanae Vitae* as did many in either the rest of western Europe or the United States. Although Pope John Paul's successful 1979 visit to Ireland indicated a lingering, enthusiastic loyalty to Rome, an increasingly well-educated laity meant more intellectual examinations of Catholicism. Cynicism concerning puritanism was evident in the less-frequent censorship of books, periodicals, and film until, for all practical purposes, it ceased to exist. Reported scandals beginning in the 1980s had a highly damaging impact on the hierarchy and regular clergy. A popular bishop of Galway's relationship with an American woman, and his fathering of a child, created a scandal that resonated among the laity. Many people were more resentful of his use of diocesan funds to support his mistress and child than they were of his sexual conduct. Numerous other examples of hypocrisy became almost commonplace as several well-known priests, known to be advocates of sexual purity, were discovered to have lived with women and fathered children. But most shocking was the evidence of priests and Irish Christian Brothers sexually abusing children and young men. Bishops were involved in the scandals because they transferred guilty clerics from one parish to another or even to different countries, where they could and did continue their illicit practices. When it was learned that the Church had operated institutions, such as laundries and orphanages, that exploited and virtually imprisoned many young women for alleged misdeeds, nuns were added to the scandals.

In May 2009, a government investigation under the direction of High Court Justice Sean Ryan, issued a 2,600-page, 5-volume report titled *Commission to In-*

quire into Child Abuse that reflected the findings of a nine-year study of the sexual, mental, physical, and emotional abuse inflicted on youngsters of both sexes during most of the twentieth century. The shocking disclosures gave added credibility to the award-winning film *The Magdalene Sisters,* as well as to the highly acclaimed television documentary *States of Fear.* The latter was a three-part production that disclosed how industrial reformatory schools, hospitals for the mentally ill, and kindred social services had exploited and abused people, most often women and children. Stark revelations of pervasive physical and sexual abuse generated such a general outcry that Taoiseach Bertie Ahern felt compelled to launch a formal government investigation following the third televised presentation in 1999. Public outrage only intensified with the screening of the *Magdalene Sisters* in 2002, a film about teenage girls who were sent to Magdalene asylums, otherwise known as "Magadelene Laundries." These were homes administered by Roman Catholic religious orders for women who were labeled as "fallen" by their families or society. It was a national scandal that would have an enduring impact. The litany of such horrific and widespread conduct generated an almost palpable sense of revulsion among people in all walks of life. Little wonder that attendance at mass, already declining in the 1990s, now fell precipitously, as did religious vocations. The country that had once sent flocks of missionaries throughout the world could no longer afford to do so. Instead, places to which Irish clerics had brought Christianity began sending priests to Ireland to remedy a shortage of local clergy.

With spiritual leadership discredited, the Celtic Tiger deflated, and emigration driven once again by rising unemployment, some features of Irish life would continue much as before. The rock band U2 completed its tour in October of several U.S. cities, where it sold a million copies of its latest album, *No Line on the Horizon.* And Irish football (soccer) fans became volubly incensed when a French spokesman for that sport lamented how disappointed he was that France had drawn a second-class opponent, Ireland, for a two-game World Cup playoff.

Concurrently, in the fall of 2009, the irrepressible David McWilliams, author of the aforementioned *The Pope's Children*, published a new title, *Follow the Money.* With the pope's children turning thirty, McWilliams decried how the generation who could have it all was betrayed by the mandarins of the financial world who pursued reckless schemes that resulted in widespread economic turmoil. McWilliams, an economist by training, became an early proponent of the Global Economic Forum that met at Farmleigh House, a Guinness family residence, outside Dublin on September 18, 2009.

The conference considered the creation of a supportive network among the Irish diaspora around the globe to promote a sustainable economy for Irish people at home and abroad. Business leaders from major international corporations participated in programs that included the taoiseach, United States Ambassador Dan Rooney, and a diverse cross-section of Irish political leaders and financial planners. It was there that the Irish minister for foreign affairs, Michael Martin, announced that the government would commit the Euro equivalent of $2.6 million in grants for Irish organizations in the U.S. through his department's Emigrant Support Program. The Farmleigh conference's attempt to harness the talents of people who are among the most successful and influential members of Ireland's diaspora echoed the similar focus of a Dublin Castle meeting in 2007. In the closing weeks of 2009, however, a keen sense of greater urgency was clearly palpable.

Twenty-first-century Ireland retains its great literary tradition. It is impressive that this geographically tiny country can boast of such highly recognized playwrights as Brian Friel, the late Hugh Leonard, Sebastian Barry, and Tom Murphy; poets like Seamus Heaney, John Montague, Paul Muldoon, Seamus Deane, Ciaran Carson, Michael Longley, Derek Mahon, Brendan Kennelly, Paul Durkin, Gerry Dawe, and James Liddy; and fiction writers John Banville, John McGahern, Roddy Doyle, John Trevor, and Dermot Healey. Women have also contributed to the high quality of Irish literature. Edna O'Brien's novels continue to attract both considerable attention and literary criticism, while lesser-known writers, such as Val Mulkerns and her graceful prose, have provided perceptive insights into a changing Ireland. Eiléan Ni Chuilleanáin, Evan Boland, and Medbh McGuckian are among the top-ranked Irish poets who bring feminist perspectives to their work. Most, but not all, members of the Irish literati are Catholic, and a surprisingly large number of them are from Northern Ireland. Some look back on the old days and echo old complaints. A few are hostile to the economic and social changes that substituted a new urban for an old rural Ireland, believing that the transformations destroyed Ireland's unique cultural identity. Others take a more cosmopolitan view of their country and rejoice in its participation in world affairs.

Change is inevitable, but in Ireland it has been so rapid and ubiquitous, at the end of one century and the beginning of another, that it is difficult to discern what fundamental developments might be imminent for Irish society. Conditions in Northern Ireland have improved substantially over the past ten years, but the mob killing of an innocent bystander in Coleraine after a sporting event in May 2009 and the violence following the Orange parade through a Catholic neighborhood in Belfast on July 12, 2009, suggest how much efforts toward peace and reconciliation must still accomplish before "The Troubles" can be truly laid to rest.

In the wake of the cultural transformation that has been spurred by the tidal wave of immigration over the past decade, in tandem with the eclipse of the Church's once-pervasive influence, any evolving new sense of national identity might still be in a gestational stage. At the close of the first decade of the twenty-first century, one cannot help but sense that whatever the future may hold for the "Irish experience," it will be anything but impassive and uneventful.

Recommended Reading

Authors' note: The first edition of this book with another publisher in 1989 precluded the use of footnotes to reference not only published scholarship but also unpublished archival sources drawn from each author's own research. Consequently, no such citations appear in the updated edition published by M.E. Sharpe in 1996 or in the 2010 edition. What this volume provides, therefore, is a synthesis of Irish studies scholarship, together with an interpretation of the Irish historical experience, and a carefully selected bibliography, which has been updated in order to reflect the most recent studies consulted for this edition. Under the title "Recommended Reading," these bibliographical entries are intended to acknowledge our debt to those whose work made this interpretative synthesis possible, and represent as much a long footnote as they do a selective bibliography. —T.E.H. and L.J.M.

Adams, Gerry. *Before the Dawn: An Autobiography.* London: Heinemann, 1996.
———. *An Irish Voice: The Quest for Peace.* Boulder: Roberts Rinehart, 1997.
———. *A Pathway to Peace.* Cork: Mercier Press, 1988.
Akenson, Donald Harman. *The United States and Ireland.* Cambridge: Harvard University Press, 1973.
Allen, Kieran. *The Corporate Takeover of Ireland.* Dublin: Irish Academic Press, 2007.
Almeida, Linda Dowling. *Irish Immigrants in New York City, 1945–1995.* Bloomington: Indiana University Press, 2001.
Arnstein, W.L. "Parnell and the Bradlaugh Case." *Irish Historical Studies* 13 (1963): 215–235.
Arthur, Paul. *Government and Politics of Northern Ireland.* New York: Longman, 1984.
Bean, Kevin. *The New Politics of Sinn Fein.* Liverpool: Liverpool University Press, 2008.
Bell, J. Bowyer. *The IRA, 1968–2000: An Analysis of a Secret Army.* London: Frank Cass, 2000.
———. *Secret Army: A History of the IRA, 1916–79.* Dublin: Academy Press, 1983.
Beresford, David. *Ten Men Dead: The Story of the 1981 Irish Hunger Strike.* London: Grafton Books, 1987.
Bew, Paul, and Gordon Gillespie. *The Northern Ireland Peace Process, 1993–1996: A Chronology.* London: Serif, 1996.
Bew, Paul, and Henry Patterson. *C.S. Parnell.* Dublin: Gill & Macmillan, 1981.
———. *Conflict and Conciliation in Ireland. 1890–1910: Parnellites and Radical Agrarians.* Oxford: Clarendon Press, 1987.
———. *Land and the National Question in Ireland, 1858–82.* Dublin: Gill & Macmillan, 1978.
———. *The Politics of Enmity, 1789–2006.* Oxford: Oxford University Press, 2007.
———. *Sean Lemass and the Making of Modern Ireland, 1945–1966.* Dublin: Gill & Macmillan, 1982.

Bishop, Patrick, and Eamonn Mallie. *The Provisional IRA*. London: Heinemann, 1987.

Boland, Kevin. *The Decline and Fall of Fianna Fail*. Dublin: Mercier Press, 1982.

Bourke, Angela, et al. *The Field Day Anthology of Irish Writing, Volumes IV & V: Irish Women's Writing and Traditions*. Cork: Cork University Press, 2003.

Bowman, John. *De Valera and the Ulster Question, 1917–1973*. New York: Oxford University Press, 1982.

Broeker, Galen. *Rural Disorder and Police Reform in Ireland, 1812–1836*. Toronto: University of Toronto Press, 1970.

Bromage, Mary. *Churchill and Ireland*. Notre Dame: University of Notre Dame Press, 1964.

Brown, Malcolm. *The Politics of Irish Literature: From Thomas Davis to W.B. Yeats*. Seattle: University of Washington Press, 1972.

Brown, Stewart J., and David W. Miller. *Piety and Power in Ireland, 1760–1960*. Notre Dame: University of Notre Dame Press, 2000.

Brown, Terence. *Ireland: A Social and Cultural History, 1922–2001*. London: HarperCollins, 2004.

Brown, Thomas N. *Irish-American Nationalism*. Philadelphia: Lippincott, 1966.

———. *Nationalism and the Irish Peasant, 1800–1848*. Chicago: University of Chicago Press, 1971.

Cahill, Gilbert. "Irish Catholicism and English Toryism." *Review of Politics* 19 (1957): 62–76.

Canning, Paul. *British Policy Towards Ireland, 1921–1941*. New York: Oxford University Press, 1985.

Carroll, Francis M. *American Opinion and the Irish Question, 1910–23*. New York: St. Martin's Press, 1978.

———. *The American Presence in Ulster: A Diplomatic History, 1796–1996*. Washington, DC: Catholic University of America Press, 2005.

Carroll, Joseph T. *Ireland in the War Years, 1939–45*. Oxford: Clarendon Press, 1985.

Clark, Samuel. *Social Origins of the Irish Land War*. Princeton: Princeton University Press, 1979.

Collins, Stephen. *The Cosgrave Legacy*. Dublin: Blackwater Press, 1996.

Comerford, R.V. *Charles Kickham (1828–1882): A Study in Irish Nationalism and Literature*. Dublin: Wolfhound Press, 1979.

———. *The Fenians in Context: Irish Politics and Society, 1848–82*. Atlantic Highlands, NJ: Humanities Press, 1985.

———. *Ireland: Inventing the Nation*. New York: Hodder Arnold, 2003.

Connolly, Linda. *The Irish Women's Movement: From Revolution to Devolution*. London: Palgrave Macmillan, 2002.

Connolly, S.J. *The Oxford Companion to Irish History*. Oxford: Oxford University Press, 2007.

Coogan, Tim Pat. *De Valera: Long Fellow, Long Shadow*. London: Hutchinson, 1993.

———. *The IRA*. New York: Palgrave Macmillan, 2002.

Cooney, John. *John Charles McQuaid: Ruler of Catholic Ireland*. Syracuse: Syracuse University Press, 2003.

Corish, Patrick. *The Irish Catholic Experience: A Historical Survey*. Wilmington: Michael Glazier, 1985.

Corkery, Daniel. *The Hidden Ireland*. Dublin: Gill & Macmillan, 1983.

Costigan, Giovanni. "The Anglo-Irish War, 1919–1922: A War of Independence or Systemized Murder?" *University Review* 5 (1968): 64–68.

———. *A History of Modern Ireland with a Sketch of Earlier Times*. New York: Pegasus, 1970.

Cronin, Mike. *The Blueshirts and Irish Politics*. Dublin: Four Courts Press, 1997.

Curran, Joseph Maroney. *The Birth of the Irish Free State, 1921–1923.* University: University of Alabama Press, 1980.

Curtis, L.P., Jr. *Anglo Saxons & Celts: A Study of Anti-Irish Prejudice in Victorian England.* Bridgeport, CT: Conference on British Studies, 1968.

———. *Apes and Angels: The Irishman in Victorian Caricature.* Newton Abbot, UK: David & Charles, 1971.

———. *Coercion and Conciliation in Ireland, 1880–1892.* Princeton: Princeton University Press, 1963.

Daly, Mary E. *Industrial Development and Irish National Identity, 1922–1939.* Syracuse: Syracuse University Press, 1992.

Dangerfield, George. *The Damnable Question: One Hundred and Twenty Years of Anglo-Irish Conflict.* Boston: Little, Brown, 1976.

David, Fitzpatrick. *Harry Boland's Irish Revolution.* Cork: Cork University Press, 2004.

Davis, Troy. *Dublin's American Policy.* Washington, DC: Catholic University of America Press, 1998.

Dawe, Gerald, and Edna Longley (eds.). *Across a Roaring Hill: The Protestant Imagination in Modern Ireland.* Belfast: Blackstaff Press, 1985.

Deane, Seamus (ed.). *The Field Day Anthology of Irish Writing.* 3 vols. New York: Norton, 1991.

Deane, Seamus; Seamus Heaney; Richard Kearney; Declan Kiberd; and Tom Paulin. *Ireland's Field Day.* Notre Dame: University of Notre Dame Press, 1986.

Desmond, Fitzgerald. *Desmond's Rising: Memoirs 1913 to Easter 1916.* Dublin: Liberties Press, 2006.

Dezell, Maureen. *Coming into Clover: The Evolution of a People and a Culture.* New York: Doubleday, 2001.

Donnelly, James S., Jr. *The Great Irish Potato Famine.* London: Sutton, 2005.

———. *The Land and People of Nineteenth Century Cork.* London: Routledge & Kegan Paul, 1975.

Doyle, David. *Irish Americans, Native Rights, and National Empires: The Structure, Divisions and Attitudes of the Catholic Minority in the Age of Expansion.* New York: Arno Press, 1976.

Dunne, Mary Lee. *BallyKillcline Rising: From Famine Ireland to Immigrant America.* Amherst: University of Massachusetts Press, 2008.

Ebest, Ron. *Private Histories: The Writings of Irish-Americans.* Notre Dame: University of Notre Dame Press, 2005.

Edwards, Ruth Dudley. *James Connolly.* Dublin: Gill & Macmillan, 1981.

———. *Patrick Pearse: The Triumph of Failure.* London: Faber & Faber, 1979.

Elliott, Marianne. *Partners in Revolution: The United Irishmen and France.* New Haven: Yale University Press, 1982.

English, Richard. *Armed Struggle: A History of the IRA.* New York: Oxford University Press, 2004.

Fallon, Brian. *An Age of Innocence: Irish Culture, 1930–1960.* New York: Palgrave Macmillan, 1998.

Fanning, Charles (ed.). *The Irish Voice in America: Irish-American Fiction from the 1760s to the 1980s.* Lexington: University Press of Kentucky, 1991.

———. *Selected Writings of John V. Kelleher on Ireland and Irish America.* Carbondale: Southern Illinois University Press, 2002.

Fanning, Ronan. *Independent Ireland.* Dublin: Helicon, 1983.

Farrell, Brian. *Chairman or Chief: The Role of the Taoiseach in Irish Government.* Dublin: Gill & Macmillan, 1971.

Farrell, Michael. *Northern Ireland: The Orange State.* London: Pluto Press, 1986.

Farrell, Sean. *Rituals and Riots: Sectarian Violence and Political Culture in Ulster, 1784–1886*. Lexington: Kentucky University Press, 2000.

Ferguson, Sir James. *The Curragh Incident*. London: Faber & Faber, 1964.

Ferriter, Diarmaid. *Judging Dev: A Reassessment of the Life and Legacy of Eamon de Valera*. Dublin: Royal Irish Academy Press, 2007.

———. *The Transformation of Ireland*. New York: Overlook Press, 2004.

Finnan, Joseph P. *Redmond and Irish Unity, 1912–1918*. Syracuse: Syracuse University Press, 2004.

Fisk, Robert. *In Time of War: Ireland, Ulster and the Price of Neutrality, 1939–45*. Philadelphia: University of Pennsylvania Press, 1983.

FitzGerald, Garret. *All in a Life: An Autobiography*. Dublin: Gill & Macmillan, 1992.

———. *Towards a New Ireland*. Dublin: Gill & Macmillan, 1973.

Fitzpatrick, David. *Politics and Irish Life, 1913–21*. Cork: Cork University Press, 1998.

———. *The Two Irelands: 1912–1939*. London: Oxford University Press, 1998.

Flanagan, Thomas. *The Irish Novelists, 1800–1850*. New York: Columbia University Press, 1959.

———. *There You Are: Writings on Irish & American History and Literature*. New York: New York Review of Books, 2004.

Foster, R.F. *Luck and the Irish: A Brief History of Change from 1970*. New York: Oxford University Press, 2008.

———. *Modern Ireland: 1600–1972*. New York: Penguin Books, 1989.

Fuller, Louise. *Irish Catholicism Since 1950: The Undoing of a Culture*. Dublin: Gill & Macmillan, 2002.

Garvin, Tom. *The Evolution of Irish Nationalist Politics*. Dublin: Gill & Macmillan, 1981.

———. *Judging Lemass: The Measure of the Man*. Dublin: Royal Irish Academy Press, 2009.

———. *Nationalist Revolutionaries in Ireland, 1858–1928*. New York: Oxford University Press, 1988.

———. *Preventing the Future: Why Was Ireland So Poor for So Long?* Dublin: Gill & Macmillan, 2004.

Gillespie, Michael Patrick. *The Myth of the Irish Cinema*. Syracuse: Syracuse University Press, 2008.

Girvin, Brian, and Gary Murphy. *The Emergency: Neutral Island, 1939–1945*. London: Macmillan, 2006.

———. *Ireland and the Second World War*. Dublin: Four Courts Press, 2000.

———. *The Lemass Era: Politics & Society in the Era of Sean Lemass*. Dublin: University College Dublin Press, 2005.

Hachey, Thomas E. *Britain and Irish Separatism: From the Fenians to the Free State, 1867–1922*. Skokie: Rand McNally, 1977.

———. "The Rhetoric and Reality of Irish Neutrality." *New Hibernia Review* 6 (2002): 26–43.

Hachey, Thomas E., and Lawrence J. McCaffrey (eds.). *Perspectives on Irish Nationalism*. Lexington: University Press of Kentucky, 1989.

Hampton, Jill Brady. "Ireland and Irish America: Connections and Disconnections." *U.S. Catholic Historian* 12 (2004): 127–141.

Hanley, Brian. *The IRA: 1926–1936*. Dublin: Four Courts Press, 2002.

Harkness, D.W. *Restless Dominion: The Irish Free State and the British Commonwealth of Nations, 1921–1931*. Dublin: Gill & Macmillan, 1969.

Harmon, Maurice. *Fenians and Fenianism*. Seattle: University of Washington Press, 1970.

Hart, Peter. *The IRA and Its Enemies: Violence and Community in Cork, 1916–1923*. New York: Oxford University Press, 1998.

———. *Mick: The Real Michael Collins*. New York: Viking Press, 2006.

Hennessey, Thomas. *The Evolution of the Troubles, 1970–72.* Dublin: Irish Academic Press, 2007.

Heyck, Thomas William. *The Dimensions of British Radicalism: The Case of Ireland, 1874–1895.* Urbana: University of Illinois Press, 1974.

Holland, Jack. *The American Connection: U.S. Guns, Money and Influence in Northern Ireland.* New York: Roberts Rinehart, 1999.

Hopkinson, Michael. *Green Against Green: The Irish Civil War.* Dublin: Gill & Macmillan, 1992.

Horgan, John. *Noel Browne: Passionate Outsider.* Dublin: Gill & Macmillan, 2009.

———. *Sean Lemass: The Enigmatic Patriot.* Dublin: Gill & Macmillan, 1999.

Hurst, Michael. *Parnell and Irish Nationalism.* Toronto: University of Toronto Press, 1968.

Jackson, Alvin. *Home Rule: An Irish History, 1800–2000.* New York: Oxford University Press, 2004.

———. *Ireland, 1798–1998.* Oxford: Blackwell, 1999.

Jeffares, A. Norman. *W.B. Yeats: A New Biography.* London: Hutchinson, 1988.

Kearney, Richard (ed.). *Migrations: The Irish at Home and Abroad.* Belfast: Wolfhound Press, 1991.

Keatinge, Patrick. *The Formulation of Irish Foreign Policy.* Dublin: Institute of Public Administration, 1973.

———. *A Singular Stance: Irish Neutrality in the 1980s.* Dublin: Institute of Public Administration, 1984.

Kee, Robert. *The Laurel and the Ivy: The Story of Charles Stewart Parnell and Irish Nationalism.* New York: Viking Press, 1994.

Kenny, Kevin. *The American Irish: A History.* London: Longman, 2002.

Keogh, Dermot. *The Lost Decade: Ireland in the 1950s.* Cork: Mercier Press, 2004.

———. *Ireland & Europe, 1919–1948.* Dublin: Gill & Macmillan, 1988.

Keogh, Dermot, and Andrew McCarthy. *The Making of the Irish Constitution, 1937.* Cork: Mercier Press, 2007.

Krause, David (ed.). *The Letters of Sean O'Casey (Vol. III).* Washington, DC: Catholic University of America Press, 1989.

Laffan, Michael. *The Partition of Ireland, 1911–1925.* Dublin: Dundalgen Press, 1983.

———. *The Resurrection of Ireland: The Sinn Féin Party, 1916–1923.* Cambridge: Cambridge University Press, 1999.

Lanters, Jose. *The Tinkers in Irish Literature: Unsettled Subjects and the Construction of Difference.* Dublin: Irish Academic Press, 2008.

Larkin, Emmet. *The Consolidation of the Roman Catholic Church in Ireland, 1860–1870.* Chapel Hill: University of North Carolina Press, 1987.

———. *The Historical Dimensions of Irish Catholicism.* Washington, DC: Catholic University of America Press, 1984.

———. *James Larkin: Irish Labour Leader, 1876–1947.* Cambridge: MIT Press, 1965.

———. *The Making of the Roman Catholic Church in Ireland, 1850–1860.* Chapel Hill: University of North Carolina Press, 1980.

———. *The Pastoral Role of the Catholic Church in Pre-Famine Ireland.* Washington, DC: Catholic University of America Press, 1996.

———. *The Roman Catholic Church and the Creation of the Modern Irish State, 1878–1886.* Philadelphia: American Philosophical Society, 1975.

———. *The Roman Catholic Church and the Emergence of the Modern Irish Political System, 1874–1878.* Washington, DC: Catholic University of America Press, 1996.

———. *The Roman Catholic Church and the Home Rule Movement in Ireland, 1870–1874.* Chapel Hill: University of North Carolina Press, 2009.

———. *The Roman Catholic Church and the Plan of Campaign, 1886–1888.* Cork: Cork University Press, 1978.

———. *The Roman Catholic Church in Ireland and the Fall of Parnell, 1888–1891.* Chapel Hill: University of North Carolina Press, 1979.

Lee, Joseph. *The Modernization of Irish Society, 1848–1918.* Dublin: Gill & Macmillan, 1973.

Longford, Earl of, and T.P. O'Neill. *Eamon de Valera.* London: Hutchinson, 1970.

Luddy, Maria, and Cliona Murphy (eds.). *Women Surviving: Studies in Irish Women's History in the Nineteenth and Twentieth Centuries.* Dublin: Poolbeg Press, 1990.

Lynch, Timothy J. *Turf War: The Clinton Administration and Northern Ireland.* Hampshire, UK: Ashgate, 2004.

Lyons, F.S.L. *Charles Stewart Parnell.* London: Oxford University Press, 1977.

———. *Culture and Anarchy in Ireland, 1890–1939.* Oxford: Clarendon Press, 1979.

———. *Ireland Since the Famine.* New York: Scribner, 1971.

———. *The Irish Parliamentary Party, 1890–1910.* London: Faber & Faber, 1951.

———. *John Dillon.* Chicago: University of Chicago Press, 1968.

MacArdle, Dorothy. *The Irish Republic.* London: Farrar, Straus, 1965.

MacDermott, Eithne. *Clann na Poblachta.* Cork: Cork University Press, 1998.

MacDonagh, Oliver. *The Emancipationist: Daniel O'Connell, 1775–1830.* London: Weidenfeld & Nicholson, 1989.

———. *The Hereditary Bondsman: Daniel O'Connell, 1775–1829.* London: Weidenfeld & Nicholson, 1988.

———. *Ireland.* Englewood Cliffs, NJ: Prentice-Hall, 1968.

———. *States of Mind: A Study of Anglo-Irish Conflict, 1780–1980.* Boston: George Allen & Unwin, 1983.

MacIntyre, Angus. *The Liberator: Daniel O'Connell and the Irish Party, 1830–1847.* London: Hamish & Hamilton, 1965.

Magnus, Philip. *Gladstone.* New York: Dutton, 1964.

Major, John. *John Major: The Autobiography.* New York: HarperCollins, 1999.

Manning, Maurice. *The Blueshirts.* Dublin: Gill & Macmillan, 1971.

———. *James Dillon.* Dublin: Wolfhound Press, 1999.

Mansergh, Nicholas. *The Irish Question, 1840–1921* (rev. ed.). Toronto: University of Toronto Press, 1964.

———. *The Unresolved Question: The Anglo-Irish Settlement and Its Undoing, 1912–72.* New Haven: Yale University Press, 1991.

Martin, Peter. *Censorship in the Two Irelands, 1922–1939.* Dublin: Irish Academic Press, 2006.

Maume, Patrick. *"Life That Is Exile": Daniel Corkery and the Search for Irish Ireland.* Belfast: Institute of Irish Studies, Queen's University, Belfast, 1993.

McCaffrey, Lawrence J. *Daniel O'Connell and the Repeal Year.* Kentucky: University Press of Kentucky, 1966.

———. *Ireland from Colony to Nation-State.* Englewood Cliffs, NJ: Prentice Hall, 1979.

———. *The Irish Catholic Diaspora in America.* Washington, DC: Catholic University of America Press, 1997.

———. *The Irish Diaspora in America.* Washington, DC: Catholic University of America Press, 1984.

———. *Irish Federalism in the 1870's: A Study in Conservative Nationalism.* Philadelphia: American Philosophical Society, 1962.

———. *The Irish Question: Two Centuries of Controversy.* Lexington: University Press of Kentucky, 1995.

———. *The Irish Question, 1800–1922.* Lexington: University Press of Kentucky, 1968.

———. "Sean O'Faolain and Irish Identity." *New Hibernia Review* 9 (2005): 144–156.

McCarthy, John P. *Kevin O'Higgins: Builder of the Irish State.* Dublin: Irish Academic Press, 2006.

McCartney, Donal. *The Dawning of Democracy: Ireland, 1800–1870.* Dublin: Helicon, 1987.

———. *The World of Daniel O'Connell.* Cork: Mercier Press, 1980.

McDowell, R.B. *The Irish Administration, 1801–1914.* Toronto: University of Toronto Press, 1964.

———. *The Irish Convention.* Toronto: University of Toronto Press, 1970.

———. *Public Opinion and Government Policy in Ireland.* London: Faber & Faber, 1952.

McGarry, Fearghal. *Eoin O'Duffy: A Self-Made Hero.* Oxford: Oxford University Press, 2007.

McGuire, Maria. *To Take Arms: My Year with the IRA Provisionals.* London: Macmillan, 1973.

McMahon, Timothy. *"Grand Opportunity": The Gaelic Revival and Irish Society.* Syracuse: Syracuse University Press, 2008.

Meloy, Elizabeth S. "Touring Connemara: Learning to Read a Landscape of Ruin, 1850–1960." *New Hibernia Review* 13 (2009).

Miller, David W. *Church, State and Nation in Ireland, 1898–1921.* Pittsburgh: University of Pittsburgh Press, 1973.

Miller, Kerby A. *Emigrants and Exiles: Ireland and the Irish Exodus to North America.* New York: Oxford University Press, 1988.

———. *Ireland and Irish-America: Culture, Class and Transatlantic Migration.* Dublin: Field Day, 2008.

Mitchel, Arthur. *Labour in Irish Politics, 1890–1930.* Shannon, Ireland: Irish University Press, 1974.

———. *Revolutionary Government in Ireland: Dail Eireann, 1919–22.* Dublin: Gill & Macmillan, 1995.

Mokyr, Joel. *Why Ireland Starved: A Quantitative & Analytical History of the Irish Economy, 1800–1852.* Boston: George Allen & Unwin, 1983.

Moloney, Ed. *A Secret History of the IRA.* New York: W.W. Norton, 2002.

Moody, T.W. *Davitt and the Irish Revolution: 1846–1882.* New York: Oxford University Press, 1982.

Moody, T.W., and F.X. Martin (eds.). *The Course of Irish History.* Cork: Mercier Press, 1978.

Moody, T.W.; F.X. Martin; and F.J. Byrne. *A Chronology of Irish History to 1976.* New York: Oxford University Press, 1982.

Morgan, John. *Irish Media: A Critical History Since 1922.* London: Routledge, 2001.

Morrissey, Thomas. *William J. Walsh, Archbishop of Dublin, 1841–1921: No Uncertain Voice.* Dublin: Four Courts Press, 2001.

Mulvey, Helen. *Thomas Davis & Ireland: A Biographical Study.* Washington, DC: Catholic University of America Press, 2003.

Murphy, James H. *Ireland: A Social and Cultural History.* Dublin: Four Courts Press, 2003.

Murphy, John A. *Ireland in the Twentieth Century.* Dublin: Gill & Macmillan, 1975.

Murphy, Michael A. *Gerry Fitt: Political Chameleon.* Cork: Mercier Press, 2007.

Norman, E.R. *The Catholic Church & Ireland in the Age of Rebellion: 1859–1873.* Ithaca: Cornell University Press, 1965.

Nowlan, Kevin B. *The Politics of Repeal.* Toronto: University of Toronto Press, 1965.

O Tuathaigh, Gearoid. *Ireland Before the Famine, 1798–1848.* Dublin: Gill & Macmillan, 1972.

O'Brien, Conor Cruise. *Parnell and His Party: 1880–1890.* Oxford: Clarendon Press, 1960.

O'Brien, Justin. *The Arms Trial.* Dublin: Gill & Macmillan, 2000.

O'Brien, Mark. *De Valera, Fianna Fail and the Irish Press*. Dublin: Irish Academic Press, 2001.

O'Brien, William, and Desmond Ryan (eds.). *Devoy's Post Bag, 1871–1928*. Dublin: Fallon, 1953.

O'Broin, Leon. *Fenian Fever: An Anglo-American Dilemma*. New York: New York University Press, 1971.

O'Clery, Conor. *The Greening of the White House*. Dublin: Gill & Macmillan, 1997.

O'Faolain, Sean. *De Valera*. New York: Penguin, 1939.

———. *The Irish*. Harmondsworth, UK: Pelican, 1969.

———. *King of the Beggars: A Life of Daniel O'Connell*. Dublin: Poolbeg Press, 1986.

O'Farrell, Patrick. *Ireland's English Question*. New York: Schocken Books, 1972.

O'Grada, Cormac. *Ireland Before and After the Famine: Explorations in Economic History, 1800–1925*. Manchester: Manchester University Press, 1994.

———. *Ireland's Great Famine: Interdisciplinary Perspectives*. Dublin: University College Dublin Press, 2006.

O'Halpin, Eunan. *The Decline of the Union: British Government in Ireland, 1892–1920*. Syracuse: Syracuse University Press, 1987.

———. *Defending Ireland: The Irish State & Its Enemies Since 1922*. Oxford: Oxford University Press, 2000.

O'Malley, Padraig. *Biting at the Grave: The Irish Hunger Strikes and the Politics of Despair*. Boston: Beacon Press, 1990.

———. *The Uncivil Wars: Ireland Today*. Boston: Houghton Mifflin, 1978.

O'Neill, Kevin. *Family and Farm in Pre-Famine Ireland: The Parish of Killashandra*. Madison: University of Wisconsin Press, 1984.

O'Toole, Fintan. *The Lie of the Land: Irish Identities*. New York: Verso, 1997.

Patterson, Henry. *Ireland Since 1939: The Persistence of Conflict*. London: Penguin Books, 2006.

Quinn, Peter. *Looking for Jimmy: A Search for Irish America*. New York: Overlook Press, 2007.

Rafter, Kevin. *Sinn Féin, 1905–2005: In the Shadow of Gunmen*. Dublin: Gill & Macmillan, 2005.

Regan, John. *The Irish Counter-Revolution, 1921–1936: Treatyite Politics & Settlement in Independent Ireland*. Dublin: Gill & Macmillan, 1999.

Reynolds, James A. *The Catholic Emancipation Crisis in Ireland, 1823–29*. New Haven: Yale University Press, 1954.

Ryan, Desmond. *Fenian Chief: A Biography of James Stephens*. Dublin: Gill & Macmillan, 1967.

Ryder, Chris. *The Ulster Defence Regiment: An Instrument of Peace?* London: Methuen, 1991.

Salman, R.N. *The History and Social Influence of the Potato*. Cambridge: Harvard University Press, 1949.

Savage, Robert (ed.). *Ireland in the New Century: Politics, Culture & Identity*. Dublin: Four Courts Press, 2003.

———. *Irish Television: The Political and Social Origins*. Cork: Cork University Press, 1996.

Shannon, Catherine. *Arthur J. Balfour and Ireland, 1874–1922*. Washington, DC: Catholic University of America Press, 1988.

Shannon, William V. *The American Irish*. New York: Macmillan, 1963.

Sharrock, David, and Mark Devenport. *Man of War, Man of Peace? The Unauthorized Biography of Gerry Adams*. London: Macmillan, 1997.

Smith, James. *Ireland's Magdalen Laundries and the Architecture of Containment*. South Bend, IN: University of Notre Dame Press, 2007.

Smyllie, R.M. "Unneutral Neutral Eire." *Foreign Affairs* 24 (1946): 317–326.

Stewart, A.T.Q. *Edward Carson*. Dublin: Gill & Macmillan, 1981.

———. *Narrow Ground: Aspects of Ulster, 1609–1969*. London: Faber & Faber, 1977.

———. *The Ulster Crisis*. London: Faber & Faber, 1967.

Taylor, Peter. *Provos: The IRA and Sinn Fein*. London: Bloomsbury, 1998.

Townend, Paul A. *Father Mathew, Temperance and Irish Identity*. Dublin: Irish Academic Press, 2002.

Townshend, Charles. *Easter 1916: The Irish Rebellion*. Chicago: Ivan R. Dee, 2006.

———. *Political Violence in Ireland: Government and Resistance Since 1848*. London: Oxford University Press, 1993.

Valiulis, Maryann Gialanella. *Almost a Rebellion: The Irish Army Mutiny of 1924*. Cork: Tower Books, 1985.

———. *Portrait of a Revolutionary: General Mulcahy and the Founding of the Irish Free State*. Lexington: University of Kentucky Press, 1992.

Ward, Alan J. *The Easter Rising: Revolution and Irish Nationalism*. Wheeling, IL: Harlan Davidson, 2003.

———. *Ireland and Anglo-American Relations, 1899–1921*. London: Weidenfeld & Nicolson, 1969.

———. *The Irish Constitutional Tradition: Responsible Government and Modern Ireland*. Washington, DC: Catholic University of America Press, 1994.

Whelan, Bernadette. *Ireland and the Marshall Plan, 1947–1957*. Dublin: Four Courts Press, 2000.

Whyte, John. *Church and State in Modern Ireland*. Dublin: Gill & Macmillan, 1971.

Williams, T. Desmond (ed.). *The Irish Struggle*. Toronto: University of Toronto Press, 1966.

———. *Secret Societies in Ireland*. New York: Barnes & Noble Books, 1973.

Wills, Clair. *That Neutral Island: A Cultural History of Ireland During the Second World War*. Cambridge: Harvard University Press, 2007.

Wilson, Andrew J. *Irish America and the Ulster Conflict*. Washington, DC: Catholic University of America Press, 1995.

Woodham-Smith, Cecil. *The Great Hunger: Ireland, 1845–1849*. New York: Harper & Row, 1962.

Index

Italic page references indicate illustrations and captions.

Abbey Theatre riots, 115
Abdication crisis in England (1936),
    172–173
Aberdeen, Lord, 72
Abortion issue, 199–200, 207–208,
    249–250
ACA, 178
Act of Abdication (1936), 172–173
Act of Union (1800), 27, 34, 87
Adams, Gerry, 237–242
Adebari, Rotemi, 247
Adrian IV (pope), 3
Agar-Robartes, T.G., 124
Agricultural Credit Corporation, 154
Agriculture
    coal-cattle pact and, 170–171
    DATI and, 109
    famine and, 18, 29–30, 60, 65–68, 71,
        230
    hoof-and-mouth disease outbreak and,
        185
    in Irish Free State, 154, 170–171
    land annuities and, 166–167, 175–176
    Land War and, 70–73, 77, 93–96, 102
    landlordism and, 16–18, 31–32, 37, 63,
        73, 90
    New Departure strategy and, 90
    potatoes in, 30, 65
    tenant rights and, 71–72
    Wyndham Land Act and, 120
Ahern, Bertie, 240, 244, 245, 247–248,
    254–256, 257, 260
Aiken, Frank, 146
Alexander VIII (pope), 11
Aliens Act (1935), 169
Allen, W.P., 79
Alliance party, 221, 224
Amending Bill, 125–126
American note, 183, 188
American revolution, 20, 22, 34
Amnesty Association, 79, 83–84

Anglesey, Lord, 42
Anglicization, 4–5, 47, 114
Anglo-Irish, 19–23, 25–27, 50, 60, 159,
    227–228
Anglo-Irish Accord (1985), 203, 225–228
Anglo-Irish Agreement (1985), 202
Anglo-Irish Agreements (1938), 174–177,
    186
Anglo-Irish Intergovernmental Conference
    (1985), 226
Anglo-Irish Protestants, 156, 158–159. *See
    also* Protestants and Protestantism
Anglo-Irish Treaty (1921), 146, 161,
    166–169, 172, 175, 183
Anglo-Irish war, 134–137, 139
Anglo-Norman conquest. *See* English
    imperialism
Anglo-Protestants, 19, 112. *See also*
    Protestants and Protestantism
Anne (British queen), 13
Annuities, land, 166–167, 175–176
Anti-Catholicism in Northern Ireland, 216
Anti-Corn Law League, 54
Anticlericalism, 68–69, 77–78
Army Comrades Association (ACA), 178
Arrears Act, 95
Artwork, 177
Ashbourne Act (1885), 98, 109
Asquith, Herbert H., 121, 123, 125,
    129–130, 132, 134
Attlee, Clement, 190–191

B-Specials force, 218
Bachelor's Walk incident, 126, 129, 144
Bagenal, Sir Henry, 5, 7
Baldwin, Stanley, 148, 175
Balfour, Arthur J., 108, 119–120, 123
Balfour, Gerald, 108–109
Ballot Act (1872), 81
Banim, John, 50–51
Barton, Robert, 137

Bentham, Jeremy, 41
Bettern Government of Ireland Bill, 215
Biaggi, Mario, 232
Biggar, Joseph, 84, 87–89, 104
Birkenhead, Lord, 123, 138
Birrell, Augustine, 120
Black and Tans (radical group), 135–136, 230
Blair, Tony, 240, 244
Blaney, Neal, 196
Bloody Sunday (1972), 220
Blueshirts movement, 178–179, 186
Blythe, Ernest, 157
Boer War, 107, 119
Boland, Harry, 134
Boland, Kevin, 196
Bolívar Simón, 34
Bonar Law, Andrew, 123–125, 130, 148
Borderers, 126
Boundary Commission (1924–1925), 138, 148–150
Bowen, Elizabeth, 159
Boycott, Captain Charles, 93
Boycotting, 93–94
Boyle, Patrick, 217
Boyne, Battle of (1690), 11
Breakespear, Nicholas. See Adrian IV (pope)
Breecher, John, 234
Brehon law, 4, 7
Breslin, Jimmy, 230–231
Bridges, George Rodney, 22
Bright Clause, 80
Bright, John, 73, 80
British civil war (1641), 9, 11
British National Debt commissioners, 167
British Nationality Act (1948), 191
British Parliament, 13, 26, 28, 39, 41–43, 45, 66. See also specific legislation, party and statesman
Brooke, Sir Basil, 215
Brown, Thomas N., 74
Browne, Dr. Noel, 191–192
Brugha, Cathal, 138
Bruton, John, 208, 239–240
Bryce, James, 99
Buckinghamshire, Lord, 20
Buckley, Donald, 168
Burke, Edmund, 16
Burke, T.H., 96, 103
Butler, James, 9
Butt, Isaac, 70, 82–87, 90–91, 97
Byrne, Gay, 251

Campbell-Bannerman, Sir Henry, 119, 121
Camus, Albert, 66–67
Canada, 83
Canary Wharf bombing (1996), 240
Canning, George, 37
Capitalism, 178, 216
Carey, Hugh, 233
Carey, Sarah, 256
Carleton, William, 30–31, 47
Carnarvon, Lord, 98
Carroll, Francis, 242
Carroll, Joseph, 84
Carson, Edward, 122–125, 130
Carter, Jimmy, 223, 233
Casement, Sir Roger, 129–130, 132
Casey, John, 70
Castlereigh, Lord, 26–27
Catherine of Aragon (British queen), 4–5
Catholic Association, 36–37, 39, 42, 56
Catholic Defense Association, 72
Catholic emancipation (1801–1829)
    Catholic Association and, 36–37, 39, 42, 56
    Catholic-Protestant conflict and, 40
    Catholics and, 39–40
    consequences of, 39–40
    Grattan and, 35
    Great Famine and, 68
    O'Connell (Daniel) and, 32–37, 40, 51
    Peel and, 37–39
    Penal Laws and, 28, 35
    rural Catholic Ireland and, 28–32
    triumph of, 37–39, 67
    union and unionism and, 26–27
    United States and, 40
Catholic-Protestant conflict, 17–18, 24, 40, 216. See also Northern Ireland
Catholic relief bill (1829), 38
Catholics and Catholicism. See also Catholic emancipation
    abortion issue and, 207–208, 249–250
    consolidation of Irish, 67–70
    contraception issue, 200–201
    decline of influence of, 259
    divorce issue and, 155, 201–202, 208–209
    education and, 23–24, 251–252
    during English imperialism, 5, 17–18, 23
    in Irish Free State, 155–156
    Irish identity and, 70
    land ownership by, 10, 12, 14
    literature and, 70
    in Modern Ireland, 209–213
    nationalism and, Irish, 61, 69–70

Catholics and Catholicism *(continued)*
  in Northern Ireland, 214–218
  Orange terrorism and, 24
  peasantry and, 15–17, 28–32
  Penal Laws and, 13, 15–16, 28
  sexual abuse scandal, 259–260
  social change and, 200–201
  state relations with, 207–209
Cavendish, Lord Frederick, 96, 103
Celtic Ireland and Celticism, 50, 113
Celtic Tiger (ca. 1998–2008), 244–247,
  252–254
Censorship of Publications Act (1967), 200
Chamberlain, Austen, 138
Chamberlain, Joseph, 95, 98, 104
Chamberlain, Neville, 175, 182
Charlemont, Lord, 21
Charles I (British king), 9
Charles II (British king), 9, 11, 13
Chartism, 50
Chichester-Clark, James, 218
Childers, Erskine Hamilton, 197
Childers, Robert Erskine, 137, 139, 146
Christopher, Warren, 241
Church of Ireland, 15, 19, 80
Churchill, Randolph, 98, 120
Churchill, Winston, 124, 138, 182–185
Civil rights movement in Northern Ireland,
  218–220
Civil War
  American (1860s), 76, 83
  British (1641), 9, 11
  Irish (1922–1923), 144–148
Clan na Gael, 77, 84, 89–94, 117,
  129–130, 134
Clan system, 3–4
Clann na Poblachta (Children of the
  Republic), 188–189, 191–192
Clann na Talmhan (Children of the Land),
  187–189
Clare, Lord, 26
Clarke, Thomas J., 117
Clericalism, 40, 77
Clinton, William Jefferson, 237–238,
  240–241
Clontarf meeting (1843), 55–57
Coal-cattle pact (1935), 170–171
Cohalan, Judge Daniel, 134–135
Coleraine killing (2009), 261
Colleges Bill, 59–61
Collins, Michael
  Anglo-Irish Protestants and, 156,
    158–159
  Boundary Commission and, 148, 150

Collins, Michael *(continued)*
  de Valera and, 134, 162
  Free State Army and, 145–146
  IRB and, 144
  London talks and, 137–139
  power of, 152
  Sinn Féin and, 134–135
  treaty establishing Irish Free State and,
    162
Colonialism. *See* English imperialism
Comhairle na Poblachta (Central Council
  of the Republic), 162–163
Comisky, Brendan, 259
Common law, 7
Communism, 178
Confederation of Kilkenny, 9
Congested Districts Board, 109
Connacht, 4, 7, 31–32, 159
Connolly, James, 118, 129, 131–132, 147,
  162
Constitution (Amendment) Bill, 163,
  173–174
Contraception issue, 200–201
Coogan, Tim Pat, 218, 241
Corish, Brendan, 197
Corkery, Daniel, 209
Corn Laws, 50, 54, 60
Cornwallis, Lord Charles, 22, 26–27
Corrigan, Miss Mairead, 223
Cosgrave, Liam, 195–197, 221, 231
Cosgrave, William T.
  Anglo-Irish Treaty and, 169
  end of era of, 165, 186
  linguistic issue and, 157
  as president of Irish Free State, 146, 148,
    150, 152–153, 160–164
  retirement of, 188
  treating establishing Irish Free State and,
    162
Costello, John A., 172, 189–193
Coughlin, Mary, 258
Council of Ireland, 149, 221–222
Council of Three Hundred, 55
Cowen, Brian, 254, 256–257
Craig, Sir James, 122–124, 130, 214–215,
  221
Crawford, William Sharman, 72
Crimes Act, 105, 108
Croke, Thomas William, 98
Cromwell, Oliver, 9, 11
Cullen, Paul (archbishop), 43, 59, 68–70,
  69, 73, 77–80, 97
Culture. *See also* Literature
  Anglo-Irish influences on, 27

Culture *(continued)*
    artwork, 177
    assimilation and, 4–5
    in Éire, 177, 185–186
    English imperialism and, 3–4
    film, 250–251
    in Irish Free State, 157–159
    in Modern Ireland, 200–201
    nationalism and, Irish, 115
    in twenty-first-century Ireland, 250–254,
        261
Cumann na nGaedhael (Community
    of Irishmen), 151–153, 157–158,
    160–161, 163–164, 172, 174
Curragh internment camp, 180
Cusack, Michael, 114

Dáil Éireann
    Boundary Commission and, 138
    de Valera and, 134, 137–138, 143,
        151–153, 163, 169
    establishment of, 134–135
    Fianna Fáil and, 152–153, 163
    IRA and, 135, 137, 143
    IRB and, 135
    in Irish Free State government, 160
    linguistics issue and, 157
    MacNeill (Eoin) and, 149
    Sinn Féin and, 151
    treaty establishing Irish Free State and,
        139, 143, 147–148
    Volunteers and, 135
Dalton, C.F., 150
Darwinism, 112
DATI, 109
Davis, Thomas Osborne, 47–49, *48,*
    61, 78
Davitt, Michael, 92, 104
Dawson, Geoffrey, 1234
De Chastelain, John, 241, 243
De Clare, Richard fitz Gilbert (known as
    Strongbow), 3
De Ginkel, Godbert, 11
De Grey, Lord, 54–56
De Valera, Eamon
    Act of Abdication and, 172–173
    American note and, 183
    Anglo-Irish Agreements and, 174–177
    Anglo-Irish war and, 134
    Blueshirts movement and, 178–179
    Churchill (Winston) and, 182–185
    Clann na Poblachta and, 188
    Collins and, 134, 162
    Constitution Bill and, 173–174

De Valera, Eamon *(continued)*
    Dáil Éireann and, 134, 137–138, 143,
        151–153, 163, 169
    Easter Week rebellion and, 132–133
    era of (1932–1959), 165–193, 213
    Fianna Fáil and, 151, 162–164,
        192–193
    Hitler's death and, 184–185
    Irish civil war and, 144
    Irish Nationality and Citizenship Act
        and, 191
    Irish Press and, 153
    land annuities and, 166–167
    later years of, 193
    legacy of, 165, *166,* 247
    military tribunal and, 179–180
    neutrality in World War II and, 181–182,
        254
    oath of allegiance to crown and,
        152–153, 166–167
    partition and, 181
    personal background of, 132
    as president of Irish Free State, 146,
        164–193
    successor to, 194
    trade war and, 176–177
    treaty establishing Irish Free State and,
        139, 166–170, 183
    in United States, 134–135
    World War II and, 181–185
Deane, Seamus, 217
Declaratory Act (1720), 19, 22–23
Defenders, 18, 24, 30
Democratic Unionist party (DUP), 224,
    241–242, 244
Department of Agricultural and Technical
    Instruction (DATI), 109
Derrig, Thomas, 158
Devlin, Bernadette, 218
Devlin, Joseph, 134
Devolution schemes, 220–224, 233
Devon, Lord, 59
Devoy, John, 78, 84, 90, 129, 134–135
Diamond, Battle of (1795), 18
Dicey, A.V., 123–124
Dickinson, P.L., 159
Dilke, Charles, 113
Dillon, James, 186
Dillon, John Blake, 47–48, 65, 73, 93, 102,
    107–108, 111, 133
Disestablishment Act, 80–81
Disraeli, Benjamin, 81, 85, 113
Divorce issue, 155, 201–202, 208–209
Doheny, Michael, 76

Downing Street Declaration (DSD) (1993), 238–240
Doyle, Roddy, 203
Drummond, Thomas, 45–46
DSD (1993), 238–240
Dublin, 23, 55, 114, 161, 177, 195, 228
Dublin Castle meeting (2007), 261
Duffy, Charles Gavan, 47–48, 56, 62–65, 70–72, 85, 90
Duffy, George Gavan, 137
Duggan, Eamon, 137
Dukes, Alan, 203
Dunlop, Frank, 248
Dunne, Finley Peter, 77
DUP, 224, 241–242, 244

Easter Week rebellion and rebels (1916), 131–134, 139, 253–254
EC, 203
Ecclesiastical Titles Bill, 72
Economic crisis (1929–1932), 162
Economic crisis (2008), 245, 256
Economy. *See also* Agriculture
    Celtic Tiger, 244–247, 252–254
    in Éire, 185–188
    during English imperialism, 20–22
    information technology bubble and, 256
    in Irish Free State, 153–155, 170
    in Modern Ireland, 194–196, 201, 204
    New Departure strategy and, 90
    self-sufficiency and, 176–177
    trade war and policies and, 170, 176–177
    in twenty-first-century Ireland, 244–247, 252–261
    unemployment and, 204, 215–216, 244
Eden, Anthony, 183
Edgeworth, Maria, 31
Education
    Catholic, 23–24, 251–252
    Colleges Bill and, 59–61
    Irish education bill (1831) and, 42–43
    Irish University Bill and, 80–81, 84–85
    liberal reform and, 119–120
    linguistics issue and, 157–158
    national, 42–43
    in Northern Ireland, 215, 217
    Peel and, 119
    in twenty-first-century Ireland, 235, 251–252
Edward VI (British king), 5
Edward VIII (British king), 172
EEC, 194–195, 197, 212–213
Éire
    Anglo-Irish Agreements and, 174–177

Éire *(continued)*
    constitution forming, 173–174
    culture in, 177, 185–186
    economy in, 185–188
    neutrality in World War II and, 181–182
    partition and, 181
    Republic of Ireland Act and, 189–191
    unrest in, social and political, 177–180
    World War II and, 181–188
Eisenhower, Dwight D., 241
Electric Supply Board (1927), 155
Elizabeth I (British queen), 5, 7
Elliot, Walter, 171
Emergency Powers Act (1940), 180
Emigration
    during English imperialism, 16
    during famine, 71, 74
    during Modern Ireland, 204–205, 209
    nationalism and, Irish, 74–75
    to United States, 73–75
Emmet, Robert, 34, 65, 76
English imperialism
    Battle of Boyne and, 11
    Catholic-Protestant conflict and, 17–18
    Catholics and Catholicism during, 5, 17–18, 23
    civil war in England and, 9, 11
    Confederation of Kilkenny in, 9
    culture and, 3–4
    economy during, 20–22
    emigration during, 16
    geography, 8
    Irish insurrections and, 5, 7
    land ownership by Catholics and, *10, 12, 14*
    landlordism and, 16–18
    onset of, 3–5
    the Pale in, 4, *6*
    peasant revolt during, 25–26
    Penal Laws and, 13, 15–16, 18–19, 21
    plantations and, 7, *8,* 9, 11, 13
    Protestant Ascendancy and, 16, 18–27
    Protestants and Protestantism during, 5, 18–27
    Stuart restoration and, 9, 11
    trade embargo and, 20
    Treaty of Limerick and, 13
    Treaty of Paris and, 23
    Tudor England and, 5, 7, *8,* 9, 19
    union and unionism and, 26–27
ERP, 189
European Community (EC), 203
European Economic Community (EEC), 194–195, 197, 212–213

European Economic and Monetary Union, 244–245
European Monetary System (EMS), 197
European Recovery Program (ERP), 189
Ewart-Biggs, Christopher, 197
Executive (External Relations) Bill, 173
External Relations Act (1936), 189–191

Famine, 18, 29–30, 60, 65–68, 71, 230
Farmleigh House conference (2009), 260–261
Faulkner, Brian, 218–219, 221
Federalism, 50, 83–84
Feetham, Richard, 148
Fenian Brotherhood, 76–77
Fenianism (1858–1870), 76–79, 82, 93
Ferguson, Samuel, 113–114
Ferns Report (2005), 259
Fianna Fáil (Warriors of Fál)
    abdication crisis and, 172
    abortion issue and, 199
    Ahern and, 247–248
    Clann na Poblachta and, 188–189
    Dáil Éireann and, 152–153, 163
    de Valera and, 151, 162–164, 192–193
    economic self-sufficiency policy of, 176–177
    elections
        1927, 152–153
        1932, 163–164
        1973, 196–197
        1987, 202
    establishment of, 151
    foundering and disgrace of, 192–193, 248
    Haughey and, 198, 202–203, 206, 247–248
    IRA and, 179
    Lemass and, 185, 194–196
    Lynch (Jack) and, 196–198, 247
    Nice treaty and, 245
    Northern Ireland policy of, 196–197
    power of, 152–153, 163–164, 186, 247–248
    protests of treatment of Irish Catholics by, 220
    Reynolds and, 206–207, 237–238, 247
    treaty establishing Irish Free State and, 162
Film, 250–251
Films Appeal Board, 200
Fine Gael (formerly Cumann na nGaedhael), 174, 179, 186–187, 188–189, 196–199, 253

Fisher, J.R., 148–149
Fitt, Gerry, 221
Fitzgerald, C.E. Vesey, 37
Fitzgerald, Desmond, 161, 172
FitzGerald, Dr. Garret, 198–202, 225, 231, 233, 236, 254, 257
Fitzgerald, Lord Edward, 25
Fitzgibbon, John (earl of Clare), 26
Flannery, Michael, 231–232
Flood, Patrick, 22, 24
Flood Tribunal (1999–2000), 248
Foley, Thomas, 255
Ford, Patrick, 90
Foreign policy, 195–196
Forster, W.E., 94–95
Fortune, Sean (father), 259
Four Courts (building), 23, 144–145
"Four Horsemen," 233
Fox, Charles J., 22–23
Foy, Dr. Lydia, 250
Framework Document, 239
France, 5, 22, 30, 33
Franco, General Francisco, 179
Fransoni, Cardinal, 58
Fransoni Directive, 68
Free State. See Irish Free State
Free State Act (1933), 168
Free State Army, 144–145, 149–150
French Revolution, 30, 33
Friel, Brian, 198, 217

Gaelic Athletic Association (GAA), 114–115, 117, 119
Gaelic language, 157, 186
Gaelic League, 114, 117, 124, 186
Gaelicization, 114, 117, 124, 157–158, 186
Gaeltacht Commission (1925), 157
Gallicanism, 68
Galvin, Martin, 231
Geldof, Bob, 202
George, David Lloyd, 120, 239
George I (British king), 13, 19
George II (British king), 13
George III (British king), 21
George IV (British king), 39
George, Lloyd (prime minister), 132–139, 144–145, 148
George V (British king), 121–122, 125, 168
George VI (British king), 172, 183
Geresford, Lord George, 37
Gladstone, Herbert, 98
Gladstone, William E.H.
    Arrears Act and, 95

Gladstone, William E.H. *(continued)*
  Fenianism and, 77
  Home Rule and, 84–85, 98–100,
    106–108
  Land Act and, 94
  nationalism and, Irish, 60, 73, 79–81
  Parnell and, 105
  Peace Preservation Act and, 94–95
  unionism and, 102
  University Bill and, 80–81, 84–85
Global Economic Forum (2009), 260–261
Goldsmith, Oliver, 16
Good Friday Agreement (1998), 236,
    241–244, 253, 255
Government of Ireland Act (1920), 149
Graham, Sir James, 54–55, 57
Grand Alliance, 11
Grattan, Henry, 21–22, 24, 26, 34–35
Gray, David, 183
Gray, Dr. John, 71–72
Great Famine (1845–1851), 18, 29–30, 60,
    65–68, 71, 230
Great Hunger. *See* Great Famine
Green party, 245
Gregory, Lady Augusta, 115
Gregory XVI (pope), 57
Grey, Lord Leonard, 7, 42, 45
Grey, Sir Edward, 126
Griffin, Gerald, 50–51
Griffith, Arthur, 116–117, 134, 137–139,
    143, 145, 148, 154

Halifax, Lord, 180
Handlin, Oscar, 228
Harney, Mary, 248
Harrington, Timothy, 102
Hartington, Lord, 100
Haughey, Charles
  Ahern and, 255
  Anglo-Irish relations and, 227
  Fianna Fáil and, 198, 202–203, 206,
    247–248
  Lynch (Jack) and, 196, 198
  NORAID and, 231
  as prime minister of Ireland, 198–199,
    202–203, 206, 236–237
  scandal and, 247–248
  successor to, 206–207
Health care issue, 192
Health Service Executive (HSE), 249
Healy, Timothy, 104, 108, 118
Heaney, Seamus, 217
Hempel, Dr. Edward, 183–184
Henry II (British king), 3

Henry, Mitchel, 86
Henry VIII (British king), 4–5, 7
HGA, 83–85
Hickey, Neil, 230
Hillsborough Agreement. *See* Anglo-Irish
    Accord (1985)
Hitler, Adolf, 175, 184
Hobson, Bulmer, 117, 130
Hogan, James, 178
Holkeri, Harri, 241
Holocaust (1930s-1940s), 66–67,
    184–185
Home Government Association (HGA),
    83–85
Home Rule (1870–1906)
  alternative to, 116–117
  Asquith and, 125
  Butt and, 82–87, 97
  Carson and, 122–123
  Churchill (Winston) and, 124
  Craig and, 122–123
  creation of, 82
  crisis (1912–1914), 214
  decline of Butt's version of, 91–93
  Duffy and, 72
  Fenianism and, 79
  Gladstone (William) and, 84–85, 98–100,
    106–108
  House of Lords crisis and, 121–122
  improved prospects of, 111–112
  Land War and, 93–96
  limits on advances of, 84
  low priority of, 118–119
  nationalism and, Irish, 108
  New Departure strategy and, 89–91,
    93–94
  Parnell (Charles) and, 87–89, *88*, 91,
    100
  politics and, polarizing, 101
  recruiting party candidates and, 86
  Redmond (John) and, 105, 107, 119,
    121–126, 132–133
  success of, 81, 105
  Ulster Unionists and, 214
  Unionist Irish strategy and, 108–110
Home Rule Confederation of Great
    Britain, 84, 86–87, 89
Home Rule League, 85, 89, 92, 98
Hoof-and-mouth disease outbreak (1941),
    185
HSE, 249
Humbert, Jean Joseph, 25
Hume, John, 225, 233, 236–239, 241
Hyde, Douglas, 114, 186

IMC, 243
Independent Irish party, 73
Independent Monitoring Commission (IMC), 243
Information technology bubble (1990s), 256
INLA, 226
Inskip, Sir Thomas, 169, 171
Invincibles (radical group), 95–96
IRA. *See* Irish Republican Army
IRB, 76–79, 94, 117, 119, 124–125, 129–130, 135, 144
Ireton, Henry, 9
Irish Americans
  American revolution and, 20
  emigration from Ireland, 73–75
  influence of, in Modern Ireland, 200
  IRA and, 230–231
  nationalism and, Irish, 74–75, 228–229, 232–233
  Northern Ireland issue and, 228–234
  Parnell (Charles) and, 91
Irish Bill of Rights, 160
Irish Catholics, 9, 44. *See also* Catholics and Catholicism
Irish Censorship of Publications Act (1929), 155
Irish Christianity, 3. *See also* Catholics and Catholicism; Protestants and Protestantism
Irish civil war (1922–1923), 144–148
Irish Coercion Bill, 98–99
Irish Confederation, 62–64
Irish Constitution (1922), 159–164, 173–174
Irish Convention (1917–1918), 133
Irish Council, 119
Irish education bill (1831), 42–43
Irish Free State (1922–1932). *See also* Éire
  abdication crisis in England and, 172–173
  agriculture in, 154, 170–171
  Anglo-Irish Protestants in, 156
  army mutiny and, 149–150
  Catholicism in, 155–156
  civil war and, 144–148
  constitution of, new, 159–164, 173–174
  Cosgrave (William) as president of, 146, 148, 150, 152–153, 160–164
  crises facing, 147–150
  culture in, 157–159
  Dáil Éireann in, 160
  de Valera as president of, 146, 164–193
  dismantling, 165–174

Irish Free State (1922–1932) *(continued)*
  early years, 143–153
  economic crisis and (1929–1932), global, 162
  economy in, 153–155, 170
  financial agreement of, 150–151
  government in, 144–145, 160
  IRA and, 143–144, 162
  land annuities and, 166–167, 175–176
  in League of Nations, 161
  linguistics issues in, 157–158
  literature in, 159
  myth and legend in making of, 139–140
  Northern Ireland's option out of, 148–149
  oath of allegiance to crown and, 138–139, 151–153, 166–167
  Protestants in, 156, 158–159
  religious life in, 155–156
  renaming of, 174–175
  treaty establishing, 139, 143, 146–148, 162, 166–170, 172, 183
Irish Home Rule. *See* Home Rule
Irish-Ireland, 113–116
Irish-Liberal alliance, 100–102
Irish municipal reform bill (1840), 44–45
Irish National Caucus, 232
Irish National Federation, 111
Irish National Liberation Army (INLA), 226
Irish Nationality and Citizenship Act (1935), 169, 191
Irish Parliament, 19–28, 66. *See also specific legislation, party and statesman*
Irish party, 86–87, 97–99, 111–112, 121
Irish Press (party newspaper), 153
Irish question. *See* Nationalism, Irish
Irish Republic (1948–1959), 188–193. *See also* Modern Ireland (1959–1998); Twenty-first century Ireland
Irish Republican Army (IRA)
  arms supplies to, 230–232
  articles about, 233–234
  cessation of military operations by, 238–239, 243–244, 253
  challenge of, to British, 136
  control of operations and, inability of, 243–244
  Dáil Éireann and, 135, 137, 143
  Fianna Fáil and, 179
  imprisonment of members of, 223–224
  Irish Americans and, 230–231
  Irish Free State and, 143–144, 162

Irish Republican Army (IRA) *(continued)*
negotiation and, inclusion in, 240
Official, 219
Provisional, 219, 230–232
resurgence of, 193
Sands and, 224, 230, 233
Sinn Féin and, 225, 227, 244
split within, 219
violent campaigns of, 135, 179–180, 193, 217, 219
Irish Republican Brotherhood (IRB), 76–79, 94, 117, 119, 124–125, 129–130, 135, 144
Irish Situation Committee, 165, 171, 174
Irish Transport Workers Union (ITWU), 118
Irish University Bill, 80–81, 84–85
Irish War for Independence (1919–1921), 147
Irregulars force, 145–147
Israeli-Palestinian conflicts, 226–227
ITWU, 118

Jackson, Andrew, 25
James I (British king), 7
James II (British king), 11
John Paul II (pope), 198, 252, 259
Joyce, James, 70, 106, 199
Judicial Committee to the Privy Council, 99, 168–169

Keatinge, Patrick, 254
Kelly, Thomas J., 79
Kennedy, Edward, 232–233, 241
Kennedy, John F., 201
Kenny, James, 253
Kenny, Pat, 251
Keogh, William, 72, 78
Kickham, Charles J., 78, 83–84, 94
Kiely, Benedict, 217
Kilmainham Treaty, 95, 104
Kipling, Rudyard, 124
Kitchener, Lord Horatio Herbert, 129

Labor disputes, 117–118
Labour party, 120, 152–153, 172, 187–189, 197, 199–200, 202, 205, 253
Ladies Land League, 97
Lake, Anthony, 241
Lake, Gerard, 24
Lalor, James Fintan, 63–64, 90–91
Land Acts, 80, 85, 93–95, 103, 109
Land annuities, 166–167, 175–176
Land League, 94, 97

Land Purchase Acts (1891–1909), 167
Land Purchase Bill, 109
Land War, 70–73, 77, 93–96, 102
Landlordism, 16–18, 31–32, 37, 63, 73, 90
Larkin, James, 118, 187, 203
Larkin, Michael, 79
Lavelle, Patrick, 78
Lavin, Mary, 178
League of Nations, 161
Leinster, 3–4, 21, 31–32, 71, 93
Lemass, Sean, 176–177, 185, 194–196, 247
Leo XIII (pope), 97–98, 178
Leopold (Holy Roman Emperor), 11
Liberal party and liberalism, 40, 85, 89, 94, 99–102, 106, 118–121
Lichfield House Compact (1835), 43–44
Linehan, Brian, 254–255
Linguistics issue, 157–158, 186
Lisbon treaty, 245–246, 254
Literature. *See also specific writer*
Abbey Theatre riots and, 115
Catholicism and, 70
Dublin and, 114
Gaelic tradition and, 114–115
in Irish Free State, 159
landlordism and, 31
in Modern Ireland, 198–199, 209–210
in *Nation*, 47
nationalism and, Irish, 114–115
post-revolutionary, 209–210
in twenty-first-century Ireland, 261
unrest in 1930s and, 177–178
Long Kesh internment camp, 219
Loreborn, Lord, 124
Louis XIV (French king), 11, 13
Loyalty oaths, 23. *See also* Oath of allegiance to crown
Lucas, Frederick, 71
Lynch, Jack, 196–198, 247–248
Lynch, Liam, 144, 146
Lynch, Timothy, 241

MacBride, Séan, 162, 180, 188–189, 192–193
MacDermont, Sean, 117
MacDonagh, Thomas, 128, 130, 132
MacDonald, Malcolm, 171, 174–175
MacDonald, Ramsay, 148, 165
MacHale, John (archbishop), 43, 46–47, 58–59, 67–68, 78, 94
MacMurrough, Dermot, 3
MacNeill, Eoin, 114, 124, 128, 130, 132, 148–149, 157

MacNeill, James, 167–168
MacNevin, Thomas, 47
Macready, General Sir Neville, 145
MacSwiney, Terence, 137
Madden, Daniel Owen, 47
Maffey, Sir John, 185
Magadene asylums, 260
Maguire, Frank, 224
Major, John, 237–238, 240
Manchester martyrs, 79
Mangan, James Clarence, 47
Manning, Henry Cardinal, 104
Mansergh, Martin, 237
Marshall Plan, 189
Martin, John, 65, 77
Martin, Joseph, 87
Martin, Michael, 260–261
Mary (British queen), 11, 13
Mary Tudor (British queen), 7, 19
Mathew, Theobold (father), 52
Maunsel publishing company, 159
Maxwell, General Sir John, 131
Maynooth bill, 58–60
Maze Prison, 224
Mazzini's anticlericalism, 68–69
McAleese, Mary, 213, 246, 249, 253
McAnespie, Aidan, 228
McBride Principles, 227
McCann, Eamon, 218
McCarthy, Justin, 105–106
McCartney, Donal, 159
McCullough, Denis, 117
McDermott, Sean, 130
McGee, Thomas D'Arcy, 47, 65, 77
McGilligan, Patrick, 161, 164
McGuigan, Barry, 227
McGuiness, Martin, 244
McGuire, Maria, 230
McKechnie, Liam, 250
McManus, Sean, 232
McManus, Terence Belew, 78
McNamara, Dr. Kevin, 201–202
McQuaid, John (archbishop), 192
McWilliams, David, 252–253, 260
Meagher, Thomas Francis, 47, 62, 64–65, 77
Melbourne, Lord, 42, 44, 46
Mellows, Liam, 146
Members of the Legislative Assembly (MLAs), 242
Military Operation Bill, 124
Milner, Lord, 123
Mitchel, John, 47, 62–65, 77, 90, 117
Mitchell, George, 241

MLAs, 242
Modern Ireland (1959–1998)
    Catholicism in, 209–213
    challenges and opportunities in, 196–200
    church-state relations in, 207–209
    culture, 200–201
    economy in, 194–196, 201, 204
    emigration during, 204–205, 209
    European Economic Community
        membership and, 194–195, 197,
        212–213
    Haughey's leadership of, 198–203,
        206–207
    identity of Irish and, 205, 209–213
    Irish American influence on, 200
    Irish Catholicism versus Irish-Ireland in,
        209–213
    Lemass's leadership of, 194–196
    literature in, 198–199, 209–210
    Lynch's leadership of, 196–198
    modernization in, 203–206
    politics in, 200–203, 206–207
    Protestants in, 210
    social changes in, 200–203
    unemployment in, 204
    United Nations membership and,
        212–213
    urbanization and, 203–205
Modernization, 203–206, 244
Molly Maguires, 30
Molyneaux, James, 239
Molyneux, William, 19
Monster Meetings, 53–55
Montague, John, 43, 213, 217
Moore, Brian, 217
Moore, George Henry, 72–73, 83
Moore, Thomas, 34, 78
Moran, D.P., 154
Moriarity, David (bishop), 77, 79
Morley, John, 105, 107
Morrison, Bruce, 240
Mother-and-child scheme crisis, 191–192
Moylan, Sean, 144
Moynihan, Daniel Patrick, 233
Mulcahy, Richard, 144, 146, 150, 159,
    164, 172
Munster, 4, 31–32, 71, 93, 159
Murphy, John (father), 25
Murphy, William Martin, 118
Murray, Daniel (archbishop), 46, 58, 60,
    67–68

Nation (newspaper), 47–52, 61–64, 86
National Land League, 92

National League, 153
National Volunteers, 128–129. *See also*
    Volunteers force
Nationalism, Irish
    Butt and, 91–92
    Catholicism and, 61, 69–70
    crises in (1880–1914)
        civil war, brink of, 122–126
        Home Rule alternative, 116–117
        House of Lords, 121–122
        Irish Ireland, 113–116
        Irish party's aging, 111–112
        labor disputes, 117–118
        Liberal reform, 118–121
        racism, 111–113
    Cullen and, 69–70
    culture and, 115
    emigration and, 74–75
    Fenianism and, 76–79
    Ford and, 90
    Gladstone (William) and, 60, 73, 79–81
    Home Rule and, 108
    Irish Americans and, 74–75, 228–229,
        232–233
    landlordism and, 31
    literature and, 114–115
    O'Connell (Daniel) and, 32–37, *39*, 43,
        50, 61, 90
    Parnell (Charles) and, 102
    peasant revolt and, 25
    Peel and, 54–55, 60
    Sinn Féin and, 147
    violent, 79
    Whigs and, 41–42
NATO, 193, 254
Neave, Airey, 224
Neutrality issues, 181–185, 254–255
New Departure strategy, 89–91, 93–94
New Ireland Forum (1983), 225
Newman, John Henry, 59
Nice treaty, 245
Nicholls, George, 45
Nonconformists, 15–16, 22, 24, 50, 112,
    120, 124, 139
NORAID, 231–232
North American Act (1867), 83
North Atlantic Treaty Organization
    (NATO), 193, 254
North, Lord, 20
Northern Aid Committee (NORAID),
    231–232
Northern Ireland
    Anglo-Irish Accord and, 225–228
    anti-Catholicism in, 216

Northern Ireland *(continued)*
    background of "troubles" and, 214–218
    Bloody Sunday in, 220
    British troops in (1969–1971), 219–220
    Catholics in, 214–218
    civil rights movement in, 218–220
    confrontation of crisis in, 232–234
    devolution schemes in, 220–224, 233
    education in, 215, 217
    Fianna Fáil's policy on, 196–197
    Good Friday Agreement and, 241–244
    Irish Americans and, 228–234
    Irish Free State and, option out of,
        148–149
    NORCAID and, 231–232
    perception problem for British and,
        230–231
    politics in, 215
    power-sharing attempts and, 220–224
    Protestants in, 214–218
    Regan's comments on, 201
    Reynolds and, 208
    sectarian violence in, 216, 219–220,
        222–227
    Sinn Féin in, 225–227
    Spring and, 207
    in twenty-first century, 235, 261
    unemployment in, 215–216
    World War II and, 181, 216–217
Northern Ireland Assembly, 221
Northern Ireland Civil Rights Association,
    218
Northern Ireland Constitutional Proposals
    (white paper), 220–222

Oath of allegiance to crown, 138–139,
    151–153, 166–167
Obama, Barack, 258
O'Brien, Conor Cruise, 195, 220, 231–233
O'Brien, Michael, 79
O'Brien, William Smith, 62–65, 77, 90,
    102, 108, 111, 187
Obstruction, 98
O'Casey, Sean, 115, 117, 209
O'Ceallaigh, Séan T., 188
O'Connell, Daniel
    in British House of Commons, entering,
        41–43
    Butt and, 82
    Catholic emancipation and, 32–37, 40,
        51
    death of, 62
    legacy of, 106
    Lichfield House Compact and, 43–44

O'Connell, Daniel *(continued)*
Nation and, 50, 61
nationalism and, Irish, 32–37, *39*, 43, 50, 61, 90
Peel and, 37, 42, 53–55
personal background of, 33–34
power of, 36–37, 68
reform bill (1832) and, 42
Repeal Association and, 46
Repeal of union and, 41–44, 46, 51–57
slavery and, criticism of, 53
Whig alliance and, 43–46
wife of, 34
Young Ireland/Irelanders and, 44, 49–50, 61–62
O'Connell, John, 62, 64
O'Connell, Mary, 34
O'Connor, Fergus, 42
O'Connor, Frank, 43, 177–178, 209
O'Connor, Rory, 145–146
O'Connor, Thomas Power, 98
O'Donnell, F. Hugh, 93, 103
O'Donnell, Hugh, 5
O'Donnell, Peadar, 162
O'Duffy, General Eoin, 150, 178–179
O'Dwyer, Paul, 231–232
O'Faoláin, Sean, 27, 106, 157, 177–178, 186, *187*, 209–212
Offences Against the State Act (1939), 180
Official IRA, 219
O'Flaherty, Liam, 177
O'Grady, Standish, 113–114
O'Hagan, John, 47
O'Hagan, Thomas, 65
O'Higgins, Kevin, 146, 150, 152, 161
Old English Catholics, 9, 17. *See also* Catholics and Catholicism
Old Ireland/Irelanders, 60
O'Mahoney, John, 76–77
O'Malley, Desmond, 248
O'Malley, Ernie, 144
O'Neill, Hugh, 5, 7
O'Neill, Terence, 196
O'Neill, Thomas "Tip," 233, 236
OPEC, 195
Orange Order and Orangemen, 18, 24, 46, 99, 218, 242
O'Reilly, John Boyle, 90
Organization of Petroleum Exporting Countries (OPEC), 195
Ormond, Earl of, 9
Osgood, Molly, 137
O'Shea, Captain William, 95, 103–104
O'Shea, Katherine, 95, 102–104, 106

Packenham, General, 25
Paisley, Ian, 218, 221, 224, 227, 241–242, 244
the Pale, 4, *6*
Palmerston, Lord, 73
Paramilitary organizations. *See specific name*
Parliament Act (1911), 121–122
Parnell, Charles Stewart
Clan na Gael and, 91
daughter's death and, 95
fall of, 102–106
Gladstone (William) and, 105
Home Rule and, 87–89, *88*, 91, 100
imprisonment of, 95
Irish Americans and, 91
Land Act and, 93–95
Land League and, 97
Land War and, 93
legacy of, 106
lover of, 95, 102–104, 106
nationalism and, Irish, 102
personal background of, 87
Phoenix Park murders and, 96–97
Plan of Campaign and, 103
power of, 68, 92–93
Redmond and, 105
Parnell, John Henry, 87
Parnell, Sir John, 87
Parnell, William, 87
Partition, 148–149, 181, 226. *See also* Northern Ireland
Patrick, Nicholas, 73
Peace People, 223
Peace Preservation Act, 94–95
Peace process, 236–244
Pearse, Patrick, 128, 130–131, 157
Peasant revolt (1798), 25–26
Peel, Sir Robert
Catholic emancipation and, 37–39
education and, 119
Great Famine and, 66–67
integration of Ireland with United Kingdom and, 54–60
Irish policy of, 54–61
Maynooth bill and, 58–59
nationalism and, Irish, 54–55, 60
O'Connell (Daniel) and, 37, 42, 53–55
Repeal of union and, 51, 54–55, 57–60
Royal Irish Constabulary and, 31
Peelite-Whig coalition government, 72
Peep O'Day boys, 18
Penal Laws, 13, 15–16, 18–19, 21, 28, 35
Phoenix Park murders (1882), 96–97, 103

Pigott, Richard, 103
Pitt, William, 26
Pius IX (pope), 68, 79
Pius XI (pope), 178
Plan of Campaign, 102–103, 105
Plantations, 7, 8, 9, 11, 13
Plunkett, Joseph Mary, 128, 132
Police Service of Northern Ireland
    (formerly RUC), 218
Politics. *See also specific law, party and
    statesman*
  Home Rule and, 101
  in Modern Ireland, 200–203, 206–207
  in Northern Ireland, 215
  in twenty-first-century Ireland, 247–250
Poor Law, 45, 51–52
Popery Act (1704), 15
Population explosions, 30
Power, John O'Connor, 84, 93
Poynings Law (1494), 19, 22–23
Pre-Norman Ireland, 3–4
Precursor Society, 46
Privy Council (British), 99, 168–169
Program for National Recovery, 202
Protestant Ascendancy, 16, 18–27, 52
Protestant-Catholic conflict, 17–18, 24, 40,
    216. *See also* Northern Ireland
Protestant Ulster Workers Council, 222
Protestants and Protestantism
  during English imperialism, 5, 17–27
  evolution toward, 5, 18
  in Irish Free State, 156, 158–159
  in Modern Ireland, 210
  in Northern Ireland, 214–218
  Penal Laws and, 13, 15–16, 18–19
Provisional IRA, 219, 230–232

Racism, Anglo-Saxon, 112–113, 115
Radicals and radicalism, 32, 41–42, 57–58,
    60, 118, 227
Radio Telefis Éireann (RTÉ), 199–200,
    251
Reagan, Ronald, 199, 201, 236, 241
Redmond, John
  British Unionist strategy and, 123
  Home Rule and, 105, 107, 119, 121–126,
    132–133
  Irish Convention and, 133
  Irish party and, 111–112, 121
  son of, 134
  Volunteers force and, 124, 126, 128
  World War I and, 129–130
Redmond, Captain William, 134
Reform Bill (1867), 81

Reform League, 73
Reformism, British, 31
Reid, Alec, 237, 241
Relief Bill, 21
Remembrance Day ceremony bombing
    (1987), 237
Renunciation Act, 23
Repeal Association, 46, 49, 51–54,
    61–62
Repeal of union (1830–1845)
  combating rising tide of, 54–55
  defeat of, 55–57, 61
  enthusiasm for, increased, 54–55
  lobbying for, 46–47
  Monster Meetings and, 53–55
  O'Connell (Daniel) and, 41–44, 51–57
  Peel and, 51, 54–55, 57–60
  surge of, 51–54
  Whig alliance and, 43–46
  Young Ireland and, 47–51
Republic of Ireland (1948–1959),
    188–193. *See also* Modern Ireland
    (1959–1998); Twenty-first century
    Ireland
Republic of Ireland Act (1948), 189–191
Republicanism, 76–79, 83–84, 90,
    135–137, 151, 230–231
Reynolds, Albert, 206–208, 237–238, 241,
    247
Ribbon Society and Ribbonism, 18, 30
RIC, 31, 79, 100, 122, 135
Richardson, General George, 124
Rinuccini, Giovanni Battista, 9
Roberts, Earl, 124
Roberts, William R., 78
Robinson, Mary, 205–206, 213, 249
Robinson, Peter, 227, 244
Rockingham, Marquis de, 22
Romanization, 4, 68
Rooney, Dan, 260
Roosevelt, Franklin, 183–184
Rosebery, Lord, 107
Rossa, Jeremiah O'Donovan, 76
Rothschild, Lord, 124
Royal Academy, 23
Royal Irish Constabulary (RIC), 31, 79,
    100, 122, 135
Royal Ulster Constabulary (RUC), 215,
    218
RTÉ, 199–200, 251
RUC, 215, 218
Russell, Charles, 103
Russell, Lord John, 44–45, 72–73
Ryan, Sean, 259–260

Sacramental Test Clause, 15
Sadlier, John, 72, 78
Salisbury, Lord, 98–99, 108, 113
Sands, Bobby, 224, 230, 233
Saor Éire, 162
Sarsfield, Patrick, 11
Scotland, 28, 42
Scots-Irish, 7, 50
SDLP, 221–222, 224–227, 241, 248
Seanad Éireann, 160
Secret societies, 18, 30, 93. *See also* *specific name*
Self-sufficiency, economic, 176–177
Senior, Nassau, 66
Sexton, Thomas, 102
Sexual abuse scandal in Catholic Church, 259–260
Shannon Scheme, 154–155
Shaw, William, 92
Sheil, Richard Lalor, 36, 46
Silver Jubilee of British Queen Elizabeth (1977), 223
Sinn Féin
    Adams and, 242
    Anglo-Irish conflict and, 134
    Collins and, 134–135
    Dáil Éireann and, 151
    decline in representation by, 153
    in European Parliament, 236
    IRA and, 225, 227, 244
    IRB and, 119
    nationalism and, Irish, 147
    negotiations with British politicians and, 138–139
    in Northern Ireland, 225–227
    old leaders of, 145
    partition and, 226
    peace process and, 241
    public support for, current, 220
    republicanism and, 136–137
    in twenty-first-century Ireland, 248–249
    violence in Northern Ireland and, 225
    Volunteers force and, 133
Skeffington, F. Sheehy, 132
Smith, F.E. (Lord Birkenhead), 123
Smith, Jean Kennedy, 241
Smyllie, R.M., 185
Soar Éire, 162
Social Democratic and Labour party (SDLP), 221–222, 224–226, 227, 241, 248
Society for the Liberation of the Church from State Patronage and Control, 73
Society of United Irishmen, 24–25, 34, 62

Somervell, General Sir Donald, 171
Somerville, Edith, 159
Spain, 5, 7, 22, 179
Special Powers Act, 215
Spencer, Lord, 75
Spring, Dick, 207
St. Patrick's Day statement (1979), 232
St. Ruth, Marquis de, 11
Stack, Austin, 138
Stalker, John, 227–228
Stanley, Lord, 42, 45, 59
Statute of Westminster (1931), 161, 169
Statutes of Kilkenny (1366), 4, 15
Stephens, James, 76–79, 90
Stormontgate spying scandal (2002), 243
Strongbow, 3
Stuart restoration (1660), 9, 11
Stuart, Villiers, 37
Suez situation (1956), 241
Sugden, Sir Edward, 52, 55
Sullivan, A.M., 72, 77
Sullivan, T.D., 86, 92
Sunningdale conference (1973), 221–222
Swift, Jonathan, 19
Sykes, Sir Richard, 224
Synge, John Millington, 115
Synod of Thurles (1850), 59

Talbot, Richard, 11
Taylor, Dennis, 227
Tenant League-Irish Brigade coalition, 72
Tenant rights, 71–72
Terry Alts, 30
Thatcher, Margaret, 198–199, 224–228, 233, 236, 241
Thomas, J.H., 167–169, 171, 175
Tierney, Michael, 178
Tithe act (1838), 44–45
Tobin, Liam, 150
Toleration and Indemnity Acts, 15–16
Tone, Theobald Wolfe, 24–25, 173
Tories, 31–32, 35, 37, 39, 41–42, 43–44, 54, 56–57, 60
Townshend, Lord, 20
Trade war (1938), 176–177
Treason Act (1939), 180
Treaty of Limerick, 13
Treaty of Paris (1783), 23
Trevelyan, Charles Edward, 66
Tribalism, 3–4
Trimble, David, 239, 241
the Troubles. *See* Northern Ireland
Tudor England, 5, 7, *8*, 9, 19
Turbridy, Ryan, 251

Twenty-first-century Ireland
   background of, 235–236
   Celtic Tiger in, 244–247, 252–254
   change and, 235, 261
   culture in, 250–254, 261
   economy in, 244–247, 252–261
   education in, 235, 251–252
   European Economic and Monetary
      Union membership and, 244–246,
      256–257
   GNP in, 256
   immigration and, 247
   information technology bubble and,
      256
   literature in, 261
   Lisbon treaty and, 245–246, 254
   neutrality in, 254–255
   Northern Ireland and, 235, 261
   peace process in, 236–244
   politics in, 247–250
   Sinn Féin in, 248–249
   unemployment in, 244
Tyrconnell, Earl of, 7, 11

UDA, 232, 243
Ulster, 7, 31, 71, 102
Ulster Defence Association (UDA), 232,
   243
Ulster Unionist Party (UUP), 221
Ulster Unionists, 123–124, 136, 139, 190,
   198, 214
Ulster Volunteers Force (UVF), 123–124,
   126, 128–129, 243
Unemployment, 204, 215–216, 244
Union and unionism
   Act of Union and, 27, 34, 87
   British, 108, 123
   Butt and, 82–83
   Catholic emancipation and, 26–27
   debate about, 26–27
   English imperialism and, 26–27
   Gladstone (William) and, 102
   Home Rule and, 108–110
   Irish strategy, 108–110
   Kitchener and, 129
   peace process and, 241–244
United Irish League, 111
United Irishmen, The (weekly), 64
United Nations, 212–213
United States. See also Irish Americans
   Catholic emancipation and, 40

United States (continued)
   Civil War in, 76, 83
   De Valera in, 134–135
   economic crisis in (1929–1932), 162
   economic crisis in (2008), 245, 256
   Fenianism and, 78–79
   Irish emigration to, 73–75
   revolution in, 20, 22, 34
University Bill, 80–81, 84–85
Urbanization, 203–205
UUP, 221
UVF, 123–124, 126, 129, 243

Versailles Peace Conference, 134
Vinegar Hill Battle (1798), 25
Volunteers force, 21–22, 46, 124–126,
   128–133, 135

Wales, 28, 42
Wall, Mervyn, 212
Wall Street Crash (1929), 162
Walsh, William J. (archbishop), 98, 120
Warnock, William, 183–184
Webb, Sidney and Beatrice, 113
Wellington, Duke of, 37–38, 42, 53, 56
West, Harry, 224
Whelehan, Harry, 239
Whigs, 21–22, 32, 35, 39, 41–46, 50,
   56–60, 62, 66, 73
White papers, 220–223
Whiteboys, 30
Whitelaw, William, 220–221
William of Orange (British king), 11, 13
Williams, Mrs. Betty, 223
Williams, Shirley, 233
Wilson, Harold, 218, 222
Wilson, Sir Henry, 124, 144
Wiseman, Cardinal, 73
Wood, Mrs. Benjamin, 104
World War I, 118, 126–134, 139
World War II, 175, 181–188, 216–217
Wyndham Act (1903), 109
Wyndham, Charles, 109
Wyndham, George, 119–120
Wyndham Land Act, 120
Wyse, Sir Thomas, 36–37

Yeats, William Butler, 27, 106, 114–115,
   116, 132
Young Ireland/Irelanders, 44, 47–51,
   60–65, 69, 76–77, 82

About the Authors

Thomas E. Hachey is currently University Professor of History and executive director of the Center for Irish Programs at Boston College. The author or editor of seven books, as well as several dozen articles in scholarly journals on various aspects of British and Irish history, Hachey has spent numerous summers and sabbaticals researching at British and Irish archive repositories. He served as chair of the Department of History (1979–1993) and as dean of the College of Arts and Sciences at Marquette University (1993–2000) before his appointment as an endowed chair at Boston College. Professor Hachey is a past president of the American Conference for Irish Studies.

Lawrence J. McCaffrey is Professor Emeritus at Loyola University of Chicago. The author or editor of ten books and a long list of articles in American and Irish scholarly journals, Professor McCaffrey is also a past president of the American Conference for Irish Studies, an organization of some one thousand plus academics that he cofounded in 1960. Professor McCaffrey taught history for a number of summers at the School of Irish Studies, Dublin, and at the Irish Studies Summer School, University College Cork. Among his many honors and awards is an honorary degree presented by the National University of Ireland in 1987.